The Epistemological Basis for Belief according to John's Gospel

The Epistemological Basis for Belief according to John's Gospel

Miracles and Message in Their Essentials as Nonfictional Grounds for Knowledge of God

DAVID A. REDELINGS

◆PICKWICK *Publications* • Eugene, Oregon

THE EPISTEMOLOGICAL BASIS FOR BELIEF ACCORDING TO JOHN'S GOSPEL
Miracles and Message in Their Essentials as Nonfictional Grounds for Knowledge of God

Copyright © 2011 David A. Redelings. All rights reserved. Except for brief quotations in critical publications or reviews, no part of this book may be reproduced in any manner without prior written permission from the publisher. Write: Permissions, Wipf and Stock Publishers, 199 W. 8th Ave., Suite 3, Eugene, OR 97401.

Scripture quotations taken from the New American Standard Bible®, Copyright © 1960, 1962, 1963, 1968, 1971, 1972, 1973, 1975, 1977, 1995 by The Lockman Foundation. Used by permission.

Pickwick Publications
An Imprint of Wipf and Stock Publishers
199 W. 8th Ave., Suite 3
Eugene, OR 97401

www.wipfandstock.com

ISBN 13: 978-1-61097-180-5

Cataloging-in-Publication data:

Redelings, David A.

The epistemological basis for belief according to John's gospel : miracles and message in their essentials as nonfictional grounds for knowledge of God / David A. Redelings.

xii + 226 p. ; 23 cm. Includes bibliographical references and indexes.

ISBN 13: 978-1-61097-180-5

1. God—Knowableness—Biblical teaching. 3. Bible. N.T. John—Criticism, interpretation, etc. I. Title.

BS2615.52 R45 2011

Manufactured in the U.S.A.

*For those who have been told
that no one can have knowledge of God*

"Then Moses answered and said,
'What if they will not believe me,
or listen to my voice? . . .'" (Exod 4:1)

". . . I performed my signs among them;
that you may know that I am the LORD." (Exod 10:2)

" . . . and that you may tell in the ears of your son and of your grandson,
how I made a mockery of the Egyptians . . ." (Exod 10:2)

"And Pharaoh's servants said to him,
'. . . Do you not know that Egypt is destroyed?'" (Exod 10:7)

"For if you believed Moses, you would believe me,
for he wrote of me." (John 5:46)

"If I do not do the works of my Father,
do not believe me." (John 10:37)

"If any man is willing to do His will,
he shall know . . ." (John 7:17)

Contents

Foreword by Richard Bauckham / *ix*

Acknowledgments / *xi*

1. Introduction / 1
2. Varieties of Belief in John's Gospel, and the Need for Belief / 8
3. The Character of Knowledge: General Considerations and Johannine Perspective / 22
4. The Evangelist's Concept of Knowledge: History, Fiction, and the *A Priori* Exclusion of the Possibility of Historical Miracles / 34
5. The Evangelist's Concept of Knowledge: Intended Fiction in the Case of Miracles / 54
6. The Evangelist's Concept of Knowledge: Miracles as Historical Grounds for Belief / 77
7. The Evangelist's Concept of Historical Knowledge: A Comparison with Modern Historiography / 91
8. The Extent of Nonfictional Intention in John's Miracle Accounts / 103
9. John's Use of Miracles as Grounds for Belief in Jesus / 130
10. The Essential Words of Jesus as Nonfiction in the Gospel of John / 149
11. John's Essential Message as Grounds for Belief in Jesus / 182
12. Conclusions / 197

Bibliography / 203

Ancient Documents Index / 209

Names Index / 219

Subject Index / 223

Foreword

How Christian faith in Jesus Christ may be properly grounded or warranted is clearly an issue of great importance. If we look for an account of this in the New Testament, it is perhaps the Gospel of John that seems the most promising source, because this Gospel is explicitly intended to enable its readers to come to faith in Jesus or to confirm their existing faith. The Gospel presents a series of "witnesses," including importantly the "signs" or "works" that Jesus does, which provide some kind of basis for believing in Jesus.

Can faith be based on anything as flimsy as historical reports of what Jesus said and did? Rooted in a strong modern tradition of Enlightenment rationality, many a New Testament exegete or theologian has sought to secure the substantial independence of faith from history. Moreover, even within the realm of historical knowledge, miracles can surely have no place, since the basic epistemological assumptions of modern historiography make it impossible to affirm that anything not analogous to general human experience has happened in history. Rudolf Bultmann's project, as one of the most influential of modern commentators on John, was to accommodate these requirements of Enlightenment epistemology by extracting the purely existential message of John's Gospel from its mythological expression as an apparently historical narrative. As the New Testament writer who, in Bultmann's view, most clearly perceived the independence of the Christian existential message from the mythological worldview of the time, Bultmann's John teaches that miracles cannot possibly be a basis for authentic faith.

Along these lines many scholars have thought, not only that John's narratives of Jesus' "signs" have strongly symbolic resonances (as, of course, they do, especially when read in the light of the Old Testament parallels and images they evoke), but that John intended them to be read only for their symbolic significance. In that case their significance in no way depends on their historicity and John did not intend his readers to mistake them for non-fictional historical narratives. On such a view it is not difficult to suppose that John simply created many of his narratives to serve as fictional vehicles for his theology.

In the face of this trend in Johannine scholarship, David Redelings mounts a robust case for the non-fictional character both of the miracles in John's Gospel and of the Gospel's presentation of the essential message of Jesus. He is not attempting to show that the miracles actually happened or that Jesus did preach such a message, only that the Gospel claims historical status for its major content. What is most important about his argument is that it shows from the logic of the Gospel's own statements that its narratives, especially those of the "signs," must be presented as non-fiction. In the Gospel's

Foreword

understanding of the grounds for Christian faith in Jesus, the significance of Jesus' signs is inseparable from their occurrence as real events in history. Too often John's Gospel has been understood as a "spiritual Gospel" in the sense that it floats free of earthly and physical reality, locating its message in a purely spiritual realm. But that the physical reality of Jesus' signs matters is much more in accord with the Gospel's programmatic announcement that in Jesus the Word has become flesh.

Redelings is well conversant with the philosophical discussion of miracles, and is able to claim that there is not in fact, as New Testament exegetes too easily suppose, a consensus among philosophers that miracles do not occur. Certainly, to affirm that miracles have happened, one must reject assumptions that many modern historians make, but there is more than one way to write history. John, at any rate, made different assumptions—deeply informed by the Jewish tradition with its foundational narrative of the Exodus and the many miracles that attended it—and we should not be judging his purposes as a Gospel-writer by the standards of Enlightenment reason.

Redelings does not claim that, in John's view, miracles are sufficient basis for enduring faith in Jesus, but rather that they have a key place alongside other conditions of faith, especially the words of Jesus and the consistency of his words and deeds with the Scriptures. They are one proper basis of faith, capable of evoking belief or confirming existing belief. Readers of Redelings' work are bound to ask whether they can still function in that way today. That question raises further questions, not broached in this book, but Redelings' work has convincingly opened the way for those further questions by showing that John's Gospel does claim to report miraculous events and invites assessment of those reports.

Richard Bauckham
Emeritus Professor of New Testament Studies,
University of St Andrews, Scotland,
and Senior Scholar, Ridley Hall, Cambridge

Acknowledgments

THIS BOOK IS A slightly revised version of the doctoral thesis I submitted in 2002 at the University of St. Andrews, Scotland. I thank my thesis supervisor, Professor Richard Bauckham, particularly for his thoughtful and diligent critiques, his encouragement, and his continual patience. I thank Professor Alan Torrance particularly for his kind and helpful direction to several philosophical authors.

I also thank all those family members and friends who in various ways made this book possible, including especially my parents, my sister Kathy, and many friends who welcomed us to Scotland. Most of all, I thank my wife Cherie and our three sons, who all shared many difficulties without complaint.

1

Introduction

THIS BOOK DESCRIBES THE grounds on which beliefs about God are warranted, according to John's Gospel. In the modern age, both nonreligious and religious people often consider knowledge of God to be impossible to attain. If the historic influence of John's Gospel is any evidence of the depth of its insights, we may wonder how the early Christian author would respond to these modern doubts and questions.

While John's Gospel is of special interest to Christians, John's ideas address more universal concerns. As we will see, John has been largely influenced by earlier Jewish thought, to the extent that many scholars believe John was Jewish. Beyond this, John is interested in how all people can know about the one God, and on what basis they may believe. Consequently, it is congenial to pose modern questions about the knowledge of God, and describe the answers that John's Gospel gives. Members of all religious traditions, as well as religious agnostics, will find that many of the philosophical questions posed in this investigation, and some of John's answers, are congenial with their own perspectives. Standard historical method and argument are used in this investigation to describe and elucidate John's ideas about the grounds for knowledge, which we will refer to as John's epistemology. John's handling of this topic holds particular interest for the Christian community, since the member of any faith must at times decide what is worthy of belief and practice within his or her own tradition.

This investigation considers questions about the sources of religious knowledge, the possibility and means of attaining such knowledge directly, the dependence of religious knowledge upon reasoning, the dependence of religious knowledge upon the reports of others who claim such knowledge, and the dependence of religious knowledge on historical knowledge of such reports. In each case, questions about the nature and extent of religious certainty are involved. This investigation does not try to answer these questions using primarily philosophical approaches. Instead, we attempt to describe and understand the way that John thought about these questions in his own (often Jewish) categories of thought, and to explain his rationale in terms that a modern audience could comprehend. John's Gospel is perhaps the most important for understanding early Christian thought, and his reflections on the grounds for belief are the most developed of the four Gospels.

This investigation argues that the Gospel of John respects the prior need for evidence as a foundation for belief. Such respect is apparent already in the words that John attributes to Jesus, "If I do not do the works of my Father, do not believe me, but if I do them, though you do not believe me, believe the works . . ." (John 10:37–38). Here Jesus does not simply demand that he be believed because he makes claims, or because he is telling the truth, or even because he speaks God's words. Jesus does not assume that people have the innate ability to perceive directly the truth or divine origin of someone else's words. Instead, Jesus recognizes the reasonable need of his audience to base their assessment of his claims upon grounds that they are able to know and regard as sure. As we will try to show, John's epistemological methodology proves to derive largely from the Books of Moses, particularly Genesis, Exodus, and Deuteronomy.

Scholars have proposed a number of theories for the history of editing and the underlying sources of this Gospel, however this investigation treats the book as a literary unit. Readers who approach with a different understanding can generally read references to John the Evangelist as references to the implied author of the Gospel (in its final form). References to John the Evangelist in the specific sense of the historical or real author can be understood as references to the real author who was the primary creator of the work. The identity and name of the author are not an assumption of the argument. One advantage of treating the work as a literary unit is that such treatment does not ignore apparently meaningful thematic and conceptual relationships between various parts of the work. These relationships, in turn, must be considered prior to final decisions about the sources and editing of the Gospel, especially where those decisions imply that the apparent meaning is only a literary accident.

What is the place for this book among others on the same subject? Edward Malatesta's (1966) and Gilbert van Belle's (1985) cumulative bibliographies on John's Gospel list no entries of substance under "epistemology," and list few relevant entries under related topics (e.g., revelation, knowledge). The situation apparently has not changed much, so there is much room for further study. Two recent works are worth noting. Cornelis Bennema has written a chapter on John's epistemology in *The Bible and Epistemology*, edited by Mary Healy and Robin Parry (2007). Whereas Bennema focuses on internal illumination of believers, this investigation focuses on John's direct claim that signs and testimony are grounds for an objective and public basis for knowing, and grounds the argument in John's own vocabulary and conceptual world. (This focus on signs and testimony somewhat neglects other means of knowing, as my student David Hodges has noted, but the investigation may serve as an entry point to wider investigations of John's epistemology in the future.) Also of note is philosopher C. Stephen Evans' chapter, "The Historical Reliability of John's Gospel," in *The Gospel of John and Christian Theology* (2008), edited by Richard Bauckham and Carl Mosser. Evans's chapter addresses epistemological questions about John's historical claims, rather than focusing directly on John's own epistemology. The conversation partners in this investigation have been selected for their relevance to the topic of John's direct claims about his epistemology.

Unfortunately, establishing John's own epistemology proves to be difficult, for there is currently a pervasive doubt among many scholars that any single part of John's Gospel was clearly intended as historical nonfiction. As will be explained below, an author's epistemology cannot be determined with high confidence on the basis of fictionally intended or metaphorical narrative. Establishing portions of John's Gospel that scholars of all persuasion may accept as nonfictional and not metaphorical requires lengthy argument. That argument encompasses the majority of the chapters in this book. The need for this argument, and a more detailed description of the topics covered by this book, are given under the two headings below.

THE NEED TO IDENTIFY THE LIMITS OF FICTION

In order to identify John's epistemology, the investigation begins by identifying a part of this Gospel that nearly all can agree is nonfictional. Why is this necessary? Since before the composition of the canonical Gospels during the first century, those outside the Christian community have questioned the historical reliability of the Christian tradition that the Gospels embody. In particular, the New Testament itself tells of many who questioned the reports of Jesus' resurrection. However, an investigation of John's epistemology does not rest on such controversial reports. Instead of deciding whether an element in John's Gospel is actually historical, we need only decide what John *regarded* as historical. Similarly, instead of deciding what metaphysical statements are actually true, we need only decide what John *regarded* as true. Furthermore, we need only decide this to the extent needed to describe John's epistemology.

Since a large number of John's statements are controversial if taken as historical claims, many people have interpreted them as nonhistorical claims. Such nonhistorical interpretations include: symbolic statements to express metaphysical or spiritual realities, legend that is not central to the message, dramatic embellishment, story as a medium for artistic expression, or something like a historical novel.

Since it is John's understanding of history, rather than history itself, that is central to this investigation, the terms *fiction* and *nonfiction* typically do not refer in this investigation to whether John had his facts right. If we ask, for example, whether the resurrection of Jesus was a fiction, we will not usually be asking whether it was a historic fact, but whether John intended his readers to regard the resurrection as historic fact. Consequently, the terms *fiction* and *nonfiction* will typically refer to two alternate ways that John's readers might be expected to understand his historical narratives.

Historical and metaphysical knowledge are important parts of epistemology, and John's epistemological practice cannot practically be determined until one knows what kinds of things he regards as historical or real. In the current proliferation of doubt about John's historical intent, it is likely that some would consequently question any reconstruction of the author's actual system of epistemology as reconstructed from this Gospel. Such questioning could argue that fictional narratives need not fully and accurately represent the author's own real view of the epistemological world, but might rather express his fictional viewpoint or the viewpoint of a fictional narrator. For this reason we begin by identifying material that the author intended as nonfiction.

To address the concerns of those who doubt John's historical intention, this reconstruction of John's epistemology rests only on an identified core of themes that the author most obviously intended to be understood as nonfiction. These themes are identified in the following way. We first show that the entire composition of the Gospel is driven by the author's central purpose: to persuade his readers to believe, or continue believing, in Jesus. Where the author offers particular grounds as a persuasive argument for such belief, we argue that in some cases such grounds must be intended as nonfiction. Nobody will be persuaded by an argument when its grounds are plausibly understood as mere fictions.

THE MAIN ARGUMENT

There are two main lines of argument that rest on this recognition of the Evangelistic purpose of the author. First, when the historical aspect of the ground of an argument is essential to the persuasive force of the argument, that historical aspect is clearly intended as nonfiction. As will be shown, John uses miracles as a ground supporting one argument for belief, and that argument depends on Jesus' miracles being regarded as nonfictional historical events. The persuasive force of such an argument does not depend on John's miracle accounts being free of all historical error, but it does require that the miracle itself is not regarded as a historical error. Again, the argument is not that the miracles were historical events, but rather that John *regarded* them as essentially historical events.

The second line of argument is different. When John portrays characters in his Gospel as turning away from Jesus because of Jesus' claims, John cannot intend such offense as arising from a simple misunderstanding of fiction or metaphor. If that were the case, John's concern to promote belief in Jesus would then require him to clarify his true meaning to the reader, in order that the reader not be unnecessarily offended and turn from belief in Jesus. Otherwise, John would not fulfill his purpose in writing the Gospel, which is to promote belief in Jesus. Consequently, this controversial aspect of Jesus' claims cannot be metaphorical or fictional.

The effect of reconstructing John's epistemology only from his central persuasive purpose is to narrow this investigation primarily to the Evangelist's claim that belief in Jesus is warranted (along with any knowledge and beliefs that belief in Jesus presupposes). This has disadvantages. Focus on such a primary theological claim does not allow the same appearance of neutral and fair handling that analysis of less theological claims might give. Furthermore, such a limited case study does not allow a full survey of John's system of epistemology and belief. Nevertheless, this focus actually provides a more secure basis for conclusions, due to its reliance only on clearly nonfictional elements of the author's message. Furthermore, the grounds warranting such religious belief reveal the main structure of John's entire epistemology. The results are at least indicative of, and sometimes directly show, the grounds that John would recognize as warranting any belief. Lastly, the results of this narrow investigation show that the extent of intended nonfiction in John's Gospel is much wider than those passages and themes upon which the investigation was based. This provides a much larger basis on which expanded studies of John's epistemology could be carried out in the future.

We will next argue that John's appeal to nonfictional miracles as evidence warranting belief reveals the place of historical events and testimony in John's epistemology. The rationale for an epistemology appealing to historical events and testimony as a basis for knowledge, in opposition to modern doubts about the reliability of any historical claims, will be discussed. John's particular claims to religious knowledge will also be identified, and the rationale for these claims will be discussed.

In this investigation, the foundations of John's ideas are not discovered or discussed until the final chapters. The argument begins with the evidence for John's own epistemological beliefs and investigates the basis for those beliefs down to their foundations. A simple summary of John's essential epistemological system might naturally present his thought in the reverse order, working up from foundational ideas. However this would not show so clearly that John's own perspective was guiding the analysis. The order of this investigation is therefore the former order, the order of discovery.

For this reason it will be helpful to offer here, without supporting argument, a brief explanation of the perspective of the Evangelist. The Evangelist adopts implicitly the Jewish view that the structure and qualities of the one universe give evidence of One Creator. Rather than beginning his Gospel with any extensive arguments for the Creator's existence, John simply refers to the word or plan (Greek *logos*) which established this particular order of the universe, alluding, as we shall see, to the opening words of Genesis. The Evangelist also adopts implicitly the Jewish view that this Creator has the ability to communicate just as do the people he created with that same ability, and has at times revealed himself by speaking in human language to chosen individuals, identifying himself by miracles and other phenomena that are otherwise inexplicable. In particular, John accepts the prophetic claims of Moses (and so, for all practical purposes, the covenant and teachings of Moses as preserved in the books of the Torah that were traditionally ascribed to him). Moses, as the prophet who announced God's covenant and Law to the nation of Israel, was the prophet by whom the reports of all other prophets had to be judged. Moses told Israel to obey a prophet who would come as his successor. For John, the decision to accept Jesus consequently constitutes a question of religious law. Support for this description of the Evangelist's perspective is provided in the thesis.

AN INDEX TO THE ARGUMENT

We end Chapter 1 with this index, which is provided below for readers whose interest is primarily in only a portion of the argument. Some readers may be interested only in the chapters relating directly to John's epistemology, and others may be interested only in the chapters about the limits to intended fiction in John's Gospel. The index will also serve as a convenient summary of the argument, and will provide landmarks for any who get lost in subsidiary arguments.

In chapter 2, the essential catechetical or evangelistic purpose of the Evangelist is shown. Since the Evangelist considers Jesus' commission by God to be evident, he sees a rejection of Jesus as a rejection of God, just as Jews would have seen rejection of Moses and his Law as a rejection of God. In both cases, the consequences are a matter of life and death (Deut 30:15). Jesus is seen as a Prophet like Moses. In the Torah, God wants people to "believe in you [Moses and his words] forever" (Exod 19:9). The Evangelist's purpose is to similarly encourage trust in Jesus. To avoid confusion, the argument makes a distinction. The kind of continuing trust in Jesus that is a condition of eternal life is distinguished from other kinds of belief that are not a condition for eternal life.

In chapter 3, we review basic philosophical insights into the different kinds of knowledge that exist, the definition of knowledge, and the sources of knowledge. We also describe the conception of knowledge found in John's Gospel, and compare this with modern conceptions and views about knowledge.

In chapter 4, the main argument begins. To determine the Evangelist's idea of the basis for belief, we first address questions about both the extent of nonfiction and the extent of the nonhistorical character of the Gospel. Since the miracles of John's Gospel are entangled with questions of fiction and history, and since the miracles are of evident interest to John himself, they become a key focus for understanding his epistemology. To avoid misreading a modern distaste for miracles into John's views, modern philosophical challenges against accounts of miracles are discussed. The arguments against the credibility of miracle accounts are found to lack modern scholarly consensus.

In chapter 5, we look at the earliest known readers of John's Gospel to see if they understood his miracle accounts as essentially historical or fictional events. The consistent acceptance of miracle claims among early Christians, along with our earliest readings of John's Gospel, shows that John intended his miracle accounts to be understood as essentially nonfictional.

In chapter 6, we look at the way that the Evangelist uses miracles as evidence justifying belief. Against modern exegesis to the contrary, exegetical arguments are presented to show that the Evangelist does not disdain the use of reported miracles as evidence to justify belief.

In chapter 7, general historical skepticism about the possibility of crediting any report (including miracle accounts) is discussed and criticized. The Evangelist's own ideas are compared to the seminal modern ideas of Strauss and Kierkegaard, and his greater regard for historical accounts is shown.

Chapters 4 through chapter 7 only argue that the Evangelist believes Jesus performed miracles of some kind. Chapter 8 extends this argument to say that the Evangelist regarded each of the particular miracles of the Gospel, and certain aspects of them, as essentially historical events.

Having clarified the Evangelist's use of miracles as nonfiction, chapter 9 discusses his use of them as grounds to believe in Jesus. This discussion interacts with many scholars, among whom there has been resistance to such a portrait of the Evangelist.

In chapter 10, the presence of nonfiction is extended from the miracle claims of Jesus to what is here called the *essential message* of Jesus. This message is the part of the Gospel's teachings that are the immediate occasion for characters in the Gospel to turn from Jesus. It is called essential because the Evangelist is otherwise needlessly turning people away from Jesus by advocating offensive but trivial ideas. Each point of offense for the characters in the Gospel is the point of offense for the Jewish community when the Evangelist wrote. The views of several scholars about a Johannine kerygma are discussed.

Chapter 11 explains the underlying Jewish theology that gave rise to the belief that God speaks to people. The Evangelist adopts implicitly the Jewish view that existence of the one ordered world gives evidence of one Creator, and that this Creator has at times communicated to people, and revealed himself in language spoken to selected individuals. Such speech being incapable of natural explanation is then seen as credibly from God. Moses was the foremost prophet, since the covenant and law he brought formed the standard by which the authenticity of other prophets had to be judged. The rationale for such Jewish beliefs is given in detail. Consequently, the decision to accept Jesus constitutes a Jewish legal question. On this basis the Evangelist appeals to the miracles of Jesus and Jesus' own words as grounds for accepting Jesus as a prophet from God, and as more than a prophet. This assumes the view that reports of miracles and divine speech are potentially credible, just like other kinds of reports. The grounds for belief in Jesus' message are then discussed.

Biblical quotations are from the very literal New American Standard Version, except where I have offered my own translation to emphasize another aspect of the original Greek. The version used generally makes little difference in the argument. Abbreviations follow the *SBL Handbook of Style*.

2

Varieties of Belief in John's Gospel, and the Need for Belief

ANY ATTEMPT TO DETERMINE the epistemological views held by the author of John's Gospel must address the widespread opinion that this Gospel contains fictionally intended elements. A reconstruction of the Evangelist's epistemology, if based upon material regarded as intentionally fictitious, will be subject to the objection that the Evangelist himself may not have really held to all the claims that his Gospel made. To avoid this objection, we will base our reconstruction on a clearly nonfictional element of the Evangelist's work, an element that underlies his entire purpose in writing. This nonfictional element is the Evangelist's catechetical and evangelistic purpose to persuade his audience to trust in Jesus as the Messiah.

Our first task in this chapter will be to show the seriousness with which the author expresses this purpose. We will argue that the author's language, insofar as its purpose is to persuade others to trust in Jesus, cannot reasonably be understood as fictionally intended. Our accompanying task will be to clarify the author's conception of the kind of belief in Jesus that was needed. In later chapters we will describe the epistemological grounds offered for such belief. We will also provide arguments showing that the Evangelist cannot be offering intentionally fictional grounds to secure a nonfictional belief in Jesus.

The Evangelist's claims about Jesus were inherently controversial, just as Jewish claims about Moses were controversial. According to the Torah, the law of God was revealed to the nation of Israel through the prophet Moses (Deut 5:27–33), so that a rejection of Moses amounted to a rejection of God's law and, consequently, a rejection of God himself. This perspective is evident in the books of Exodus and Deuteronomy, and so was widely adopted by first century Jews. The Evangelist sees the revelation of God through Jesus as of comparable importance to the revelation of God through Moses, indeed, as of greater importance (John 1:17, 18). We will even argue later that the Evangelist thought of Jesus as the Prophet foretold by Moses, who would someday speak to the people of Israel as Moses had spoken, and who must likewise be obeyed (Deut 18:18–19). Just as Moses' claims had been disputed, so Jesus' claims were disputed.

The Evangelist does not portray these controversial claims about Jesus as claims that require no justification. For example, the Evangelist carefully portrays Jesus as one who remains faithful to Moses (John 5:46; 8:46), so that unfaithfulness to Moses should not arise as a plausible ground for objecting to Jesus. Furthermore, just as Moses' revelation was confirmed by miracles (e.g., Exod 4:1–9; Deut 34:10–12), so the Evangelist confirms Jesus' revelation by miracles (e.g., John 20:30). The Evangelist's full rationale for these justifications and others will be described later. The point to be noted is that the Evangelist makes Christian claims along with supporting arguments, and he would dispute the allegation that his claims lack justification.

WHY THE EVANGELIST CALLS FOR BELIEF IN JESUS

To perceive the seriousness of the author's purpose, it will be helpful to understand his rationale. This is made partially evident by comparing the Evangelist's portrayal of Jesus with the Torah's portrayal of Moses.

The Evangelist's call for belief in Jesus has precedents in the account of Moses' life in the book of Exodus. Such precedents would be important for readers who accepted the claims of Moses given in the Torah. Moses is told that he would be "as God to" Aaron, while Aaron "shall be your prophet" (Exod 7:1). Aaron would be Moses' "mouth" to the people of Israel, while Moses would be to Aaron "as God" (Exod 4:16). God tells Moses that He would come down to Mount Sinai in order that the people of Israel "may hear when I speak with you, and may also believe in you forever" (Exod 19:9). The people have seen the miracles performed by Moses' hand, and they directly hear God's voice at Mount Sinai. Consequently, the people have sufficient grounds to believe Moses' own testimony about God's appearances and messages to him, and to believe that Moses' laws are actually given to him by God. For that reason, belief in (or lack of belief in) Moses is implicitly seen as acceptance or rejection of God himself. Moses summarizes this as a choice between "being careful to do all his commandments which I command you today" and not being careful to do them (Deut 28:1, 15). The respective consequences for these alternate choices are "life and good, or death and evil" (Deut 30:15). The basis for these consequences is not the rejection of Moses, but the rejection of God. Since God has clearly spoken, and has offered the people a life full of joy and blessings, any rejection of God is attributed to reckless desire or self-will.

The Torah calls the nation of Israel to "believe in" Moses (Exod 19:9), and consequently to accept all the innovations revealed by Moses as part of this first covenant between Israel and God. The Evangelist, in similar fashion, calls for his readers to "believe in" Jesus. Just as Moses is portrayed as standing in the place of God, so the Evangelist portrays Jesus as standing in the place of God. The Evangelist sets forth what he considers sufficient grounds to believe that Jesus really has been sent by God. Consequently, the Evangelist sees rejection of Jesus as a rejection of the God who had revealed himself through Jesus. This identity of Jesus with God's authority is expressed, for example, in Jesus' saying, "I did not speak from myself, but the Father himself who sent me has given me commandment, what to say, and what to speak" (John 12:49).

THE EPISTEMOLOGICAL BASIS FOR BELIEF ACCORDING TO JOHN'S GOSPEL

BELIEF THAT GIVES ETERNAL LIFE

In one specialized and prominent usage of the term *believe*, the Evangelist accentuates the distinction between believing and not believing, by positing the existence of only two groups of people in the world, groups marked respectively either by belief in the Son of God, or by turning away in unbelief. Here the idea of belief entails the idea of trust, and unbelief entails a refusal to trust. The division of humanity into two by this criterion of belief is most striking in passages where antithetical parallelism is used, or where antonyms are set in opposition. Such language is reminiscent of the blessings and curses of the covenant given through Moses (Deut 28). Moses announces that blessings fall on those who "obey the LORD your God, being careful to do all his commandments which I command you today" (Deut 28:1). However curses fall on those who violate this charge. In similar fashion, the Evangelist says, "The one who believes in the Son has eternal life; but the one who does not obey the Son shall not see life, but the wrath of God rests on him" (John 3:36). Or again, "The one who believes in him is not judged; the one who does not believe has been judged already . . . and this is the judgment, that light is come into the world, and men loved darkness rather than light, for their deeds were evil" (John 3:18–19). Or again, Jesus "knew from the beginning who they were who did not believe" (John 6:64). Such belief is regarded in these citations as one without degree. Each person either believes in the Son or does not believe.

As indicated above, these two groups are also differentiated by their hope of eternal life. Eternal life is promised to those who believe in Jesus, while those who do not believe are tacitly or explicitly excluded from the promise (e.g., John 3:15, 16; 11:25; 17:2, 8, 9). The Evangelist's extraordinary use of antithetical parallelism arises from his perception of the situation's urgency. Jesus has appeared (John 3:19; cf. 1:6–9), and the Evangelist writes because people have the opportunity to believe in him (John 20:31). Eternal life and the judgment of God hang upon the presence or absence of such belief, and the Evangelist cannot allow his readers to ignore or sidestep this demand. Since this belief has such great consequences, the rest of this chapter clarifies its place among other varieties of belief.

BELIEVING AS EITHER MERE ASSENT OR AS TRUST

For clarity in our discussion, it is important here to observe two distinct meanings that have been attributed to the Greek word *pisteuō* (πιστεύω), the word that is regularly translated in most English versions of John's Gospel as *believe*. Walter Bauer's lexicon says that (with rare exception) *pisteuō* can have one of three distinct meanings: believe, trust, or entrust.[1] For our purposes, it is important simply to distinguish the first meaning from the other two.

The first meaning of *pisteuō* given by Bauer refers either to acceptance of the truth of statements, or to acceptance of the truth of a person's claims. This meaning of *pisteuō* refers merely to belief in the sense of mental *assent*. For example, it is a meaning found

---

1. Bauer, *Greek-English Lexicon*, 660–62.

in John's Gospel in the passage (John 9:18) where the Jewish authorities "did not believe" the claim of the man who said he had formerly been blind. Another example in John's Gospel is in the passage where Jesus questions his opponents' belief in Moses' writings. Jesus asks, "If you do not believe his writings, how shall you believe my words?" (John 5:47). In both examples, believing means *assent* to the truth of what is said.

A second meaning of *pisteuō* refers instead to the choice to *trust* a person. This meaning was also used in the time of the Evangelist. For example, we read, "And we have come to know and have believed the love that God has for us" (1 John 4:16). In this passage the author speaks both of "having come to know" (ἐγνώκαμεν) the love of God, and of believing the love of God. One who has come to know God's love for people would normally assent to the statement or claim that "God has love for us." Indeed, the author of this passage himself assents to that claim. Consequently, having knowledge of God's love already means that one believes (in the sense of mere *assent*) that God loves people. Why then does the author add, "and have believed the love"? This addition indicates some further aspect or emphasis other than knowledge and mere assent. The author is evidently emphasizing his consequent *trust* in God's love. One can more naturally trust in a love that one has come to know well. Furthermore, the phrase "believe the love" is intelligible if we understand it as "*trust* the love," whereas the reading "*assent* to the love" is not intelligible. The meaning *trust* also accords well with the fact that, in John's Gospel, people are the object of belief more often than are particular statements. These people are often believed, not in regard to a single statement, but rather in regard to an entire perspective or narrative or body of teaching. For example, it is only after Jesus has spent a few days with the Samaritans that many of the Samaritans believed in Jesus as the Messiah "because of his word" (John 4:41). Consequently, *pisteuō* can mean *believe* in this second sense of *trust*.

Here it is to be noted that *trust* has usually been understood to include some element of *assent*, even though trust goes beyond mere assent. For example, Otto Kirn concludes that Augustine and Aquinas conceived of true faith as the giving of assent at the instigation of the will.[2] Karl Barth, in a detailed discussion about faith, concludes that the older Reformers never accepted "the possibility of excluding the element of *notitia* or *assensus*, i.e., the element of knowledge from faith."[3] Trust requires knowledge of the person trusted, at least knowledge of their identity.

In summary, it is important to keep in mind that, in John's Gospel, the English translation *believe* (which is typically given for *pisteuō*) can mean *trust*, rather than mere *assent*. The meaning of *trust* is even the more common meaning, and so should be considered first as a possible meaning, wherever the word *believe* is encountered.

OTHER KINDS OF BELIEF IN JESUS?

Some commentators have claimed that there exists a kind of belief in Jesus that does not result in eternal life. For example, with regard to the Gospel's pronouncement about the

---

2 Kirn, "Faith," 269–70.

3. Barth, *Church Dogmatics*, 1:234.

belief of certain leaders (John 12:42), Wescott says, "the belief only lacked confession, but this defect was fatal."[4] Likewise, Hoskyns refers to a "false belief " (John 8:31) just as he earlier refers to a group that "'believes' but does not believe" (John 2:23).[5] This is reminiscent of the concern James expresses about faith that is dead and not able to save (Jas 2:14), or of Luke's reference to people who "believe for a while, and in time of temptation fall away" (Luke 8:13). Barrett asks in his commentary (John 20:31), "was the gospel written to deepen, instruct, and confirm the faith of believers, or to convert unbelievers?"[6] To confirm faith suggests that there are some kinds of faith, or stages of faith, which could prove unstable. Does the Evangelist ever think of people as believing in Jesus in some way that is inadequate to give eternal life? Can these references to belief be understood as meaning an inadequate belief, or a temporary belief?

On its face, this conception of belief seems to violate the Evangelist's antithetical and dualistic understandings about belief, which were described earlier. Why does the Evangelist present *belief in Jesus* as alone determining whether one receives eternal life rather than judgment, if this *belief in Jesus* might be confused for some other sort of belief in Jesus? The question strikes at the Evangelist's declared purpose for writing the gospel: that the reader should believe "that Jesus is the Christ, the Son of God, so that believing you might have life in his name" (John 20:31). Such life is given to some, and not others, belief being the only stated requirement. The Gospel's statement of purpose implies that there is one kind of belief about Jesus that gives life, and that no other belief in Jesus is worthy of the name *belief*. The Evangelist seems to have no conception there of a person believing "that Jesus is the Christ, the Son of God" in such a way as not to secure life. In that text there is only one kind of belief in Jesus, a belief that gives life. Are there contextual signals we have not yet identified which differentiate the two?

UNSTABLE BELIEF IN JESUS: JOHN'S FIRST PASSOVER ACCOUNT

To illuminate this question, we will examine at length one text that suggests there is a belief in Jesus that does not save. This text is from John's first account of the Passover festival:

> Now when he [Jesus] was in Jerusalem at the Passover, during the feast, many trusted in his name, beholding the signs that he was doing. But Jesus, on his part, was not trusting himself to them, for he knew everyone, and because he did not need anyone to bear witness about man, for he himself knew what was in man. (John 2:23–25)[7]

A proper understanding of this passage requires consideration of many features. For clarity, we will examine this text in the light of its ties to the immediately subsequent passage:

---

4. Westcott, *Gospel According to John*, 2:136.
5. Hoskyns, *Fourth Gospel*, 338.
6. Barrett, *Gospel According to John*, 134.
7. My translation.

> Now there was a man of the Pharisees, Nicodemus by name, a ruler of the Jews. This person came to him by night and said to him, "Rabbi, we know that you have come as a teacher from God, for no one is able to do these signs that you are doing unless God should be with him." . . . Jesus responded, ". . . What is born from the flesh is flesh, and what is born from the spirit is spirit." . . . Nicodemus responded and said to him, "How is it possible for these things to be?" Jesus responded and said to him, "You are the teacher of Israel, yet do not understand these things? Truly, truly, I say to you, we tell what we know, and testify about what we have seen, and you do not accept our testimony." (John 3:1–2, 6, 9–11)[8]

As a first observation, there is widespread agreement among commentators that, though the people "trusted in his name," their belief was in some respect inadequate. Calvin, Westcott, Bultmann, Morris, and Beasley-Murray share this view.[9] It is important, however, to determine whether this belief was inadequate to secure eternal life, or whether it was merely inadequate to reach some ideal state of belief. It is also important to determine whether the belief was a different kind of belief, or whether it was the same kind but only held temporarily.

To clarify how the belief was inadequate, we must first note the irony of expression in this text. Although these people "trusted in his name," Jesus was not in turn "trusting himself to them." The Evangelist, by repeating the word *trust*, and using the translation "but" and "on his part," pointedly notes that the trust is not reciprocated.[10] The point here is not that the people's trust is to be misunderstood as ironically meaning *false trust*, but that there is irony in Jesus' response. This irony is brought out by the Evangelist's repetition of *trust*. The irony clearly focuses Jesus' mistrust upon the people who trusted him.

According to our main text, the cause of Jesus' mistrust lies in the defective nature of these same people. Jesus cannot trust them because he knows "what was in man" and so he knows that their belief is unreliable. As Barrett cogently puts it, "Jesus has divine knowledge and is not misled by appearances."[11] The defective nature of these people does not refer merely to the kinds of deficiencies common to both believer and unbeliever. When the Evangelist concerns himself with the deficiencies of human nature, with "what was in man," it is overwhelmingly with deficiencies that keep people from a saving belief in Jesus (e.g., John 7:7; 8:40–47; 13:10; 15:17–25).

There are several reasons to link this mention of human deficiency to that mentioned in the following narrative with Nicodemus, and so to consider the deficiencies to be of the same kind. Overt mention of defective human nature is first introduced in this Passover account (John 2:23–25), and sets the stage for the following account of Jesus' conversation with Nicodemus, where the inability of human nature (flesh) to secure entrance into the kingdom of God is given as the reason that people must be born

---

8. My translation.

9. See Calvin, *Gospel of John*, 1:57–58; Westcott, *Gospel According to John*, 1:97; Morris, *Gospel According to John*, 181; and Beasley-Murray, *John*, 47.

10. Barrett, *Gospel According to John*, 204. That this is an unexpected response to the people's trust is supported by the presence of the mild adversative δε (translated above as "but" rather than "now") and the emphatic αὐτός (translated above as "on his part" rather than "himself").

11. Ibid.

"of the Spirit" (John 3:6). Another of the narrator's themes is continued by Nicodemus, when he repeats (John 3:2) the narrator's prior mention (John 2:23) of belief that arose from signs. The repetition of "man" (John 2:25 and John 3:1) may also tie these passages together.[12]

One other tie between these two passages is the situation of Nicodemus himself. Nicodemus calls Jesus a teacher from God, and says that God is with him. Jesus' enemies never offer this acknowledgment, but instead question or deny that God is with Jesus. Consequently, (contra Bultmann, and following Brown)[13] Nicodemus himself is one who has such a belief in Jesus, and yet is also one who may not be entirely trusted. Nicodemus comes "by night." This is such a distinctive and unusual time to visit that the reader who has forgotten Nicodemus's name is reminded later of his identity (or character) as "the one who had first come to him by night" (John 19:39). It does not, therefore, seem explicable merely as common practice of the studious rabbi.[14] As other evidence for Nicodemus' belief in Jesus, he is the only person explicitly identified as a "ruler" whose name we have, and so is a strong candidate for being one of the "rulers" who "believed in him" but was not confessing (John 12:42). This description also ties in well with his coming to Jesus "by night."

In view of this evidence linking Nicodemus to the people who believed, we may conclude that the Evangelist attributes the unreliability of the people's belief to the inadequacy of human nature. This inadequacy can be overcome only if they are "born of water and the spirit" (John 3:5), rather than merely "born of flesh" (John 3:6). Consequently, their belief is inadequate to secure eternal life, but only because they will not hold to their belief. These same people, of whom Nicodemus is a representative, are addressed as those who as yet "do not receive" (John 3:11) the witness of Jesus, John the Baptist, and Jesus' disciples, and do "not believe" (John 3:12) even the simpler teachings of Jesus. Hoskyns says, "These casual believers may be the stuff out of which disciples are made, but they are not disciples, and may never become so. They stand outside the truth . . ."[15]

It is the inadequacy of human nature, rather than regard for miracles, that the Evangelist criticizes. Strictly speaking, Hoskyns is correct when he says about this passage that belief arising from Jesus' signs could not be relied on.[16] The belief could not be relied on and it was a belief that arose from seeing signs. Consequently, belief arising from signs may not always be trusted. Yet the Evangelist does not say that the belief could not be trusted *because* it arose from signs. Throughout the Gospel, the Evangelist favorably regards belief arising from signs. Earlier in this same chapter of the Gospel, the disciples believe in Jesus after seeing the miracle at Cana (John 2:11). In the face of Jesus' signs, the Evangelist considers unbelief to be remarkable, and even evidence of blindness (John 12:37). Signs are included throughout the Gospel rather than simply being omitted. Jesus performs the miracles because they are signs. The Evangelist says

---

12. Ibid.
13. Brown, *Gospel According to John*, 1:xx.
14. cf. Barrett, *Gospel According to John*, 204.
15. Hoskyns, *Fourth Gospel*, 202.
16. Ibid.

Varieties of Belief in John's Gospel, and the Need for Belief

that he has included the signs to instill a belief that will secure eternal life (John 20:31). Consequently, the Evangelist evidently believes that signs play a positive role in bringing people to eternal life. It is only the inconstancy of human nature that the Evangelist overtly criticizes in this account of the Passover crowds, referring to "what was in man" (John 2:25).

This positive assessment of signs as grounds for belief is confirmed in another way. We are probably to understand Jesus' distrust for these people as distrust for them as a group, rather than as distrust of every individual member of the group. Since Jesus is already known as a rabbi with his own disciples (John 1:38), the reader can reasonably expect that Jesus has not merely performed signs in Jerusalem, but also has taught the people. It is implausible in such a scenario that every one of those who believe, without exception, should believe in a way that would later prove superficial. Consequently, there is no sufficient reason to suggest, as in Hoskyns' discussion of the passage, that every person who believed at this time was unworthy of Jesus' trust.[17] The Evangelist's concerns are merely to declare the general unreliability of human nature, the folly of trusting in human belief indiscriminately, and Jesus' divine knowledge of the human heart. So the rise of belief in response to signs is not here construed as a different kind of belief.

The Evangelist does not provide any details to indicate in what respects Jesus was unwilling to "trust himself to them." This silence suggests that it is simply the relationship of trust itself, with all the specific manifestations that trust would entail, which is primarily in mind. In other words, Jesus would not trust himself to them because their belief in him was unstable.

ATTEMPTS TO DISTINGUISH UNSTABLE BELIEF AND SAVING BELIEF

The idea that *belief in Jesus* does not always secure eternal life requires an explanation, because it seems to contradict other conceptions about belief that are found in this Gospel. The blessing of eternal life is offered explicitly or implicitly throughout the Gospel on the condition of belief. If belief in Jesus, without further qualification as to its kind, is considered sufficient for eternal life, a belief in Jesus that does not save lies outside the Evangelist's normal idea of such belief. To make sense of the text, the reader will naturally look for contextual clues that would differentiate between belief in Jesus that saves, and belief that does not.

To distinguish belief in Jesus that saves from a belief in Jesus that would not save, we might expect the Evangelist to use qualifying adverbs with *believe* (πιστεύω). Perhaps surprisingly, we do not find this kind of contextual clue. The Evangelist does not speak of people who *truly believe*, nor of *true believers* as does Abbott,[18] nor does he speak of *saving faith* as does Bultmann.[19] The absence of qualifying adjectives is particularly apparent in antithetical clauses where the sole criterion for eternal life is belief in Jesus. However

---

17. Ibid., 210.
18. Abbott, *Johannine Vocabulary*, 48.
19. Bultmann, "πιστεύω," 6:212.

their absence is not limited to the antithetical clauses; the blessing of eternal life is offered explicitly or implicitly throughout the Gospel solely on the condition of belief.

Westcott, citing Origen, suggested that the expression "believe in his name" (John 2:23) differed in meaning from the expression "believe in him" and referred to a belief for which eternal life was not promised.[20] Abbott also follows Origen, but does not adequately explain how those who "believe in his name" are elsewhere considered possessors of eternal life (cf. 1 John 5:13). Furthermore, Abbott's suggestion that the expression "in his name" is a baptismal allusion does not secure his argument for a "rudimentary faith" which does not save. The New Testament evidence indicates that the church did not regard baptismal faith as faith that is inadequate to save (e.g., Mark 1:4; 16:16, Acts 2:38; 16:31–33, 1 Pet 3:21). In addition, he must acknowledge that Chrysostom (who like Origen was fluent in Greek) saw no distinction in the two expressions.[21] Origen's distinction seems unjustifiable in view of the Evangelist's earlier statement which uses the same expression: "But to as many as received him, he gave the right to become children of God, to those who believe in his name, who were born . . . of God" (John 1:12, 13). In this statement, those who "believe in his name" are placed in antithesis to those described in an immediately preceding statement as "his own [who] did not receive him." As Calvin points out, "belief in his name" is here attributed only to those who "are already born of God."[22] To suggest that "belief in his name" refers to a belief which does not save raises unacceptable difficulties in understanding the text. Consequently, Origen's suggestion has not been widely accepted by other commentators. The distinction is not recognized by Barrett,[23] and is plainly denied by Bultmann, who points to examples where similar expressions are used interchangeably (e.g., John 3:18).[24]

Another suggestion is that occurrence in this first Passover account of the phrase "believed in his name" (John 2:23) is to be understood ironically as meaning "did not believe in his name." Hoskyns' discussion of the group that " 'believes' but does not believe" suggests this solution.[25] Let us assume that the reference to people who believe refers ironically, in some instances, to people who do not believe. In each of the most likely occasions where such ironic "belief " can be suggested (John 2:23; John 8:30, 31; John 12:42), the Evangelist distinguishes such believers from others who do not believe. Consequently, there is no point in ironically ascribing faith to these believers, unless they at least give an appearance of believing which the Evangelist wishes to discount as inadequate. While under this scenario the Evangelist does not view their faith as adequate, he acknowledges the reality of these outward indications; that is what objectively distinguishes this group from other unbelievers. So if irony is being used, it does not express a simple contrast of belief to unbelief. The added allusion to unbelievers would then be unexpected, as it reduces the sting of an ironic reference to believers.

20. Westcott, *Gospel According to John*, 1:98.
21. Abbott, *Johannine Vocabulary*, 34–37.
22. Calvin, *Gospel of John*, 1:18.
23. Barrett, *Gospel According to John*, 163, 164.
24. Bultmann, *Gospel of John*, 59.
25. Hoskyns, *Fourth Gospel*, 338.

Under this assumption that the Evangelist uses *believe* in an ironic sense, this separate mention of unbelievers as a different class can perhaps be best explained as reflecting more accurately the real differences among those who heard Jesus. If the Evangelist uses *believe* in an ironic sense, he views such belief as not adequate, but nevertheless as being a real phenomenon that shares some of the outward characteristics of adequate belief. Ironic usage alone, in the absence of a real phenomenon that appears to be belief, cannot explain the Evangelist's omission of qualifying terms with *believe* (πιστεύω). The question then arises as to whether it is not simpler and more convincing to view *belief* as referring to this *appearance of belief* without irony. It is difficult to argue that a phenomenon having an appearance of belief would fall outside the semantic range of *believe*. It is perhaps for these reasons that commentators on this passage (John 2:23–25) have not generally expressed the view that *belief* is used with simple irony to mean *unbelief*.

In summary, the inadequacy of the crowd's belief, as narrated in John's first Passover account, cannot be attributed to its basis in Jesus' miracles, or to a special meaning of "believe in his name," nor to the use of qualifying adjectives, nor to its use in an ironic sense to mean "unbelief." How then is some belief incapable of securing eternal life?

A PROPOSAL FOR TWO CONCEPTIONS OF *BELIEF IN JESUS*

Instead of these suggestions, it is proposed that the Evangelist refers to *belief in Jesus* in two different ways. In the first usage, he refers indiscriminately to whatever appears to be belief in Jesus. In this usage, the Evangelist describes as *belief* any behavior that would normally be described by the word *belief*. Under this usage, belief may or may not prove to continue; the term is applied descriptively to all who appear to believe, without determining whether they will continue to believe. Presumably, some people who believe in Jesus will continue to believe, while others will stop believing. This usage reflects the normal range of meaning of the Greek verb *pisteuō*, which is the word regularly translated as *believe* in English versions of John's Gospel. In the second usage, the Evangelist refers to this same kind of belief, but conceives of it more narrowly as a *customary* belief in Jesus. In this usage, belief is conceived of as without end, and consequently is viewed as securing eternal life.

One indication of the narrower sense, *customary belief in Jesus*, is the Evangelist's use of the present participle of *pisteuō*. This is typically rendered in English as "the one who believes" or "he who believes." Fanning says, "Also very common is the customary sense for the present participle." [26] Such a usage of the participle is not unique to the Evangelist, but is shared, for example, by Paul (e.g., Rom 1:16; 3:22; 4:5,11, 24; 9:33, 10:4, 11). The usage is pervasive in 1 John (e.g., 1 John 3:6, 7; 4:7, 8). Bultmann acknowledges "the common use of the present participle [of *pisteuō*] in Paul and John" which is to be understood as either "to come to believe" or as "to be believing." [27] But whether salvation is promised to convert or Christian, it is not promised except in anticipation that one remains in the faith.

---

26. Fanning, *Verbal Aspect*, 410.
27. Bultmann, "πιστεύω," 6:214.

The present participle does not always have a customary sense in Greek usage, even when it expresses the durative idea of the present tense.[28] The non-customary sense may occur with an adverbial use, as when Pilate addressed the crowd, wanting (θέλων) to release Jesus (Luke 23:20). In an attributive use, the participle may refer to actions that are not customary, but only of brief duration, as when John the Baptist saw the Spirit "coming down" (John 1:33). The durative idea may be limited to a past situation, as when we read that "all the ones believing were of one heart and soul" (Acts 2:44). Abbott notes that the present participle can refer to a future situation, citing the words, "This is he that baptizes in the Holy Spirit" (John 1:33), since the Holy Spirit was "not yet" present until Jesus was "glorified" (John 7:39).[29] This use arises partly because the future participle was rare in the New Testament.[30] In spite of these other uses, the customary sense is common enough in John's use of *pisteuō* that this frequency can be understood as part of John's own style.

In this gospel, several contextual factors show when the present participle of *pisteuō* is to be understood as a continuing state of belief. Following the Mosaic teaching about covenantal blessings (or life) and curses, the Evangelist frequently juxtaposes *believing* with the resulting state of eternal life (John 3:15, 16, 36; 5:24, 6:40, 47; 11:25, 26). At the same time, he often places it in antithesis to both *not believing* and judgment, thus requiring us to understand *believing* as a state, rather than as an action occurring at a single moment in time, which might later be reversed. The identifying characteristic of those receiving eternal life is not merely belief that happens for a moment, nor belief that continues for a time, but belief that is customary.

An examination of the context for the 19 instances of the present participle shows that the present participle of *pisteuō* is always used in this gospel in a customary sense. The Evangelist indicates a customary sense of the participle by differentiating the believing from the unbelieving communities solely by use of the present participle of *pisteuō* (e.g., John 3:18). Westcott says of one text (John 1:12), "the faith is regarded as present and lasting"; he also contrasts the present tense of the participle with the aorist tense used elsewhere.[31] Morris says of one text (John 3:36), "the present participle indicates a continuing trust" and of another text (John 3:16) he speaks of "a continuing state of belief."[32] In several texts (e.g., John 3:36), those receiving eternal life are differentiated from others simply by the formula description "the one believing in him," that is, by the present participle of *pisteuō* with the article, together with *eis* [εἰς] and some reference to Jesus as the object of this belief. This same formula occurs 13 times in the Gospel of John, always in contexts where it effectively differentiates the believing from the unbelieving community (John 1:12; 3:16,18a, 36; 6:35, 40; 7:38; 11:25, 26; 12:44, 46; 14:12; 17:20). However that entire formula is not even necessary to identify this group. The present participle with the article and the dative of the object is sufficient (John 3:15; 5:24), as is the present

28. Brooks and Winbery, *Syntax*, 143–44.
29. Abbott, *Johannine Grammar*, 368.
30. Blass and Debrunner, *Greek Grammar*, 178.
31. Westcott, *Gospel According to John*, 1:17.
32. Morris, *Gospel According to John*, 248, 232.

participle and article without any explicit object at all (John 6:47, 64). In the latter case, the object is implied. The only other instance of the present participle with the article also refers to belief that secures eternal life (John 3:18b), as does the only instance of the present participle without the article (John 20:31). Westcott describes the latter instance as "belief, held as a present power." [33] In each instance, the existence of two groups of people shows that we are to understand a customary sense of the present participle. The force of these contextual factors is such that even an aorist participle must sometimes be understood as customary, when the destiny of two groups are expressed antithetically: "He who has believed and is baptized shall be saved; but he who has disbelieved shall be condemned" (Mark 16:16).

The Evangelist favors use of the present participle of *pisteuō* (which occurs 19 times) over both its perfect participle (which occurs only once—John 8:31), and its aorist participle (which occurs only twice—John 7:39; 20:29). While even the aorist participle could be used to express a state of belief, the present tense usually includes the ideas of duration, continuation, or of being incomplete, while the aorist tense does not.[34] The idea of duration is easily adopted to express customary action. The perfect tense, though expressing the idea of continuation, also expresses the idea of commencement, and so tends to express a temporal idea. Avoidance of the perfect participle may also help the Evangelist express the idea that people who believe in Jesus at one particular time may later prove to be untrustworthy, and that continuity of belief is crucial.

FAITH THAT SECURES ETERNAL LIFE

The Evangelist writes about belief using a variety of terms, so that we might hesitate to regard any two instances of belief as being of the same kind. Abbott, for example, concludes that believing "is to be regarded, in different aspects, not as a consummation or goal, but as a number of stages . . ."[35] However such an approach prevents us from seeing any larger or richer conception of belief. The Evangelist declares a criterion, this *customary believing in Jesus*, which divides the whole community into two groups, just as did the blessings and curses of Moses. By this means the Evangelist reveals many relationships between his various conceptions of belief. Any kind of belief that differentiates people into these same two groups cannot be equated with any belief that would divide people along a different line. For example, Jesus says that the disciples, in contrast with the (unbelieving) world, do believe that God sent Jesus (John 17:8). But it is not until after the resurrection that they believe Jesus' words, spoken long before, "Destroy this temple and in three days I will raise it up" (John 2:22). However their failure to believe these particular words of Jesus does not place the disciples in the category of those not believing in Jesus. The existence of these two groups helps us to distinguish *customary believing in Jesus* from other kinds of belief.

---

33. Westcott, *Gospel According to John*, 2:357.
34. Brooks and Winbery, *Syntax*, 82, 83, 98.
35. Abbott, *Johannine Vocabulary*, 80.

Conversely, any belief that would divide people along the same line as *customary believing in Jesus* must be identical with or inseparable from that belief. Believing in Jesus is therefore characterized variously by its different aspects in the phrases, "believing in him" as God's "only begotten Son" (John 3:16), "believing . . . in the name of the only begotten Son of God" (John 3:18), "believes in the Son" (John 3:36), "believe that Jesus is the Christ, the Son of God" (John 20:31), "they believed that you sent me" (John 17:8), "hears my word, and believes him who sent me" (John 5:24), "believes in me (as Resurrection and Life)" (John 11:26), "believe in the light" (John 12:36), and "He who believes in me does not believe in me, but in him who sent me" (John 12:44). All of these kinds of belief are attributed to the entire group believing in Jesus and to them alone. In each case, belief in one of its aspects is presented as the sole condition for receiving the eschatological blessing. However, such belief in one aspect entails such belief in all its aspects and effects. The unitary nature of *believing in Jesus*, manifested in the existence of the one believing group, is such that even if it has various aspects, or even if there is any kind of variation or change in it, these do not change its essential nature as faith that procures eternal life.

We may extend this conception of belief by observing the relationship between the believing group and eschatological blessings. Since certain blessings are promised to the group *believing in Jesus* and denied to the unbelieving group, these blessings correlate without exception to the presence of such belief. The members of the believing group are partakers of all these blessings: having eternal life (John 3:15), being saved (John 3:17), not perishing (John 3:16), not being judged (John 3:18), living even if one dies (John 11:25), having life in his name (John 20:31). As a consequence and corollary, promises of these same blessings to those who satisfy some single condition other than belief, indicate that only those who believe will satisfy this other condition. For example, Jesus says, "unless you eat the flesh of the Son of Man and drink his blood, you have no life in yourselves. The one eating my flesh and drinking my blood has eternal life, and I shall raise him at the last day" (John 6:53, 54). Since they have eternal life, it is clear that the group believing in Jesus must be coextensive with the group "eating my flesh and drinking my blood." Conversely, those who do not "eat my flesh and drink my blood" are identical with the group of those not believing. As another example, it is only those hating their life in this world, who will "keep it to eternal life" (John 12:25).

In like fashion, each calamity that falls upon the unbelieving group can be correlated with any condition whose fulfillment would result in that same calamity. The unbelieving group partakes of all these calamities: being lost (John 3:16), being condemned (John 3:16), not seeing life (John 3:36), having the wrath of God abide on them (John 3:36), being in death (John 5:24). Following the reference to being lost there is a related text, which says that they love their life and so "will lose it" (John 12:25). Together all these references clarify the nature of the groups believing or not believing in Jesus. The groups constitute two loci that tie together various conceptions and descriptions of belief that are used by the Evangelist.

In any examination of belief in the Gospel of John, the preeminent position of saving belief must be kept in mind. In a number of passages the Evangelist says that belief is absent (e.g., John 3:12, 18; 4:48; 5:38, 44, 46, 47; 6:36, 64a; 7:5, 48; 8:24, 45, 46; 9:18; 10:25, 26, 37, 38; 12:37–39, 44; 16:9). The heightened anxiety or concern for belief, which is evident in these passages, can only be explained if eternal life is at stake. This is particularly clear where Jesus is calling for belief. The sort of belief that is in mind is therefore either a belief that gives eternal life, or at least a belief that acts as a precursor to such life-giving belief. In either case, the belief that gives eternal life is ultimately the driving concern. A person who does not believe at all, certainly does not believe in the way that secures eternal life. Such an interpretation of these passages is consistent with the Evangelist's portrait of Jesus' purpose in preaching, as well as with the Evangelist's explicitly stated purpose in writing the Gospel (John 20:31). It is also consistent with Jewish readings of the Torah, in light of its promised blessings and curses. Once this underlying concern for eternal life is noticed, it becomes clear that many of these references to unbelief refer directly to unbelief that precludes the possession of eternal life (e.g., John 4:48; 5:38, 44; 6:36, 64a; 7:48; 8:24; 10:25, 26; 12:37, 39, 44b; 16:9). References to belief in this Gospel, especially belief connected in some way with Jesus, must be considered in the context of an evangelist's purpose: to secure in his readers a saving belief in Jesus.

THE BASIS FOR BELIEF IN JESUS

Belief in Jesus is evidently conceived of as trust in Jesus. Trust is not to be given without justification, however trust begins where such justification ends. Trust involves not merely beliefs about Jesus, but also individual commitment to Jesus. The sharply defined alternative between belief in Jesus and unbelief is explained in part by the necessarily sharp distinction between commitment and lack of commitment. Trust also entails, however, some beliefs about Jesus, since one must have some conception of Jesus in order to have made any kind of commitment to him. To understand the basis for such belief requires a discussion of the knowledge by which such belief can be warranted.

CHAPTER CONCLUSIONS

Any reconstruction of John's epistemology requires that we first determine what John intends to be understood as nonfiction. The Gospel of John is manifestly a work that seeks to promote and confirm trust in Jesus as the Christ. In the Evangelist's eyes, failure to trust in Jesus is an open refusal to trust in and follow God, having terrible consequences similar to the curses of disobeying the covenant given by Moses. Trust in Jesus, if only it does not fail, is consequently seen as sufficient to secure eternal life. Consequently, John cannot intend his readers to understand as mere fictions his basic claims and arguments that are given to persuade his readers to believe. It is in these persuasive claims that we will find a clearly nonfictional core of John's beliefs, and so discover his epistemology of belief.

3

The Character of Knowledge

General Considerations and Johannine Perspective

IN ORDER FOR OUR analysis of John's epistemology to avoid conceptual confusion, we pause in this chapter to provide a summary of relevant insights from philosophers about knowledge, belief, and certainty. We will also identify various ways that, according to philosophers, knowledge in general is secured, and will discuss the relation of knowledge to both belief and certainty. We will then compare this understanding with John's conception of knowledge and the sources of knowledge, according to the evaluation of various Johannine scholars.

KINDS OF KNOWLEDGE: GENERAL PHILOSOPHICAL CONCEPTIONS

In a general synopsis of philosophers' ideas about knowledge, Anthony Quinton presents several pertinent observations about the various kinds of knowledge that exist. Quinton says that the phrase *knowing that* refers to a different kind of knowledge than does the phrase *knowing how to*. Only the first phrase, he says, has as its objects propositions about the world, even though both kinds of knowledge must be learned.[1] He also comments that *knowledge of*, such as knowledge of a person or of an animal or of art, is not the same as *knowledge that*.[2] *Knowledge of* can be a far more comprehensive knowledge than could be expressed in a single proposition, and it may sometimes even prove impractical to reduce such knowledge to propositions. Furthermore, *knowledge of* can be a knowledge that comes in various degrees, because the object of such knowledge may be so complex. In John's Gospel, *knowledge of* persons is an important kind of knowledge. For example, the Evangelist says, "This is eternal life, that they may know you, the only true God . . ." (John 17:3). Here, as elsewhere in John's Gospel (e.g., John 17:25), knowledge of God is not conceived of as occurring in various degrees, but in distinction from not knowing God. In addition to these various senses of knowing, language even allows for the expression "I knew it!" where *knew* does not refer to genuine knowledge, but rather to some

---

1. Quinton, "Knowledge and Belief," 4:345.
2. Ibid., 346.

strongly held opinion which in fact the person did not yet actually know.[3] In summary, the word *know* can refer to various and distinct kinds of knowing.

DEFINITIONS OF KNOWLEDGE

In Plato's dialogue *Theaetetus*, Socrates asks what knowledge is. Is knowledge the same as perception, or is it any true belief, or is it true belief having a plausible account for its truthfulness?[4] Although Socrates discounts all three explanations, many philosophers today define knowledge as *justified true belief*, a definition corresponding to this third idea of the character of knowledge. Here, belief is not referred to in the sense of *trusting in*, or *believing in* a person, but only in the sense of *accepting a particular view*. Quinton observes that this definition of knowledge as a kind of belief excludes *knowledge how to do* something, and *knowledge of* persons.[5] Similarly, in Plato's *Theaetetus*, belief is generally to be understood as a *belief that* some proposition is true, not as *belief in* a person. In John's Gospel these two concepts can both be evoked in the Evangelist's call to "believe that Jesus is the Christ" (John 20:31), since in practice this entails trust in Jesus as well as belief that he is the Christ. Though Plato wrote several centuries before Jesus, modern philosophical discussion has largely accepted Plato's understanding of the problems of epistemology.

Some philosophers have denied that knowledge is a kind of belief, or have denied more generally that knowledge can be derived from what is not knowledge. As one consideration against this denial, Quinton observes that people do mistake their own beliefs for knowledge. Conversely, he asks whether we can mistake knowledge for mere belief. Experiments on human perception have shown that in some conditions people predictably have reliable knowledge even when they are unsure. Such knowledge does not require that one believes without having any doubt. Quinton also points out that we may come to know something that previously we only believed, and that there may be beliefs that we can never know to be true.[6] Some philosophers have argued that the concept of knowledge is "primitive and indefinable." This view necessarily dissents from the view that knowledge can be adequately defined as *justified true belief*.

Since words are defined largely by their usage, it is important to observe that John's Gospel uses the word *know* in cases that some philosophers would say exhibit mere belief. The words translated in John's Gospel as *know* are, in nearly all cases, either of the two Greek words, *ginōskō* (γινώσκω) or *oida* (οἶδα). These two words can be used in regard to the kinds of facts that one would testify to in a legal proceeding. We find in the inquiry of the man born blind, for example, the latter word used in the sentence, "We know that this is our son, and that he was born blind" (John 9:20). Similarly, we find the same word used in the sentence, ". . . one thing I do know, that, whereas I was blind, now I see" (John 9:25). The claim to knowledge can be made in cases where the Evangelist

---

3. Ibid.
4. Plato, *Theaetetus* xxiii.
5. Quinton, "Knowledge and Belief," 346–47.
6. Ibid., 348.

would not accept the claim as true. For example, the Pharisees are portrayed as saying of Jesus, ". . . we know that this man is a sinner" (John 9:24). It is noteworthy that these claims to knowledge are claims that would be seriously considered in a courtroom. Some philosophers, who doubt the reliability of human perception, memory, and testimony, might argue that such claims to know are merely beliefs, and not knowledge at all. These kinds of claims to know are not portrayed as a fallacy of characters within the Gospel, a fallacy avoided by the Evangelist himself. The narrator also claims such knowledge, saying that "the servants who had drawn the water knew" where the wine came from (John 2:9), and saying that "the Jews knew that he [Jesus] was there" (John 12:9). Further, the Evangelist portrays Jesus himself making claims to such knowledge, saying, "I know that you are Abraham's seed" (John 8:37) and "these know what I said" (John 18:21). Normal usage in John's Gospel of the word *know* does not defer to skeptical claims about normal human reporting, but adopts instead the provisional viewpoint commonly adopted in courtrooms.

John even indicates that knowledge is possible in regard to some matters that in our era would be commonly ascribed to belief alone. He portrays Jesus as saying about his teaching, "If anyone is willing to do his will, he shall know of the teaching, whether it is of God, or whether I speak of myself" (John 7:17). He portrays the Pharisees saying, "We know that God has spoken to Moses" (John 9:29). John entertains the possibility of knowledge in matters that are now often relegated to mere belief. However this does not show that John is confusing the concepts of *knowing* and *believing*, but rather is easily understood as an indication of his own understanding about the possible limits to human knowledge.

INFERENCE AND PERCEPTION AS TWO SOURCES OF KNOWLEDGE

According to Quinton, many philosophers hold that there is some knowledge which is not inferred, but which constitutes first premises. These premises include self-evident truths, such as the axioms of logic. They also include perceptual or introspective truths, such as "I am in pain" or "I am having the experience of seeing something green." Quinton says that such statements "are logically immune from falsification by the results of any further experience" since their truth "follows from the fact that it is believed by the person to whom it refers."[7] These sorts of claims to know are hardly controversial. However the Gospel of John portrays some additional kinds of knowledge as "seeing." For example, Jesus says "we bear witness of what we have seen" (John 3:11, 12). Similarly, the Evangelist portrays the absence of some kinds of knowledge as "blindness." For example, the man born blind, speaking to the Pharisees about Jesus, says it is "an amazing thing, that you do not know where he is from, and yet he opened my eyes . . . if this man were not from God, he could do nothing" (John 9:30, 33). Jesus then indicates that these Pharisees are blind (John 9:39; cf. 12:38–40). This suggests the idea that there are certain kinds of spiritual insight that have a self-evidential quality or that there are certain esoteric visions that have a perceptual quality.

7. Ibid., 346–47.

The Character of Knowledge

In a discussion of what constitutes justification of a true belief, Quinton himself argues that some knowledge must be self-evident rather than inferred. He points out that when knowledge can be justified only by other knowledge, the result may be an unreasonable requirement for an infinite regress of justification. Any item of knowledge A can only be justified by other knowledge B. However we can only say that "B justifies A" if we can give a reason "because C" where "C" is something else we know. In other words, we must introduce C saying "C justifies 'B justifies A.'" The rigid requirement to find justification for every argument consequently leads to an infinite regress of arguments for justification.[8] Since this is not how people ever know things, some knowledge must be self-evidently justified.

KNOWLEDGE AS PROVISIONALLY KNOWN

Quinton discusses how some philosophers have said that it is the coherence of beliefs about the sensory world, which provisionally justify the beliefs as knowledge. These philosophers have denied that any beliefs about the external world are self-justifying.[9] To avoid circularity of argument, the proposal has been made that some beliefs about the external world, such as those arising from sight, are *relatively basic*, by which is meant that, unlike other beliefs, they deserve to be accepted until contrary evidence arises that discredits them. Such beliefs constitute knowledge of only a provisional kind, since such beliefs may in some cases not prove to be true, and the justification for such beliefs does not itself require that they be actually true. In John's Gospel such provisional knowledge is never treated in practice as uncertain. For example, a person's testimony is considered a way of providing knowledge, even though human testimony is known at times to be unreliable. Similarly, in both the miracle of healing the man born blind (chapter 9) and the miracle of Lazarus' resurrection (chapter 11), little allowance is made for the legitimacy of doubt (on the part of characters in the narrative) about the two miracles that are personally witnessed. When the weight of evidence is so great, a denial that one has knowledge is considered by the Evangelist to be unreasonable, and an indication of biased judgment.

CERTAINTY

Quinton mentions two current schools of thought about the possibility of certainty. On one side, there are those who say that we can never have certainty about perceptions, memory, testimony, inductive logic, or introspection, even though these are accepted as common knowledge of fact. This kind of view he attributes to Bertrand Russell, C. I. Lewis, and A. J. Ayer.

On the other side, G. E. Moore and his adherents have argued that the very idea of being *certain* is learned on the basis that sensory knowledge is really knowledge, and that the idea of certainty that has been proposed by the first camp is excessively strin-

---

8. Ibid., 346.
9. Ibid., 347.

gent, requiring that something be "impossible to doubt."[10] Moore argued that certainty, in at least one sense, applies to fundamental sensory experience like "seeing a pencil," providing knowledge more certain than any of the arguments against its possibility.[11] More generally, Moore argued that the skeptical contention that any experience may be a dream is based on the knowledge that dreams occur, implying knowledge that not all experience is a dream. This in turn shows that people can really know that they are not dreaming when they are seeing an object.[12] Wittgenstein, arguing from our use of language to describe knowledge and doubt, maintains that the external world's existence is beyond doubt.[13] Moore labels propositions about reality whose truth depends on the real and actual situation as "contingent propositions." Moore denies that the contingency of any proposition implies, of itself, that the proposition is not known to be true, or is not absolutely certain, and takes some care to distinguish the senses of the word *possible* that have been confused.[14] As Quinton explains it, doubt about a proposition can only be justified under this view when similar propositions, made in similar situations, and based on similar evidence, are known to be false. It is notable that doubt also needs justification to be worthy of acceptance. Quinton notes that this view of doubt explains how necessary truths are not always certain, so that this view does not require a foundation of incorrigible propositions. In this camp Quinton places, along with G. E. Moore, L. Wittgenstein, J. L. Austin, and Norman Malcolm.

It might be questioned whether the Gospel of John advocates certainty in an absolute sense. However, it is evident that this Gospel does not in any practical way acknowledge the legitimacy of an anti-Christian perspective on the grounds that the Christian claim is doubtful. Furthermore, John's Gospel does not generally suggest any criticism against people for having excessive certainty in their faith in Jesus or God. It would be alien to the text, for example, if the Samaritan woman (John 4), were to be criticized for believing too easily in Jesus. While again it might be questioned whether the Gospel actually regards the knowledge given by perception and by legal procedure as inherently certain, in practice the vocabulary and ideas used in the gospel make no distinctions between absolute certainty and the certainty that such means can provide. It is the very certainty of perception and legal procedure, which is the basis for the Gospel's criticism of those who ignored the miracles of Jesus (e.g., John 9 and 11).

SUFFICIENCY AND VALIDITY OF EVIDENCE

Closely related to the idea that knowledge must be justified are questions about what constitutes sufficient or valid evidence to justify a true belief as knowledge. We here propose that some knowledge (such as knowledge from reports or testimony) is justified provisionally. It is frequently supposed, to the contrary, that a valid justification for

10. Quinton, "Knowledge and Belief," 351.
11. Moore, *Philosophical Papers*, 226.
12. Ibid., 249.
13. Stroll, *Moore and Wittgenstein*, 123.
14. Moore, *Philosophical Papers*, 230–36.

knowledge must absolutely guarantee the truth of what is known. Such a stringent requirement makes the scope of what can be called knowledge far less than what would be allowed either by normal linguistic usage, or by normal courtroom usage, both of which are usages adopted in the Gospel of John.

In our modern era the suggestion has been made that religious faith is "belief in something for which there is no evidence." [15] Both the ancient Jewish and the Johannine understandings of belief and knowledge differ from such a view, for they argue against opposing religious beliefs precisely on the basis of religious or legal considerations which they offer as argument and evidence. The real difference between the earlier views and this modern view is that the latter does not admit most religious evidence to be valid. Religious evidence is discounted because it is not usually physical evidence, and also because it is evidence that persuades some, but not an overwhelming majority of people who are well educated about the subject. Religious beliefs and evidence are in this respect similar to controversial beliefs in politics, in the courtroom, or a controversial theory in a new field of science. Descartes criticized those who gave assent to beliefs before they had been given sufficient evidence to justify acceptance of them. More stringently, W. K. Clifford is cited as saying that, "It is wrong, everywhere and for anyone, to believe anything upon insufficient evidence." [16] Such a maxim ignores the legitimacy of provisional beliefs, but it has a certain scope of validity. A person who accepts false beliefs often tends to give less serious consideration to evidence favoring alternative (and true) beliefs. However the Gospel of John certainly portrays its own religious claims as supported by sufficient evidence, even to the point of portraying the unbelief of its opponents as explicable only by blindness or stubbornness (e.g., John 9:39 and 12:40).

MODERN DISCUSSIONS: THE IDEA OF KNOWLEDGE IN JOHN'S GOSPEL

The remainder of this chapter will be of interest primarily to Johannine scholars. Here we will review relevant current scholarship that describes the idea of knowledge in John's Gospel. This review will present current insights, provide an opportunity to clarify points of confusion, and provide a sense of the scholarly range of views about this topic.

James Gaffney examines the identity of those who are said to have religious belief or knowledge. Jesus is always portrayed as knowing, never as believing, and never as not knowing or not believing. Gaffney sees in this an indication that knowing is more perfect than believing. The disciples are variously said to know, to believe, and not to know, or not to believe. Unfortunately, Gaffney's analysis here does not simultaneously take into consideration the thing that is known or believed, and the person who knows or believes. Gaffney instead considers the object of knowledge or belief separately from the person who knows or believes. This leads to some confusion. For example, Gaffney suggests that "not believing" was the most deplorable offense, and yet this is what he ascribes to the apostle Thomas, whereas the Pharisees, John the Baptist, and Mary Magdalene at various

---

15. Quinton, "Knowledge and Belief," 352.
16. Ibid.

points merely do "not know," which he considers a lesser offense.[17] Why believing and knowing should always be considered obligatory, regardless of the object of that belief or knowledge, is not made clear; Gaffney does not clearly distinguish between *knowledge about* Jesus and *knowledge of* Jesus, but everywhere focuses on knowledge and belief as contributing to salvation.

Gaffney also discusses the causes or conditions for knowing and believing. Unfortunately, he does not distinguish the causes of knowing from the causes of believing, but lists them without distinction in a single chart. Causes of "believing and knowing" are listed as testimonies, moral predisposition, divine influence, and seeing the risen Jesus. Causes of "not believing and not knowing" are listed as "misinterpreted scripture, divine influence, moral predisposition, and diabolic influence."[18] He distinguishes testimonies that are words (such as reports) from testimonies that are works (such as the evidence of miracles).

Gaffney argues that testimony and signs provide a moral incentive to believe, rather than "strict objective evidence" to believe. In this regard, he offers many incisive comments. The significance of the evidence can, in his understanding of the Evangelist, "be resisted with a certain display of objective reasonableness." Although Gaffney says that the works are "undeniable" and the words "irrefutable," he also says that the "conclusion to be drawn" is not rationally "inescapable."[19] On the other hand, Gaffney argues that these motivations cannot be resisted "without a certain intimation of subjective bad faith or bad will."[20] This indicates that these people in John's Gospel are unable to defend their unbelief as being a reasonable response, given what they know about Jesus' undeniable and irrefutable works and words. Gaffney acknowledges that "these words and works are, in fact, all that will be given" and that Jesus "reproaches them" for unbelief in the face of these things. Gaffney says that Jesus "does not complain of their illogic but of their irreligion."[21] Yet this remark does not capture the full scope of Jesus' complaint. Their irreligion is not considered defensible, and yet they defend it with faulty arguments, so these arguments are themselves a manifestation of their irreligion. Consequently, Jesus' complaint against their irreligion is also a complaint against their arguments. Whether or not they are conscious of the fallacies in their arguments, Jesus recognizes no justification for their use of such arguments.

In a lengthy article, Rudolf Bultmann discusses the way that the Greek word *ginōskō* (γινώσκω) was used. After discussing the underlying idea of knowledge found among Greek philosophers, Bultmann discusses general usage of *ginōskō* among the Greeks, and then the special usages among the Gnostics, in the Old Testament, among the Jews, among early Christians, and afterwards. Bultmann says that linked usage of *ginōskō* and *oida* (the two Greek words commonly translated as *know*) shows that "knowledge is re-

17. Gaffney, "Believing and Knowing," 223–26.
18. Ibid., 234.
19. Ibid., 232.
20. Ibid.
21. Ibid.

The Character of Knowledge

garded as a mode of seeing."[22] According to Bultmann, Gnostic usage adopted a special technical sense, which referred only to the knowledge of God, an esoteric knowledge distinct from all other kinds of knowledge because of its divine object, and a knowledge given only by the revelation of God to man, distinct from rational thought. Bultmann characterizes the use of *ginōskō* and *oida* in the Septuagint as broader than Greek usage, not always connoting a sense of objective *verification*, and often expressing the idea of subjectively *experiencing* some situation.[23] Dodd agrees that the Septuagint, by situating *ginōskō* in contexts where the Hebrew word *yada'* (יָדַע) was originally used, has changed the meaning of *ginōskō* toward the Hebrew, which emphasizes experiential knowledge more strongly.[24] Bultmann says that Jewish usage is characterized as following Septuagint usage, but often emphasizing the knowledge of Torah, and in Hellenistic forms, tending toward rationalistic uses. He concludes that the early Christian idea of knowledge "is thus largely determined by the Old Testament."[25] In the Johannine writings, Bultmann says about *ginōskō*, "the word here denotes emphatically the relationship to God and to Jesus as a personal fellowship."[26]

Gaffney offers a comparison of the Fourth Gospel's ideas of religious belief and religious knowledge.[27] He begins his study by identifying texts of the gospel that use the Greek words normally translated as *believe* or *know* (and their cognates and antonyms). Gaffney then identifies other texts that seem to refer to belief and knowledge figuratively (e.g., as seeing, coming, receiving, learning, loving, drinking, keeping, and confessing).

Gaffney claims that in John's special usage, such figurative references, together with the words translated as *believe* and *know*, are all functionally equivalent, though not exact synonyms. This position seems confused. On one hand, Gaffney acknowledges that such figurative language does not constitute a synonym for belief and knowledge, and even criticizes Rudolf Bultmann for the tendency to assume total synonymity where it does not occur.[28] However Gaffney himself still tends to obscure any distinction between believing and knowing, as well as between those words and their figurative parallels. He lists the figurative parallels to both words in a single chart, without distinction as to whether a word is used as a parallel to believing or to knowing. In reference to John 8:43, he identifies *hearing* Jesus' word as synonymous with *knowing* Jesus' speech, even though the absence of hearing is given in that verse as the *cause* of not knowing. He says that *believing* can be "identified" with *receiving* in John 1:12. He says that "Receiving, knowing, and believing are all three joined together in 17:8."[29] In that verse the parallelism of "they truly knew that I came forth from you" with "they believed that you sent me" leads

---

22. Bultmann, "γινώσκω," 1:691.
23. Ibid., 1:697.
24. Dodd, *Historical Tradition*, 152.
25. Bultmann, "γινώσκω," 1:707.
26. Ibid., 1:713.
27. Gaffney, "Believing and Knowing," 215.
28. Ibid., 222–23, citing Bultmann in *Theology*, 2:70–74; *Das Evangelium des Johannes*, and *Gnosis*, 48–50.
29. Gaffney, "Believing and Knowing," 220–22.

Gaffney to claim, "believing and knowing are, in some instances, simply synonymous."[30] He summarizes by saying that believing and knowing "are not used quite as synonyms."[31] Here Gaffney is arguing for the prevalence of a special use of these words in John. What Gaffney inadequately clarifies is that the same real event (e.g., conversion) may include belief and knowledge and other characteristics as well, all as distinct but inseparable elements or aspects. How, after all, can a person believe without also knowing either what or whom they believe? Granted, there is a functional equivalence if believing in Jesus requires knowing Jesus. But this does not require us to think of believing and knowing as at all synonymous in meaning.

KNOWLEDGE OF GOD IN JOHN'S GOSPEL

Though we have been considering knowledge of all kinds in John's Gospel, it will be helpful to look at C. H. Dodd's more restricted discussion about the concept of knowledge that John uses in reference to knowledge of God. Dodd observes that John's idea of knowing God cannot be assumed to be simply equivalent with the ideas of the Hermetists, the Gnostics, or Philo. Even allowing for these influences, Dodd denies that such influences can ". . . decide the question, what this writer meant by γινώσκειν τὸν θεόν ['to know God']."[32] Following Rudolf Bultmann, he accepts the idea that the Greek conception of *knowing God* has a different character than the Hebrew.[33] For the Greek mind, the knowledge of God consists in perception and contemplation of the objective reality or essence of God. Dodd writes, "Accordingly, for the Greek, to know God means to contemplate the ultimate reality, τὸ ὄντως ὄν, in its changeless essence."[34] In the Hebrew conception, on the other hand, Dodd states that knowing God "is essentially intercourse with God; it is to experience His dealings with men in time."[35] Dodd, again following Bultmann, views the Gnostic literature as holding an idea of knowledge which requires a person to be divine, and which implies experiential knowledge in accordance with the Hebraic conception of knowing. Dodd summarizes, "It makes a man no longer that superior type of humanity, the philosopher, living the βίος θεωρητικός [the informed life] but a being like God, or even a god himself."[36] Of course a god is a "being like God," but Dodd indicates here that there was a conception of exalted humanity, which lay between the concept of god and the concept of ideal man.

Dodd finds substantial affinities between the idea of knowing God in John's Gospel and this same idea in the Old Testament (Septuagint). The knowledge of God is considered accessible in the Old Testament, so that the lack of such knowledge in God's people is considered to be not an inherently human limitation, but rather human

30. Ibid., 231.
31. Ibid., 239.
32. Dodd, *Historical Tradition*, 151.
33. Bultmann, "γινώσκω," 701–8.
34. Dodd, *Historical Tradition*, 152.
35. Ibid.
36. Ibid., 153.

ignorance. Citing Wis 13, Dodd writes, ". . . the charge is precisely that God is knowable through the world He has made, but that men are too stupid (ματαίοι φύσει) to perceive Him."[37] Dodd writes, "That God's people *ought* to know Him is always assumed: it is unnatural that they should not know Him."[38] Furthermore, such ignorance of God is considered the result of a willful act, for which the people are culpable. This concept arises from the understanding that God has revealed Himself. The same Old Testament theme is taken up in John's Gospel. Dodd says of those who reject the Messiah in John 8:41–42, "Those who have been declared to have no knowledge of God are now said to be no children of God."[39]

In the Old Testament, human knowledge of God is not directly discussed with any frequency. Dodd remarks that "There are so few passages in the Old Testament which categorically assert that man knows God."[40] However in one striking passage, David exhorts his son Solomon, as the ascendant king, to know God (1 Chr 28:9). The meaning of this charge is that Solomon should be faithful to God, rather than be estranged from him. It is not primarily referring to the neutral and objective philosophical knowledge that was prominent in later Hellenistic thought.

It is important to distinguish between those ideas about the knowledge of God that are original to John, and those ideas which had already been expressed in the literary work of his time. The order of our examination of these ideas will depend in part on the relative influence we ascribe to each of them. Dodd's own discussion of *the knowledge of God* in John's Gospel begins with the ideas of such knowledge common in the literature of the period, before looking at John's particular ideas.[41] Dodd begins by discussing Hellenistic and Jewish parallels to the terminology and concepts found in the Gospel. Where the Evangelist uses similar terminology, Dodd ascribes to the Evangelist many of the concepts that such terminology carried in the Hellenistic literature. Dodd allows, however, that the Evangelist was not himself fully conscious of the way he used these concepts.[42] The terminology in John is similar to that in the Hermetic literature, and Dodd's primary concern is to determine the extent to which John's concepts are taken from Hellenistic ideas or Jewish ideas, and so to understand John's meaning. However Dodd wrote his analysis before the first English translation of the Dead Sea Scrolls had been published in 1955.[43] His analysis of the extent of Hellenistic influence is in need of reconsideration in the light of this new evidence about the origin and meaning of the terminology used by John.

---

37. Ibid., 156.
38. Ibid., 157.
39. Ibid., 158.
40 Ibid., 160.
41 Ibid., 151ff.
42 Ibid., 159.
43. Burrows, *Dead Sea Scrolls,* and Bartholémy and Milik, *Judean Desert* 1.

LITERARY INFLUENCE AND AUTHOR'S MEANING

How relevant is other literature of the time for understanding John's concept of knowledge? The assessment of the importance of background literature as an indication of the author's meaning constitutes a hermeneutical problem. Werner Jeanrond characterized Hans-Georg Gadamer's hermeneutic as "truth manifests itself to every well-intentioned reader of a classic text without any need for an explicit method of interpretation."[44] Whatever the merits of this approach, it is clearly a fallacy to require for the understanding of every text prior familiarity with another text, for this would prevent any initial entry into the family of texts.

Stephen Prickett touches on an equally serious exegetical question. Pricket, criticizing what he sees as excessive confidence by biblical translators in their methodology, says "the Bible is *not about* things that are natural, clear, simple, and unambiguous."[45] An associated question is whether we can correctly understand John even after we have reviewed the extant literature from his era. This problem arises not only because of the fragmentary character of the literary remains of that age, but also because there is no guarantee that any writer can be rightly understood simply because we have identified the background concepts prevalent in his own time. If we can understand the author, we may find that any significant understanding of him is largely to be derived from his own work rather than from the thought of his own age. Consequently, until we have actually looked at the author's text, there is no way to know whether the author's own thought, or whether instead the thought of his own age, or particular authors within his age, should provide the primary framework in which to understand him. For these reasons, in the next chapter we may legitimately proceed to examine John's own idea of knowledge and the knowledge of God, without first discussing in greater detail the religious influences of Hellenism, Judaism, and early Christianity.

CHAPTER CONCLUSIONS

Several conclusions from this chapter are worth noting. There is more than one kind of knowledge. We can distinguish *knowledge that* some statement is true from *knowledge of* a person or of an art. We can distinguish both of these from *knowledge how to do* something. Some knowledge can be understood as *justified and true belief*, but only when belief is not understood in the sense of *trust*, and only when knowledge is understood as *knowing that*. The Evangelist sometimes accepts the idea of some philosophers that there are kinds of knowledge that cannot be defined this way, notably when the Evangelist is thinking of *knowing a person*. The Evangelist at times indicates acceptance of the idea that some kinds of knowledge are self-evidently true. For example, he describes both seeing, and human testimony or reports as sources of knowledge. These two examples indicate his view that some beliefs deserve to be accepted as knowledge, and called knowledge, on a provisional basis. Doubt about what one sees is not usually justified, and

---

44. Jeanrond, "After Hermeneutics," 93.
45. Prickett, *Words and The Word*, 10.

would not be regarded as reasonable by John. Doubt sometimes requires justification, just as belief sometimes requires justification. John adopts the Hebrew conception of knowledge of God as experiential, rather than as merely mental contemplation, and he accepts the possibility of having such knowledge. He deserves to be read independently of Hellenistic parallels, and on his own terms. With the foregoing concepts of knowledge and belief set forth, we may now consider how John thinks knowledge can arise from historical accounts.

4

The Evangelist's Concept of Knowledge

History, Fiction, and the A Priori *Exclusion of the Possibility of Historical Miracles*

THE EVANGELIST'S IDEAS ABOUT knowledge of God are closely tied to his idea of the historical truth of his Gospel's statements. If we do not distinguish his statements about historical reality from his other statements, we may misunderstand his idea of what one can know about God's historical words and works. We may consequently misunderstand both his conception of historical fiction (including his use of symbols), and his conception of the historical accuracy intended in his accounts. The existence of this problem is illustrated by Rudolf Bultmann's comment on the miracle at the wedding in Cana. Bultmann says,

> The question whether the Evangelist believed the miracle to have been an actual historical occurrence may not, it seems to me, be answered so obviously in the affirmative as usually happens . . . [1]

Bultmann's comment suggests two questions about the historical character of assertions in the Fourth Gospel. First, to what extent does the Evangelist intend his statements as fiction, as only symbolic of nonhistorical truths, or as having limited historical accuracy, instead of as exact claims to knowledge of historical realities? Second, to what extent could the Evangelist plausibly have believed he is telling us about historical realities, about events that had actually occurred, or situations that really existed? The second question is related to the first. Fiction and symbolism are often indicated when a statement, which might otherwise refer to the real world, clearly claims something that the author could not believe to be true of the real world. A reader must then evaluate whether a text can be more cogently explained as an author's historical belief, than as symbolic or fictional usage. The answers to both of these questions will clarify the intended limits of fiction, symbolism, and historical accuracy in this Gospel. However we will not answer these

---

1. Bultmann, *Gospel of John*, 119.

questions by deciding the historical and factual character of John's particular claims, due to the inherently controversial character of such decisions.

THE HISTORICITY OF JOHN'S GOSPEL: CONTRARY VIEWS

The historical character of John's Gospel has always been controversial. The Gospel was a Christian work, and it made claims about Jesus that were not generally accepted outside the Christian community. (Here the term *Christian* includes Jesus' direct disciples, who were all Jews). The controversial character of this Gospel's historical claims is even acknowledged within the Gospel. Jesus himself was not accepted by "his own" (John 1:11) as being the one he claimed to be. The Judean leaders do not initially believe a blind man's testimony that Jesus healed him (John 9:18). Jesus' own disciple Thomas does not believe the reports of Jesus' resurrection (John 20:25). Just as, among characters described within the Gospel, there is controversy about the facts, we can be sure that the Evangelist encountered controversy about Christian historical claims in his own proclamation of Christian teaching, and in the public response to other Christian teachers.

The controversial character of Christian beliefs is suggested, first of all, by the early estrangement of Jews in the Christian community from the larger Jewish community. E. P. Sanders lists, as one of several "almost indisputable facts" about the early church that "at least some Jews persecuted at least parts of the new movement (Gal 1:13, 22; Phil 3:6), and it appears that this persecution endured at least to a time near the end of Paul's career (2 Cor 11:24; Gal 5:11; 6:12; cf. Matt 23:34; 10:17)." [2] We may ask, then, whether these groups held different accounts of Jesus' history.

As one instance of controversy, the first century Christians and the larger Jewish community did not equally credit the resurrection of Jesus. According to Matthew, Jewish leaders had promoted a report that the disciples stole Jesus' body from the tomb (Matt 28:12–15). For three reasons, this report appears to have been really circulating before Matthew wrote his Gospel. First, Matthew troubles to discredit the report with his accusation that it was promoted by means of lying and bribery. The accusation looks like Matthew's attempt to discredit a real report. Second, Matthew makes a publicly verifiable claim to knowledge of the report's current circulation, saying the report was "*widely spread* among the Jews *to this day*." Matthew would be seriously discredited as an informed source of knowledge about Jesus, if no such report had been currently circulating. His bribery accusation would then be suspect, and would look like baseless slander against Jewish religious leaders. Matthew's accusations were in writing, so it would have been difficult to later deny or reconstrue his meaning. All this would bring unnecessary embarrassment about Matthew's Gospel, discouraging its acceptance by the Christian community, and needlessly reducing its credibility among those inquirers Matthew wished to bring to the Christian faith. Third, if Jesus' body was truly missing, the suggested explanation was possibly the most plausible natural explanation. It appears then

---

2. Sanders, *Jesus and Judaism*, 11.

that the report of a stolen body was circulating within the Jewish community for some time before Matthew's Gospel was written.[3]

Another example of the difference between Christian and official Jewish views is that in the book of Acts there are Sadducean leaders who "say that there is no resurrection" (Acts 23:8–9). In contrast, it would be hard to imagine anyone remaining in the Christian community who denied the resurrection of Jesus in the same sense that these Jewish leaders denied it. The Christian claim about the resurrection was also controversial in Gentile communities, as is indicated, for example, by the Athenians' reception of Paul, "And having heard of a resurrection of the dead, some mocked . . ." (Acts 17:32). Because of the nature of these claims, the historical claims of the Gospels will predictably remain controversial.

For our purpose, however, no decision about the actual historical character of the particular miracles in John's Gospel is necessary. We will instead argue merely that the Evangelist believed such miracle accounts were substantially historical. Unfortunately, modern skepticism about the miraculous is so deeply held that (as will be argued) it has led many to erroneously suppose or suspect that John himself could not really have believed in the miracles he recounts. Any historical argument that John did accept miracles as basically factual appears futile without first addressing this inability to imagine how such a belief might appear plausible to the Evangelist.

HISTORICAL INTENTION: THE IMPORTANCE OF MIRACLES AS A TEST CASE

For several reasons, an examination of miracles provides an ideal initial test case for understanding John's use of history and fiction. The examination is unavoidable for review of the influential principle that miracle accounts are never credible. If we know that miracles cannot occur, or at least cannot be reported credibly, then it is more easily argued that John had no evidence for miracles that even he could have found historically convincing. This alone would not be fatal to our main argument about John's own historical beliefs, but would weigh against it. Miracles also provide an important test case for examination of the principle that historical reports in general cannot provide adequate evidence to become a basis for religious knowledge and belief. Furthermore, focusing upon the limited case of miracles as events will also eliminate the need to reach agreement about the historical or fictional character of every word in selected passages from the Gospel. Even if such agreement could ever be reached, the discussion needed to address all viewpoints would be impossibly long. If, however, John's intention to portray the miracles as essentially historical events can be shown, it becomes clear that many statements in his Gospel should be understood as essentially historical claims. Lastly, as we will discuss in a later chapter, miracles are a useful test case for understanding the Evangelist's idea of how people can have knowledge about God, since the Evangelist himself claims miracles are one of the primary means for such knowledge.

---

3. See also Byrskog, *Story as History*, 192–93.

The Evangelist's Concept of Knowledge: Possibility of Miracles

The argument of this chapter has four parts. First, the importance of understanding the Evangelist's view about miracles will be discussed, showing that our understanding in this case strongly influences the way in which the Evangelist's historical beliefs will be understood more generally. Second, various concepts of *miracle* will be broadly surveyed, described, and compared with the Evangelist's conception, so that our argument will not rest upon confused assumptions or misunderstandings about the concept of *miracle*. Third, a historical survey will describe the various arguments that have been made against the credibility of miracle reports. Lastly, it will be argued that, assuming there is a God who could perform a miracle, there is no modern consensus including theistic scholars that there could be no credible historical account of the miracle. It will be argued in consequence that, in the absence of such a consensus, modern concerns about the credibility of miracle accounts should not be allowed to influence our judgment about whether the Evangelist thinks miracles are impossible or are a means of knowing about God.

By the term *miracle*, we are here referring only to events that have no plausible natural cause. In the view of many current scholars, many of Jesus' healings could be plausibly ascribed to psychosomatic or other natural explanations. Marcus Borg characterizes the situation, saying, ". . . on historical grounds it is virtually indisputable that Jesus was a healer and exorcist."[4] E. P. Sanders has said, "Smith and I—and more or less everyone else—think that Jesus claimed to be a spokesman for God and performed what were viewed as miracles."[5] However, our concern here is with the miracles for which there exist no plausible natural explanations. Such miracles are especially prominent in John's Gospel.

THE HISTORICAL SIGNIFICANCE OF DENYING ALL MIRACLE REPORTS

The denial of the credibility of all miracle reports, as a principle consistently applied, significantly invalidates the historical character of the canonical Gospels. Under this principle, the reports of miracles must be regarded as historically unreliable, whether intentionally or unintentionally on the part of the author. If the author intended to tell of miracles that he believed did not occur, then he either expected his audience to understand his work as fictitious (e.g., like a historical novel or as a symbol for some non-historical reality), or he knew his report would mislead his audience (e.g., he "fabricated" and "invented" his claim, as Reimarus had suggested in the eighteenth century).[6] If, on the other hand, the author intended to tell of miracles that he (erroneously) believed did occur, then he was himself mistaken in that belief. Such an error could arise from a credulous use of unreliable sources (e.g., the author believed erroneous reports). Alternatively it would arise from a lack of care in the interpretation of facts and sources (e.g., the author misunderstood a report, or did not inform his readers of its doubtful character). The nineteenth century scholar David F. Strauss, citing particularly Paul's reported vision

---

4. Borg, *Jesus, a New Vision* cited in Habermas, "Did Jesus Perform Miracles?" 124.
5. Sanders, *Jesus and Judaism*, 170.
6. Reimarus, "The Intention of Jesus," 243.

of Jesus, thought it possible that the other apostles (still regarded by him as authors of the Gospels) likewise "proclaimed what they themselves believed" and so "were guilty of self-deception at most, not of lying."[7] If it is actually possible to deceive oneself about what one has seen, so as to believe it despite imprisonment or death, that must also be counted as genuine (if erroneous) belief. Error and misunderstanding are susceptible to a wider variety of explanations if we can further show that the real author did not receive his information firsthand, but secondhand, or thirdhand, or was even dependent upon an amalgam of tradition whose sources cannot be traced.

More particularly, a definitive demonstration that miracle reports are never credible will influence our reading of John's Gospel in regard to its historical veracity, accuracy, reliability, and fictional or symbolical intention. Not only would the removal of miracles itself change the character of the Gospel, but the narrative, dialogue and discourse which are often intertwined with the miracles become historically dislocated, which tends to diminish their historical character. As Graham Twelftree has observed, ". . . the Gospel writers placed so much emphasis on the miracles of Jesus that if they did not occur, a large question mark is placed against all the Gospel writers' fundamental understanding of Jesus and their message about him."[8] Here Twelftree assumes that the Gospel writers did promote the belief that Jesus performed historical miracles. The importance of miracles to historical and interpretive questions is suggested in Richard Swinburne's comment,

> It is an interesting exercise to read different New Testament commentaries and books about New Testament times, including those listed above, and note how different authors make different background assumptions about whether there is a God capable of intervening in nature and prepared on occasion to do so, and in consequence reach quite different conclusions about whether an apparent miracle really occurred, while using the same detailed historical evidence. This is as it should be, but what is to be regretted is that the different writers do not make explicit how their conclusions are determined largely by background assumptions.[9]

In a similar vein, Ernst and Marie-Louise Keller, while discounting the possibility of Jesus' miracles, agree that one's view of Jesus' life, and even the dating of the Gospels, depends in part on one's view of the possibility of miracles.[10] The credibility of miracle accounts has been a guiding criterion for historical evaluation of the Gospels. Although exorcisms and healings are sometimes credited as possible through unknown natural means, Hendrik van der Loos, in an extensive review of such claims, concluded that all of Jesus' miracles will never "be finally 'explained' in some physical, medical, or psychological laboratory."[11]

---

7. Strauss, "Hermann Samuel Reimarus," 51.
8. Twelftree, *Jesus the Miracle Worker*, 247.
9. Swinburne, *Miracles*, 207.
10. Keller and Keller, *Miracles in Dispute*, 192–93.
11. van der Loos, *Miracles of Jesus*, 303.

The Evangelist's Concept of Knowledge: Possibility of Miracles

THE CONCEPT OF *MIRACLE* AMONG SCHOLARS

Denial of the possibility of miracles, or of reports that they have been seen, necessarily invoke some concept of miracle in this denial. While the concept of miracle held by the Fourth Evangelist will be fundamental to our investigation, any evaluation of the criticism against miracles must be aware of other conceptions that have been held by scholars. Joseph Houston and Colin Brown have described the conceptions of miracle that have been held by a variety of influential historical figures.

Colin Brown's observations about Augustine's ideas are of special interest. Brown notes first that Augustine differentiated miracles that were merely stupendous from those (as in the Gospels) which conferred important benefits upon their recipients. Like many other theologians, Augustine viewed miracles as signs of God's gracious promises.[12] Brown also observes the limits that Augustine places on the idea of natural law. Suggesting an immanent rather than a transcendent view of God, Augustine says of miracles, "When such a thing happens, it appears to us as an event contrary to nature. But with God it is not so; for him 'nature' is what he does."[13] In Augustine's mind, a miracle contrary to nature is really only "contrary to what we know of nature."[14] However, as our discussion of Houston will show, this does not mean that Augustine sees all causes as residing in nature, but rather that God's purposes established and expressed in natural causes do not conflict with his purposes expressed in other causes. Augustine is hesitant to identify what we know of nature with all of nature's true laws. Augustine also observes the greater wonder of the creation in comparison to miracles, and remarks, "Now any marvellous thing that is wrought in this universe is assuredly less than this whole universe, that is heaven and earth and all things that in them are, which God assuredly made."[15]

Summarizing the views of theologians from Origen to Calvin, Brown observes that miracles were not set forth as a prime evidence for belief that God exists; other reasons were given to believe in God's existence. Brown notes also that the church observed the differences in character and in compelling evidential force of the various biblical miracles.

Joseph Houston provides a penetrating survey of the thought of Augustine, Aquinas, Locke, and Hume on miracles. According to Houston, Augustine conceives of some miracles as attributable to unknown natural laws, and conceives of others as due to God's direct intervention (sometimes by way of permanently changing the nature of previously created things). Augustine is doubtful that natural laws can be fully known, though he thinks it is beyond reasonable doubt that some events cannot be attributed to natural causes. We can have a provisional knowledge of at least some natural laws, according to Houston's understanding of Augustine. Some events are outside natural causes, for Augustine says, "In the first created order God did not pre-establish every cause, but

---

12. Brown, *Miracles and Critical Mind*, 19.
13. Augustine, *Genesis*, 6.13.24, cited in Brown, *Miracles and Critical Mind*, 9.
14. Augustine, *Faustus the Manichaean*, 26.3, cited in Brown, *Miracles and Critical Mind*, 8.
15. Augustine, *City of God* 10.12, cited in Brown, *Miracles and Critical Mind*, 328–29.

retained some in his own will, and those which he has kept in his own will assuredly do not depend on the necessity of created causes."[16] Even when God, rather than nature, is the direct cause, "those causes which he retained within his own will cannot be contrary to those which he laid down by his will, because the will of God cannot be contrary to itself."[17] For Augustine, a miracle must be a historical report, rather than a fable. Human dullness can only be overcome by a credible historical report, even though God discourages demands for the sensational. For Augustine, some miracles are remarkable enough to provide unbelievers a reason to come to faith in Christ.

Houston continues with a discussion of Thomas Aquinas. Aquinas differs from Augustine both by additions and by emphasis. Aquinas defines miracles as being performed by God alone, "since whatever an angel or any other created thing does by its own power takes place in accordance with the ordinary processes of nature and so is not miraculous."[18] Without criticizing this conception of miracle, it is noteworthy that this distinction does not seem to be a usage of the term *miracle* that would be recognized in the biblical literature, since false prophets can there perform miracles by means of evil spiritual powers. Aquinas agrees with Augustine that direct intervention by God would never be contrary to nature. However Aquinas apparently would not regard as a miracle an event that was caused by an unknown and never before observed natural law. Aquinas does not think miracles have the power of generally compelling belief because he thinks that belief and faith require the exercise of the will. Miracles are only reasons for a believer's faith. The believer "would not believe unless he saw that they [the matters of faith] are worthy of belief on the basis of evident signs or something of the sort."[19] Here Aquinas seems to regard belief as trust, not as mere assent.

Houston also cites a number of developments introduced by John Locke. Locke emphasizes more highly the importance of miracles. For him they are "that foundation on which the believers of any divine revelation must ultimately bottom their faith."[20] In other words, special divine revelation, which informs the essential content of religious faith, depends for its credibility upon attesting miracles. Locke understands belief to operate directly upon the evidence, without interposition of the will. This assumes a cognitive definition of belief as assent, rather than the definition of belief as trust. Consequently, Locke also regards belief as having degrees of intensity that should ideally correspond to the strength of the evidence. This is notably different from the conception of saving belief in John's Gospel, where our argument in an earlier chapter was that saving belief is not conceived of as a matter of degree, but as simply present or not present in any life. However, John generally thinks of belief as trust, not as cognitive assent, so the primary difference lies in the definition of belief that is adopted. Locke is interested in the credibility of historical testimony, and especially about miracle accounts.[21] In Houston's view,

16. Augustine, *Genesis*, 9.18.33, cited in Houston, *Reported Miracles*, 15.
17. Augustine, *Genesis*, 6.18.29, cited in Houston, *Reported Miracles*, 17.
18. Aquinas, *Summa Theologiae*, 1a, 110, 4. cited in Houston, *Reported Miracles*, 25.
19. Aquinas, *Summa Theologiae*, 2a, 2ae, 1,4. cited in Houston, *Reported Miracles*, 31.
20. Locke, *Discourse of Miracles*, cited in Houston, *Reported Miracles*, 34.
21. Locke, *Human Understanding*, cited in Houston, *Reported Miracles*, 35.

The Evangelist's Concept of Knowledge: Possibility of Miracles

Locke holds in *A Discourse of Miracles* a subjective definition of miracle. Locke defines miracle from the observer's standpoint as "in his [the observer's] opinion contrary to the established course of nature" and "taken by him to be divine."[22] Locke uses a subjective opinion about natural law because, like Augustine, he regards our human capacity to discover natural law as quite limited. In particular, since he defines miracle as something that "no created being has a power to perform,"[23] he is concerned that people cannot be sure that an apparent miracle was not performed by some other power (e.g., an angel). However Locke appeals to God's providential care in preventing anyone from being misled about authentic miracles. Houston criticizes Locke here for inconsistently encouraging the observer to credit miracles when he has no sufficient and reasonable grounds for the belief, in violation of Locke's ethic of responsible belief. Locke criticizes irresponsible belief as Enthusiasm. Houston notes that, in contrast, an objective theory of miracle is given in Locke's *Essay Concerning Human Understanding*.[24] Like the church fathers, Locke argues for the existence of God on the grounds of our own existence, rather than from the evidence of miracles. Locke also adopts the skeptical historical principle that "any testimony, the further off it is from the original truth, the less force and proof it has."[25]

After this survey of the most important views about miracles, Houston provides a comprehensive discussion of the concept of miracle. He begins with Hume's definition of a miracle as "a transgression of a law of nature by a particular volition of the Deity, or by the interposition of some invisible agent."[26] Houston offers instead the more qualified definition of a miracle as "what would be a transgression of natural law, were it not for extraordinary divine action."[27] The purpose of his qualified definition is to eliminate two assumptions. First, it removes any assumption that the divine purpose expressed in natural laws is necessarily in conflict with the divine purpose expressed in miracles.[28] Second, it removes any assumption that a miracle would be a transgression of natural law. In particular, this means the assumption that natural laws include laws about God's own actions, or alternatively, the assumption that God is not equally active in both natural law and in miraculous events.[29] In Houston's assessment, Hume's argument is directed against "the apologist, whose non-believing audience makes no theistic assumptions" and yet tries to make "a case for his religious system by appealing to reported proposed miracles."[30] Houston uses his modified definition to preserve Hume's emphasis on miracles as the tool of apologists, without excluding from discussion parties that have plausible objections to Hume's definition. Houston notes that Hume's definition requires one

---

22. Locke, *Discourse of Miracles,* cited in Houston, *Reported Miracles*, 35.
23. Ibid.
24. Locke, *Human Understanding* 15.5, cited in Houston, *Reported Miracles*.
25. Locke, *Human Understanding* 16.10, cited in Houston, *Reported Miracles*, 47.
26. Hume, *Human Understanding* 10.12.n23, cited in Houston, *Reported Miracles*, 103.
27. Houston, *Reported Miracles*, 112.
28. Ibid., 107.
29. Ibid., 108–11.
30. Ibid., 127–28.

to prove that a god performed the anomalous event, before calling the event a miracle. A similar definition to Houston's is adopted by Hendrik van der Loos who says, ". . . the very characteristic of miracles is the abrupt end of a status quo, an immediate change, a break in the existing state of affairs, i.e. the occurrence of a new and inexplicable situation."[31]

While the concept of miracle as an event inexplicable by natural law is useful, Mary Hesse reminds us that miracles popularly include cases of remarkably improbable coincidence, not merely supernatural interference.[32] As indicated above, Augustine also accepted this view. In similar fashion, George MacRae tells us, Josephus viewed God as alternately "working in and through the world."[33] MacRae especially notes how Josephus sees the natural order within events like the descent of quails into the midst of the hungry Israelites. This view of miracle was probably common in the first century Christian communities as well. In the Biblical traditions God is seen variously as immanent or transcendent. While it is not clear that nature is generally viewed as existing independently of God's power, God is often portrayed as acting upon nature, just as people, in a far more limited fashion, act upon nature. Indeed, it is the natural course of events, which shows that a supernatural agent (God) must have intervened when events follow a different course than would be naturally expected. This eliminates the objection that "the Hebraic worldview had no formal notion of 'laws of nature.'"[34] It is precisely by the knowledge that events are not natural that the presence of God is revealed in many of the Exodus miracles. Hesse notes that miracles that do not violate the laws of nature, whether coincidental or making use of unknown laws, are more easily accepted as historical.[35] This is notable for its potential influence on New Testament historiography, although it is almost impossible to imagine any plausible extension of natural laws that could explain all Biblical miracles. Similarly avoiding a machine model of the universe, C. F. D. Moule suggested that the universe, like our bodies, has mechanical qualities, but is likewise subject to influences that cannot be predicted mechanically.[36] Nevertheless, the rise of quantum theory does not mean that the universe is entirely unpredictable, but only unpredictable in certain quite limited respects.

THE CONCEPT OF MIRACLE IN JOHN'S GOSPEL

With this understanding of various conceptions of miracle, we can now understand more clearly the Evangelist's own conception, beginning with his terminology. John's standard term for miracle is *sēmeion* (σημεῖον), regularly translated into English as *sign*. Walter Bauer gives as one meaning of *sēmeion*, "*the sign or distinguishing mark* by which something is known, *token, indication*."[37] Bauer illustrates this usage with the text, "I,

---

31. van der Loos, *Miracles of Jesus*, 289.
32. Hesse, "Laws of Nature," 35.
33. MacRae, "Antiquities of Josephus," 142.
34. Purtill, "Defining Miracles," 63.
35. Hesse, "Laws of Nature," 41.
36. Moule, *Miracles*, 16.
37. Bauer, "σημεῖον," 747.

Paul, write this greeting with my own hand, and this is a distinguishing mark (*sēmeion*) in every letter" (2 Thess 3:17). The second meaning given by Bauer is, "*a sign consisting of a wonder or miracle.*"[38] This usage has a precedent in the account of miraculous plagues sent by God against Egypt (e.g., Exod 10:1–2), which are referred to as "signs" (*sēmeia* in the Septuagint). Raymond Brown has summarized the Old Testament parallels to John's Gospel, where the people do not trust in God "despite all the signs which I have performed among them" (Num 14:11), and where the importance of Moses' life is also finally epitomized in the signs which God gave him to do (Deut 34:11).[39]

While the term *sign* (*sēmeion*) has two common meanings, in the Gospel of John the context normally shows that *sēmeion* refers to miraculous signs, rather than to Jesus' works generally.[40] This is evident, for example, where Jesus clears the temple with a whip while making public accusation against the temple authorities (John 2:13–25). In response to this action, the Jewish leaders ask for a sign, since a miracle would give proof that Jesus has divine authority for his actions. In their mind at least, the action of clearing out the temple is not itself a sign, for they seek a sign that has a miraculous character, as proof of Jesus' authority. Here the Evangelist probably shares this idea of sign. The question, "What sign do you show us . . . ?" seems to portray the question of an entire group of people in language which is summarized in the Evangelist's own words, rather than in the words of a chief spokesman. In any case, the Evangelist's usual understanding of *sēmeion* as miracle is indicated from the narrator's characterization of Jesus' signs as the cause of the people's belief (John 2:23; 12:9–11), by the contrasting claim that John the Baptist "performed no sign" (John 10:41–42), and as the grounds by which Nicodemus knows that Jesus acted with divine assistance and authorization (John 3:2). Schnackenburg notes that about seven "great miracles" in John have often been referred to as signs, and that a number of other miracles are also described collectively as *sēmeia*.[41] While some have suggested that Jesus' death is a *sēmeion*, Schnackenburg notes that "the linguistic usage of John is different."[42] Barrett similarly says of Jesus' death, "it is not a σημεῖον [*sēmeion*] and is not called a σημεῖον [*sēmeion*]."[43]

John's typical use of the term "sign," rather than "miracle," reflects the same usage as the book of Exodus, and similarly emphasizes that the miracles give a divine message. The signs are not merely bare demonstrations of God's power to prove his presence, but are also expressions of God's character and his purposes for the world. In John's Gospel, signs take the forms of feeding, healing, and resurrection from the dead, which are all expressions of God's goodness. They are a cause for hope, for they foreshadow the same kinds of goodness promised for the Messianic Age. The signs, as a personal expression of Jesus' own power, also express John's Christological message, being, as in Barrett's words,

---

38. Ibid., 748.
39. Brown, *New Testament Essays*, 239.
40. Ibid., 236.
41. Schnackenburg, *Gospel According to John*, 1:516.
42. Ibid., 1:520.
43. Barrett, *Gospel According to John*, 78.

"a manifestation of the glory of Christ' (2.11)."[44] The signs are also special marks of God's presence because miracles are extraordinary events, and were best known to the Jews from times of rare national crisis. In the Old Testament, the two main clusters of miracles are performed by Moses at the Exodus, and by Elijah and Elisha in a time of Israel's apostasy from God. In the former instance, the deliverance of Israel from Egypt (and an affirmation of Moses' credibility) is secured by the miracles (Exod 3–14). In the latter, the worship of God is restored to the nation, after the murderous imposition of Baal worship (1 Kgs 16—2 Kgs 10). In John's Gospel, the signs are appealed to as evidence that Jesus has been sent by God as Messiah, one greater than Moses, and so an historic event in God's dealing with his people Israel.

The miraculous character of John's signs are emphasized by details which show that the signs are miraculous rather than naturally explicable: the wine made from water is of the best quality and is provided in enormous quantities (John 2); the official's son is healed at a distance, and at the very hour Jesus said he would be healed (John 4); the man healed of blindness had been blind from birth, as is testified by his parents (John 9); Lazarus had been dead for four days (John 11:17), Jesus was raised to life after his death was publicly witnessed, a spear in his side releasing blood and water (John 19:34–35).

THE RISE OF CHALLENGES AGAINST MIRACLES

Given the above clarifications of the concept of miracle used by John and others, we can now clearly document modern objections against the credibility of miracle reports in the Gospels. We will then describe the historical origin and rising influence of these ideas.

Perhaps the most elaborate early case for the unhistorical character of the Gospel miracles was made in the nineteenth century by David F. Strauss. It is noteworthy that Strauss excluded the possibility, not of most of the Gospel miracles, but all of them. Such a broad conclusion reflects his philosophical beliefs, rather than merely historical judgments. In 1835 Strauss wrote:

> Indeed no just notion of the true nature of history is possible, without a perception of the inviolability of the chain of finite causes, and of the impossibility of miracles. This perception which is wanting to so many minds of our own day was still more deficient in Palestine, and indeed throughout the Roman empire.[45]

Strauss clearly denied the possibility of miracles. More importantly, he made this denial a principle of valid historical method. Strauss expressed this as follows:

> That an account is not historical—that the matter related could not have taken place in the manner described is evident,
> *First.* When the narration is irreconcilable with the known and universal laws which govern the course of events.... When therefore we meet with an account of certain phenomena or events of which it is either expressly stated or implied that they were produced immediately by God himself (divine apparitions—voices from

---

44. Ibid., 75.
45. Strauss, *Life of Jesus*, 74–75.

heaven and the like), or by human beings possessed of supernatural powers (miracles, prophecies), such an account is *in so far* to be considered as not historical.[46]

In Strauss's judgment, the non-miraculous character of history means that "either Jesus was not really dead, or he did not really rise again."[47]

The philosophical foundation for Strauss's views has been delineated by Niels Thulstrup and is summarized and supplemented here.[48] Cicero, under the influence of ancient skepticism, denied the possibility of miracles.[49] Colin Brown notes that early seventeenth century "skepticism received its strongest encouragement from religious apologists who sought to demolish all claims to knowledge of their opponents in order to make way for their own views."[50] In particular, he cites a skeptical sixteenth century philosophical movement, the New Pyrrhonism, named after the Greek skeptic Pyrrho. This movement, says Brown, was "forged for the destruction of Calvinism" by seeking "to undermine all human claims to rational, objective knowledge, including the claims to know Scripture to be the Word of God and to be able to interpret it correctly."[51] Brown cites La Placette, Bouiller, and Chillingworth as Protestants who in turn used such arguments against Catholic authors. Lord Herbert of Cherbury published a seminal work for Deism, criticizing revelation and miracles, *On Truth, as it is Distinguished from Revelation, from the Probable, the Possible, and the False* (1645 edition).[52] Benedict (Baruch) de Spinoza, in his *Tractatus Theologico-Politicus* of 1670, subsequently promoted the denial of miracles.[53] Later, the seventeenth century philosopher Gottfried Leibniz proposed a distinction between truths known by reason, and those known by experience. Truths of reason are true of necessity, but truths of historical fact are considered by Leibniz to be contingent, since the world might have been different. In the following century, David Hume's essay *On Miracles* (1748) argued that reports of miracles could not be plausibly credited. Later in that century, Carl Bahrdt argued for explanations of all miracle reports by means consistent with the natural course of events. Bahrdt was particularly concerned that faith not be based on the miraculous, but on what he considered to be the divinity of the Gospel.[54] From Hume's idea of the unreliability of historical reports, the dramatist Gotthold E. Lessing argued in *Über den Beweis des Geistes und der Kraft* (1777) that the truths of reason have a greater validity than truths of experience. Lessing maintained this idea after his publication of *Fragments* from Hermann Samuel Reimarus' posthumous *Apologie; oder, Schutzschrift für die vernünftigen Verehrer Gottes*. According to Lessing, all reports, including those in the New Testament, are only probable at best, and so are

46. Ibid., 87–88.
47. Ibid., 736.
48. Kierkegaard, *Philosophical Fragments*, xlvi–lx. For a broader historical outline yielding similar conclusions, see Kee, *Early Christian World*.
49. van der Loos, *Miracles of Jesus*, 7.
50. Brown, *Miracles and Critical Mind*, 23.
51. Ibid., 24–25.
52. Ibid., 25.
53. Keller and Keller, *Miracles in Dispute*, 30.
54. Ibid., 67–69.

inherently unreliable, and so can only be believed by a resolution or "leap." Consequently, Lessing does not accept reports of miracles as grounds for Christian belief. Similarly, Immanuel Kant, in his *Religion within the Limits of Pure Reason* (1793), counts knowledge of morality as the essence of religion, and historical truths of religion as unimportant. The relative insignificance of history was accepted also by Johann Fichte (1806) and Friedrich Schleiermacher (1799). Hegel considered the truths of history to be merely poor duplicates of what could be seen by reason. Strauss, who explicitly acknowledges his debt to Hegel, then proposed his own theory that the New Testament accounts are myths. Ludwig Feuerbach, another Hegelian, argued that religion is merely wishful and imaginative thinking, and that gods are merely an image reflecting human nature.[55] Against this trend, another Hegelian, Carl Daub, argued for a return to traditional church orthodoxy.

It is evident from this summary that Strauss drew from philosophical movements that antedated him by at least a generation. His decision to exclude the possibility of any miracles was made on the basis of these ideas. At least from the time of Kant, it is evident that many writers doubted the historical incarnation and the historical resurrection of Jesus. This philosophical trend against the miraculous is the more remarkable for having gained ascendancy prior to the publication of Darwin's *Origin of the Species* in 1859. Without an accepted scientific theory to account for the origin of mankind, these philosophers were at least provisionally dependent upon a Deistic account of the creation, which suggested that at least the one miracle of the creation of the human race had occurred.

Albert Schweitzer, in his review of the progress of nineteenth century German Gospel scholarship, indicates that Strauss's view of miracles became widespread in Germany. Schweitzer remarked,

> What has been gained is only that the exclusion of miracle from our view of history has been universally recognized as a principle of criticism, so that miracle no longer concerns the historian either positively or negatively. Scientific theologians of the present day who desire to show their "sensibility," ask no more than that two or three little miracles may be left to them—in the stories of the childhood, perhaps, or in the narratives of the resurrection. And these miracles . . . have at least no relation to those in the text, but are . . . too insignificant to do historical science any harm, especially as their owners honestly pay the tax upon them by the way in which they speak, write, and are silent about Strauss.[56]

Schweitzer apparently refers to the incarnation and resurrection of Christ as the "two or three little miracles" which were still accepted by many. In Schweitzer's judgment they were accepted on the basis of theological tradition, rather than on the basis of the evidence of the Gospels, since the miracles in his view had "no relation to those in the text." In other words, this scientific and critical understanding of history did not accept the claims of the text as historically adequate evidence for the occurrence of any of the miracles it reported.

55. Ibid., 105.
56. Schweitzer, *Historical Jesus*, 111.

The Evangelist's Concept of Knowledge: Possibility of Miracles

Keller suggests that important twentieth century developments in theology are dependent upon a naturalistic explanation of miracles.[57] As he describes it, Hermann Gunkel, a member of the *history of religions* school, argued early in the century that the miracles in the Bible should be understood like the folk tales found in many cultures and religions. Martin Dibelius and Rudolf Bultmann, leaders of the form-critical approach, attempted to understand the miracles by analyzing the function of their literary and oral forms, including comparisons with folk literature. Bultmann also construed the world to be "immune from the interference of supernatural powers."[58] He separately argued for the importance of the miracle stories, not as history, but as embodying a message that can give our own lives meaning.

That the German debate was not yet over in Schweitzer's time is suggested, however, by the comment of Käsemann half a century later, that the battle was only then complete:

> Over few subjects has there been such a bitter battle among the New Testament scholars of the last two centuries as over the miracle-stories of the Gospels. . . . We may say that today the battle is over, not perhaps as yet in the arena of church life, but certainly in the field of theological science. It has ended in the defeat of the concept of miracle which has been traditional in the church.[59]

The traditional concept of miracle, which Käsemann finds defeated, is apparently the concept of a miracle that was inexplicable from natural causes, which could be known as a historical event. Käsemann's portrayal of the controversy as a battle among New Testament scholars is unconvincing, for it suggests that New Testament scholars have made this determination alone, or by means of their special expertise. The impossibility of miracles occurring is a question concerning which New Testament scholars are not expert, if only because miracle traditions from other religions are conceivably true. The possibility of miracles is a question belonging primarily to the disciplines of Philosophy of Religion and Philosophy of History, rather than to New Testament scholarship. New Testament scholars do have special expertise in the evaluation of the particular evidence for the Gospel miracles, however it seems unlikely that Käsemann has this in mind. The merely historical evidence can hardly prove that each and every individual miracle has no historical basis. Furthermore, in the judgment of a scholar like E. P. Sanders, the historical evidence itself suggests that Jesus himself saw his own miracles as testifying to his commission from God.[60]

An anti-miraculous view of the world remains influential. Joseph Houston, in a book arguing against Hume's anti-miraculous views, concedes that the acceptance of Hume's arguments by professional philosophers is "the consensual philosophical wisdom," supported in recent times most notably by J. L. Mackie, T. Penelhum, and John Hick.[61] The

---

57. Keller and Keller, *Miracles in Dispute*, 109–44.
58. Bultmann, "New Testament and Mythology," cited in Ellis, "Gospels Criticism," 27.
59. Käsemann, *New Testament Themes,* 48, 50–51, cited in Helms, *Gospel Fictions,* 62.
60. Sanders, *Jesus and Judaism,* 173.
61. Houston, *Reported Miracles,* 3.

anti-miraculous view also enjoys popular influence. A 1998 study reported that in both 1933 and 1997 only 40 percent of American scientists believed in "a God in intellectual and affective communication with man ... to whom one may pray in expectation of receiving an answer."[62] The remainder said they did not believe, or were unsure. Among the 1,800 scientists of the prestigious American National Academy of Sciences surveyed in 1997, with over fifty percent of those polled responding, fewer than ten percent of the respondents said they believe in this kind of God.[63] It seems unlikely that many who doubt the existence of such a God would credit the possibility of miracles.

NO CONSENSUS THAT MIRACLE REPORTS ARE NEVER CREDIBLE

In this section we will argue first that, assuming there is a God who could perform a miracle, there is no full consensus among modern philosophers that there could be no credible historical account of a miracle. We will show that any philosophical judgment on this matter is neither simple nor trivial, so that it should not be assumed that the Evangelist would adopt the modern disaffection for the possibility of any miracles.

In spite of its influence, the philosophical view that the world is ruled solely by natural law has achieved no consensus that includes theistic scholars. In the recently issued *Routledge Encyclopedia of Philosophy*, the philosopher David Basinger includes a synopsis of the major arguments currently advanced, and cites in the bibliography several authors who advance arguments in support of the possibility of miracles, including works by R. F. Holland, J. Houston, R. A. H. Larmer, and Richard Swinburne.[64] Houston in turn, in his recognized critique of Hume, notes the continuing presence of philosophically "sophisticated challenges" to the Humean consensus from "highly reputable centres of learning," including challenges by William Alston, Alvin Plantinga,[65] William Rowe, and Richard Swinburne. Both Larmer's and Swinburne's works include edited collections of essays, showing further support for the credibility of miracles. Within German scholarship, Wolfhart Pannenberg[66] and Peter Stuhlmacher have supported the reality of miracles. John Hick, an influential philosopher of religion, has argued that the laws of nature are tentative generalizations of our experience of the world which must be revised when our experience violates them, saying, "Without regard to the relevant evidence, it cannot be said that the story, for example, of Jesus's healing the man with the withered hand (Lk 6:6–11) is untrue, or that comparable stories from later ages or the present day are untrue."[67] J. P. Moreland argues that allowing miracles within certain limits does not itself undermine the concept of natural law, since that concept was developed in times

---

62. Larson and Witham, "Scientists and Religion," 90. Also, Larson, "Scientists Still Reject God," *Nature*, 313.

63. Larson and Witham, "Scientists and Religion," 90.

64. Basinger, "Miracles," 411–16. See Holland, "The Miraculous," 43–51; Larmer, *Water into Wine*; idem, *Questions of Miracle*; and Swinburne, *Miracles*.

65. See Alston, *Perceiving God*; and Plantinga, *Warranted Christian Belief*, 394–404.

66. See Pannenberg, *Philosophy of Science*, 400.

67. Hick, *Philosophy of Religion*, 38.

when God's action in the world was widely accepted.[68] Theistic arguments favoring the possibility of miracles should not be dismissed as trivial, before a hearing of the more cogent proponents.

While support for and against the miraculous can be found among scholars, the mere prevalence of opinion cannot decide which view is correct. This is not only evident on logical grounds, but is supported by the documented change of philosophical opinions through the centuries. Houston remarks that "it is surprising to see any professional philosopher appealing, as Williams does, to assured results, those of Hume and Kant, in philosophy; it is the more surprising when much of their Enlightenment anti-theology has come to be challenged in recent years."[69] Since philosophers, like others, often argue against prevailing opinion, they do not recognize prevailing opinion alone as decisive. For those who lack the expertise or time to form an independent judgment, the disparity of opinion among professional philosophers of religion means that the opponents deserve a hearing before one denies the possibility of miracles upon philosophical grounds.

HOUSTON'S ARGUMENT AGAINST HUME'S VIEW OF MIRACLES

The purpose of this chapter is not to argue that miracles can occur, but rather to present arguments showing that the possibility cannot be dismissed as trivial. If theists cannot see a rejection of miracles as a trivial philosophical decision, much less can it be argued that John the Evangelist would have dismissed miracles as philosophically trivial. The arguments of Joseph Houston against David Hume, and against Hume's current advocate J. L. Mackie,[70] will be briefly presented here.

Houston focuses on the key figure of David Hume. Hume had argued that there could not, even in principle, be compelling evidence to accept any report of miracles. More particularly he wrote,

> That no testimony is sufficient to establish a miracle, unless the testimony be of such a kind, that its falsehood would be more miraculous, than the fact, which it endeavours to establish.[71]

This seems reasonable, provided that by "more miraculous" Hume means "more highly improbable." The criterion, however, is possibly incapable of application, since it does not indicate how this relative improbability can be measured. Is the probability that any event was miraculous equal to the proportion of past miracles to all past events? Instead of all past events, should only events that have the non-miraculous elements of miracles (e.g., human significance or divine purpose) be compared? If an ostensibly divine purpose is a requirement, how is such a purpose to be differentiated from other purposes? Similarly, how are past miraculous events to be first identified so that the probability of any other reported miracle being authentic might be calculated? Houston, similarly,

---

68. Moreland, *Nature of Science*, 226.
69. Houston, *Reported Miracles*, 2–3.
70. Mackie, *Miracle of Theism*.
71. Hume, *First Enquiry*, Section 10, p. 109, as cited in Houston, *Reported Miracles*, 53.

asks if Hume's manner of assessing a single miracle neglected consideration of "reports of other miracles supposedly accomplished by, or on, or in some relation to the same person as is alleged to have worked" the miracle in question.[72]

Another difficulty is that Hume's criterion may call into question every report of an anomalous event. Hume remarks about testimony to miracles,

> The reason why we place any credit in witnesses and historians, is not derived from any *connexion*, which we perceive *a priori*, between testimony and reality, but because we are accustomed to find a conformity between them.... The very same principle of experience ... gives us also, in this case, another degree of assurance against the fact ... from which contradiction there necessarily arises a counterpoize, and mutual destruction of belief and authority.[73]

Hume may be correct about the absence of any *a priori* connection between testimony and reality, yet it seems that a genuinely pervasive doubt about the existence of such a connection would be a step into madness. However Hume's doubt about the credibility of testimony would also seem to apply to all anomalous events, even if they were anomalous simply because of one's limited experience. Hume, following the philosopher John Locke, mentions an Indian prince who, having never seen ice, does not believe reports that rivers in Moscow freeze over in the winter. Hume is sympathetic to such disbelief, but seems not to take into account that the first time this prince himself sees ice with his own eyes, his prior uniform experience will also be violated. Consequently, violation of uniform experience cannot, by itself, provide adequate grounds for the prince to doubt his own senses. Similarly, a child initially has no experience, and many new experiences are unparalleled by prior experiences, yet the child must provisionally believe these new experiences. Why then should anyone doubt the report of an event solely because the event was anomalous? As Houston says concerning historical investigation generally, "the reply of the anti-sceptic is that since the field of investigation incontestably does provide knowledge and understanding, its presuppositions are thereby vindicated."[74] Consequently, a charitable reading of Hume requires a supplemental condition for doubting reports. This condition must be that the reported event is a more improbable cause of the report than is some alternative explanation—as Hume indicates in the first above citation from his work. Alternative explanations would include: that the witness was in error; that the witness was lying; or that the report had been misunderstood. This leaves us again, however, with the problem of determining the probabilities of alternate explanations, rather than knowing by simple inspection which events are more improbable and so deserve to be doubted. As Colin Brown notes, A. E. Taylor has voiced a similar criticism of Hume to the effect that one must first examine all claims for miracles in order to know the natural law that would not have allowed them to occur.[75]

---

72. Houston, *Reported Miracles*, 70.

73. Hume, "Of Miracles," Section 10 of *An Enquiry concerning Human Understanding*, cited in Houston, *Reported Miracles*, 112.

74. Houston, *Reported Miracles*, 71.

75. Brown, *Miracles and Critical Mind*, 92.

Houston warns against a misunderstanding of Hume's conception of natural law. Hume does not simply exclude the possibility of the miraculous by defining natural law so as to exclude anomalous events. Houston argues instead that Hume asks for the most reasonable way to evaluate reports, when those reports differ from all similar reports. This evaluation, Houston argues, makes no implicit assumption that a reported miracle is the same kind of event as those by which a natural law is determined.[76]

It is only one's experience that reports of anomalies are usually unreliable that justifies one in thinking that new reports of that kind are unreliable. However everyone's experience will show that some reports of anomalous events are to be credited, and some are not. This means that the probability of the event can be only one factor in determining whether it is credible. Lack of absolute certainty does not justify a presumption of doubt. In general, the necessity to act on available information may require one to provisionally believe or disbelieve a report on the balance of the probabilities, even if one knows that the basis for belief or disbelief is weak. Following Francis H. Bradley and Ernst Troeltsch, Houston argues that "we are constrained to accept whatever is a presupposition" of any "intelligibility-giving activity."[77] Maximizing intelligibility of the world seems the right way to approach anomalies. Rather than limiting our understanding merely to our direct past experiences, Bradley argued that we must and ought to critically evaluate and understand all our experiences against a theory which best explains them by causes analogous to our own experience, or at least not violating those analogous causes.[78] Colin Brown similarly concludes that the assessment of reports cannot be isolated from one's larger judgments about the character of the report, and what is possible.[79]

Houston notes Hume's observation that any appeal to testimony requires a general trust in common experience, as a basis for knowing when testimony is of a reliable sort. In other words, we assess the veracity of reports by our previous experiences of the reliability of similar reports. Points of similarity in two reports might include the characteristics of each witness, the characteristics of what is reported, and agreement or disagreement between the reports. Agreement by independent witnesses about the events reported (especially in cases of dispute), and characteristics of the way the report was delivered, may both reflect indirectly upon the character of a report. The preponderance of evidence will in some cases indicate "no contest."

Hume's main argument seems to be that all knowledge comes by experience, so that a claim that challenges the validity of experience cannot be accepted without undermining the ground of all our knowledge. Hume defined a miracle as "a violation of the laws of nature."[80] Colin Brown adds that Hume argued *a posteriori* that the witnesses of miracles are never competent, that reports of miracles arise only from exaggeration, that such reports are prevalent among the ignorant, and that reports of miracles can be

---

76. Houston, *Reported Miracles*, 129–30.
77. Ibid., 71.
78. Ibid., 72, 75.
79. Brown, *Miracles and the Critical Mind*, 99.
80. Ibid., 84.

found among rival religions, undermining their importance as evidence.[81] Hume's case, however, remains controversial.

Joseph Houston argues that Hume made two mistakes. One error was to argue that the evidence for natural law is so vast that it proves that a miracle could not have occurred. If miracles sometimes occur, Houston says, it is invalid to exclude miracles arbitrarily from all the reports by which natural law is determined. He argues further that we might know some natural laws on the basis of comparatively limited evidence, so that a miracle supported by very powerful evidence would outweigh the evidence for the natural law.[82] Hume's second error, according to Houston, was to argue that the improbability of an event determines the probability of a report of the event being true. Houston observes that many people would take special care to relate accurately a report that was so unlikely. From this he concludes that Hume was mistaken to identify the improbability of an event with the improbability of a report of the event being true; mistaken also to suppose that an unlikely event is less likely to be truly reported; and mistaken further to think that the improbability of a report being true is proportional to the improbability of the event reported.[83] Houston, like other scholars, asks only that the report of a miracle may give support to theism, not provide the foundation for a system of religion or belief in God. In his view, the hypothesis that a god caused a miracle is a possibility that can be considered objectively.[84]

The philosophical debate about the plausibility of miracles has often rested on the plausibility of monotheism. As J. A. Cover has noted, monotheists have been more willing to accept the occurrence of miracles as a rational possibility.[85] In the view of many monotheists, it appears unreasonable to hold a principle that there is no amount of evidence that could justify belief in miracles. For example, assuming absolute historical accuracy of the story of the man born blind who was healed by Jesus (John 9), should one deny the possibility of miracles if one were a parent of the man (or if one were one of the judges)? Are there not scenarios where no explanation would be (for a monotheist) as coherent as that a miracle occurred? For monotheists, allowing in principle for the possibility of miracles allows for the world to be seen as more rational and intelligible in such a situation, rather than as unintelligible; the possibility of miracles is then to be decided upon the historical evidence and upon a judgment about what constitutes probable evidence of a miracle occurring. This is perhaps the reason that some are unwilling to exclude the possibility of miracle as a matter of general principle. John P. Meier, for example, says that "faith-knowledge" can only be "bracketed . . . for the sake of the scientific method employed" in order to make a "hypothetical reconstruction" which may later be correlated with faith-knowledge.[86]

---

81. Ibid., 86–87.
82. Houston, *Reported Miracles*, 133–34.
83. Ibid., 152.
84. Ibid., 157.
85. Cover, "Miracles and Christian Theism," 374.
86. Meier, *Marginal Jew*, 30–31.

CHAPTER CONCLUSIONS

The influential modern idea that miracle reports are never credible should not determine our evaluation of John's own historical or fictional intention. Given the assumption that there is a God who could perform miracles, there is no modern consensus, including theistic scholars, that the account of a miracle could never have sufficient evidence to be credible. The idea that no miracle accounts are credible is based on controversial philosophical assumptions, rather than merely on historical evidence and scientific method. Furthermore, the belief that miracles do not occur should not be accepted as determining *a priori* that John himself knew or believed that his claims about miracles were historically unsound or fictitious. Even if it should be granted that miracles are not possible, this alone would provide no decisive reason to read John's work as essentially fictional, simply because he reports miracles. If today some still credit the possibility of miracles, it can only have been easier to credit them in John's day. This will become clearer as we examine other clues to the fictional extent of his claims, and the way that early readers understood John's Gospel.

5

The Evangelist's Concept of Knowledge

Intended Fiction in the Case of Miracles

IN OUR ATTEMPT TO understand the grounds for knowledge about God that are adopted in John's Gospel, we have begun by trying to distinguish language intended as fictional or symbolic (yet nonhistorical) from language intended to refer to historical realities. Thus far, we have focused only on the important case of whether or not the Evangelist regards the miracles in his Gospels as essentially historical events. We have argued in the last chapter that, in the absence of a modern consensus among theists that miracle accounts could never be credible, we should not decide *a priori* that John would not have regarded any miracle accounts as credible. However we must now look at the historical evidence to decide whether in fact John did regard the miracle reports in his Gospel as credible accounts of essentially historical events.

FICTIONALLY INTENDED MIRACLE ACCOUNTS IN JOHN'S GOSPEL?

The accounts of miracles in John's Gospel will not be understood as claims about essentially historical events if, for other reasons, the Gospel is understood to be intended as an essentially fictional narrative, or as more likely to be fictional than otherwise. In this discussion the term *fiction* will be used, not in the sense of historical claims which are in fact false, but in the sense of statements which are intended to be understood as nonhistorical, whether as historical fiction or as symbols of nonhistorical truths. In this regard we again note Rudolf Bultmann's suggestion that the miracle at Cana was not believed by the Evangelist to be "an actual historical occurrence."[1] If the Evangelist did not believe that this miracle occurred, it suggests that at least some miracles in the Gospel were intended to be understood as historical fiction, or alternatively as merely spiritual symbolism. Bultmann wrote that the Evangelist "gives the Gospel the appearance of an historical narrative," though for Bultmann it is only this "appearance" which is certain.[2] Rudolf Schnackenburg observes that some consider John's Gospel to be "a work of pious

---

1. Bultmann, *Gospel of John*, 119.
2. Ibid., 130.

speculation with no historical value."[3] D. Moody Smith says that one arguable position taken by some scholars is that "any departure" in John's Gospel from the Synoptic Gospels lacks "historical substance" and "is a product of John's apologetic or theological interest."[4] Peter Kirchschlaeger says the expulsion of the blind man from the synagogue in John 9 "must be understood more precisely as an illustration of the denial of Jesus and his followers, not as a direct indication of a historical fact—by its very genre, the Gospel of John does not necessarily want to give us historical facts."[5] Sandra Schneiders concludes that it is "highly doubtful" that Jesus raised anyone else from the dead, and she asks what the story of Lazarus' resurrection is then intended to mean for the reader.[6] Again, a Christian inventor of miracle stories presumably would have thought either that the stories were at least *like* genuine miracles that Jesus had actually done, or alternatively that the stories' genuine meaning was only symbolical, referring to nonhistorical realities. In either case, the author's primary interest would not depend upon the miracles themselves being essentially historical events.

Even on the part of those who do not believe in the possibility of historically credible miracle accounts, there has been disagreement with the idea that the Gospel of John is written as fiction. We note that Strauss's own disbelief in miracles did not lead him to conclude that the Gospel of John was intended to be understood as fiction. To the contrary, Strauss says,

> It is not denied that what to us can appear only sacred poetry, was to Paul, John, Matthew and Luke, fact and certain history.... Those first Christians needed in their world, for the animating of the religious and moral dispositions in the men of their time, history and fact, ... [7]

Strauss himself denied the Evangelists' fictional intention. Presumably he attributed the absence of historical accuracy to the Evangelists' unwitting use of nonhistorical sources, along with what he elsewhere styled as their "self-deception."[8] Strauss "defined myth in the Gospels as a 'narrative relating, directly or indirectly to Jesus which may be considered not as the expression of a fact, but as the product of an idea of his earliest followers.'"[9] Strauss thought the Evangelists themselves regarded their reported miracles as "fact and certain history," so that to this extent they would not have intended their own works to be understood as fiction. This presumes, of course, that the Evangelists had (after their self-deception) no genuine historical knowledge of the events.

For those who do not consider any miracle reports credible, an explanation similar to Strauss's "sacred poetry" is necessary. The only difference today is that, while Strauss still thought that the Gospels were really written by (or under) the apostles, the Gospels

---

3. Schnackenburg, *Gospel According to John*, 1:3.
4. Smith, "Problem of History," 314.
5. Kirchschlaeger, "Literary and Historical Approach," 147.
6. Schneiders, "Remaining in His Word," 267.
7. Strauss, *Life of Jesus*, 776.
8. Strauss, "Hermann Samuel Reimarus," 51.
9. Kee, *Early Christian World*, 17.

are now usually seen as collections of tradition rather than as apostolic memoirs. Others would now suggest that John added to this collected history his own historical fiction (as sacred "poetry"), a suggestion that denies that John understood the historicity of his miracle accounts as essential to their importance. This explanation has been used, for example, in regard to the account of Jesus' supernatural knowledge about the Samaritan woman's five marriages (John 4:18). Schnackenburg cites Bauer as considering "the narrative in 4:1–42 as a purely literary composition of the Evangelist without historical value."[10] If John's intention to be read as fiction is not accepted as a possibility, his acceptance of historical traditions circulating at the time of the Gospels' composition are apparently the only remaining explanation for the miracle accounts in his Gospel. If the miracle reports are not accepted as credible, the use of both faulty sources and fiction, selecting each as best fitted to explain particular features of the Gospels, is the mode of explanation that would seem to offer the most flexible system of explanation. This ignores, however, the question of whether the combination has any antecedent probability in any particular case.

Strauss's main contribution, according to Albert Schweitzer, was to explain the Gospel accounts of miracles as myths. Strauss thought there was not time for such myths to develop after Jesus' ministry. He proposed instead that these myths were those already current about the Messiah, and so were simply assumed to be true of Jesus. In other words, Jesus must have performed such miracles because he was the Messiah. This solution was awkward. For a time, some scholars argued that the Gospels were much later, even mid second century, allowing time after Jesus for the creation of myth. However second century dates for the Gospels have been largely abandoned, even John's Gospel usually being dated now to the late first century. As mentioned earlier, in Borg's judgment most scholars now envisage the rise of miracle legends and reports as contemporaneous with Jesus' ministry, since the miracle tradition of Jesus has been widely accepted as having a historical basis in naturally explicable healings (e.g., psychosomatic healings) and exorcisms.[11]

Strauss's conception of myth was not well founded on the actual genres of ancient literature. The claim that the Gospels were intended as myth has been contested on this basis. Konstan, for example, argues that of three genres recognized by some ancient critics (e.g., Quintilian), the Gospels are closer to being a "nonhistorical narrative" than to being myths.[12]

The view that the Gospel miracle accounts are fictions or myths does not itself explain, however, why these particular miracle legends arose, or why they arose as a collection of myths in a collection of gospels, or why they arose when they did. Furthermore, if the Gospel accounts are regarded as historical fictions of some kind, the historical elements in the fictions deserve to be recognized. Strauss's failure to explain the origin of these myths was noted by Schweitzer:

---

10. Schnackenburg, *Gospel According to John*, 1:458.
11. Borg, *Jesus, a New Vision* cited in Habermas, "Did Jesus Perform Miracles?" 124.
12. Konstan, "The Invention of Fiction," 27.

> Strauss . . . does not see that while in many cases he has shown clearly enough the source of the *form* of the narrative in question, this does not suffice to explain its *origin*. Doubtless, there is mythical material in the story of the feeding of the multitude. But the existence of the story is not explained by referring to the manna in the desert, or the miraculous feeding of a multitude by Elisha. . . . The substratum of historical fact in the life of Jesus is much more extensive than Strauss is prepared to admit.[13]

This is not an argument against the many other historical problems raised by Strauss. Our argument is not that the Gospel's miracles are actually historical, but the much more limited historical claim that John *thought* that Jesus actually performed miracles. Strauss himself seems to allow for this possibility. For example, in regard to the blind man who is healed in John 9, Strauss refers to what he considers extensive elaborations of this miracle as creations of either "the author of this fourth gospel, or the tradition whence he drew." [14]

The possibility of fictional intention seems to be more widely accepted now than it was in the time of Strauss. At least in the case of the wedding miracle at Cana cited above, Bultmann thought that a fictional intention was plausible. Helmut Koester writes, "In many instances, the author of the Fourth Gospel did not compose these discourses *de novo*, but utilized and expanded older existing discourses."[15] Koester's qualifying phrase, "in many instances," suggests that in several instances the Johannine discourses were composed *de novo*. In a popular treatment, Randel Helms argued recently, "The Gospels, however—and this is my thesis—are largely fictional accounts concerning an historical figure, Jesus of Nazareth. . . ."[16] In regard to the Gospels, Gareth Schmeling similarly writes, "No one work is all fact or all fiction but rather a blending of the two, in which one or the other dominates."[17] This last dictum provides no guidance, however, as to how the two are to be distinguished. In a recent discussion of the genre of John's Gospel, Lawrence Wills wrote, "Yet the gospel is not fiction, in the sense of an invented world that is recognized as such by both author and reader, but a cult narrative, and similar in some ways to the 'historical novel.'"[18] Commenting on Wills' comparison of the Gospels of Mark and John to the *Life of Aesop*, Mark Goodacre observes, however, ". . . the handful of similarities between the texts are far from striking."[19]

Modern views about the fictional intentions of John's Gospel are often vague, the extent of fiction in the Gospel being left as an open question. This failure to decide even a minimum extent of intentional fiction indicates a lack of strong evidence that fiction, rather than faulty sources, are the origin of particular passages. This impression of insufficient evidence is confirmed when commentaries and other works which make the

13. Schweitzer, *Historical Jesus*, 84.
14. Strauss, *Life of Jesus*, 451.
15. Koester, *Ancient Christian Gospels*, 257.
16. Helms, *Gospel Fictions*, 10.
17. Schmeling, "The Spectrum of Narrative," 27.
18. Wills, *Historical Gospel*, 12.
19. Goodacre, Review of *Historical Gospel*, 134.

attempt (or discuss the related question of the historical reliability of John's Gospel) are compared.[20]

The degree to which we assess John's Gospel as fictitious will affect our understanding of its major ideas. While Koester finds evidence that the Fourth Gospel is based on older traditions, he also posits a process of dialogue development in which the dialogue itself is an invention, though based upon and incorporating authentic traditions, perhaps similar to a historical novel.[21] Development implies change, and the question arises as to whether the changes have affected the meaning of Jesus' sayings, and if so, whether it is likely that such changes would have or could have been made.

Supposing that a miracle account is intended as fiction solves certain problems, however such an explanation should not be accepted if it is not itself plausible. A credible explanation must also offer a plausible nonfictional purpose for the fictional origin of the details of the account. For example, a symbolic truth might be advocated under the guise of a historical fiction, especially if the author wished to discount, or at least had no concern for, the historical character of the event. If the plausible origin of these details depends upon the circulation and evolution of successive discrete versions of the account, the viability and use of intermediate versions of the account must also be shown plausible. Similarly, a fictional account should not be simply assumed to be *wholly fictitious*, rather than a *historical fiction*. Instead, the mix of demonstrably historical and fictional elements in any historical fiction should be identified, and a plausible explanation of the origin and use of this mix of elements must be provided. In other words, plausible purposes must exist if we are to account for the origin of the details of a historical fiction or of nonhistorical symbols.

FICTION AND JOHN'S VIEW OF THE HISTORICITY OF JESUS' MIRACLES

Whatever may be the historical veracity or intention of John's Gospel in general, or of any underlying sources, John's own intention to convey the essentially factual and historical character of the reported miracles is hard to deny. This view is strongly maintained by Rudolf Schnackenburg:

> But it would be a grave misapprehension to see in these signs (according to the mind of the evangelist) merely vivid representations or symbolic illustrations of certain Christological and soteriological truths. It is remarkable how strongly he emphasizes their real and factual nature. . . . No matter how criticism judges the historical credibility of the events attested by the fourth evangelist, it cannot fail to admit his intention of attesting and confirming actual events.[22]

This judgment gives due weight to the Evangelist's declaration that he recounts the signs to secure a belief in Jesus which will give eternal life:

---

20. e.g., Dodd, *Historical Tradition,* and Meier, *Marginal Jew.*
21. Koester, *Ancient Christian Gospels,* 256, 257.
22. Schnackenburg, *Gospel According to John,* 1:18.

The Evangelist's Concept of Knowledge: Intended Fiction

> Now Jesus performed many other signs before his disciples, which are not written in this book, but these are written that you might believe that Jesus is the Christ, the Son of God, and that believing you might have life in his name. (John 20:30–31)

Judging from the New Testament writings, in the first century church there was a widespread belief in Jesus' miracles. Similarly, outside the church, there was a widespread belief in the possibility of miracles. John has undeniable literary gifts, and shows evidence of considerable experience as an Evangelist. He must have known that he would be widely understood as claiming that Jesus actually performed signs, signs that at the least were similar to the signs he recounts, including Jesus' resurrection. This historical intention in his claims is also shown by the Evangelist's inclusion in his Gospel of many signs, which he might simply have omitted if he was not interested in affirming the historical reality of Jesus' miraculous powers. The importance of signs is also shown by their key role in the climax of the first half of the Gospel. The unbelief of Jesus' opponents, in the face of the great signs he has performed up to that point, is considered explicable only by their blindness to reality (John 12:37–43). Indeed, any reading of the Gospel of John which denies its historical claims about Jesus' miracles must explain why both Christian and non-Christian readings of the Gospels have from the earliest times treated the miraculous claims as historical claims.

Gerd Theissen also argues that miracle stories were intended to be understood as nonfiction. Theissen cites Origen's arguments against Celsus to show that belief in the Christian miracles contributed "to the establishment and legitimation of a new way of life," and in particular to the persuasion of Jewish believers to "reject the immemorial customs and practices of their fathers."[23] Theissen argues that the Christian miracle stories "have a missionary intention," writing:

> It is the task of the apostles to preach and heal (Lk 10.8f; Mt 10.7; Mk 3.15; 6.15ff.). Miracles are associated with missionaries (Mk 6.12; 2 Cor 12.12; Heb 2.4). Acts bears witness to this throughout . . . The missionary intention of miracles makes it very probable that the miracle stories have a similar intention. . . . Acts shows that conversions resulted, not directly from miracles, but from the spread of news of them in narratives: 'It became known throughout all Joppa, and many believed in the Lord' (9.42; cf. 19.17f). Similar remarks about the dissemination of knowledge of miracles (κηρύσσειν ["proclaim"] Mk 1.45; 5.20; 7.36; ἀκοή ["report"] Mk 1.28; λόγος ["word"] Mk 1.45; Lk 7.17) can be found in the gospels; no conversions are reported, but the language is clearly primitive Christian missionary terminology (cf. Rom 10.10–17; Acts 2.41), which enables us to say that the tellers of miracle stories perform missionary activity. Miracle stories were probably part of primitive Christianity's καινὴ διδαχή ["new teaching"].[24]

Theissen argues for the historical intention in the miracles stories, without implying that all their features are reliable. He refers to the account of Lazarus' resurrection as hav-

---

23. Theissen, *Early Christian Tradition*, 259.
24. Ibid.

ing "baroque overloading" but still seems to understand it as having been put forth with the intention that it be understood as an essentially historical event.[25]

That miracles are to be understood historically is indicated also by the Evangelist's understanding of Old Testament miracles. Both the narrator and the characters within the Gospel regard these miracles as historical. Neill notes that Jesus himself lives "in the categories of the Old Testament, which is the record of the great acts of God in history."[26] Jesus is asked to miraculously bring manna out of heaven as Moses had done (John 6:30–31), and he is considered by some characters in John's Gospel to have performed as many miraculous signs as could be expected of the Messiah (John 7:31). Even if John's Gospel were to be understood as a kind of historical novel, the need for historical verisimilitude would necessitate that this mindset of the Gospel's characters was indicative of the historical mindset of many readers of that era. More generally, both the author and the characters in John's Gospel simply presume that reports of signs should be considered at least possibly historical. This presumption is thereby shown to be the same that would likely be made by original readers, who otherwise would lose rapport with the characters. These observations support the idea that John sees the deeds of Jesus as a continuation of God's works in history. John's reading of the Old Testament is not atypical of the period. Josephus, in his late first century *Jewish Antiquities*, reads the book of Genesis as historical, even describing the record of the antediluvians of Genesis 5 as a record made by those who were accustomed "to note with minute care the birth and death of the illustrious men."[27]

FICTION AND EARLY READINGS OF JOHN'S MIRACLES AS HISTORICAL

That the author's general intention is to be understood historically is also supported by the way he actually was understood, according to the earliest readings of John. Tatian, in his second century harmony of the four Gospels, the *Diatessaron*, interleaves narratives from John's Gospel with those of the Synoptic Gospels, as though John's account is of a historical character similar to the other Gospels. Although there are variations in the harmonization sequence among the various manuscript witnesses to the *Diatessaron*, Louis Leloir has prepared sequence tables of the major witnesses that show this interleaving of John's Gospel in all cases.[28] Although William Peterson warns us in his standard introduction to the *Diatessaron* that there are currently no reliable editions or texts of the *Diatessaron*,[29] a true sense for this interleaving of John's Gospel with the Synoptic Gospels can still be obtained from the available English translations. With regard to the surviving versions of the Diatessaron, Hogg noted in 1895 that, "the Latin, Armenian,

---

25. Ibid., 175.
26. Neill and Wright, *Interpretation*, 233.
27. Josephus *Antiquities* 1.82 (Thackeray, LCL).
28. Leloir, "Le Diatessaron de Tatien," 208–31.
29. Peterson, *Tatian's Diatessaron*, 137.

and Arabic *Diatessarons* correspond pretty closely in subject matter and arrangement," and in their "order and contents." [30]

This evidence is consistent with our broader knowledge of the *Diatessaron*. According to Peterson, Tatian was a student of Justin Martyr in Rome.[31] That Tatian's harmonization was accepted is indicated by the *Diatessaron*'s influence. Peterson says that Tatian's *Diatessaron* was written in Syriac, and influenced the text of the Old Latin and the Sinaitic and Curetonian Syriac Gospels; we also have a Syriac and an Armenian recension.[32] It is first actually mentioned by Eusebius, who says that it was in circulation in his time.[33] Aland confirms this, listing a third century fragment of the *Diatessaron*, ms 0212.[34] It might be thought that Tatian's subsequently expressed "gnostic" tendencies would support a nonhistorical reading of John. Irenaeus says that, after Justin Martyr's death, Tatian separated from the church and, like the Valentinians, held to a doctrine of invisible aeons. Theodoret, a fifth century bishop in Syria says that Tatian removed the genealogies and other evidence of Jesus' descent from David. It is evident, however, from the order of events in his *Diatessaron*, that Tatian considers John's Gospel to be of a historical character similar to the Synoptic Gospels.[35] Indeed, his use of a chronological framework shows that he treats his sources as primarily historical in character; this is why he thinks it does not violate the Gospels' genuine individual character to break up their original literary contexts and set them in a single chronological framework.

Papyrus Egerton 2 provides similar evidence for a historical reading of John in early times.[36] This manuscript is dated by Koester to about 200 AD (others had ascribed an earlier date), and combines Johannine and Synoptic traditions (perhaps arising independently from our canonical Gospels) to form a single narrative. The narrative does not distinguish the historical value of the Synoptic and Johannine traditions.

It might be thought that an early exception to a historical reading of John is to be found among the group whom the fourth century Epiphanius of Salamis calls the Alogoi. The Alogoi were noted for their rejection of both the Gospel of John and the Apocalypse of John, ascribing them instead to the gnostic Cerinthus. Epiphanius says of the Alogoi, ". . . for they say the mysteries are not from John but from Cerinthus, and they say these mysteries are not worthy to exist in the church."[37] The early third century Roman pres-

---

30. *Diatessaron* (ANF 9:38). This older English trial translation by H. Hogg is taken from an uncritical edition of the Arabic version based on two known Arabic manuscripts. The Syriac original from which they are translated had not been found.

31. Peterson, "Tatian's Diatessaron," 404.

32. Ibid., 406, 408, 428.

33. Eusebius, *Ecclesiastical History*, 4.29.6.

34. Aland, *Novum Testamentum Graece*, 700.

35. Tatian, *Fragments*. (ANF 2:154).

36. Papyrus Egerton 2, in Cameron, *Other Gospels*, 72–75.

37. My translation, from Epiphanius, *Panarion* 51:3 cited in Aland, *Synopsis Quattuor Evangeliorum*, 544. The Greek text of Aland (including the prior sentence for clarity) is: . . . ὢ ἀξίως τὰ μυστήρια ἀπεκάλυπτεν καὶ ἐπὶ τὸ στῆθος αὐτοῦ ἀνέπεσε, καὶ ἕτεροι αὐτὰ ἀνατρέπειν πειρῶνται. λέγουσι γὰρ μὴ εἶναι αὐτὰ Ἰωάννου ἀλλὰ Κηρίνθου καὶ οὐκ ἄξια αὐτὰ φάσιν εἶναι ἐν ἐκκλησία.

byter Gaius also attributed these two works to Cerinthus.[38] Irenaeus (*Against Heresies* 1.26.1) describes as the teaching of Cerinthus the idea that "the world was not made by the primary God, but by a certain power far separated from him." If Cerinthus were a gnostic of some kind, would this require a nonhistorical reading of the text?

There are several reasons to dismiss any suggestion that this attribution shows that the Evangelist intended this Gospel to be read fictionally. First of all, Beasley-Murray remarks, "there is no ground for questioning the name of the author of the Book of Revelation as *John*; virtually all are agreed that there is no case for pseudonymity in the Book of Revelation."[39] This means that Gaius and the Alogoi were using unreliable methodology to determine the authorship of the books. Also weighing against the attribution is the uniform naming of John in the title of all our early manuscripts of the Gospel. Of more importance, however, is testimony of Irenaeus and Polycarp that Cerinthus was regarded as a heretic, and one who was particularly opposed by John. Irenaeus, before the time of Gaius, claims that John wrote his Gospel to refute Cerinthus (*Against Heresies* 3.9.1). The origin of such a strong statement is difficult to account for, if Cerinthus had written the Fourth Gospel. Irenaeus also notes (*Against Heresies* 3.3.4) an account by the second century Polycarp, disciple of John, that John called Cerinthus "the enemy of the truth". Irenaeus's account of Cerinthus's teachings also indicates that the views expressed in the Fourth Gospel are opposed to those of Cerinthus. We may note last of all that there is no modern scholarly interest in ascribing the authorship of the Gospel to Cerinthus.

Irenaeus, our next early reader of the miracles, likewise treats the miraculous signs in John as historical. Irenaeus writes as follows:

> For many believed in him, when they saw the signs which he did, as John the disciple of the Lord records. Then again, withdrawing himself, he is found in Samaria; on which occasion, too he conversed with the Samaritan woman, and while at a distance, cured the son of the centurion by a word, saying, "Go thy way, thy son liveth." Afterwards he went up, the second time, to observe the festival day of the Passover in Jerusalem; on which occasion he cured the paralytic man who had lain beside the pool thirty eight years, bidding him rise, take up his couch, and depart. Again, withdrawing from thence to the other side of the sea of Tiberias, he there, seeing a great crowd had followed him, fed all that multitude with five loaves of bread, and twelve baskets of fragments remained over and above. Then when he had raised Lazarus from the dead, and plots were formed against him by the Pharisees, he withdrew to a city called Ephraim. . . .[40]

Note here how Irenaeus, writing about 180 AD, reads John's accounts of even Lazarus' resurrection as historical.

Clement of Alexandria, who is said to have called John's Gospel a "spiritual gospel"[41], also writes of the resurrection of Lazarus as historical:

---

38. Bareille, "Gaius," 544.
39. Beasley-Murray, *John*, lxix.
40. Irenaeus, *Against Heresies* 2.22 (ANF 1:391).
41. Clement of Alexandria, *Hypotyposes*, cited in Eusebius, *Ecclesiastical History*, 6.14 (NPNF 1:261).

The Evangelist's Concept of Knowledge: Intended Fiction

> But the good Instructor, the Wisdom, the Word of the Father, who made man, cares for the whole nature of His creature; the all-sufficient Physician of humanity, the Savior, heals both body and soul. "Rise up," he said to the paralytic; "take the bed on which thou liest, and go away home;" and straightway the infirm man received strength. And to the dead he said, "Lazarus, go forth;" and the dead man issued from his coffin such as he was ere he died, having undergone resurrection. Further, he heals the soul itself by precepts and gifts—by precepts indeed, in course of time, but being liberal in his gifts, he says to us sinners, "Thy sins be forgiven thee."[42]

Upon inspection, it is apparent that Clement's characterization of John as a "spiritual gospel" refers to its emphasis on God in his essence, rather than to any idea that the physical world is not of religious significance, or that miracles were physical and therefore unimportant. This is also evident from a remark Clement made on 1 John regarding the incarnation. Clement said that this letter of John also has the "spiritual principle" simply because John claims (1 John 1:1) to have "seen and heard" and "handled" the one who "was from the beginning."[43] His idea seems to be that, through the incarnation, the reality of the spiritual world fills the lesser though genuine reality of the physical world. It is implausible to imagine that John's Gospel would not be understood by many in the ancient world as a work promoting the miraculous. It is therefore implausible that the Evangelist did not know he would be understood in this fashion by a great part of the public.

Could it be, however, that this concern for miracles shows the same lack of understanding or misunderstanding that is often portrayed in John's Gospel? One of several commentators on Johannine irony, Jakob Jónsson notes that a characteristic method for understanding John's Gospel recognizes "a play with words and ideas, where two or more senses or meanings are expressed in the same 'sign' at the same time,—and on the other side the human intellect reveals its shortcomings by asking questions, quid pro quos, that lack understanding and insight."[44] Could it be, then, that this concern for miracles constitutes a misunderstanding of the Evangelist's concerns, in a way actually anticipated by the Evangelist? This is implausible, for several reasons.

In this Gospel the failure to understand usually arises by understanding the reference to a physical object literally, rather than by analogy. One may compile a substantial list of misunderstood metaphors, without finding any miracle that is the symbol for a purely non-miraculous reality. To illustrate, a representative list will be given here which pairs physical objects and their analogical reference, along with the corresponding misunderstanding. For our first example, Jesus refers to his body as the temple of God, yet the Jewish leaders he addresses misunderstand him quite understandably (John 2:18–21). The Evangelist as narrator explains Jesus' meaning to the reader, who would otherwise (quite naturally) misunderstand Jesus just as the Jewish leaders had misunderstood. When Nicodemus does not understand what Jesus means by being

---

42. Clement of Alexandria, *The Instructor* 1.2 (ANF 2:407). To the same effect is the more recent translation by Wood, *Christ the Educator*.

43. Clement of Alexandria, *Fragments*, from the Latin trans. by Cassiodorus (ANF 2:1166).

44. Jónsson, "Humour and Irony," 201.

"born again" (John 3:3), Jesus explains further. At that point Nicodemus (and the careful reader) do essentially understand Jesus' meaning (John 3:5–10), even though Nicodemus still does not believe Jesus' teaching. To the Samaritan woman Jesus offers a "drink" of "living water" (John 4:10). The reference of this symbolic language is not understood until Jesus clarifies his meaning enough to exclude literal water, and to explain that this "living water" will give eternal life (John 4:14). To his disciples Jesus says metaphorically, "I have food to eat that you do not know about" (John 4:32). Naturally his disciples misunderstand him, until he explains that by "food" he metaphorically refers to "doing the will" of God. When Jesus offers the people "bread from heaven," they do not initially know that he is referring to himself (John 6:33–41). The Evangelist even explains, as narrator to a reader who presumably will not otherwise understand, that the words of Jesus, "from out of his belly shall flow living water," refer to "the Spirit" (John 7:37–39). When Jesus says, "Our friend Lazarus has fallen asleep," his disciples do not understand that "fallen asleep" meant "died" (John 11:11–13). The Evangelist, as narrator, is careful to explain to the reader (who like the disciples could not otherwise know) that "Jesus had spoken of his death" (John 11:13). Jesus himself is then portrayed as explaining his plain meaning to the disciples (and so again to the reader). All these examples show how often misunderstanding or lack of understanding is tied to some physical object, which is metaphorically used to refer to some non-visible reality. A miracle is never used as a symbol for a purely non-miraculous reality, and characters in the Gospel never misunderstand a miracle to be literally true. To be sure, this lack of comprehension does not always arise from symbolical use of physical objects. For example, in his words, "you will seek me, and will not find me" (John 7:34) Jesus does not explain to his opponents the nature of his absence. Similarly, when speaking of "the One who sent" him, Jesus is not understood by the Judean leaders (John 8:26–27). These failures of characters in the Gospel to understand Jesus offer little basis for claiming that the early church misunderstood the "real meaning" of Jesus' miracles, by mistaking a physical for a nonphysical reality.

We can compare the relationship that the Evangelist sees between signs and his readership, to the Gospels' portrait of the relationship that Jesus sees between signs and his hearers. Fiction was not an understanding used by either Jesus' disciples or his opponents to explain Jesus' miracles. His disciples acknowledge his miracles. His opponents discredit him on the grounds that he is a sinner (being a Sabbath breaker per John 5:16, having demonic power per John 7:20, and misleading the people per John 7:12,47). The miracles are signs, and within John's Gospel reports of them are understood by Jesus and his opponents alike to be claims about historical events. For example, when Jesus says "I have made an entire man well" (John 7:23), his opponents understand him as claiming to have miraculously healed a man on the Sabbath, which they considered a violation of the law. If Jesus were not responsible for the healing, he would not have been accused of breaking the Sabbath. When Jesus refers to the day of resurrection, the day in which all the dead shall hear his voice and rise (John 5:28–29), his opponents evidently understand this as a claim of supernatural power, not as a fiction. In spite of his many cryptic sayings, Jesus was sufficiently intelligible to gain both adherents and enemies, by his claims to miraculous powers. Why should Jesus' opponents be portrayed as being offended by claims, which Jesus never actually made? The Evangelist is not portraying Jesus' enemies as opposing him by mistake, but rather as opposing him because of their defective moral character. The Evangelist must at least be claiming that Jesus actually had miraculous power, even if Jesus did not use it. But if we acknowledge the importance of Jesus' powers for the Evangelist, there is little reason to deny that the Evangelist accepted, as a historical reality, Jesus' expression of this power.

The Gospel's explanations of these misunderstandings also indicate that acceptance of miracles is not itself a misunderstanding. It is striking, when the language of Jesus is so cryptic as to be either misleading or unintelligible, that Jesus often explains to the disciples what he means, and the Evangelist further clarifies Jesus' meaning to the readers of his Gospel. The reader is not left to misunderstand. The characters often know that the literal meaning of a metaphor is doubtful, although this does not allow them to identify the reference to which the metaphor actually points. The reader is often in the same situation of uncertainty until the Evangelist makes Jesus' meaning clear, either by direct explanation as narrator, or by including Jesus' explanation to characters in the Gospel. However these explanations never serve to persuade the reader that miracles were not actually performed by Jesus. They do not persuade us that belief in transcendent realities makes belief in miracles superfluous.

Even more strikingly, Jesus is repeatedly portrayed as encouraging people to believe in miracles, when they are unwilling to do so. When the royal official comes to Cana and asks Jesus to heal his dying child, Jesus responds by criticizing the tendency of people to believe only if they see signs and wonders (John 4:46–50). Jesus requires the official to trust him, by telling him that his son will live, even though the recovery of the son (who is in another town) cannot be seen. Clearly the man believes that God has intervened so that his dying son will recover, and this belief is a notion that Jesus has encouraged the father to hold, not to suppress or ignore. The father's trust is proven to have been well placed when he returns to his home. This is a lesson to the reader, who is taught to trust in Jesus' power to heal, and not to deny that power, which would be to show unbelief. When Jesus gives sight to the blind man, the Pharisees do not believe the man had been blind until they call his parents to confirm it (John 9:18–23). Even then, they refuse to acknowledge that Jesus has come from God, some suggesting that the miracle was performed by demonic power (John 10:20). Jesus criticizes this second refusal as a sinful (willful) blindness, made in the face of the evidence. When Jesus is planning to raise Lazarus from the dead, he encourages Martha to believe that he is capable of raising Lazarus before the Day of Judgment, asking her then, "Do you believe this?" Martha's response of belief is characterized as a confession of belief in Jesus as "the Christ, the Son of God, he who comes into the world" (John 11:26–27). When Jesus appears after his resurrection to Thomas, he chides Thomas for thinking that his appearance to the other disciples was no more than a vision, and characterizes such an attitude as "unbelieving" (John 20:27). This unbelieving attitude is reproved in the immediately subsequent narrative, when the Evangelist declares his purpose of recording signs in his Gospel: "that you may believe that Jesus is the Christ, the Son of God, and that believing you may have life in his name" (John 20:31). For all these reasons, the misunderstandings in John's Gospel cannot be accepted as evidence that the Evangelist intended his accounts of miracles to be understood as essentially fictional or nonhistorical.

In summary, it is not plausible that either John's Gospel, or its account of miracles, are intended to be read as entirely or essentially fictitious. The philosophical arguments against reported miracles are not even compelling in modern times; they provide negligible evidence that the Evangelist or his readers would have been skeptical of Jesus' miracles. Whether or not miracles occur, the Evangelist believed they occurred. It is more plausible to follow Koester, where he ascribes to the Evangelist confidence in his sources, than to argue that the Evangelist intended his Gospel to be read as fictional, or to understand the miracles as inventions of the Evangelist. The intention of including the miracles is more plausibly for the purpose of persuading people to believe in Jesus, than because of the Evangelist's grudging acceptance of the tradition. Supernatural events were widely credited in that age, so they were influential in the evangelistic discourse of Christians in the larger world. Many, if not all, of the Evangelist's audience must have understood his miraculous accounts as historical and as nonfiction. This is evident from the way the Evangelist portrays Jesus' and others' understanding of the Old Testament miracles, and by the way the Gospel's own miracles are understood in its earliest Christian readings, where a fictitious or solely symbolical reading of the miracles is unsupported. There is no substantial evidence that the Evangelist would have considered belief in miracles a misunderstanding; indeed, the opposite is the case.

FICTION AND ORAL HISTORY

Here the discussion must be enlarged to include insights from the rising field of oral history. Following the pioneering work of Paul R. Thompson in oral history, a recent work by Samuel Byrskog examines the importance of oral history for our understanding of the New Testament.[45] Byrskog is particularly interested in the way that modern paradigms force the separation of history and story, the real world and the literary (or textual) world. The fundamental link of story to history in the Gospels is evident from the widespread rejection by scholars of views that entirely deny the importance of the historical Jesus. For example, Byrskog notes the recurring interest in the historical Jesus by influential scholars such as Albert Schweitzer, C. F. D. Moule, Joachim Jeremias, Ernst Käsemann, and recent scholars involved in the *Third Quest* for the historical Jesus. To replace this artificial division of story and history, Byrskog offers the model of oral histories, where the historian "must take seriously the historical character of the oral stories which the participants and/or eyewitnesses of historical events tell in all their subjectivity."[46] He traces the link of story and history in the Gospels back to early witnesses, citing Martin Dibelius and Vincent Taylor in support of the view that stories in the Gospels were constrained by and motivated by the historical claims which were part of the stories of the earliest witnesses. As Byrskog notes, the model of oral history is applicable in a funda-

---

45. Byrskog, *Story as History*.
46. Ibid., 18.

The Evangelist's Concept of Knowledge: Intended Fiction

mental way to the Gospel stories, since it is otherwise difficult to explain the conflicting purposes between "the author's apparent faithfulness to tradition, on the one hand, and his allegedly unreflective use and addition of fictional elements, on the other."[47]

While it is not possible to conduct oral interviews of the original Evangelists, Byrskog is interested in the Evangelists as preservers of earlier traditions that they had themselves learned by inquiry or oral tradition. While some scholars argue for a radical discontinuity between the oral and written Gospel, Byrskog considers that view to make only a superficial (and misleading) use of the methods of oral history. Byrskog argues that the written Gospels did not wholly depart from the traditions of the oral Gospel, and offers his own work as a more comprehensive utilization of the techniques of oral history.[48]

Byrskog finds the historiographical methods of oral history superior to solely documentary methods. The latter methods, which discountenanced as prejudiced the reports of historians who were also observers, thereby stripped itself of the richer insights of direct observation.[49] With reference to the modern interview techniques of oral historians, Paul Thompson has argued for the inevitability that "professional historians will return to their earlier view of the acceptability of oral evidence as one of many kinds of historical source."[50] Thompson also notes the capacity of oral testimony to discredit or reformulate conclusions that have been formed on the basis of documentary evidence alone.[51] The common ability to remember some details for a period of fifty years is supported by Thompson in his discussion of psychological experiments. Similarly, the ability to pass down oral traditions with a core of accuracy through many generations is documented in the case of African traditions and children's chants.[52] The genuine historical value of memory and oral tradition must be acknowledged, even though it has limitations. Oral historians do not accept stories uncritically, but do not exclude the stories' importance simply because of the observers' interests or prejudices.

Byrskog surveys the practices of ancient Greek and Roman historians, including Herodotus, Thucydides, Polybius, Josephus, and Tacitus. Byrskog notes their strong preference for information obtained either by "being present themselves," or "by seeking out and interrogating other eyewitnesses," a method he refers to as *autopsy*.[53] He notes, in particular, the work of a "leading expert on autopsy among ancient historians," Guido Schepens, in support of this view of the ideals of ancient historiography.[54]

Byrskog notes the importance to oral history of focusing on individuals who are representative of a group, rather than merely on any group collectively. Byrskog notes that Jesus' disciples would be such a group, but thinks there was no "collective oral history"

47. Ibid., 9.
48. Ibid., 33.
49. Ibid., 23, 27.
50. Thompson, *Voice of the Past*, 78.
51. Ibid., 116–17.
52. Ibid., 134–35.
53. Byrskog, *Story as History*, 64.
54. e.g., Schepens, *L' 'autopsie'*.

and no training "in the techniques of memory and transmission."[55] Birger Gerhardsson had argued earlier that the later rabbinic handling of tradition offered analogies to the handling of the Gospel traditions by Jesus' disciples. Byrskog makes it explicit that the analogy does not apply so far as the adoption of rabbinic memorization techniques by Jesus' disciples. He says this, perhaps, because parallel passages in the Gospels would otherwise have fewer differences. Byrskog also notes the tradition in all the early documents about Jesus' family. He concludes that Peter, Mary Magdalene, the other women at the cross and tomb, Jesus' brother James, and Jesus' mother Mary were regarded as real figures from the past, figures whose stories were not entirely silenced or lost in other stories. Only this explains the Evangelists' portrayal of them as witnesses and informants about the past.[56]

As indicated above, Gerhardsson had already noted a possible analogy between Jesus' disciples and the rabbinic Jews of later centuries, the latter showing a strong interest in the preservation of tradition. Rabbinic Judaism expressed this interest in tradition by emphasizing memorization. For example, Gerhardsson notes that "Resh Laquish was himself in the habit of repeating his Mishnah paragraph 'forty times' before presenting himself to R. Johanan; R. Adda bar Ahabah used to repeat his work 'twenty-four times' before coming to Raba." Of the reputation of others Gerhardsson notes, "that they were able to reproduce the Mishnah, Sifra, Sifre and Tosefta" from memory. He notes further a tradition (*b. Ketubbot 103b*, *b. Bava Metzi'a 85b*.) about an elder who could from memory reproduce the Torah (Pentateuch) and the Mishnah.[57] Even the early second century rabbi Akiba was reputed to have said,

> *And These are the Ordinances*, etc. Why is this said? Since it says: 'Speak unto the children of Israel and say unto them' (Lev 1.2). I know only that he was to *tell them once*. How do we know that he was to *repeat* (שנה) it to them a second, a third and a fourth time until they *learned* (ילמדו) it? Scripture says: 'And teach thou it the children of Israel' (Deut 31.19).[58]

Gerhardsson also notes that Hellenistic educational practices throughout antiquity required that children recite classical texts like Homer by heart.[59] Whether or not Jews practiced such memorization in the time of Jesus, it becomes difficult to imagine that there was not already a strong interest in preserving the authentic teaching of one's rabbi. The twelve apostles were Jews who would naturally have a strong interest in carefully preserving the teachings and way of life taught by their Rabbi.

Byrskog criticizes the traditional separation of Jesus' words (which are heard) from Jesus' deeds (which were seen), in the analysis of tradition by form critics. Such a procedure unreasonably assumes that word and deed were never held together in the earliest traditions about Jesus. Byrskog adopts Heinz Schurmann's proposal that Jesus'

---

55. Byrskog, *Story as History*, 70.
56. Ibid., 91.
57. Gerhardsson, *Memory and Manuscript*, 105, 106, 114.
58. Mekilta ad Ex. 21.1, in Lauterbach, 3:1, cited in Gerhardsson, *Memory and Manuscript*, 135.
59. Gerhardsson, *Memory and Manuscript*, 124.

disciples must have been provided certain narrative historical material about Jesus. They would need this material as the context for the sayings of Jesus, which they proclaimed, when Jesus first sent them out to preach. Byrskog also adopts Rainer Reisner's further arguments that Jesus' behavior was part of the message, that some of Jesus' deeds taught symbolically and so must also be part of the message, and that logia sayings as a genre typically referred to known persons. Of even more importance, Byrskog observes that "the deepest continuity with the past was not in memory as such but in mimesis, not in passive remembrance but in imitation."[60] Here he observes the influence of such imitation not only in the ritual of the Eucharist, but in what Gerhardsson calls "the behavioural tradition" which would accompany and embody an interpretation of the "verbal tradition."[61]

In a related vein, Byrskog criticizes Werner Kelber for the view that the oral genre of gospel has no interest in past history. Gerhardsson had earlier criticized the view that "men who shaped the gospel tradition had no wish to preserve memories for posterity, but *instead* wished their proclamation to arouse faith in Christ." Gerhardsson thought this "a false alternative."[62] Against this supposed lack of historical interest, Byrskog notes the existence of archaisms preserved in oral tradition, and the implausibility of assuming that every generation generates its own oral history, or that any generation has no interest in its authentic history, or that any generation's oral history accurately describes that generation's own interests. In particular, Byrskog asks why the narrative of the resurrection of Jesus was told as history, if it was not important as history to its narrators—and asks why the Evangelists retain any interest in using tradition. Byrskog argues that early Christians' belief in this miracle should not be used to justify the *a priori* assumption that early Christians had no historical interest in the matter.[63] Against the claim that historical elements are to be attributed to rhetorical invention, Byrskog reviews the ancient use of rhetoric and concludes that "persuasion and factual credibility were supplementary rhetorical virtues, not contradictory."[64]

Byrskog tests these ideas first by looking at how James, the brother of the Lord, handled tradition. Byrskog counts at least 36 textual parallels between the Letter of James and the Gospels, although James does not follow any of them exactly, nor attribute any of the parallel texts to Jesus. Byrskog's explanation is that James "as a Christian teacher" was "deeply involved in the tradition" and "had internalized it and made it his own."[65] James' use of tradition, Byrskog concludes, indicates that "an eyewitness's personal experience of and involvement in the Jesus event furthers rather than hinders a reliable account of the past." James "did not, as far as we can tell, fill in the gaps in the present perception

---

60. Byrskog, *Story as History*, 104, 105, 107.
61. Gerhardsson, "Gospel Tradition" 501–2, cited in Byrskog, *Story as History*, 107.
62. Gerhardsson, *Memory and Manuscript*, 209.
63. Byrskog, *Story as History*, 131, 135.
64. Ibid., 223.
65. Ibid., 174–75.

of the past according to his own pattern of 'what must have happened.'" In other words, James's interpretation was integrated within the tradition known to him.[66]

Byrskog notes the importance in John's Gospel of two references to witnesses (John 19:35; 21:24). He observes in the first reference that an historical event is the object for present belief, and a legitimation of present faith. In the second reference, the beloved disciple is referred to as the author of the Gospel. As Byrskog observes, "What is at stake is the authority of the written account of Jesus. . . . another account of the life and deeds of a historical person." Byrskog concludes, "The disciple's status as an eyewitness of key points in Jesus' career served, it seems, as a legitimate basis for conferring on him an authorial status, thus linking the faith that the written narrative is to encourage (cf. 20:31) to the history of the past."[67] This also argues for an essential historical interest in Jesus' miracles, though the historical interest would naturally include sayings and other deeds as well.

Here it is important to acknowledge that ancient authors included 'plausible reconstructions' more readily than would be allowed by modern historians. Thucydides, often counted as the most stringent of ancient historians, explains in his *Peloponnesian War* (1.22–1.24) that the speeches could not feasibly be remembered word for word. However this does not allow events or speeches to be simply invented; they must actually be historically probable in some sense. Certainly this should not be understood as undermining all interest in narrating historically authentic tradition. The methods of oral history show that tradition was respected, and cannot be replaced by a complete fiction.

SIGNS AS HISTORICAL TESTIMONY: BULTMANN'S OBJECTION

Although we have argued that John's miracles are intended as nonfiction, this might be treated as inconsequential if it was objected that John does not give miracles as historical claims warranting belief in Jesus. Rudolf Bultmann has raised this objection, so it is appropriate to show that this is a misunderstanding of John's thought.

In John's thought the signs are not granted only to those who actually see them, but also to those who hear report of them. Reports of signs are considered credible on grounds similar to other historical reporting, grounds that require only an attainable standard of evidence. Jesus accepts the reports of miracles found in the Hebrew Scriptures. This acceptance is partly due to confidence in the social institutions and practices that preserved the scriptural accounts; for the Torah itself declares that some customs and texts are given as memorials for later generations. The acceptance of miracles by characters in the Old Testament seems to stand as a model to the Evangelist for the way that reports of miracles are to be tested. The characters in the Gospel are portrayed as knowing on the basis of current reports that Jesus has performed signs. We find an example of this in the narrative about the healing of the man born blind (John 9). The testimony given by the blind man's parents about the miracle is undeniable. Similarly, when Thomas refuses to believe the report given by all the other disciples, a report that they had seen Jesus risen

---

66. Ibid., 171–73.
67. Ibid., 238.

from the dead, Jesus reprimands Thomas for unbelief (John 20). To automatically deny the evidence of reports about miracles is considered unreasonable by the Evangelist.

This does not mean that the Evangelist expects everyone to accept the reports of signs immediately. The Evangelist does not criticize those who question whether the blind man who was healed is the same man who before sat as a blind beggar (John 9). Instead, the Evangelist includes the undeniable testimony by the blind man's parents that he was born blind. It is because this testimony is undeniable that those who then excommunicate the blind man for following Jesus are called blind. Similarly, some Samaritans do not initially accept the report of the Samaritan woman that Jesus had supernatural knowledge of her past (John 4:39–42). However the Evangelist does not criticize them for believing only after hearing Jesus himself. Perhaps some had more reason to doubt this woman than others.

Some deny that the Evangelist expects people to believe, on the basis of reports, that these miracles happened. Commenting on Jesus' reprimand of Thomas (John 20), Bultmann questioned whether the Evangelist expects reports to justify belief in Jesus' resurrection. Here Bultmann expresses a degree of historical skepticism:

> Does the story teach that faith in the Risen Lord is demanded on the basis of the utterance of the eye-witnesses? Should no one desire that the same experiences be given to him as were given to the first disciples, who are now for all time the trustworthy witnesses? . . . And above all, does not the reproach that falls on Thomas apply to all the other disciples as well? All of them indeed, like Mary Magdalene, believed only when they saw. . . . [So] . . . the Easter narratives . . . [are] neither . . . narrations of events that he himself could wish or hope to experience, nor as a substitute for such experiences of his own, as if the experiences of others could, as it were, guarantee for him the reality of the resurrection of Jesus; rather they are to be viewed as proclaimed word, in which the recounted events have become symbolic pictures for the fellowship which the Lord, who has ascended to the Father, holds with his own.[68]

While Bultmann's concerns are in part understandable, his characterization of the Evangelist's meaning ignores the fact that in this Gospel Thomas is reprimanded. The Evangelist does not excuse Thomas. Since Thomas is a Jew who followed Jesus, we may assume that he believes in an afterlife for the human spirit. Although Thomas hears the testimony of many witnesses whom he knows to be reliable, he refuses to believe that Jesus' resurrection was physical, that Jesus had actually shown the disciples his wounded hands and side (John 20:20). It was not reports of a vision, but reports of the physical resurrection of Jesus back into our world, which Thomas would not believe. That is why his unbelief was expressed in the demand to touch the actual wounds of Jesus. It is even plausible that he credits the disciples with seeing a vision, or a spirit. That is, at least, the initial understanding which the disciples themselves generally had of their experience, according to another early Evangelist. Luke writes, "they were startled and frightened and thought that they were seeing a spirit" (Luke 24:37). Thomas was reprimanded for not believing the report of a resurrection into this physical world, and this unbelief was un-

---

68. Bultmann, *Gospel of John*, 696.

acceptable to the Evangelist. Just as the Evangelist emphasizes the real physical death of Jesus by appealing to a witness of Jesus' death (John 19:33–35), the Evangelist emphasizes the necessity of believing in Jesus' real physical resurrection.

Bultmann also misconstrues the Evangelist's view by denying that any other disciples had believed before seeing. In the words, "blessed are those who have not seen and have believed (μὴ ἰδόντες καὶ πιστεύσαντες)" (John 20:29), Jesus specifically contrasts Thomas with disciples who had believed without seeing Jesus. The participle "have believed" (πιστεύσαντες) is in the aorist tense, which at least allows for reference to other disciples who believed in the past, especially because John usually uses the present tense for participles of this verb. The beloved disciple himself believed when he saw the linen burial cloths, and the face cloth folded up by itself, inside the empty tomb, before seeing the risen Jesus (John 20:8). The beloved disciple's response differs from that of Thomas, because the former believed only upon seeing the empty tomb, and it was public knowledge ultimately available to the Jewish leaders and Thomas alike that the tomb was empty. While the beloved disciple arguably saw the additional evidence of the linens and the cloth, this hardly compares in force with the testimony about the risen Jesus, which Thomas later received from the ten disciples whom he knew. Thomas's faith was in a state of crisis as the beloved disciple's was not. If we suppose that this story of Thomas is to be read as a historically realistic portrayal, it would be hard to doubt that the ten disciples' vision of the risen Jesus the previous week would already have been told throughout the group of Jesus' disciples in Jerusalem, and that some, like later Christians, had credited the reported resurrection simply on the basis of the disciples' testimony. It is not necessary to make the unnatural assumption that, before this admonition to Thomas, no disciples had ever believed without seeing, when they could only believe in all later ages without seeing. The first readers of John's Gospel already live in an age when belief without having seen has long been normative in the Christian community. While Jesus (and the Evangelist) gives a promise of blessing for believers of all time, this does not require us to ignore the historical setting, where the Evangelist portrays the words as spoken to Thomas, and calls him to respond more reasonably, just as others had responded. The point is not that future disciples' grounds for faith should imitate the beloved disciple in believing without seeing anything at all. Rather, the point is that it is unreasonable to set, as a condition for belief in Jesus, the condition of *personally* seeing the risen Jesus, since people have the testimony of what the disciples have seen, which has been passed on to the readers of John's Gospel.

Bultmann's concerns about the ability of historical evidence to serve as grounds for belief are widely shared concerns. However, a denial of the Evangelist's own perspective cannot resolve this modern concern about historical certainty. Barrett offers a far more perceptive assessment of the Evangelist's thought:

> The miracles of this gospel are a function of its Christology. Rightly to understand them is to apprehend Christ by faith (10.38; 14.11). The miracles once grasped in their true meaning lead immediately to the Christology, since they are a manifestation of the glory of Christ (2.11).[69]

---

69. Barrett, *Gospel According to John*, 75.

Not only does Barrett acknowledge that the Evangelist relates miracles to belief, but he acknowledges the relationship of miracles to the revealing of God's glory in Jesus. For the Evangelist, then, reports of miracles are considered credible.

Bultmann not only devalued reports about signs, but also denied that signs themselves were part of the "real work" of Jesus. The effect of this denial was to imply that it was not important to the Evangelist that his readers accept the reports about the signs as essentially historical reports. Bultmann said,

> The astonishing thing is that the ministry of Jesus is described here by means of the expression σημεῖα ποιεῖν, ["performed signs"] although his σημεῖα ["signs"] were subordinated to the discourses, and his real work was achieved in the revelatory word.... the concepts σημεῖα ["signs"] and ῥήματα (λόγοι) ["words"] flow together: the σημεῖα ["signs"] are deeds that speak, and their meaning is developed in the discourses; moreover the ῥήματα ["words"] are not human words, but words of revelation, full of divine and miraculous power—they are indeed miraculous works.[70]

Bultmann found the Gospel's emphasis on signs astonishing because he believed that God is revealed only in "the revelatory word," exclusive of deeds. The belief that God does not reveal himself in historic acts is alien to Jewish thought generally, and to the thought of John's Gospel in particular. It is also alien to Jewish thought and John's to think of signs as bare works of power, devoid of their character as signs, and given apart from God's word. Bultmann himself observes that the signs are "deeds that speak" of God. Bultmann merely obscures the unique revelatory character of signs by the confusing and romantic claim that the words of Jesus are "indeed miraculous works." While it is arguable in some sense that it is miraculous for God to be speaking in the world through Jesus, this is not the sense in which John, or other Christian writers of his time, used the term *miracle* or *sign*. For example, in the Evangelist's enumeration of Galilean signs (John 4:54), Jesus' words are not counted as either sign or miracle.

Unlike Bultmann, the Evangelist does not distinguish signs from Jesus' "real work." Indeed, as Barrett says, in this Gospel Jesus' miracles "are described as his works."[71] Jesus offers the works as an objective basis for belief, "If I do not do the works of my Father, do not believe me; but if I do them, though you do not believe me, believe the works . . ." (John 10:37–38). Even when Jesus looks back upon his life's work, he includes the glorification of God that was aroused by the signs. Jesus says, "I glorified you on the earth, having accomplished the work which you gave me to do" (John 17:4). The reference to glorification must include the miracles, if it does not primarily refer to them. The Evangelist says "this beginning of signs Jesus did in Cana of Galilee, and manifested his glory, and his disciples believed in him" (John 2:11). The relationship of miracles to glory is attested also in Matthew's gospel, "But when the multitudes saw, they were filled with awe, and glorified God, who had given such authority to men" (Matt 9:8).

---

70. Bultmann, *Gospel of John*, 452.
71. Barrett, *Gospel According to John*.

For the Evangelist, miracles constitute one of at least two grounds on which Jesus' claim to be the Christ (John 18:33) is considered credible. Another ground lies in Jesus' own character, testimony, and promises (John 4:9–24; 7:40–41; 14:9–11). These are considered valid on the basis that no evidence can be found to discredit Jesus (John 3:11; 7:51; 8:30, 45–49; 9:30–33; 10:19–21, 32), and because his words are supported by scripture (John 5:39, 40, 46, 47). However Jesus often appeals to the evidence of miraculous works (John 10:25), which are given for the sake of those who find Jesus' own testimony doubtful. (John 5:36; 10:38; 14:11). These works are typically and repeatedly referred to as God's, emphasizing the Son's dependence on the Father, as is customary in John's Gospel. They are works "shown" by the Father (John 5:20), works "given" by the Father (John 5:36), the works of the one who "sent" Jesus (John 9:4), works "from my Father" (John 10:32), and "works of my Father" (John 10:37). Indeed, Jesus says, "the Father dwelling in me, does his works," (John 14:10), even though they are also works that Jesus himself does (John 10:25). As portrayed in this Gospel, the miraculous works, by showing that Jesus' claims are not merely of human origin, offer an objectivity which Jesus' own testimony does not. They are even considered a more compelling sort of evidence than the testimony of John the Baptist (John 5:33–36), since they constitute more direct testimony by God. They are frequently mentioned as a cause for belief (John 1:49, 50; 2:11, 23; 4:29, 53; 5:36; 6:14; 7:31; 9:30–31; 10:21; 10:42; 11:45; 12:10–11; 20:26–29, 31).

While the Evangelist's signs, and particularly the sign of Jesus' resurrection, were not generally accepted in the first century, the Evangelist does not view this as justifiable grounds to doubt his reports. Offering the reports as factual, the Evangelist understands his situation to be similar to a party in court. His use of legal terminology (e.g., testimony, witness, judge, excuse) shows his consciousness of the controversial character of his message. Courts do not find the facts agreed upon by both parties to be more certain than disputed facts, but base their decision on all the facts they deem reliable, even those facts disputed by one party. The court decides which representation of the facts is justified, based upon a full investigation and a hearing of the evidence. An example of this way of resolving controversy may be seen in the description of Paul's defense before the governor Felix in Caesarea, against the charges of Tertullus the Orator (Acts 24). Even if in religious questions a court may be unable to reach a decision, this does not itself show that the decision is unclear. John believes that only those who were (metaphorically) blind could have ignored the messianic claims of Jesus (John 12:40; cf. John 9:39–41). Human courts are susceptible to human blindness. John's hope for vindication hangs on the divine judgment at the future resurrection of all people, at which Jesus will either give life to or condemn each person (John 5:26–29). The Evangelist writes out of this traditionally Jewish understanding that religious claims can be warranted, even though there is no agreement upon them in the nation or community. This understanding is found, for example, in the tradition of the persecution of prophets (e.g., Elijah and Jeremiah), and of the dissensions between the Pharisees and Sadducees (Acts 23:6–10), and of the Qumran community being "separated" from other Jews.[72] It is also evident in the conflict

---

72. 4Q397 [4QMMT 92] in García Martínez, *Dead Sea Scrolls Translated*, 79.

between Jewish and pagan religion, as expressed in the persecution of the Jews under Antiochus Epiphanes (1 Macc 1; 2 Macc 5:21—7:42),[73] and in a decree of about 40 AD by the Roman Emperor Gaius 'Caligula' to place idols in the Jerusalem temple, and kill any who resisted.[74] In this same tradition, John considers his own reports of Jesus' signs to be credible reports, which discredit opposing viewpoints, even majority viewpoints.

In part, the Evangelist portrays his opponents as eventually acknowledging the factual character of the signs. When the man born blind is healed, the Pharisees justify their unbelief by condemning the man as "born entirely in sins" (John 9:34). This expresses the idea that the man had been born blind as the result of sin, a possibility raised earlier in the chapter by Jesus' disciples. The Pharisees acknowledge by this remark that the man who now sees was indeed born blind, just as his own parents had testified. This acceptance of Jesus' signs as factual is even more evident in Jesus' raising of Lazarus from the dead. The Evangelist writes:

> Many therefore of the Jews, who had come to Mary and saw what he had done, believed in him. But some of them went away to the Pharisees and told them the things which Jesus had done. Therefore the high priests and the Pharisees convened a council, and were saying, "What are we doing? For this man is performing many signs. If we let him do this, all men will believe in him, and the Romans will come and take away both our place and our nation." (John 11:45–48)

The Jewish leaders acknowledge (for the moment, at least) that Jesus performed signs. However the main Jewish leaders do not believe that Almighty God has really sent Jesus, since they think the Romans would quell Jesus' messianic rule.

The Jewish acknowledgment of Jesus' signs as genuinely supernatural does not itself imply an acknowledgment of his divine authority, for Moses also warns of signs given by false prophets (Deut 13:1–5). In this Gospel Jesus' adversaries seem to agree among themselves that he was a sinner and a deceiver, accusing him variously of breaking the Sabbath (John 5:16, 9:16), or of "calling God his own Father" (John 5:18; 10:36), or of leading the people astray (John 7:12,47). Indeed, the Evangelist acknowledges the first two accusations, but finds Jesus guiltless (John 5:18; 7:23–24). It is not clear on what legal grounds Jesus' adversaries individually conclude that Jesus is nevertheless guilty (John 7:51, 52; 9:24, 25). Indeed, that becomes a problem for them when they can offer to Pilate no specific grounds for Jesus' condemnation. They only say, "If this man were not an evildoer, we would not have delivered him up to you" (John 18:30). It is also implied that they pass on to Pilate the accusation that Jesus claimed to be "King of the Jews," but this also is not itself a cause for condemnation under the Mosaic law, at least not unless the claim is both false and seditious. In spite of this acceptance of signs, there is little doubt that the main Jewish leaders did not believe reports about the resurrection of Jesus, especially since Jesus' own followers were initially reluctant to believe it (Luke 24:36–43; John 20:25).

---

73. Josephus *Antiquities* 12.246–56.
74. Josephus *War* 2.184–98.

CHAPTER CONCLUSIONS

We began this chapter asking whether the Evangelist regularly intends miraculous events to be understood as nonhistorical fiction or metaphor. The extent of fiction in John's Gospel is a controversial question among Johannine scholars. Nevertheless, for our purposes we have argued that the presumption must be that John intends his miracles to be understood as historical events. It is widely documented that the first generation of Christians believed that Jesus performed miracles (particularly Jesus' resurrection), so it is to be expected that the Evangelist also believed that Jesus performed miracles. The Evangelist also portrays characters in the Gospel as reasonably believing in reports of Jesus' miracles. In general, the Evangelist gives much space for miracles in this Gospel, which is consistent with belief in their historical significance. The earliest Christian readings of John's Gospel consistently understand its miracles as historical, so that it is difficult to imagine that the Evangelist intended to be understood by everyone as speaking only metaphorically.

6

The Evangelist's Concept of Knowledge

Miracles as Historical Grounds for Belief

IN OUR QUEST TO understand the Evangelist's epistemology of belief, we are still focusing on the test case of belief arising from reports of miracles. We have already argued that the Evangelist did not intend his miracle accounts to be understood as fiction or nonhistorical metaphor. We can now argue that, having already accepted the plausibility of monotheism, the Evangelist sees essentially historical reports of Jesus' miracles as providing a sufficient ground for belief. Again, we are not arguing here that the miracles are historical, but only that the Evangelist understood them as such, so that they reflect his understanding of how historical accounts can be a basis for knowledge and belief. This claim that belief can be based on miracles is sharply criticized in many circles, it being alleged that, in the view of the Evangelist, belief based on miracles is tainted or devoid of authenticity. This chapter will look closely at texts in the Gospel that are used to support such allegations, so that the Evangelist's own views can be seen.

SIGNS USED AS GROUNDS FOR FAITH: BULTMANN'S OBJECTION

Bultmann distinguishes two grounds for faith: "the revelatory word" and "miracle." By "the word," Bultmann means a message that makes no claim to historical knowledge. For Bultmann, even the physical authentication of Jesus' resurrection is not essential to the Evangelist's meaning. Bultmann writes,

> The fact that the Risen Jesus, as it were, authenticates himself and proves his identity with the man crucified two days earlier through showing his hands . . . and his pierced side is not only surprising with regard to the Gospel itself, but is also quite unmotivated within the narrative before us. . . . In any case for him the story has primarily a symbolic meaning: it sets forth the fulfilment of the promise ἔρχομαι πρὸς ὑμᾶς [I come to you] 14.18ff.[1]

This devaluation of the physical reality of the events is not true to the Evangelist's understanding, as was discussed earlier in regard to the reprimand of Thomas. Bultmann

---

1. Bultmann, *Gospel of John*, 691.

further portrays the Evangelist as knowing that the actual history of the events has no real significance. Bultmann writes,

> While he certainly has no need to contest the reality of the events narrated, it is plain that both in this one and in the story of Thomas he would have us understand that these events do not establish the genuine Easter faith. . . . The miracles of the substantial and mundane appearance of the Risen Lord, which in v. 30 are comprehended under the term, σημεῖα [signs], have only the relative worth of σημεῖα [signs], generally, and their real significance is a symbolic one.[2]

Bultmann supposes in the first citation above that the Evangelist is only concerned about a coming (ἔρχομαι) of Jesus which is a nonphysical reality. This reality is Jesus' presence with his disciples in spirit, though Bultmann would presumably deny the scientific character of any belief in a personal afterlife, even of the human spirit. The presence of Jesus' spirit is itself, then, seen as a symbol for Jesus' influence on his followers. Since, in the second citation, Bultmann considers the events in the Gospel to be symbolical, rather than physical realities, for him the events can only symbolize such spiritual realities.

As cited earlier, Bultmann says that Jesus' "σημεῖα [signs] were subordinated to the discourses, and his real work was achieved in the revelatory word."[3] Here he identifies the "revelatory word" with the message of the discourses, though he perhaps alludes to the message of the gospel or kerygma. But of course it is the discourses in particular which show that the Evangelist treats the miracles as physical realities. If on the other hand, we understand "the revelatory word" as the Word that became flesh, it seems also that we must acknowledge the Evangelist's understanding that this revelation has a physical character. In either case, Bultmann's contrast of the evidence provided by word and sign is an imposition upon the Evangelist. The Evangelist values the evidence of both sign and word (John 20:31), and portrays Jesus himself as adopting this same view (John 10:38; 14:11). The signs do not provide a basis for faith apart from Jesus' word, for they attest to Jesus as a teacher. Similarly, Jesus' word is attested by the words of other prophets, and by Jesus' own persuasive arguments.

Against the view that signs sometimes form a basis for genuine belief in Jesus, Bultmann promoted the view that *true faith* can never, in the mind of the Evangelist, be faith that arises from miracles, not even partially from miracles. Bultmann says, "faith based on miracle has only a relative value as a stepping stone to true faith, which once awakened will see 'something greater' than such miracles (v. 50)."[4] He is followed by Koester, who says, "belief in the miracles is not only insufficient; it falsifies what true belief in Jesus ought to be."[5] Here we must understand *true faith* as the kind of faith that gives eternal life (John 3:16; John 20:31). The denial of the value of signs as a partial basis for true faith is an absolute denial, which earlier commentators did not strictly make. John Calvin, commenting on Nicodemus' visit in John 3:2, says that the signs have the effect of ". . . preparing us for faith and then of further strengthening what has been conceived

2. Ibid., 688.
3. Ibid., 452.
4. Ibid., 104.
5. Koester, *Ancient Christian Gospels*, 251.

by the Word."⁶ While Calvin in these words indicates that faith cannot arise out of signs alone, he allows that faith may in some cases not arise without the additional evidence of signs, saying "the children of God are indeed helped by miracles to reach faith."⁷

The claim that there is a separate faith arising from miracles, which is never true faith, has led to incoherent readings of John's Gospel. For example, John Painter argued in his unpublished thesis:

> Consequently faith is often spoken of as a consequence of having seen Jesus' "signs" 2:23; 4:45; 6:2; 6:14; 7:31; 9:16; 11:45, 47f.; 12:37–43. But although the faith resulting from seeing "signs" should be recognized, it is to be regarded as inadequate, and only a beginning which may become fully authentic faith. The inadequacy of this faith is indicated by Jesus' refusal to trust those who believed as a consequence of having seen "signs" 2:24f.; and the reception given to Jesus (4:45) is brought into question 4:48. Those who make "signs" a condition of belief distort the meaning of "signs."⁸

In a dissertation that is otherwise persuasive, Painter portrayed this false belief as being so extensive that the apostles themselves had no "fully authentic faith" before Christ's resurrection.⁹ Does the absence of "authentic faith" mean that the apostles have fallen short of that faith which secures eternal life (John 3:16; 20:31)? Does it mean instead that they have such life-giving faith but that it needs to develop? For the Evangelist, this question is fundamental, since belief that did not result in eternal life would not achieve the Evangelist's purpose. It appears that Painter favored the former viewpoint. This reading brings enormous incoherency into the text. Do the disciples who follow Jesus and baptize have any life-giving faith themselves (John 4:1, 2)? Jesus refers in prayer to his disciples as those who "believed that you sent me," and as people "not of the world, even as I am not of the world," and as people whom he has sent "into the world" (John 17:8, 14, 18). That this kind of language would be used of disciples lacking life-giving faith is incoherent. When we talk about the kind of faith that can arise from signs, it is crucial to determine whether or not we are referring to faith that, in the Evangelist's mind, will give eternal life.

The argument that faith "arising from miracles" can never be *true faith* rests primarily upon five main texts, which will be individually discussed and critiqued below. First, based on the unreliability of those who believe in Jesus after seeing miracles at the Passover (John 2:23–25), it has been argued that faith arising from miracles is not *true faith*. A second text cited is the claim of those Samaritans whose belief is transformed so as to rest, no longer on the demonstration of Jesus' supernatural knowledge that was reported to them, but on his own word (John 4:42). A third text cited is the reproach of Jesus, "Unless you see signs and wonders, you will not believe" (John 4:48). In the fourth text, Jesus denies the request for manna (John 6:30–31). The last major text to be discussed is the reprimand given by the risen Jesus to Thomas, and Jesus' affirmation of

6. Calvin, *Gospel According to John*, 1:62.
7. Ibid., 1:58.
8. Painter, *Idea of Knowledge*, 215.
9. Ibid., 216–20.

the faith of those who believe without seeing firsthand (John 20:26–29). Discussion of these arguments requires detailed exegesis of the Evangelist's viewpoint.

THE SOURCE OF BULTMANN'S COMPLAINT

Much of the following discussion will interact with Rudolf Bultmann's work. Bultmann remains one of the most important critics of the conception of belief and miracles that we are proposing, because of his detailed exegetical arguments for opposing views in his recognized commentary on John's Gospel. Other scholars also accept many of his exegetical conclusions.

Bultmann was interested in finding a *kerygma* (proclaimed message) in the Gospels that was free of what he considered to be mythic elements. This myth he characterizes as that, "God sent forth his Son, a pre-existent divine Being, who appears on earth as a man. He dies the death of a sinner on the cross and makes atonement for the sins of men. His resurrection marks the beginning of the cosmic catastrophe."[10] Like earlier liberal theologians, Bultmann is concerned to preserve the religious value of the Christian faith that remains after the supernatural elements are discounted. Yet against the idealism of the earlier liberal theologians, Bultmann wishes to salvage this kerygma as an event, rather than timeless principles. Affirming the historical importance of the Christian Church as a religious institution, as was emphasized by the History of Religions School, he thinks that school nevertheless ignored the church's existence as part of "salvation history and eschatology" and ignored "the decisive act of God in Christ proclaimed as the event of redemption"[11] By this Bultmann seems to affirm that God was genuinely revealed in the historical event of Jesus' life and in the rise of the church, even though he considers the supernatural elements in the New Testament to be nonhistorical. Bultmann thinks there is a Christian kerygma or message within these myths which still offers profound insights, but which must be recovered from the myth. He is interested in interpreting the myths "anthropologically, or better still existentially," that is, he wants to find the importance of their meaning for people.[12] Bultmann holds to "the incredibility of a mythical event like the resuscitation of a dead person—for that is what the resurrection means"; yet he admits that "Paul tries to prove the miracle of the resurrection by adducing a list of eye-witnesses (1 Cor 15:3–8)."[13] But since Bultmann regards it as impossible that the resurrection could tell us "about the eschatological fact of the destruction of death," he thinks Paul mistaken in this attempt. Instead, Bultmann thinks that faith should arise only from "the word of preaching," there being no possibility of any historical warrant for faith. In Bultmann's judgment, one that is common, "All that historical criticism can establish is the fact that the first disciples came to believe in the resurrection."[14] For Bultmann, the destruction of death does not refer to the death we see in this world.

10. Bultmann, "New Testament and Mythology," 2.
11. Ibid., 15.
12. Ibid., 10.
13. Ibid., 39.
14. Ibid., 40–42.

SIGNS AS GROUNDS FOR FAITH: THE FIRST PASSOVER (JOHN 2:23–25)

In his commentary on the passage about Jesus' reception in Jerusalem because of his signs, Bultmann invoked a distinction between faith and *true faith*:

> This is not, of course, to say that faith aroused by miracles is false, but that such faith is only the first step towards Jesus; it has not yet seen him in his true significance, and it is therefore not yet fully established. Later the example of the healing of the blind man will be used to show how such a first step towards Jesus, if it turns into trust in him, can issue in true faith (9.35ff.). Here however v.24 teaches that such a turning towards Jesus, simply on account of his miracles, is suspect. Jesus does not trust himself to these believers, i.e. he considers them unreliable, for he sees through them all.[15]

Bultmann argues first that faith aroused by miracles is not false, but then he contrasts such faith with *true faith*. However in John's mind a faith that is not *true faith*, whatever merit it might have, falls short, since only true faith will give eternal life. For John to ignore this would be for him to ignore his fundamental conception of the human situation, and his fundamental concern in writing and publishing his Gospel (John 20:31). Barrett rightly recognizes the fatal defect of those in John 2:23 whose faith was mistrusted by Jesus. Barrett comments, "Jesus has divine knowledge and is not misled by appearances, even by the appearance of faith."[16] Unfortunately, Barrett also implies that the faith is not real, but only an appearance, even though the Evangelist explicitly says that "many believed in his name, beholding his signs" (John 2:23). In some sense the belief certainly was real, or there would have been no distinction between the "many" who believed, and the rest who did not believe (John 2:23). Schnackenburg has similarly denied that the faith was real, commenting on this passage, "Jesus knows everybody and sees into the hearts of all (cf. on 1:48), especially of those who do not believe in him (cf. 5:42)."[17] There are good reasons, however, to think that the commentators' characterization of this belief as not *true faith*, as a mere appearance of faith, and as lack of belief, are all alien to the Evangelist's plain statement that the people believed.

This passage does not support the view that the Evangelist conceives of two kinds of faith: *faith* and *true faith*. As discussed in our earlier chapter about belief, the Evangelist never uses the term "truly believing" in distinction from mere "believing," for in his mind there is only the one concept of "believing," and the only distinguishing feature from a retrospective stance is whether or not a person is still "believing" (John 3:16; 20:31). We would naturally expect such an inclusive use of this term in the early church, for descriptions of peoples' belief are not generally informed by divine knowledge of the authenticity or future tenacity of their belief, and there must have been many occasions in which the response of people to the proclamation of the gospel was described as "believing." An observer simply sees believers, and would not know which of them would eventually turn back. An observer such as the Evangelist would have often seen, when the

---

15. Bultmann, *Gospel of John*, 131.
16. Barrett, *Gospel According to John*, 202.
17. Schnackenburg, *Gospel According to John*, 1:359.

Christian faith was proclaimed, that some did not believe, some believe for a while, and some believe without turning back.

Even if this time in Jerusalem is understood merely as a historical novel, it deserves to be read with the historical verisimilitude and conceptual language which would describe the standard situation when the gospel was proclaimed. It is historically implausible, when so many in Jerusalem were not yet persuaded to believe in Jesus by these signs, that every single person who did believe in Jesus should later turn back. Indeed, Nicodemus seems to be an exception. It may be, of course, that most did turn back, and the Evangelist might have in mind Jesus' ultimate lack of support in Jerusalem on Palm Sunday (John 12:12–19; 19), but why would the Evangelist claim knowledge that every one who evidenced belief in Jesus on this occasion later turned away from Jesus?

The more plausible meaning of the Evangelist is that the believing members of the crowd could not, in their entirety as a crowd, be trusted by Jesus, since many (but not necessarily all) of those who believed did not have a faith which would endure. This is a more natural reading. Jesus has incurred the hostility of the religious leaders due to his actions in the temple, as evidenced by the subsequent clandestine night visit of Nicodemus. Jesus cannot trust his safety to the acclaim of his supporters among the crowds. This reading of the belief as inclusive of both enduring and temporary belief is confirmed, contra Bultmann,[18] by the role of Nicodemus. Nicodemus is representative of these same people in Jerusalem who were so impressed by the signs Jesus performed (John 3:2). Although Nicodemus is initially a secret supporter of Jesus, he eventually associates with Jesus publicly, even after Jesus' criminal conviction and crucifixion (John 19:38–42). This shows at least that the first faith of Nicodemus, which was initiated in part by the miraculous signs, led to the eventual faith of Nicodemus. If signs are even a partial cause of bringing people to genuine faith in Jesus, then signs cause faith, and we can understand the Evangelist's declared interest in including them so prominently (John 20:31).

In this passage there is little reason to understand the people's faith as arising from miracles alone, since it is to be understood that Jesus' miracles were accompanied by teaching. Jesus has publicly condemned the sale of animals in the holy temple of the Jewish nation, and the Evangelists typically give in their portrayal of events mere summaries and selections of Jesus' teaching. That Jesus is not to be understood here as a silent miracle worker is evident also in the subsequent passage, where Nicodemus knows him as a "teacher come from God, for no one can do these miracles that you do unless God is with him" (John 3:2). Jesus is addressed as "Rabbi (which is being interpreted, Teacher)" (John 1:38) even from the beginning of this Gospel, before we are specifically informed that he has taught. Jesus is probably to be understood as still accompanied by his disciples in Jerusalem. Jesus' defense of his actions in the temple was probably to be understood as more extensive than the brief summary given by the Evangelist. The reader is to understand, therefore, that the miracles were accompanied by teaching. The Evangelist's emphasis on signs as a cause of the people's belief does not entirely discredit signs as a valid ground for belief. Instead, he emphasizes the essential role which the

---

18. Bultmann, *Gospel of John*.

signs had for eliciting belief, but discredits the fickleness of human nature, which is the stated basis on which Jesus mistrusts the crowd. The emphasis in the passage is that "what was in man" (John 2:25) was corrupt, not that the people have a different kind of faith. This theme of the ineffectiveness of the signs in the face of human obstinacy surfaces again later (cf. John 12:37–40). It cannot be shown that those who turn away from Jesus are only those who believed because of Jesus' signs.

SIGNS AS GROUNDS FOR FAITH: THE SAMARITANS (JOHN 4:39–42)

A second text cited to distinguish "faith" based on miracles from *true faith* is the account of the Samaritans. Many Samaritans "believed in him on account of the words of the woman who testified, 'He told me everything I have done.'" In John's account, Jesus' supernatural knowledge of this woman's past history is one essential basis for their belief. After Jesus speaks with the Samaritans directly, more of them believe, and the Samaritans say their belief was transformed so as to rest, no longer on the reports of Jesus' supernatural knowledge and claims, but on Jesus' own words. Jesus' words provide more persuasive evidence for belief. It is speculative, however, to claim with Schnackenburg that the belief of those Samaritans who had first trusted in Jesus simply after hearing about his prophetic powers were "would-be believers."[19] Indeed, the Evangelist's claim that "many more believed in him on account of his words," suggests that these new believers are conceived of as added to the original group of believers, and so have the same kind of belief. The Evangelist's emphasis is on the more compelling basis of Jesus' words as a ground for belief, not on the inadequacy of the Samaritan woman's report as a ground for belief. Belief that is initially justified by sufficient evidence, upon the discovery of much weightier evidence, will naturally rest more heavily on the latter. In the same way, Jesus elsewhere declares that after Nathanael sees the greater signs of Jesus, the demonstration of prophetic knowledge which had originally evoked Nathanael's faith would be seen as a less compelling reason to believe (John 1:50). Furthermore, it would be a mistake to think that this more strongly justified belief of the Samaritans means that none of these Samaritans would ever turn away from believing in Jesus. The latter belief, too, would not give eternal life, if it did not continue.

For this same text, some argue for a distinction of miracle-based faith from *true faith*". This is argued on the grounds that all human testimony, including testimony about the miraculous, is unreliable and so provides an inadequate basis for belief. Barrett comments about the Samaritan woman's report of the miraculous, "human testimony has its value, yet it is also secondary."[20] He then cites in support Bultmann's comment, "Thus we are faced with the strange paradox that the proclamation, without which no man can be brought to Jesus, is itself insignificant, in that the hearer who enjoys the knowledge of faith is freed from its tutelage, is free, that is, to criticize the proclamation which brought him to faith."[21] But in what sense does the Evangelist portray human testimony as sec-

---

19. Schnackenburg, *Gospel According to John*, 1:455.
20. Barrett, *Gospel According to John*, 244.
21. Bultmann, cited in Barrett, *Gospel According to John*, 244.

ondary? If human testimony is secondary, why does the Evangelist testify through his Gospel? In this Gospel, Jesus says in regard to John the Baptist's testimony,

> The witness which I receive is not from man, but I say these things that you may be saved.... But the witness which I have is greater than John; for the works ... bear witness of me that the Father has sent me. (John 5:34–36)

While secondary, human testimony is here sufficient "that you might be saved." Saving faith may be caused by miracles, at least as an indirect cause. In the Evangelist's thought there is no reason to deny the status of *true faith* to belief simply because the belief arises from human testimony. Furthermore, the supernatural works of Jesus, works that the Jewish leaders knew about by means of human reports, are nevertheless considered a divine witness, and are here specifically distinguished from human testimony. The report of the Samaritan woman that Jesus demonstrated supernatural knowledge cannot therefore be simply dismissed as incapable of securing a belief that gives eternal life. It is too simplistic as well to think of her testimony as a mere report of the supernatural. She argues that the Messiah has come to Samaritans (John 4:29), and it is this claim that is believed on the basis of her report.

SIGNS AS GROUNDS FOR FAITH: THE OFFICIAL'S SON (JOHN 4:46–54)

A third text cited to discredit faith arising from miracles is the reproach of Jesus, "Unless you see signs and wonders, you will not believe" (John 4:48). Bultmann considered this text to be the main point of the passage, and to be a criticism of faith arising from miracles.[22] Indeed, Jesus does indicate by these words that the people would not believe without seeing signs, and Jesus does imply that this reveals a moral deficiency of character. However this text does not mean that those who saw signs would believe, for elsewhere in the Gospel people see signs and do not believe (John 9 & 11). Rather, in this text Jesus appeals to the people, especially the official, to trust him, based on the compelling reports they have heard from others, instead of unreasonably demanding to see signs personally. There were other grounds to believe than seeing personally, grounds which were sufficient for people of good will, but which would be resisted by people of ill will. The man to whom Jesus spoke believed Jesus' promise before seeing the sign (John 4:50). In violation of the view that faith from miracles is not *true faith*, we are also told that the man believed after he saw the sign (John 4:53). While the man did believe Jesus' word beforehand, it is evident that his faith after seeing his son's healing was the climax of his faith, not the diminishing of his faith. Knowledge of the sign was also the cause that his household believed. There is no indication in the passage that this belief arising from miracles was not itself *true faith*. Such an interpretation ignores the climax of the story.

Commenting on this passage, Schnackenburg also devalued faith which arises from miracles. He spoke of "Jesus' denunciation of a faith which clings to miracles."[23] But the severe assessment of "denunciation" misses the context of the story. An official whose son is dying has heard of Jesus' power to heal. He considers the reports credible. Leaving

---

22. Bultmann, *Gospel of John*, 112.
23. Schnackenburg, *Gospel According to John*, 1:466.

The Evangelist's Concept of Knowledge: Miracles and Belief

his town, he comes and asks Jesus to heal his son. He believes that Jesus, as one sent from God, may be able to come to his home and heal the child. However Jesus does not agree to go with the man, but instead declares that the child will live, and tells the man to return home. By doing this, Jesus demands that the man trust Jesus' promise (and God's), the promise that the child will live. The man has heard reports of Jesus' healings, and has been told by Jesus in front of many people that the child will live. The man responds to all this by believing Jesus' promise that the child will live, even though he cannot see whether this healing has taken place. This is the response of trust that Jesus was seeking from the official. That the official should have responded in this way was not certain. Jesus had warned him just beforehand against the common attitude of believing only what he could see, an attitude which showed, not trust based on miracles, but no trust in Jesus (or God) at all. Although Jesus warns against an attitude of unbelief held by the people generally, he must primarily be addressing the official who is requesting his son's healing. The Evangelist says that it is in response to this request that Jesus "therefore" addressed the official with these words, and the official is the one who is then called upon to believe Jesus in a matter so grave as the impending death of his child. It was the official's own problem, though it was a problem many others shared, that he was not inclined to trust Jesus. It required no trust to ask Jesus to heal the child, only a belief that Jesus might be able to heal. Jesus' concern was not that the man's faith arose from miracles, but that the man's belief was limited to what he could see. This is confirmed by Jesus' expression of the same concern later with Thomas, whom he criticizes for not believing until he saw (John 20:29). There are other grounds for belief than seeing. The official who asked of Jesus a miracle was therefore required first to trust in Jesus (and God) to grant it. While believing a promise need not in general constitute trust in the person who promises absolutely, the official shows a trust in Jesus as one sent by God, and as one who promises to save his child from death. What greater trust can be demanded? There is reason, then, to see this man as trusting in Jesus already at this point with an authentic faith. The people would not believe (οὐ μὴ πιστεύσητε) that Jesus would perform a sign, unless they saw the sign performed, because they did not trust in Jesus. The verb *believe* is in the aorist tense of the subjunctive mood, not the future tense of the indicative mood; this indicates that the people do not currently believe *in Jesus*, and would not be willing to trust Jesus to perform the miracle, even if they do believe it possible that Jesus will perform a miracle. The verbal form indicates, not that the people might cease to believe, but that they would not believe at all without first seeing. Belief in the possibility that Jesus might perform a miracle may arise from reports of Jesus' miracles. However such a belief amounts neither to trust in Jesus, nor even to trust in Jesus' promise to perform another miracle.

Schnackenburg's exegesis leads into difficulties. The story concludes with the official's faith being confirmed by seeing the miracle of his son's healing take place. This forms a climax to the story, but it violates Schnackenburg's idea that the Evangelist is criticizing faith "which relies exclusively on the spectacular, the visible, the external elements of the miracle" since "the purely sensational is not a valid motive for faith."[24] Schnackenburg then finds that this favorable view of miracles at the end "brings a peculiar tension into

---

24. Ibid., 1:467.

the rest of the story, since on the one hand the official believes the mere word of Jesus (v. 50) and comes, on the other hand, to full faith (v. 53b) only when he has verified exactly the healing at a distance (v. 53a)."[25] Schnackenburg finds the ending scene "all the more remarkable, since it attaches importance to the exact verification of the miracle and thus, after all, favors once more the motive supplied by the external experience of miracles (cf. v. 53)." Schnackenburg finds it "strange to find so much stress laid on the exact verification of the healing at a distance," and "[w]hat follows is still more awkward" because the faith which arises from the miracle must be "a weak type of faith, which corresponds to the attitude blamed by Jesus and is no longer on the level of faith in the mere word of Jesus (v. 50)."[26] The incoherence of Schnackenburg's reading is so palpable that he is then forced to suppose that the Evangelist clumsily "took over the story in substance from a source which also contained the first Cana miracle, and inserted it into his narrative with some redactional additions." Schnackenburg argues that the redaction is so poorly executed because of the Evangelist's regard for the integrity of his sources.[27] If the Evangelist selects from the sacred Old Testament, why would he not select from this source? If he would not even abbreviate this source out of respect for its integrity, would he not accept its view of miracles? It is far more credible to abandon the idea that the Evangelist finds belief to be tainted by having originated from reports of miracles.

The phrase "signs and wonders" (σημεῖα καὶ τέρατα) occurs 16 times in the New Testament, without any generally pejorative connotation. The two words occur together about 25 times in the Septuagint (e.g., Exod 7:3,9; 11:9; Deut 4:34; 6:22; 7:19; 11:3; 13:1, 2; 26:8; 28:46; 29:3; 34:11; Neh 9:10; Pss 78:43; 105:27; 135:9; Wis 8:8; 10:16; Isa 8:18; 20:3 Jer 32:20,21; Bar 2:11). In the Septuagint the words refer with few exceptions to the signs and wonders of the Exodus. John uses the phrase only in this text (John 4:48); he perhaps uses it here to emphasize the demand for miracles of greatness similar to those performed by Moses. This would parallel the unreasonable demand for Jesus to provide manna, after already having fed the five thousand (John 6). The only other time that this phrase is attributed to Jesus (Matt 24:24; Mark 13:22), it refers to false prophets, but this evidence by itself is too slight to draw any inferences about the phrase having a pejorative connotation.

SIGNS AS GROUNDS FOR FAITH: MANNA DENIED (JOHN 6:14–59)

A fourth text cited to discredit faith arising from miracles is the account of Jesus' denial of a request to bring down manna from heaven, as Moses was believed to have done. The sign is demanded to prove Jesus' divine commission. Jesus' refusal to perform this sign indicates that signs do not necessarily elicit an enduring faith, and are not always the best way to elicit an enduring faith. Jesus himself refers to other factors that drew people to him, saying in that passage, "you seek me not because you saw signs, but because you ate of the loaves and were filled" (John 6:26). The limited value of signs is also shown by their partial acceptance by Jesus' opponents. In John's Gospel, even Jesus' opponents

25. Ibid., 1:467.
26. Ibid., 1:468.
27. Ibid., 1:469.

eventually acknowledge that "this man is performing many signs" (John 11:47). They believe Jesus performed the sign, but they do not trust in or believe in Jesus. They apparently attribute the signs to demonic power, even though it is a repeated point of public contention whether anyone but God could give such power (John 3:2; 9:16, 32, 33; 10:21, 38). A common belief in the limits of demonic power is implied also by the continued requests for signs of adequate power (or character) to definitively show that God sent Jesus (John 2:18; 6:30).

Signs may attract the temporary allegiance of mercurial people. After the feeding of the five thousand, people first wish in response to make Jesus king, but after listening to Jesus further they repudiate him (John 6:14–15, 58–66). This erratic response shows that miracles are of limited usefulness for eliciting an enduring faith. The religious leaders are convinced of Jesus' popularity, as shown by the premise of their argument that "all men will believe in him, and the Romans will come and take away both our place and our nation" (John 11:48). Again, however, this need not mean that everyone who believed in Jesus because they saw signs had a mercurial disposition. A belief that Jesus performed miracles could nevertheless be an important cause of *true belief* in Jesus, even though those who credited Jesus with performing "many signs" did not necessarily believe in him. Indeed, if the Evangelist understands God to be the source of the signs, it would be senseless to deny the value of their message to evoke belief.

SIGNS AS GROUNDS FOR FAITH: THOMAS'S DEMAND (JOHN 20:24–31)

The last text used to discount the importance of miracles is taken from Jesus' resurrection appearance to Thomas. According to Bultmann,

> While he certainly has no need to contest the reality of the events narrated, it is plain that both in this one and in the story of Thomas he would have us understand that these events do not establish the genuine Easter faith. . . .[28]

Bultmann indicates here that it was unimportant whether or not the resurrection was a historical event. Perhaps in particular it was unimportant whether the disciples merely saw Jesus in a vision, as Thomas suggests by his refusal to believe without touching Jesus. Bultmann's comment suggests that he is discounting the importance of signs as historical events, since they are for him only signs directing us toward greater realities that stand outside of history. This view about signs does not agree with the Evangelist's view. This concern to prevent faith arising from signs is not shared in John's Gospel by either Jesus or the Evangelist. Both Jesus who performs the miracles, and the Evangelist who retells them do so to lead many to *true faith*, not to inauthentic faith. If faith arising from signs is not *true faith*, why did the Evangelist include the signs? Unlike Bultmann, the Evangelist is not concerned to deny the historical character of the miracles, as Bultmann admits. Another problem with Bultmann's reading is that Bultmann himself does not believe that the miracle here recounted occurred, and yet that is exactly what Thomas is reprimanded for doubting that God had done. It is likewise the Evangelist's reason in other passages for condemning the Pharisees as "blind" (John 9:39), and for warning

---

28. Bultmann, *Gospel of John*, 688.

the royal official about needing to "see" signs to believe they had occurred (John 4:48). There are compelling reasons to understand Jesus' words to Thomas as an admonition to one who hesitates to believe compelling evidence that God has performed a unique miracle in history. Thomas is specially criticized because, refusing to trust the eyewitness testimony of friends he knows to be reliable, he unreasonably demands to see and touch Jesus personally before he will acknowledge the miracle of Jesus' resurrection. Unbelief in the sign here implies unbelief in the word of Jesus' own disciples, and in Jesus' earlier claims to have the power of raising the dead. The story of Thomas is given to encourage trust in the apostolic testimony about Jesus' resurrection, not a story teaching the reader to ignore all testimony as unreliable.

EXEGETICAL CONCLUSIONS

While it is true that miracles may engender a belief that later proves spurious, only a selective reading of the texts can support the view that miracles have no legitimate place in the formation of faith. Jesus himself admonishes his audience, if they will not believe his words, to believe the works that he does (e.g., John 14:11). In narrative context, these works must particularly include, and probably solely refer to, signs which are miraculous. The disciples are said to believe in Jesus after seeing his transformation of water into wine (John 2:11). It is clear from the development of the Gospel's plot, which shows Jesus' growing influence, that this belief is referred to approvingly. The belief is merited by the signs, and is not a hindrance, but rather an influence that brings some to a life giving belief in Jesus as Christ. Conversely, it is Jesus' detractors who, after the climax of signs in the resurrection of Lazarus, are criticized by the Evangelist for not believing in Jesus "though he had performed so many signs" (John 12:37). Since Jesus' opponents express concern that the Romans will destroy their nation if it follows Jesus, it is evident that they do not accept Jesus' raising of Lazarus from death as showing God's authorization of Jesus. This in turn suggests that they are doubtful either about the reports they heard, or of the significance of those reports. Thomas is admonished for doubting, in his despondency, reports of Jesus' resurrection (John 20:29), since Thomas knows the witnesses as reliable friends. The Evangelist's inclusion of select miracles cannot be explained as carelessly adopted from sources in spite of his own belief that they are not a proper source for faith. Instead, they show his genuine acceptance of the importance of signs for eliciting faith. Indeed, all of the earliest Christian texts show a widespread belief and acceptance of Jesus' miraculous powers as a historical reality. According to Theissen, G. Klein claimed that both Mark's and John's Gospels were written to deter readers from belief in miracles. Theissen comments, "Can Mark really have told sixteen miracle stories solely in order to warn against belief in miracles? It seems a rather clumsy way of doing it."[29]

Based on our exegesis of these passages, what is the difference between believing in Jesus and believing that Jesus performed miracles? Here the examples of Caiaphas and Nicodemus will be instructive. Upon the testimony of those who reported to the

---

29. Theissen, *Miracle Stories*, 294.

Pharisees about the resurrection of Lazarus, the high priests and Pharisees declare that Jesus was performing "many signs." The evidence for the latter miracle confirms the credibility of prior reports of miracles. At the same time, Caiaphas says he does not consider Jesus' powers to be a match for the Romans. Caiaphas thinks the people will acclaim Jesus as Messiah and so draw the wrath of Rome upon the nation. Caiaphas seems to believe that Jesus has raised a man from death, yet not to believe that Jesus would have any power to stop the Roman suppression of a revolt. While it might be suggested that Caiaphas is speaking insincerely, the plan of the gospel indicates that even the leaders know (at least for the moment) that the miracles of Jesus were authentic. This is what gives bite to the accusation of blindness (John 12:40). Caiaphas, then, apparently differs from Nicodemus in not attributing Jesus' miracles to God's power. Nicodemus has earlier declared that Jesus' miracles showed that he was a teacher from God (John 3:2). Jesus, however, did not regard Nicodemus as one who believes in him, for he is told by Jesus "you do not receive our testimony" (John 3:11). If Nicodemus does not yet believe in Jesus, then Caiaphas, who arranges for Jesus' death, certainly does not believe in Jesus. Merely seeing Jesus' miracles, or hearing reliable reports of them, and believing they occurred, does not necessarily evoke faith in Jesus.

What did people have to believe about Jesus' signs, for the signs to be a ground of faith in Jesus? We might first consider those beliefs that are expressed about the signs by characters in John's Gospel who are sympathetic to Jesus. Nicodemus says, "you have come from God as a teacher, for no one can do the miracles you do unless God is with him" (John 3:2). Some of the people say, "He is a good man" (John 7:12). Again, "Many of the people believed on him and said, 'When the Christ comes, will he do more miracles than these which this man has done?'" (John 7:31). Some Pharisees say, "How can a man that is a sinner do such miracles?" (John 9:16). The man healed of blindness says, "Now we know that God does not hear sinners; but if any man be a worshiper of God, and does his will, he hears him. Since the world began it was not heard that any man opened the eyes of one that was born blind. If this man were not from God, he could do nothing" (John 9:31–33). Others say, "These are not the words of him that has a demon. Can a demon open the eyes of the blind?" (John 10:21). While these are not necessarily the views of people who already believe in Jesus, they are the views of those who are sympathetic to Jesus, of whom some will come to believe. This is their line of reasoning: The accounts of Jesus' miracles can be credited. Such miracles are beyond human power to perform. It is true that false prophets can perform miracles that would lead the people to other gods (Deut 13:1). However Jesus is a good man rather than a sinner, a teacher who follows God, rather than a deceiver (John 7:12). The beneficence of his miracles shows the favor of God. Consequently, Jesus must be performing the miracles by God's power and with God's approval. The miracles are just as great as we might expect of the Messiah. All of this shows that God has approved Jesus and sent him as a teacher. We should therefore give heed to him and his teaching.

It might be replied that the Evangelist is not endorsing this line of reasoning, but merely describing the (confused) response of the people. However it should be observed that the Evangelist is also providing models for belief. Characters who come to believe in

Jesus are first sympathetic to Jesus for various reasons. John would also be aware of typical reasons for sympathy through his own experience as an Evangelist. While he might include examples of people believing for poor reasons, he has an incentive to distinguish these so as to encourage his readers to believe on better grounds. One would naturally expect that sympathizers to Jesus would hold reasons for sympathizing that would often be shared by the Evangelist. These sympathetic views are often set forth in contrast to the views of Jesus' opponents, and it seems unlikely that the Evangelist would repeatedly portray Jesus' opponents as holding the more reasonable view.

It is also implausible that characters who come to believe in Jesus would be generally portrayed as believing on grounds that the Evangelist considers unwarranted. Yet their apparent reasons for belief seem the same as for people who were sympathetic to Jesus, as listed above. Nathanael knows only of Jesus' prophetic powers and a claim that he is the messiah. The woman of Samaria has a similar knowledge. The royal official initially knows only Jesus' reputation for miracles, and that he was sent from God. The man born blind knows little more. It seems, then, that these beliefs about miracles are regarded as sufficient to evoke a genuine belief in Jesus. It might be thought that some belief about Jesus' divinity must be evoked by miracles. For example, when Jesus makes water into wine, John says that Jesus' "glory appeared" (John 2:11), language reminiscent of the phrase "the glory of the Lord appeared" (Exod 16:10; cf. John 1:14). However since the divine glory is always revealed in miracles, it is not obvious how the divine glory was made evident in this miracle, differently than in miracles performed by others (e.g., by Moses, Elijah, Elisha, or Peter). So even if Jesus' glory does appear in his miracles, it does not appear that belief in Jesus required an explicit belief that Jesus' divinity was shown in the miracles. Jesus' divine claims seem to be of more importance for shaping this aspect of his disciples' belief. The beliefs relating to miracles, which were held by those sympathetic to Jesus, seem to be regarded by John as adequate grounds to believe in Jesus.

CHAPTER CONCLUSIONS

This chapter asked whether belief based on miracles is promoted by the Evangelist's teaching. It has been alleged that the Evangelist denigrates faith based on historical reports, especially reports of miracles. A close examination of the texts normally used to support such a claim shows otherwise. The Evangelist instead criticizes both the fickleness of human nature, and the refusal to accept any miracle reports not seen personally. For the Evangelist, some miracle reports are so well documented that it is unreasonable not to accept them. Belief in Jesus can legitimately arise in response to such reports, at least among those who accepted Jewish monotheism. The Evangelist's epistemology clearly allows for knowledge and belief based on historical reports, even for some reports of miracles.

7

The Evangelist's Concept of Historical Knowledge

A Comparison with Modern Historiography

WE HAVE NOW COMPLETED our argument that miracle reports are not only offered by the Evangelist as objective historical evidence justifying belief that the miracles occurred, but also that they are offered as evidence to elicit a saving belief in Jesus as the Christ sent by God. While the Evangelist recognizes the limited persuasive effectiveness of miracles, he often regards this as a limitation due to willful human blindness, not as a doubt justified by the evidence. Signs are not always seen firsthand, but are often known only from people's reports. They nevertheless constitute for the Evangelist the divinely appointed evidence which people have no excuse to reject.

In view of the uncertainties characteristic of historical knowledge, how can the Evangelist consider any kind of historical evidence to be such an important basis for religious belief? In this chapter we will describe the historiographical method of the Evangelist and compare it with modern perspectives. This will help us in two ways. First, this comparison clarifies the exact character of the Evangelist's claims to historical knowledge, and relates his view to modern concepts that have shaped our thought. Second, the miracle claims made by any religious tradition can be partly evaluated by considering the plausibility and coherency of the religion's historical methods. There is no reason to assume in advance that each community will support their claims by an equally plausible historiography. We can examine the coherency of the Evangelist's perspective in light of modern insights.

HISTORICAL METHOD: CONFLICTING VIEWS AND THE EVANGELIST'S VIEW

Miracle reports that uniquely support a particular religious tradition will generally be doubted by members of alternative religious traditions. The validity of the reports of Jesus' miracles has been denied since the time of the Evangelist. It appears that no historiographical method for determining the validity of the Evangelist's reports would be fully accepted by both the Evangelist and his opponents. The basis for any methodology can always be questioned. We should not expect, therefore, that any historiographical method for determining the historicity of miracles would necessarily be accepted across all communities.

Nevertheless, it is sometimes thought that historical agreement among those with differing religious and philosophical beliefs is the best criterion for what is historical. In his history of Jesus, John P. Meier says that he writes a history that "a Christian, a Jew, and an Atheist" could all agree on.[1] This is certainly a legitimate and valuable kind of historical endeavor. By first identifying the commonly held historical ground, miracle claims that are specific to particular religious traditions can be more easily discussed and evaluated. The risk of Meier's approach is that what is known by agreement might be confused for all that can be known. Alvin Plantinga likens Meier's approach to the views of the early twentieth century scientist Pierre Duhem. Plantinga challenges Duhem's claim that metaphysical and religious assumptions should always be restricted to those held by all accepted parties, arguing that any reasons for such assumptions "are extraordinarily well hidden."[2] For example, claims brought to a court are not dismissed simply because there is not agreement between the parties. The Evangelist does not regard his claims about Jesus' miracles to be deniable simply because many doubted those claims.

In a similar way, the Evangelist does not accept criteria of historical proof that would negate his claim of the essentially historical character of Jesus' miracles. Graham Twelftree argues along similar lines about acceptance of the burden of historical proof as a criterion for deciding the limits of historical certainty. Acceptance of this criterion, says Twelftree, "does not mean that if I cannot prove historicity in any particular case, the story—or elements of it—must be discarded as necessarily historically unreliable. It must be stressed: We cannot move from '*un*proven' to '*dis*proven.'"[3] We may similarly ask whether *unproven* means *not known*, for people can know things even when they are uncertain about their knowledge. For example, people may recall factual information correctly, without being sure that their recollection is correct. The decision about what is reasonable to demand as a criterion of proof is an essential issue. For example, the Evangelist does not accept (or even address) the reasonability of dismissing his miracle reports on a priori grounds. To his mind this would be a refusal to consider the historical evidence he offers, and so decides prejudicially against his credibility.

In the evaluation of miracle reports, non-theistic methods often seem to take a privileged place above all theistic approaches. This is a situation that is antipathetic to the Evangelist. The Naturalistic claim that accepting reports of miracles violates proper historiography has, as an unsupported claim, no decisive force for monotheists. Monotheistic historiography, which in principle allows for the possibility of revelation or miracles, cannot be decisively discredited simply because it violates agnostic historiographical principles. Instead, reports of miracles must be discredited on grounds which themselves are also held by monotheists. For example, if monotheists themselves can find no meth-

---

1. Meier, *Marginal Jew*, 1:1.
2. Plantinga, *Warranted Christian Belief*, 403, 415.
3. Twelftree, *Jesus the Miracle Worker*, 250.

The Evangelist's Concept of Historical Knowledge: A Comparison

odological grounds to support the miracle claims of one monotheistic tradition over the claims of alternative monotheistic traditions, then they must explain why no such grounds exist, and why their particular claims are still to be considered credible.

Modern doubts about the possibility of giving credible reports of miracles are alien to the Evangelist's thought. A widely held principle for resolving contradictory miracle claims is the theory that historical evidence, being inherently uncertain, can never provide adequate evidence for us to know that historical reports (especially reports of miracles in John's Gospel) are a reliable basis for knowledge and religious belief. As mentioned in the earlier discussion on miracles, there are influential philosophical views (notably those argued by David Hume) that maintain that historical knowledge is insufficiently reliable to validate reports of miracles. This philosophical situation was largely established in the early nineteenth century.

A related view, which we will argue is antipathetic to the Evangelist, is that one cannot expect others who stand outside one's faith to believe that the miracles occurred. Some who believe that particular miracles have occurred nevertheless hold this view. As John Hick relates, the current view of many theologians is that "miracles belong to the internal life of a community of faith; they are not the means by which it can seek to evangelize the world outside."[4] Reports about miracles often have been used by religions to attract converts. Hick's point is that, in the opinion of many, such reports cannot be confirmed by those outside the community. This opinion may stem from a view that only those with faith can "see" the historical reality of a miracle, as suggested by Kierkegaard:

> . . . a miracle does not exist for immediate apprehension, but only for faith, if it be true that whoever does not believe does not see the miracle . . .[5]

Alternatively, as Strauss suggested, the opinion may stem from the view that the miracles have not in fact happened but can be declared "true" only in some merely non-historical sense, which has only religious value for the community of faith that holds to the miracle.

SKEPTICISM AND HISTORICAL KNOWLEDGE: KIERKEGAARD'S RESPONSE

The modern denial of our capacity to have historical knowledge, because this denial is so influential, deserves a more detailed description of its driving concerns and arguments. As representatives of modern doubts about the possibility of historical knowledge, we will here describe the seminal views of three early nineteenth century religious thinkers: Søren Kierkegaard, Gotthold Lessing, and David F. Strauss.

Rather than arguing narrowly against a skeptical view of reports about miracles, Søren Kierkegaard argued that the entire Socratic conception of the human capacity for knowledge is flawed. Kierkegaard, a Danish philosopher, published his *Philosophical Fragments*[6] in 1844, nine years after David F. Strauss published his *Life of Jesus Critically*

---

4. Hick, *Philosophy of Religion*, 38.
5. Kierkegaard, *Philosophical Fragments*, 116.
6. Kierkegaard, *Philosophical Fragments*.

Examined, (eight years after publications of its principal parts in Danish). Living in the same period as Strauss, Kierkegaard wrote against the current ideas that so influenced Strauss, particularly the ideas of Lessing, who had published the *Fragments*[7] from Reimarus's work.[8] Kierkegaard argues that people are dependent on God as a source of knowledge. He argues that the root of Lessing's error is his adoption of the Socratic view that all knowledge is directly accessible to each individual, without any continuing dependence upon another person as the source of knowledge.

In the Socratic view, the learner is not fundamentally dependent upon any other person teaching or giving them knowledge. In Plato's *Meno*, Socrates theorizes that when people learn, they do not actually learn what they don't know, but simply recollect what their souls have already learned in past lives and have forgotten.[9] This theory is offered to explain how people could recognize truth when they found it, unless they already knew it.[10] Socrates demonstrates this by a controlled experiment, wherein he teaches a young slave boy a truth of geometry: that the area of a square is half of the area of a second square whose sides are the length of the diagonal of the first square. The young boy learns simply by answering a long series of questions from Socrates. Socrates' point is that the boy recognizes all of the correct inferences himself, because "without anyone having taught him, and only through questions put to him, he will understand (ἐπιστήσεται), recovering the knowledge (ἐπιστήμην), out of himself."[11] People can be trained to do things in any number of ways, depending solely on the particular impression that the external trainer wishes to make. They can also remember reports or statements they have heard, and use them to compose histories or to testify in courtrooms. However in Socrates' portrayal, the learning of knowledge must come from within, for a person must also recognize the knowledge as actually true, rather than merely repeat a formula without understanding, or accepting a report. Kierkegaard says that in the Socratic idea of recollection "the Truth is not introduced into the individual from without, but was within him."[12]

The idea that the capacity for knowledge lies solely within each individual has important implications for any philosophy of history, since the acceptance of perceptions and reports forms the basis for legal, historical, and scientific analysis. Without a presumption that reports are credible and reliable, law and history and science cannot even begin to use their techniques of critical analysis; reasoning must have data before it can evaluate data. It might be questioned whether Socrates really held to his theory as consistently as Kierkegaard indicates. But in any case, a consistent application of that theory underpinned ideas about the inherent unreliability of history, as held by Lessing and others in the era of Kierkegaard. This is part of the reason that the late eighteenth

---

7. Reimarus, *Fragments*.
8. Thulstrup, cited in Søren Kierkegaard, *Philosophical Fragments*, lv.
9. Plato, *Meno* 86b.
10. Ibid., 80d–e.
11. Ibid., 85d (Lamb).
12. Kierkegaard, *Philosophical Fragments*, 11.

century philosopher Immanuel Kant said, "it is superstition to hold that historical belief is a duty and essential to salvation."[13]

In lieu of the Socratic idea that learning is internal recollection, Kierkegaard proposes that human knowledge is limited, that not all knowledge is directly accessible, and that some knowledge remains dependent upon outside sources.[14] Beyond the limits of human knowledge lies the Unknown, which human reason cannot comprehend, because it knows nothing at all about the Unknown. Human reason mistakenly attempts to understand the Unknown in terms of the known "so that Reason no longer knows itself and quite consistently confuses itself with the unlikeness" of the Unknown.[15] In particular, Kierkegaard argues that there are limits to the knowledge which human reason can reach, and that even the existence of God is beyond demonstration by such reason.[16] Knowledge of God, when declared to human reason, cannot even be understood by human reason, for it is absolutely different from all that human reason knows, and so cannot be understood in terms that human reason can understand; indeed even the knowledge of this absolute unlikeness of God is not accessible to human reason, because it cannot conceive of an unlikeness which is different from all that it knows.[17] Kierkegaard warns that human reason too easily claims (erroneously) knowledge of things it can never know. He says that ". . . the Reason, in attempting to determine the Unknown as the unlike, at last goes astray, and confounds the unlike with the like. . . ."[18] Here Kierkegaard's terminology is difficult, for one might think that, by definition, *Reason* cannot err. For Kierkegaard, *Reason* refers to common human reason as it is actually used by human inference, which is subject to error in its conception of the entities about which it argues.

By denouncing the claim of human reason to give knowledge of God, Kierkegaard does not mean that the knowledge of God can have no basis. Kierkegaard says that another kind of vision is granted by faith: "God gave to the disciple the condition that enables him to see Him, opening for him the eyes of Faith."[19] Kierkegaard refers to faith as the necessary "condition" for such knowledge of God.[20] Only the disciple is enabled to see, and the object of faith is God, rather than the teaching God gives. However the possibility of vision remains only while the disciple continues to have faith. Under the Socratic method, it was assumed that every learner could recollect the truth, and so could "thrust the teacher aside" upon having perceived the truth directly. In contrast, "Faith must steadily hold fast to the Teacher."[21] In particular, Kierkegaard argues for the possibility of learning by faith about the historical entry of God into the world, primarily in the Incarnation, but also in miracles and other historical acts of God. Kierkegaard openly

13 Kant, *Conflict of the Faculties*, 76–77, cited in Green, "Kierkegaard's Philosophical Fragments," 11.
14. Kierkegaard, *Philosophical Fragments*, 16–17.
15. Ibid., 56.
16. Ibid., 49–56.
17. Ibid., 57–58.
18. Ibid., 56–57.
19. Ibid., 80.
20. Ibid., 73.
21. Ibid., 77.

acknowledges his debt to historic Christian theological ideas, yet he is innovative in framing his argument within the terms and narrative structure of Platonic philosophy.

In agreement with Lessing and Strauss, Kierkegaard argues that belief in this incarnate God cannot be secured by an exhaustive historical account, not even one by an ideal historian with ideal sources who was contemporary with the incarnate God.[22] For Kierkegaard, the entry of God into history cannot be proven by the means available to the modern historian, because these means are limited to what can be known by finite and fallacious human reason. Beyond what is accessible to human Reason is the Unknown or the Paradox, which can only be seen by Faith.[23] Kierkegaard's argument for the limits of human reason is, on his own theory, incapable of demonstrating its truth by argument, or at least by argument apart from faith. This is perhaps why he presents his view as a mere proposition. Kierkegaard portrays his book as being authored by a certain Johannes Climacus, and as being published by Kierkegaard. Consequently, the argument of the book may in some respects not represent Kierkegaard's own views.

Kierkegaard's claim that faith is a kind of vision, influences his understanding of historiography. The knowledge of God's acts in history cannot be passed on by standard historical methods, because not all have the faith to see the truth. Writing about the relationship of the contemporary witness to the successive generations that rely on that witness for their knowledge of the incarnation, Kierkegaard writes:

> *What then can a contemporary do for a successor?* (a) He can inform him that he has himself believed this fact ... (b) In this form he can relate the content of the fact. But this content exists only for Faith, in the same sense that colors exist only for sight and sounds for hearing.[24]

For Kierkegaard, those who do not believe can indeed see all that history can reveal to human Reason, but since God's revelation of Himself in history is always devoid of his Eternal character (history being limited to the temporal and changing), merely historical knowledge about God's presence in history cannot by itself give anyone genuine faith or knowledge that the Eternal God is present.

C. Stephen Evans, commenting on the theory that faith in the observer is a necessary condition for knowing, observes that "not everything in the world is as easy to perceive as a color patch, and it is a commonplace of theories of perception today that accurate perception requires the perceiver to have certain subjective qualities."[25]

Kierkegaard's ideas have much wider import than a mere discussion of whether historical knowledge about miracles is possible. Here it suffices to note that, in Kierkegaard's view, the denial of the miraculous is an error of reasoning. According to Kierkegaard, this error arises from confusing limited human experience, and our correspondingly limited imagination, with the extent of reality.

---

22. Ibid., 115.
23. Ibid., 48, 49, 73.
24. Ibid., 128.
25. Evans, "Historical Religious Knowledge," 153.

The Evangelist's Concept of Historical Knowledge: A Comparison

In 1840–41 Strauss published his *Die Christliche Glaubenslehre*.[26] In this work, Niels Thulstrup tells us, Strauss borrowed from Lessing, having in one important passage "used the pertinent passage from *Uber den Beweis des Geistes und der Kraft* almost word for word."[27] In that passage Strauss writes:

> Even suppose that the Biblical narrative were established on the level of historical evidence, on the same level as the most indubitable historical facts . . . , even then those who know the nature of the historical world would not be able to avoid seeing that the so-called certainty in this sphere is only a high degree of probability, never absolute certainty, and consequently remains in a permanent misrelationship to religious faith, which requires unconditional certainty on the basis of which it can live and die. . . . If, however, I have no historical objections to Christ's resurrection from the dead, must I therefore (dogmatically) hold to be true that precisely this resurrected Christ has been the Son of God?[28]

Strauss thought that the inference from Jesus' resurrection to his being the Son of God was a confusion of historical knowledge, which was always uncertain, with metaphysical knowledge, which must be certain. Commenting on Lessing's version of the same passage, Merold Westphal observed that Kierkegaard would oppose the idea that "human reason contains an a priori knowledge of God that is so ultimate and definitive that nothing God could possibly do in history could affect it." This would be "locking God out of a world preinterpreted in our own image."[29]

JOHN'S IDEAS ABOUT HISTORICAL KNOWLEDGE AND MODERN IDEAS

There are both similarities and differences between the ideas of Kierkegaard (or his assumed persona of Johannes Climacus) and the ideas of John the Evangelist. First, Kierkegaard incorporates into his thought the idea of human blindness to truth. Kierkegaard proposes that people do not all have a natural capacity to grasp the truth.[30] He concludes that without this capacity, the truth will seem foolish, and people who know the truth will also be seen as foolish. Kierkegaard here follows the Johannine and Pauline themes that those who know the truth will be considered blind, mad, foolish, and ignorant. These themes are in turn drawn from the Old Testament. The rationalist movement claimed in response to the biblical assertions of truth that its own ideas were the genuinely enlightened ones. Strauss, for example, attributed the opposition against his own ideas to blindness arising from religious "piety" or superstition. Any claim to have the truth necessarily has rhetorical overtones, and has as a corollary the blindness or unreasonableness or mistake of one's opponents. Kierkegaard's basic categories of thought are largely reminiscent of the categories in John's Gospel: God, sin, error, faith, sight, the moment of gain-

---

26. Thulstrup, in Kierkegaard, *Philosophical Fragments,* 150.
27. Ibid., 151.
28. Strauss, cited in Kierkegaard, *Philosophical Fragments,* 150, 151.
29. Westphal, "Johannes and Johannes," 23.
30. Kierkegaard, *Philosophical Fragments,* 16–20.

ing faith, and the new birth.[31] Kierkegaard, however does not clearly distinguish truth from The Truth, and so his view is not sufficiently developed to explain how people can learn even simple nonreligious information, such as the geometrical truths mentioned by Plato. Furthermore, Kierkegaard's conception of Reason is drawn from his own time, rather than being a category of thought shared by the Evangelist. It is doubtful that the Evangelist would separate the concept of reason from his idea of faith, in the way they were separated by Kierkegaard.

The Evangelist emphasizes more strongly than Kierkegaard that Jesus' opponents willfully turn away from truth that has been made known to them. Although Jesus' opponents are blind (John 12:40), they also have some limited perception. For example, they hate Jesus because they have seen him. Jesus says, "If I had not done among them the works which no one else did, they would not have sin, but now they have both seen and hated me and my Father as well" (John 15:24). If their blindness is so absolute that they cannot see at all, could they have "seen and hated" Jesus? In the Evangelist's mind, it is because they genuinely hear Jesus and genuinely hate him in consequence that they are shown to be of ill will toward the truth. Jesus himself says to his opponents, "If you were blind, you would have no sin" (John 9:41a). An absolute blindness would at least partially excuse the behavior of Jesus' opponents. However it is not at all obvious that an absolutely total blindness to this revelation would be ascribed by John to Jesus' opponents, as Kierkegaard seems to do. When John says that "light has come into the world" he declares that men, in response, "loved darkness rather than light," and this he explains, not by their blindness, but because "their deeds were evil" (John 3:19). To think of blindness here would violate the point of declaring that light has come into the world. Furthermore, it is this deliberate turning away from the light which he characterizes as mankind's "condemnation," and he elaborates further that they do not come to the light because they do not wish their evil deeds to be reproved (John 3:20). Jesus himself says that his opponents "know me and know where I am from" (John 7:28), even though he denies that they know him in a fuller sense (John 8:19). In a limited way, they do know him. Kierkegaard agrees with the Evangelist that people turn away from the truth and are unwilling to reform. Yet the Evangelist more strongly emphasizes that this willful turning away from truth is actually shown in particular by their turning away from the revelation of truth that is given to them in Jesus, and by Jesus' miraculous signs.

A similarity to the Evangelist's thought is found in Kierkegaard's view that "belief is not a form of knowledge, but a free act, an expression of will."[32] This differs from the primarily cognitive sense of belief that is used in the widely accepted philosophical definition of knowledge as "justified, true, belief." But is it possible to show by lexical usage that the word *believe* (*pisteuō*) always holds in John this merely cognitive sense? It seems not. The phrase *pisteuōn eis auton* (John 3:18) must be understood not merely as "believing in him," but also as "trusting in him," since the object of belief is not an idea or a statement, but a person. But is simply believing that a person is worthy of trust identical to trusting in that person? The latter seems to include, in the referenced text, a decision

---

31. Ibid., 16–23.
32. Ibid., 103.

or personal commitment. All who "believe in him" are given eternal life, and this belief always corresponds with the rejection of evil (John 3:16–21). This personal commitment explains why Kierkegaard considers belief to be a kind of passion or sense and "the opposite of doubt" rather than a "form of knowledge."[33] John enlarges the idea of belief in this text so that "belief in him" also requires the rejection of evil.

One way in which John differs from both Kierkegaard and Strauss, is that John does not advocate the principle that historical reports are inherently unreliable. In this respect Kierkegaard is closer to John than is Strauss, for Kierkegaard at least argues approvingly that, according to the Greek philosophers, "immediate sensation and immediate cognition cannot deceive." Kierkegaard warns also that "the Hegelian doctrine of a universal doubt" itself calls into question "whether they have doubted anything at all."[34] Nevertheless, Kierkegaard differs from John by viewing historical reports as incapable of warranting committed belief, a view for which Joseph Houston criticizes him.[35] Houston observes that there are many situations in which even life will be risked on the basis of information that is uncertain and even unlikely to be correct; clearly the person risking their life considers the information to be credible in some sense. While there has never been a general consensus among all people that John's signs are essentially factual, there need be no disagreement that John and most of his readers understood John to be making that claim, and that he expected his claim to form one basis for his audience to believe.

The credibility of reports has received recent support from C. A. J. Coady. Coady has argued that testimony should not be viewed as more suspect than other modes of knowledge. He concludes,

> In treating testimony as epistemically more problematic than individual perception, memory, or inference, these attempts rest inevitably upon the sense of an individual's orientation to reality through others as somehow tacked on to his more fundamental orientation via his private intellectual powers. This implies that testimony is sufficiently separable from them to be capable of presentation for independent judicial arraignment. There is much to question in this picture.[36]

Coady notes that modern English Courts accept even uncorroborated testimony as evidence, and that English, Scottish, and some Continental courts often accept hearsay testimony as admissible evidence.[37]

Strauss objected to miracles not only on the philosophical grounds that they would be impossible to adequately document, but also on the historical grounds that reports of miracles are known in some cases to be false or fictitious reports. While the Evangelist would not agree with the first criticism, he recognizes the need for a hearing of the evidence. Indeed, his work is offered as the evidence that he knew his readers would need to hear. Strauss himself did not evaluate the evidence for these reports, for he did not

---

33. Ibid., 105.
34. Ibid., 102.
35. Houston, *Reported Miracles*, 102.
36. Coady, *Testimony, a Philosophical Study*, 133.
37. Ibid., 39.

think that any historical evidence was adequate to substantiate such reports. Schweitzer acknowledged, and said that Strauss himself acknowledged, that Strauss' own work ignored the genuine historical elements in the gospel, and that these were not explained until Ferdinand C. Baur addressed the problem. However false reports of miracles cannot show that all reports of miracles are false, as Strauss seemed to assume. The specific historical evidence must be heard before determining whether any one, or any group, of John's reported miracles are worthy of belief.

C. K. Barrett discounted the historical weight of Biblical sources by a different criterion. Barrett claimed that secondhand information is inherently unreliable:

> There is, of course, only one sort of authority of real worth in the realm of history: sound, accurate, first-hand information. Ideally it will come from the historian's own observation and recollection, though even here he may find that he cannot entirely trust his own memory. And even eye-witnesses are not necessarily to be credited.[38] [Barrett then quotes Thucydides *Hist.* 1.22, as an illustration of the historian's problems].

Barrett denies the "real worth" of any information that is not both "first-hand" and "accurate." Since he quotes Thucydides, it may be that under the term "first-hand information" he includes reports that are gathered by an investigating historian from other witnesses. Since the gospels are widely regarded as secondhand sources based on traditions rather than on known witnesses, Barrett's view might seem to deny the "real worth" of the information in the gospels. However the denial of all value to secondary sources would be indefensible, since historians often have only secondary sources to work with, and still write histories. Barrett himself makes use of secondary sources, though with restraint. He presumably means, by his use of the expression "real worth," that the value of firsthand sources is usually much greater than secondhand sources, since firsthand sources usually include considerably more detail and fewer errors can be attributed to those details. Following this remark, he lists several genuine causes of historical error. However Barrett's comment leaves room for the false impression that historical information is always doubtful merely because there is in principle a possibility of error. The theoretical possibility of error does not itself justify doubt; instead, evidence that error is likely must be shown. To use examples from Barrett's own citation, every historian regularly trusts his own memory in many respects, and eyewitnesses are also generally credited; this trust can be reasonably abandoned only to the degree that evidence is brought forward to justify doubt. The Evangelist, like Kierkegaard, would acknowledge that human certainty is fallible, since people have no direct ability to detect or remove their blindness. In the Evangelist's thought this provides no justification for a universal doubt, especially since people are to believe, rather than doubt, that Jesus is the Christ.

As illustrated in these examples from Kierkegaard, Strauss, Schweitzer, and Barrett, there are several modern objections to the possibility of historical knowledge, which differ from the Evangelist's ideas. These modern objections are based on questionable general principles for evaluating historical evidence, rather than on the evidence itself.

---

38. Barrett, *Essays on John*, 118.

The Evangelist's Concept of Historical Knowledge: A Comparison

The use of these principles is not always accompanied by a justification of their use. They are not principles that would have been accepted by the Evangelist, nor would he regard evaluation of his evidence by those principles as reasonable.

CHAPTER CONCLUSIONS

In previous chapters we have drawn several conclusions. John's idea of knowledge is related to his ideas of history, fiction and belief. Miracles form an important test case for understanding the Evangelist's views about history, fiction, and the relation of knowledge to belief. Although the possibility of miracles has been widely discounted in the modern era, this should not cause us to assume that the Evangelist, who wrote in a different time, intended his report of miracles to be understood as fictional. Moreover, the foundation for modern skepticism about miracles rests in still disputed philosophical ideas. Strong support for the possibility of miracles remains among philosophers who are monotheists, so that it would be prejudicial to simply assume that everyone should discredit the reported miracles. While some scholars have suggested that John does not intend the miraculous elements in his Gospel to be understood as historical events, this violates John's own use of the miracles as an incentive and basis for belief. A reading of the miracles as fiction also assumes that early readings of the Gospel uniformly misunderstood the fiction as nonfiction. The rising field of oral history also indicates the likelihood that the Evangelist had a genuine historical interest in Jesus' miracles and deeds, whether or not the miracles really occurred. The Evangelist actually offers Jesus' miracles as a ground for belief. Against modern readings that the Evangelist counts faith arising from miracles as inauthentic, a closer reading shows that the Evangelist criticizes instead human obstinacy in the face of credible evidence, such as the demand to personally see a miracle instead of accepting credible reports of miracles. While the miracle accounts will not likely be credited except by those within the Christian community, it should be clear to all that the Evangelist sets forth an account of miracles as essentially historical events, and as events which provide an important reason to justify belief.

This chapter has compared the Evangelist's concept of the human capacity for historical knowledge with modern conceptions. Modern conceptions express much greater doubt about the possibility of having historical knowledge. While the actual historicity of Jesus' miracles will always be disputed, the mere absence of consensus does not by itself show that they did not occur. Such a proof instead demands evaluation of the historical evidence. An unwitting adoption of historiographical methods that are hostile to the mere possibility of miracles will prejudice evaluation of the historical evidence for particular miracles. Our discussions of Kierkegaard and Coady have shown that such methods, which take an overly skeptical view of historical knowledge in comparison with other kinds of human reasoning, are philosophically questionable. The Evangelist's own principles for the evaluation of historical evidence differ from many of these modern principles. He would consider their skepticism a denial of reasonable evidence, and while this view is antipathetic to modern skepticism, it also finds some support among modern scholars. The Evangelist's use of miracles reveals a number of important characteristics of the way that the Evangelist understands fiction, historical fact, knowledge of historical reports, and belief based upon such knowledge.

Although this discussion has argued against depreciating historical evidence on the basis of these modern principles, this merely makes the historical intention of John's Gospel conceivable. We have not examined the evidence supporting the historical intention of particular miracles. If it can be shown that the Evangelist knew that early Christian readers would understand any of his miracle accounts as historically incredible, this would be evidence that particular miracles were to be understood as merely symbolic or fictional. There is no way to know whether the historical evidence has internal contradictions, or contradicts external evidence, without looking at the specific historical problems of the Gospel. Although there is good reason to believe that the Evangelist's claims about signs were not essentially intended as fiction, the degree to which the Gospel should be understood as nonfiction cannot be determined apart from a closer examination of the evidence about specific miracles. This discussion has set forth, however, the essentially historical manner in which the Evangelist believed his miracle claims should be evaluated. In the next chapter we will discuss evidence for the Evangelist's nonfictional intention with regard to particular miracle accounts. From this nonfictional core of historical claims by the Evangelist, we will basis our description of his epistemology, an epistemology rooted in his view of history.

8

The Extent of Nonfictional Intention in John's Miracle Accounts

GIVEN OUR EARLIER CONCLUSION that John intends his reports of Jesus' miracles to be understood as *essentially* nonfiction (i.e., real miracles occurred), it will be helpful to first determine more carefully just how far this essential character extends. Is each miracle in John's Gospel intended to be understood as nonfiction? To understand John's idea of how we know about God, historical claims about God's acts and works must be distinguished from fiction, and from fictional embellishment. Otherwise, if God has ever made himself known by acting or speaking or appearing in some way at any time, John's claims to such knowledge might not be understood as genuine claims. It is of particular concern to our current discussion that John's historical claim for miracles be distinguished where possible from any intentionally fictional elements in his narrative. The importance of this distinction is best understood by comparing the typical views about John's Gospel in the scholarly literature. The views to be examined include a sampling of those expressed most cogently, or cited in recent literature reviews, such as those by Robert Kysar[1] or Gerard Sloyan.[2] Here we shall look particularly at authors who have also expressed opinions on the use of signs to evoke belief, because those views will be discussed in a subsequent chapter. This literature review also allows us to discuss our earlier conclusion within the context of a broader range of current opinion.

THE RANGE OF VIEWS ABOUT MIRACLES AS NONFICTION

Scholars of the Fourth Gospel hold a variety of differing judgments about the intentionally fictional character of its miracles, ranging from total fiction, to total nonfiction. By way of reminder, it is noted again that fiction and nonfiction do not refer here to whether the miracles actually happened, but only to whether the author intended his readers to believe they happened. At one end of the spectrum of opinion, some scholars think it possible that the miracles in John are intended as entirely fiction, a notion that has been extensively argued against above. Other scholars say that some miracles are wholly fic-

---

1. Kysar, *The Fourth Evangelist*. Also, Kysar, "The Fourth Gospel," 2389–2480.
2. Sloyan, *What are they Saying?*

tional, but that other miracles are drawn from traditions regarded by John as authentic. A third set of scholars says that all the miracles are presented as nonfiction, but that they have been edited with substantial fictional embellishments. A fourth viewpoint allows no significant role to intended fiction, explaining the origin of the miracle narratives as deriving from accepted miracle traditions and other sources (the author's recollections and interpretive judgments, and any identifiable errors in historical transmission).

ALL MIRACLES AS FICTIONAL? MCCASLAND, STIBBE, AND HINDLEY

Among scholars who suggest that all the miracles may be wholly fictional, are McCasland,[3] Stibbe,[4] and perhaps Hindley.[5] McCasland, in a paper discussing the idiom *signs and wonders* (σημεῖα καὶ τέρατα), held that John's Gospel advocated the use of miracles as proof warranting faith, although he thought it at least possible that the miracles are intended in John's Gospel as fiction. He argued that, in comparison with the Hellenistic world and the Old Testament, the New Testament downplays the importance of the miraculous. In support, he says the New Testament uses the phrase *signs and wonders* to refer "almost entirely to ordinary deeds of healing performed by faith," even to the extent that he thinks the meaning of the phrase is changed in the New Testament.[6] For McCasland, the use of miracles as a basis for faith was a popular practice which Jesus and other "sophisticated persons" scorned.[7] In McCasland's view, this popular interest in miracles increasingly infected the gospel traditions, reaching its peak influence in John's Gospel, where the structure and declaration of purpose indicate that "Jesus is preoccupied with giving signs from heaven, and the purpose of this Gospel is to record them." This understanding of the development of the gospel traditions, and of John's Gospel particularly, contrasts with Bultmann's view that John was minimizing the importance of miracles which he found in a *signs source*. However McCasland is ultimately undecided about the intent of the miraculous in John's Gospel, for he still thought it at least possible that the *signs and wonders* in the Gospel of John were "purely symbolical" rather than miraculous. By "purely" he apparently means that the *signs and wonders* may have been fictional, rather than intended to be understood as historical miracles.

McCasland's arguments have several deficiencies. Although the phrase *signs and wonders* (σημεῖα καὶ τέρατα) often refers in the New Testament to healings, reference is not so uniform as to show that the phrase itself takes the limited meaning of "healings." This is evident even from McCasland's own reference to the "signs and wonders" of false prophets (Mark 13:22; 2 Thess 2:9). Also, the traditional meaning had not fallen out of usage in society at large, so that readers cannot have been addressed as though they would automatically understand this term to indicate a new Christian meaning. Josephus (*Wars*, 6.288–309) refers to eight non-healing miracles, as "signs,"

---

3. McCasland, "Signs and Wonders," 149–52.
4. Stibbe, "Tomb with a View," 38–54.
5. Hindley, "Witness in the Fourth Gospel," 319–37.
6. McCasland, "Signs and Wonders," 151.
7. Ibid., 151–52.

as McCasland admits.[8] McCasland seems to be motivated by an interest to rescue the historical tradition from fabulous additions, but this suggests that he sees the text as nonfiction which has been corrupted by false or fictional (miraculous) elements. His conclusion that the New Testament tradition downplays the role of the supernatural is unwarranted, a point more recent scholarship has emphasized.[9] The miraculous even has an arguably greater role in the New Testament than in the Old Testament. There are a great number of New Testament miracles that are not healings. It is also doubtful that the miraculous character of the healings is really of no interest to either the Jesus of the Gospels, or the Evangelists. And it could at least be questioned whether belief in miracles was really less common among the sophisticated, since McCasland offers no supporting evidence of this. McCasland treats the miracles as fabulous, and possibly fictional, additions. Though he argues that the New Testament redefines *signs* (σημεῖα) to mean *faith healings* instead of *signs*, his supporting linguistic argument is deficient.

Another scholar who suggests that the miracles are all fictional is Mark Stibbe. In Stibbe's discussion of the raising of Lazarus, his narrative-critical approach intentionally ignores the historical aspects of the text, and focuses separately upon its literary effects. Stibbe is interested in how the reader of the story interacts with the story as a story. His reader of the Gospel treats the text as the work of one author whose own voice is always present, even if the author uses sources. Modern source critics, insofar as they read as source critics, are excluded as readers. Stibbe also ignores the common reader's need to decide which parts of the story of Lazarus' resurrection are fictional, which is unfortunate in view of his focus on the reader's experience. Stibbe is only concerned that in the miracles the reader should see "a sign of glory" and "a greater reality."

Apart from the historical claim that Jesus raised Lazarus, and that Jesus had the capacity and desire to raise someone from death, what is the "glory" that is shown, and what is the "greater reality" that is evident in the miracle? Suppose that the "authority and power of the Father and the Son over the great human enemy, death" was not a historical claim for the raising of Lazarus.[10] How would the readers perceive that this "authority over death" would ever have any factual presence in the readers' own lives, or the lives of those they love? Indeed, how would the readers know what "authority over death" even meant? The readers must be intended to learn from the story about a reality that actually affects their own life histories, as Stibbe would seem to agree. Certainly it is plausible that a hope for physical resurrection from death persuaded many readers to hold the Christian faith, just as this hope persuaded many to hold the faith in later generations.

Stibbe suggests that the "true death" is *spiritual death*, and that it is essentially (perhaps solely) this that the Evangelist has in view. For Stibbe, it is only this spiritual death which God promises to overcome in the reader's own life.[11] This reading presents serious difficulties. Even if we were to read the death of Lazarus as *spiritual death*, the

---

8. Ibid., 151.

9. See Meier, *Marginal Jew*, 2:11, 554, 618; See also especially, Smith, *Jesus the Magician*; Aune, "Magic in Early Christianity."

10. Stibbe, "Tomb with a View," 49.

11. Ibid., 51.

raising to *spiritual life* is not based on a historical claim about Lazarus returning to God. Indeed, the narrative itself says that Lazarus is an example of the person who "believes in me, [who] though he dies, yet shall he live" (John 11:25). This means that the reader would have no historical precedent from the story for hoping that *spiritual death* can be overcome in the reader's own historical life. The reader would expect someone coming to spiritual life to become the focus of the story, if *spiritual life* were the sole interest of the story. This, however, is not the case even for the only other characters on whom the author focuses, Mary and Martha. They are already portrayed as disciples of Jesus, even if Martha's faith matures through the experience of seeing her brother Lazarus raised up from death. Many of those who observe the miracle also believe, however they are mentioned in only a single verse. There is no assurance given that they will all remain faithful to Jesus, just as at the first Passover (John 2:23–24) the Evangelist gives no assurance that all who believed after seeing miracles would continue in faith. The central place in the dramatic narration is taken by the resurrection of Lazarus, rather than the coming to faith of these observers. For these reasons the reader must be intended to see Jesus' offer of life as a promise of physical life. This reading is consistent also with the Evangelist's interest in physical resurrection, indicated in the later narrative about Thomas's demand to touch the risen Jesus. Indeed, the miraculous character of Lazarus' resurrection is a link to the larger plot of the Gospel, which could not be the case for a *spiritual raising* of Lazarus. The raising of Lazarus is tied to a new resolve to execute Jesus (John 11:46–53; cf. John 5:18; 11:8). Since the Evangelist presents Jesus' miracles as evidence justifying belief in Jesus, the force of that evidence is undermined if the miracle did not occur. It is more plausible that the Evangelist regards the resurrection of Lazarus as an essentially historical miracle, however mistaken one may think him to be. Stibbe's reluctance to recognize this nonfictional claim of the Evangelist is disappointing, for his understanding of the intended reader's experience is thereby vitiated.

J. C. Hindley, in his article, "Witness in the Fourth Gospel," considers the significance of the Gospel's miracles to be essentially independent of whether or not they are fiction. He does not explicitly say whether John intended his readers to accept the miracles as nonfiction. Perhaps alluding to Dodd's work *Historical Tradition in the Fourth Gospel*, Hindley does say that the addressed readers of the Gospel had "a great deal of knowledge about Jesus from other sources."[12] This probably implies that, in Hindley's view, they had some independent idea of Jesus' resurrection and of traditions about other miracles. Two miracles in the Fourth Gospel, the feeding of the 5,000 and the resurrection of Jesus, are also found in the Synoptic tradition. While Hindley is aware of a "more positive view" of the Fourth Gospel's historical value arising from "recent study," he does not rely upon this for the purposes of his own discussion.[13] It seems that Hindley is concerned to separate the divine testimony from all historical claims, due to the problems of certainty inherent in historical method, as noted by Kierkegaard. Hindley seems to consider the historical element of no primary importance to the Evangelist's message. This suggests that a

---

12. Hindley, "Witness in the Fourth Gospel," 324.
13. Ibid.

fictional view of the miracles does not undermine their essential importance, and so is basically acceptable to Hindley as grounds for belief.

The articles of McCasland, Stibbe, and Hindley treat the miracles in John's Gospel as wholly fictional in intent, or at least possibly so. However this viewpoint of the Evangelist's intent is notable for the absence of supporting argument by these authors, and the restraint with which they promote this view. Stibbe and Hindley seem to adopt this position, not because of any real evidence that the miracles are intended as fiction, but because they feel the historical character of the miracles are in doubt, and are in any case not of essential importance. The possibility that the Evangelist intends all the miracles to be considered fiction has already been argued against in more detail in a previous chapter, and found unconvincing.

SOME MIRACLES ARE WHOLLY FICTIONAL: MEIER'S VIEW

A scholar who suggests that John only intended some of the miracles to be understood as historical events is John P. Meier.[14] Meier, in a major and detailed study of Jesus' miracles, reviews the historical evidence that the reports of miracles in the four Gospels reflect a belief in Jesus' miracles widely held during Jesus' own lifetime. In support of this claim, Meier notes that the Gospel miracles are attested in multiple sources, are attested in multiple literary forms, and are coherent with Jesus' words and deeds. He also argues that the miracles could not have been merely read back into the texts by drawing from Jewish or pagan or ecclesiastical traditions.[15] Meier asks of nonbelievers that, as historians, they acknowledge that some of the healings of Jesus are unexplained. He sees belief in Jesus' miracles by Jesus' contemporaries as one explanation of Jesus' influence. Meier concludes, "For the crowds that followed Jesus, his supposed miracles were no doubt the most striking and attractive element of his ministry."[16]

Meier does not consider every miracle narrative, or every part of every miracle narrative, to be an authentic early tradition. He thinks we have enough evidence to know that the reports of some miracles were current in Jesus' own time, but enough evidence to know that the report of other miracles was a later creation. Even for those traditions of miracles that he deems to be early, he thinks that many portions of the tradition are not early, or at least cannot be known to be early.

This perspective of Meier is best illustrated in his opinions about particular miracles. When addressing the historicity of particular miracles, Meier separates the miracles into distinct types: exorcisms, healings, raising the dead, and "nature miracles." He thinks the miracle of changing the water into wine is "for the most part, if not entirely, the creation of the Evangelist."[17] On the other hand, he believes the story of the healing of the Centurion's servant (Matt 8) to have arisen from a contemporary oral account of the healing. Meier thinks the historical evidence favors the existence of such an account,

14. Meier, *Marginal Jew*.
15. Ibid., 2:622.
16. Ibid., 2:1043.
17. Ibid., 2:947.

though he allows that this may not be the case.[18] The healing of the man born blind (John 9), Meier thinks, is "more likely than not" an authentic early tradition.[19] He does not think it can be known historically whether the man was blind from birth. That is because he thinks this element could be explained equally well as having arisen from "the tendency of John's Gospel to heighten the miraculous element" or from a theological interest in providing a symbol of human blindness in general.[20] Other details, such as the calling of the blind man's parents to prove the man was blind, he considers to be simply unknown, and beyond the range of the historian. Meier accepts the resurrection of Lazarus (John 11) as reflecting "some incident in the life of the historical Jesus."[21] He thinks it likely that Jesus' disciples considered this to be a resurrection even in Jesus' own lifetime. However, with most scholars, he thinks it was not a proximate cause of Jesus' arrest in the early tradition, and that the chronological placement is not historical.

ANALYSIS OF MEIER'S VIEW OF FICTION

Meier thinks that John may have entirely created at least one miracle narrative: the turning of water into wine. Consequently, in Meier's view, John himself would regard some of his own Gospel's miracles as essentially fictional, even though he regards others as essentially historical. This view presents difficulties.

The ideology of the Evangelist is inconsistent with any fictional reading that would undermine his claims about the reality of Jesus' miracles. The Evangelist says he includes miraculous signs to persuade and encourage his readers to "believe that Jesus is the Christ" (John 20:31). Surely he believes himself that eternal life is only found in Jesus. The use of signs was a persuasive technique that was of proven influence and was widely accepted in the first century church. Consequently, the presumption should be that the Evangelist believed that some of the miracles he knew of were, essentially, both nonfictional and historical. By including miracles known in the Synoptic tradition, the Evangelist shows his acceptance of the miraculous element in that tradition. There are no compelling reasons to think that the two miracles in John's Gospel that are clearly paralleled in the Synoptic Gospels (the feeding of the 5,000 and the physical resurrection of Jesus) are understood by him as essentially fictional. Since each of the four Evangelists include collections of signs which differ largely by chance, it is probable that other miracles in the Fourth Gospel (not only those we can check by reference to the Synoptic Gospels) are also drawn from traditions which John regarded as essentially historical and nonfictional. He regarded this signs tradition so highly as to include and emphasize the importance of Jesus' signs. He portrays the signs as an important and even divine evidence of Jesus' identity, Jesus himself calling the undecided to "believe the (miraculous) works" (John 10:38). It is not rhetorically plausible then, that the Evangelist was unconcerned with the physical and historical reality of at least some of his signs.

18. Ibid., 2:726.
19. Ibid., 2:694.
20. Ibid., 2:698.
21. Ibid., 2: 831.

The Extent of Nonfictional Intention in John's Miracle Accounts

John gives no indication within the text of his Gospel that only some miracles are nonfictional. Clues that some miracles are fictional would have to be provided either within the text, or by the common knowledge of those to whom the Gospel was addressed. John could not count on a reader who, like Origen, had compared the chronology of the Gospel of John with that of the Synoptic Gospels, as a key to which parts were fictional.[22] That many would read John as historical is clear enough from Origen's defensive posture in setting forth his own views. The gnostic views of the early commentator Heracleon, cited by Origen, allegorize rather wildly, and provide no credible alternative way to understand the Evangelist's concern with miracles.

Furthermore, there is no evidence of the readers having independent external knowledge that would tell them which miracles are fiction. The Synoptic Gospels, even when read closely, do not clearly show that any miracles in John are essentially fictional. The clues to fiction must lie therefore in other common knowledge that might be expected of most readers. Unless the Gospel was originally addressed to readers who already had a far more extensive knowledge of Jesus' life than we have in the Synoptic tradition, there is no evident way that the extent of fiction in John's Gospel could be determined. There is no indication that the readers addressed by John's Gospel had this kind of familiarity with Jesus' life.

Under Meier's view, then, due to the absence of any markers of fiction, the reader would likely confuse fictional and nonfictional miracles. John's Gospel would in this way be undermined as an independent historical source for the miracle tradition. This would be a considerable rhetorical concession on the part of the Evangelist, for the early Christian rhetoric about miracles was evidently persuasive, and claims about miracles were potent only insofar as it was claimed that Jesus really performed them. Such a concession would undermine the Evangelist's persuasive purpose, for he presents miracles as grounds for belief that Jesus is the Christ. This makes the addition of fictional miracles implausible. This is not to argue that the miracle narratives are entirely and fully nonfictional, nor is it to argue that the miracles which are essentially nonfictional actually occurred. It is only to argue that the Evangelist himself presented all the miracles included in his Gospel as essentially nonfictional.

The Evangelist would not be free to undercut the historical aspects of his claims for some miracles, simply to add fictional miracles, even if these fictional miracles were similar to miracles believed to be authentic. Since he is not writing at a time when all these traditions have been lost, it is more to be expected that John is repeating only miracles that are accepted as historical within the tradition, than that he invents miracles that are merely similar to authentic miracles. If he were mixing fiction and nonfiction, he would naturally and easily have given clues to guide the reader, so as to preserve the special rhetorical force of his nonfictional claim about Jesus' resurrection and other miracles. Since the claims about Jesus' miracles could be a key reason for some readers to believe in Jesus, confusion on this issue could also expose John to the charge of being deceptive or

---

22. Origen, *Gospel of John*, 10.2–10.6.

THE EPISTEMOLOGICAL BASIS FOR BELIEF ACCORDING TO JOHN'S GOSPEL

unreliable. It is implausible that such a talented and experienced controversialist would have overlooked this weakness.

It is hard to explain the prominence of miracles in the Fourth Gospel if the Evangelist did not really believe that Jesus performed miracles, or did not believe that the particular miracles he includes in the Gospel were authentic. He portrays Jesus as calling on doubting people to believe the signs, even if they would not trust Jesus' own word. The signs are portrayed as a testimony by God that Jesus should be recognized, divinely sanctioned evidence offered especially for the skeptical. The Evangelist says that he included signs so that his readers might believe that Jesus is the Christ (John 20:31). Thomas is reproved for not believing in the physical character of a miracle attested to by a community that deserved his confidence (John 20:27). The Evangelist believes in Jesus' physical resurrection, or he would not have included in his Gospel a narrative criticizing Thomas for doubting the testimony of his fellow disciples about seeing the risen Jesus. Jewish leaders are reproved for ignoring the significance of Jesus' healing of a blind man (John 9:41). A royal official is expected to believe that Jesus will perform a miracle, on the basis of Jesus' reputation and Jesus' promise to him (John 4). The beloved disciple's belief, upon seeing the evidence of the burial clothing in the empty tomb, is implicitly approved (John 20:8). Only if the Evangelist does believe these miracles occurred, essentially as he portrays them, is this prominence of miracles quite natural.

There is one other reason to think that the Evangelist himself believed all these miracles were essentially historical. If he presented fictional miracles to others, he would certainly be aware that his own sources might be equally misleading. Consequently, he would be careful to determine whether the miracles in his own tradition were fictional. The Evangelist's own teaching and emphasis is that miracles provided a compelling evidence for belief in Jesus (John 12:37–43), a position that he would hardly have promoted if he thought Jesus performed no miracles. Given that he believed in miracles and considered them important, he would be naturally interested in using those that he found personally convincing and compelling.

Meier's argument is more cogent when amended to disallow the possibility that this miracle was "entirely" the creation of the Evangelist. Instead, Meier's idea that it was "for the most part" a creation of the Evangelist, if understood as being essentially nonfictional, allows for the Evangelist's consistency of purpose in advocating that the miracles provided reason to believe in Jesus. This concession does not seem to require a major change in Meier's overall approach. The common stylistic characteristics of John's Gospel can more plausibly be explained by his own reformulation of the existing signs tradition, than by his invention of parts of that tradition.

MIRACLES AS EMBELLISHED NONFICTION: FORTNA, PAINTER, & LABAHN

Many scholars have held that all the miracles are essentially presented as nonfiction, but that the miracle narratives have been substantially edited so as to knowingly introduce many fictional elements. This group probably includes Robert Fortna,[23] Edwin Freed

---

23. Fortna, "Source and Redaction," 151–66.

with Russell Hunt,[24] D. M. Smith,[25] John Painter,[26] and Michael Labahn.[27] Their views tend to rely upon source theories of the gospel, typically built around some kind of sign source (as proposed earlier by Rudolf Bultmann) containing reports of miracles. They distinguish the sign source from the Evangelist's own editing or use of other sources.

Fortna thought that the canonical Gospel of John is based on an earlier source, a source Fortna calls the Signs Gospel.[28] He thought this Signs Gospel contained "the seven original signs" and a passion narrative.[29] Fortna attributed to John the reformulation of this Signs Gospel into its canonical form, and seems generally to have accepted the canonical form as reflecting John's own views and interests, rather than the views and interests of earlier traditions. Since we are investigating here John's nonfictional intention, we need only concern ourselves with Fortna's evaluation of John's Gospel, and not his evaluation of the earlier Signs Gospel. Fortna said, "the fourth evangelist's interest in the true nature of faith, and its relation to Jesus' miraculous deeds, is plain enough from the gospel as it stands. . . ."[30] Fortna thought that John was trying to explain the theological problem, "Why do some, indeed most, fail to believe in the face of the signs?"[31] This indicates that, in Fortna's judgment, John and his readers accepted the miracles as being *essentially* nonfiction, and found disbelief in the face of such miracles unnatural.

Freed and Hunt argued on stylistic grounds that the Fourth Gospel has two parts. One part, which is basically Fortna's Signs Source, has few stylistic variations. The other part, which they called Johannine Material (JM),[32] has a relatively large number of stylistic variations. Typical characteristics which they attributed to the later JM include: different verbs for "saying" are used, the subject of the verb is not always given, the object of the verb is not always given, Jesus' divine office is conceived of under different titles, synonyms and synonymous expressions are used, and rare words are used at a third to half the rate as in the Signs Source material.[33] Freed and Hunt admitted that some Signs Source sections may have been edited so extensively that Johannine stylistic variation has been incorporated into them indistinguishably from the Evangelist's own (JM) material.

Freed and Hunt's thought that the Signs Source's distinctive style demonstrates, not merely a different narrative voice, but a different authorship. They considered John's Gospel to be an embroidering of this source material with John's own unique (JM) stories. They perceived examples of such embroidery in the narratives about the Samaritan woman, the healing of the man born blind, and the raising of Lazarus. This raises a ques-

---

24. Freed and Hunt, "Fortna's Signs-Source," 563.
25. Smith, "Setting and Shape," 231–41.
26. Painter, "John 9 and Interpretation," 31–61.
27. Labahn, "Tradition and Literary Art," 178–203.
28. Fortna, "Source and Redaction," 156.
29. Ibid., 151–52.
30. Ibid., 151.
31. Ibid., 159.
32. Freed and Hunt, "Fortna's Signs-Source," 564–66.
33. Ibid., 568, 572.

tion. Did they believe that the Johannine material in these same miracle stories should be understood as independent tradition and nonfictional interpretation, or as dramatic and illustrative portrayal that are fictional? Freed and Hunt may have regarded the Johannine Material as merely fictional. Their judgment that John's theology has contradictions might support a fictional reading of Jesus' theology and of Jesus' words in the Fourth Gospel. However they seem to have regarded the Signs Source as a nonfiction work that the Evangelist adopted out of respect for its historical testimony.

Freed and Hunt allowed for a considerable degree of fiction in the miracle narratives. For example, they thought Fortna might be correct to say that the "miracle of the fishes" in John 21 was "transformed from a simple miracle story" (included in Luke 5:1–11) and to say that John composed the bulk of that chapter.[34] They did not clearly say whether John reworked the miracle with embellishments he regards as fictional, or whether he adopted it as historical. However it seems that on their reading a fiction must have been intended by either John or the earlier Signs Source, in order for the miracle story to have been transformed from an account like that given in Luke 5:4 into the account given in John 21. This does not mean, however, that they thought the miracle itself, common to both accounts, was ever intended by John to be understood as fictional.[35]

Dwight Moody Smith, in a discussion of John's sources, also based his view about the Evangelist's historical intention upon his view of a Signs Source. Smith regarded the existence of this *semeia* source as widely accepted, even by those who don't agree with Bultmann's judgment that the source was adopted by John to correct its signs theology.[36] Smith noted that scholars now strongly support the view that John's miracle tradition is independent of the Synoptic tradition. Smith regarded as unattainable a full consensus that the Signs Source was a written source. However he saw a widespread acknowledgment among scholars of the strong case favoring the existence of "a single (or major) collection of miracle stories."[37] In support, Smith claimed that redaction-critical study of John has often found "simpler miracle stories" which often were "the basis for the development of distinctly Johannine discourses and dialogues."[38] Smith seems to mean by this that there is dramatic development by John that is fictional, even if it is based on historical miracles. Smith allowed that the underlying source might be part of a genre of "miracle stories for propagandistic purposes."[39] This indicates that the signs source claimed to be nonfiction.

Against Ernst Haenchen,[40] John Painter argued for the Evangelist's own composition of large portions of John 9, claiming that the Evangelist's own theological interests included "demonstrating the reality of the miracle."[41] Haenchen had attributed this chap-

34. Ibid., 568.
35. Ibid.
36. Smith, "Setting and Shape," 231.
37. Ibid., 232.
38. Ibid.
39. Ibid., 233.
40. Haenchen, *John: A Commentary*, 41.
41. Painter, "John 9 and Interpretation," 33.

ter almost entirely to a signs source. Painter, however, sees greater "literary development" in this demonstration of the evidence, in Jesus' initiative in performing the miracle, and in the emphasis on the miraculous nature of the healing. Painter notes that, "extreme care is taken to establish that the miracle actually happened (9:8ff., 18ff.)."[42]

Michael Labahn's interest in the Fourth Gospel's miracle stories rested in what he called "the creativity of the Fourth Evangelist in using his tradition."[43] Labahn saw "historical reminiscences" of the Evangelists' communities behind the healing of the paralytic (John 5) and the blind man (John 9), but considered them to have been interpreted by a theological principle of the Evangelist in a nonhistorical fashion. However Labahn did not identify any principle that can explain the details in the Evangelist's narrative.

Labahn has noted the cumulative force of the miracle claims. The Jewish leaders' problem is that Jesus "is performing many signs" (John 11:47). Here the Jewish leadership cites all the miracles in the Gospel, not merely the raising of Lazarus, as a cause for Jesus' popularity, and for the Jewish leaders' consequent decision to kill Jesus.[44] The compelling character of this great sign confirms the authenticity of Jesus' earlier signs. The cumulative evidence of the signs is more compelling for both the characters in the gospel, and for the reader, than the mere sum of the evidence. Conversely, the discrediting of particular miracles would have a cumulative effect of discouraging belief in Jesus.

Labahn thinks that the Evangelist often uses tradition in its received form, but that often "he changed it fundamentally."[45] He argues that the Evangelist accepts the basic miracle claim of his tradition, but narrates it according to his own theology. In particular, he says the Evangelist expresses a Christology of Christ as giver of life: "in so far as people are seeing the signs or are hearing the narrated stories of these signs and are understanding them as signs of the sent revealer, they receive the true life."[46] In other words, salvation comes to those who understand what the signs signify. This approach is similar to Hindley's in two ways. First, it makes an understanding of signs, that only believers have, the means of salvation, a view that was criticized in our discussion of Hindley. Second, it discounts the importance of the historical element in the Gospel's miracles, though Labahn clearly argues, unlike Hindley, that the miracles were historical even if they are now detached from their historical context. The weakness of Labahn's view is that it underestimates the rhetorical importance of retaining the historical form of the miracle traditions, and it provides no real explanation as to why the Evangelist should have to ignore the form of the received tradition in order to express his theology. One would expect that the Evangelist saw in the historical form of the tradition God's expression of this same theology, and so would have no need to have "changed it fundamentally." It is Labahn's view that "the narration of the signs repeats the *krisis* (the separation) into believers and unbelievers."[47]

42. Ibid., 43.
43. Labahn, "Tradition and Literary Art," 178.
44. Ibid., 180.
45. Ibid., 200.
46. Ibid.
47. Ibid.

FORTNA, PAINTER, & LABAHN: REASONS FOR THEIR POSITION

These scholars, from Fortna to Labahn, and Meier as well, believed that the Evangelist preserved part of a signs tradition. They apparently thought that John accepted the signs tradition as nonfiction, since he regards it highly enough to preserve parts of it, and he continues to use its signs as a reason to believe in Jesus. However, these scholars generally thought that John knowingly embroidered this tradition with substantial fictional inventions of his own. In some cases (e.g., John 21), the supposed fictional element nearly overshadows the supposed historical core. Is it justified to suppose such an extensive use of fiction? This depends upon their reasons for thinking that the Gospel incorporates fiction.

There are at least two reasons that these scholars consider John's additions to the signs tradition to be fictions, rather than independent tradition. One arises from the scholars' assessment of the differences between John's Gospel and the Synoptic Gospels. They regard many of these differences as greater than could have arisen from the use of authentic traditions, even allowing for natural confusion in the retelling of the traditions. An example of this would be John's location of a temple cleansing near the beginning of Jesus' ministry, while the Synoptic Gospels place it at the end. Most scholars identify these as one event. There is no agreement on how these two chronologies are to be resolved. Schnackenburg summarizes the situation, "A number of Catholic scholars, and some few Protestants, prefer the Johannine dating, and this appears logical, in so far as most exegetes today would prefer to follow John on the question of the date of Christ's death (14 or 15 Nissan)."[48]

As another example, in John's Gospel the resurrection of Lazarus provides an impetus for the Jewish authorities' decision to plan Jesus' death (John 11:53). It also was an impetus for Jesus' public support by the Passover pilgrims, which made possible his triumphal entry into Jerusalem (John 12:17–18). Death threats had already been made against Jesus before this decision to execute Jesus (John 5:18, 8:59; 10:31; 11:8), and the decision was only effected because of Judas' betrayal of Jesus' whereabouts (John 18:2). Still, it is surprising to many that Lazarus's resurrection is not mentioned in the Synoptic Gospels. The differences in vocabulary, Christology, and events also make the historical accuracy of the Gospel suspect in the eyes of many. Where there are large differences between John's Gospel and the Synoptic Gospels, these scholars consider John's to be generally less reliable.

A second reason they think John includes fiction arises from the internal structure of John's Gospel. They think it has features that cannot be explained as authentic traditions, not even confused traditions, but only as fiction and interpretation. For example, it has long discourses by Jesus that might seem beyond the capacity of human memory to have retained. Distinctively Johannine language and ideas are attributed to both Jesus and John the Baptist, or to Jesus and the narrator, as well as being found in the letter of 1 John. There are other distinctively Johannine elements interwoven throughout John's entire gospel, which are inexplicable if not arising from one author. These distinctive

---

48. Schnackenburg, *Gospel According to John*, 1:354.

elements include not only a pervasive uniformity of vocabulary and syntax, but also of concepts, Christology, and several themes.

Most scholars attribute such uniformity not only to John's own selection, but also to his reformulation of and additions to the traditions he received. Admittedly, some scholars deny the existence of a single written signs source.[49] Labahn, for example, follows the suggestion that there was a second (smaller) source including only two miracles: changing water into wine, and healing from a distance.[50] However the problem of explaining the pervasiveness of distinctive Johannine elements is not eliminated by the abandonment of Fortna's Signs Gospel. Fortna himself sees no need for the hypothesis of a Signs Gospel except as a way "to account for the synoptic-like matter in the Fourth Gospel" upon the assumption that the Fourth Gospel did not depend upon the Synoptic Gospels.[51] But if there was no Signs Gospel, then Fortna thinks John used the Synoptic Gospels themselves as the signs source. In addition to John's distinctive speech and thought, many scholars attribute the level of detail in the miracle and discourse narratives to fiction, or fictional elaboration, rather than to transmission of (even confused) authentic memories.

Another reason for thinking that John includes much fiction is that, apart from actually crediting miracles, the miracle narratives in John can only be explained by a limited number of other factors. On the (widely accepted) presumption that John's Gospel was not written by a direct witness, natural transmission errors in the retelling of the tradition would include: errors arising from limited or faulty memory, the addition of elements due to interpretation or plausible historical reconstruction, the addition of fictional dramatic elements not meant to be taken as historical elements, and the confusion of such added elements for genuinely historical claims.

Can such processes plausibly explain why details to prove the reality of the miracles were included? In the narrative about the man born blind, even the blind man's parents testify that he was blind from birth. In the raising of Lazarus, even Jesus' opponents testify to their own leaders that the miracle occurred. For those who do not actually credit the miracles, fiction may be the only plausible explanation remaining. Such fiction, at best, would be a sort of historical novel (with fictional proofs for dramatic effect) that was misunderstood in oral transmission as a historical report. The inclusion of apparent proofs in a historical novel suggests that real audiences often did question the evidence for the miracles, just as the religious leaders do in John 9. The explanation of some narrative features as fiction does alleviate difficulties for those who do not credit the possibility of miracles. It does not show, however, the likelihood that an Evangelist, who argued that miracles were a legitimate ground for belief, would also invent fictional polemic to emphasize the impossibility of natural explanations for the miracle.

---

49. See Van Belle, *Signs Source*.
50. Labahn, "Between Tradition and Literary Art," 192.
51. Fortna, review of Van Belle.

THE EPISTEMOLOGICAL BASIS FOR BELIEF ACCORDING TO JOHN'S GOSPEL

A RESPONSE: EVIDENCE FOR MORE LIMITED FICTION

Freed and Hunt, following Fortna, said that the story of the miraculous catch of fish in John 21 was the Evangelist's composition, a reworking of the miracle account in Luke 5:1-11. Without arguing for the historicity of John's miracle narratives, an argument will be made that their nonfictional character is considerably more extensive than has been generally indicated by such treatments of the Gospel. More specifically, it will be argued that the evangelistic and polemical character of John's Gospel is adequately recognized only when all the reasons and inducements that John offers for believing in Jesus are treated as essentially nonfiction. This means that the signs and fundamental promises of Jesus are essentially nonfiction, as will be argued below. These nonfictional reasons to believe include the signs of Jesus (with their essential parts and together with the proofs advanced that they are true miracles), Jesus' claim of divine authority, Jesus' promise of everlasting life, and the arguments Jesus gives to his opponents and inquirers within the Gospel. The following discussion, however, will be limited to the nonfictional character of the signs of Jesus.

As argued earlier in the chapter on belief, John thinks that believing in Jesus is a vital necessity for his readers, a condition of eternal life (John 3:16; 20:31). This concern to plant belief in Jesus is a driving motive throughout his Gospel, and is an expression of the continuing apostolic mission of Jesus' disciples. Just as Jesus spoke in order to call and preserve a community of disciples, so John as a Christian evangelist writes to call and preserve a community of disciples of Jesus. John is an experienced evangelist, and knows the rhetorical power of miracle claims, as is indicated by his Gospel's later historic influence.

As has already been argued, in John's view the passing on of his signs tradition is one of the principal ways to evoke and confirm belief in Jesus, and each of the signs is presented as nonfiction. By his concern to strengthen the Christian community, he is driven as an evangelist to make use of that signs tradition. Consequently, John's remarkable emphasis on miracles as one proper basis for belief in Jesus, in the context of general acceptance of miracles by early Christians, shows that John himself accepts the miracles of Jesus generally. Given this general acceptance, his use of two miracles accepted in the Synoptic Tradition must show that he accepted those specific miracles as well. Given that he sets forth all his miracles alike as nonfiction, John himself must accept each of the miracles he narrates as essentially historical. He narrates them as nonfiction because he wants his readers to believe that the miracles are essentially historical, as he himself believes. It is a mistake to think that a talented first century Christian Evangelist would not pass on the reasons for belief that he had personally found so compelling. This is not to argue that the miracles are historical, but only that the Evangelist thought they were. If the Evangelist was primarily dependent upon a single oral or written source for his miracle accounts, this source must itself have narrated the miracles as nonfiction, in order to have engendered such a belief in the mind of the Evangelist.

A general presumption should be that any beliefs which the Evangelist takes pains to inculcate in his readers as essential for a life-giving faith are beliefs which he already holds himself. This goes far to explaining his interest in spreading those beliefs and in representing them as essential for eternal life. Another way of saying this is simply to say that the Evangelist was a Christian, and held to the distinctive Christian beliefs. Where the Evangelist tells of any sign or act or saying or teaching which he regards as capable of engendering belief in Jesus, it is to be presumed that he thinks the sign, act, saying, or teaching was essentially historical, even if he is mistaken to think so. For the same reason he cannot risk having his general credibility put in doubt. On the other hand, the Evangelist is not comparably concerned that his readers accept any of his statements that are not essential to belief in Jesus. In this category, for example, many chronological details and the exact wording and vocabulary of Jesus might often be placed. They are essential to his message only to the extent that his message rests upon them being credited. Where they are not essential, the Evangelist may still expect them to be credited, but that will depend on his other purposes in writing, and so falls beyond this discussion. Here the point is that it is not the exact wording as such, but a wording which expresses the authentic message of Jesus, and also a message which can evoke authentic belief in Jesus, which is the Evangelist's driving concern.

It is quite probable that the facts that convince characters in the Gospel to believe in Jesus are essentially presented as nonfiction. If the Evangelist presented real characters who believed on the basis of fictional events, he would provoke his readers to review his other historical claims more skeptically. If the reader knew, for instance, that the tomb of Jesus was not empty, or that the apostles had never reported seeing Jesus, they would read the Gospel much differently. On the other hand, the faith of those Gospel characters who believe after receiving the divine benefit of a miracle evokes hope in the reader: God may indeed have given such gifts through the historical Jesus. The reader is brought to a decision of belief by experiencing the perspective of the characters that the Evangelist has recorded. This requires the reader to accept the facts that it is essential for the character to accept, if the reader is to be brought to faith in like manner. For similar reasons it is unlikely that any characters can be regarded as fictional, since any promises or miracles granted to fictional characters would similarly be fictional.

The Evangelist's concern for historical miracles is also consistent with the concern for testimony by witnesses in John's Gospel. Samuel Byrskog has argued recently that "ancient historians exercised autopsy directly and/or indirectly, by being present themselves and/or by seeking out and interrogating other eyewitnesses."[52] One of the uses of such testimony was "to confirm information received from various oral testimonies, from hearsay."[53] Byrskog has noted the presence of such claims in the Gospel of John, "The editor(s) adding 21:24–25 took refuge in a person who, they believed, had been an eyewitness to the ministry of Jesus."[54] Whether or not the editor was justified in this belief, it is evident that the historical character of the Gospel was important in the very

---

52. Byrskog, *Story as History*, 64.
53. Ibid., 56.
54. Ibid., 238.

circles responsible for publishing the Gospel. It would be remarkable for all interest in authentic historical tradition to have ceased. Indeed it is implausible.

There is no compelling reason to conclude that the Evangelist could not have accepted his miracle accounts as historical, as traditions to be guarded, simply because he was expressing his own Christological understanding of the miracles and of Jesus. A crucial problem in Johannine studies has been to distinguish what is basic tradition, and what is authorial elaboration. Byrskog has noted that in ancient rhetoric, "the basic material—the *fundamenta*—should be true, while its elaboration—its *exaedificatio*—should be plausible."[55] The Evangelist was certainly capable of expressing tradition within his own idiom and interpretive stance. As Byrskog has noted, even ancient historians would record oral histories from the perspective of a later time, giving their writings "a fundamental diachronic dimension."[56] The Evangelist's driving concern was not that every detail of his narrative be counted historical, but that his readers should believe in Jesus as the Christ. This made it essential that those elements of his narrative which were included to invoke belief in Jesus, and which would lose their rhetorical power to do so if found historically questionable, should be set forth as historically credible. Elaboration must lie outside these essential claims.

GENRE, AND THE LIMITS OF NONFICTION

Studies in Greco-Roman historiography and biography have shown that legend, historical supposition, and artistic elaboration were often incorporated in the absence of more reliable information. These practices have in recent years been brought to bear upon the Gospels generally, and upon the Gospel of John in particular. They raise the problem of the misrepresentation of fiction as fact, and the problem of determining the historical intention in ancient historiography and biography.

The problems raised by unreliable historical accounts were already recognized in antiquity. Thucydides, in a famous critique of historical method, said of his own writing, "It is better evidence than that of the poets, who exaggerate the importance of their themes, or of the prose chroniclers, who are less interested in telling the truth than in catching the attention of their public, whose authorities cannot be checked, and whose subject-matter, owing to the passage of time, is mostly lost in the unreliable streams of mythology."[57] Polybius criticized the historian Timaeus for careless interrogation of witnesses.[58] Plutarch accused Herodotus of "fictions and fabrications."[59] Rhetoric was the tool of orators, and as Byrskog notes, "*orator* is the Latin word for advocate. An advocate had a case to argue, a judge to persuade."[60] It was not unusual for orators to lie (if the lie was likely to succeed), and lying was promoted as part of oratory, as Byrskog adequately

---

55. Ibid., 213.
56. Ibid., 64.
57. Thucydides, *History*, 47.
58. Byrskog, *Story as History*, 61.
59. Cited in Byrskog, *Story as History*, 200–202.
60. Byrskog, *Story as History*, 205.

documents.[61] The case with biographers was no happier. Lincoln notes, "Ancient biographers operated on a continuum that stretched from history writing on one end through the encomium to the ancient novel or romance on the other."[62]

It is evident from the ancient criticism of historians that many historians violated ancient canons of authenticity. These criticisms did not arise because of the critic naively mistaking fiction for nonfiction. Neither did they arise because the critic wanted a degree of authentic historical representation that was excluded by the ancient genre of history. Particular historians were criticized in antiquity for the very reason that their accounts were actually misleading. This in turn shows that readers expected historians to abide by certain canons of authenticity and honesty, and that these historians neither abided by them, nor indicated to their readers when they were departing from those canons. Fiction was instead represented as being nonfiction. These particular historians were accordingly discredited.

In consequence, the credibility of each historian and biographer had to be evaluated on his or her own merits. An author was expected to communicate the level at which his historicity and accuracy should be evaluated. The author who significantly misled the reader would be correspondingly subject to criticism. Seneca went so far as to dismiss historians generally as being mere storytellers. Byrskog characterizes this as part of Seneca's reaction against "the increasing influence of rhetoric on the historians" in the first century.[63] Against such skeptical evaluations as Seneca's (which perhaps exhibits a bit of rhetoric itself), it must be maintained that some ancient historians and biographers had a genuine interest in communicating some core of historical reality. It must be maintained also that we can identify some part of the historical core. There is no serious scholarly acceptance of the supposition that historians and biographers such as Thucydides, Josephus, Suetonius, Plutarch, and Polybius were inventing the core of their narratives. There is no acceptance of the supposition that we cannot identify some portion of this core as historical. One must instead differentiate the reliable historian from the misleading one, and the reliable account from the unreliable. This must be accomplished by analysis of the author's own work. The reader must similarly evaluate the extent of fiction in John's Gospel on the Gospel's own merits, taking into account the particular character of the Gospel.

Consequently, it is not possible to discard the possibility that the Evangelist is making a historical claim about the miracles, simply because he writes in the genre of ancient historiography or biography. Lincoln has argued that John's Gospel cannot be considered a "witness by the canons even of ancient historiography," due to the mix of fact and fiction in ancient Greco-Roman biography.[64] However, as Lincoln acknowledges, a biographer like Plutarch could "work quite closely to the conventions of historiography."[65] Furthermore, he cites both Momigliano and Cox as acknowledging the presence of his-

61. Ibid., 203, 205–8.
62. Lincoln, *Truth on Trial*, 370.
63. Byrskog, *Story as History*, 203.
64. Lincoln, *Truth on Trial*, 370–71.
65. Ibid.

torical or real elements in ancient biography. The presence of history in ancient biography must be acknowledged, even though we cannot identify every element as either history or fiction. There is no justification to decide on the basis of genre alone that the miracle claims are not genuinely historical claims.

The different character of a Gospel from other contemporary ancient biography also suggests that genre alone cannot determine the question. This Gospel's ideas arise out of Jewish monotheism. John's understanding of God's work in history cannot be simply assumed to follow the perspective that would be found in contemporary pagan biography. The use of historically dependent polemic in John's Gospel demands a nonfictional understanding of those essential polemical claims. The religious and catechetical purpose of John's Gospel was to promote essential Christian religious ideas and to authentically represent Jesus so that the readers would believe in the authentic and essentially historical Jesus. While John is manifestly aware of aesthetics, his historical purpose differs from any strictly aesthetic value or intention to entertain such as may be found, for example, in the gossipy legends repeated by Herodotus. This difference of purpose is illustrated by the early regard for Gospel texts as authoritative scripture, which is found already in citations of the Synoptic Gospels in both *1 Clement*[66] and the letters of Ignatius.[67] Holmes says that *1 Clement* is generally dated to the end of the first century, and the Ignatian letters to the second or third decade of the second century.[68] These early citations distinguish the Gospels from other Greco-Roman biography, and suggest how seriously the miracle claims in John might be considered.

Although fiction was sometimes misrepresented as nonfiction, it would be a mistake to think that every departure from a strict historical account is misrepresentation. One must first determine the standard of expected historical accuracy. To the extent that any account was not expected to provide accurate historical representation, its imprecision would not be deceptive. There are several kinds of imprecision that should not be mistaken for misrepresentation. These are related to the limits of the literary medium, and to the purposes of the author as artist.

As one example of historical inaccuracy in ancient literature, there was no general expectation that conversations were to be regarded as complete transcripts, rather than as a matter of general recollection. An early narrative of Plato illustrates this:

> *Terpsion.* . . . but what was the conversation? Can you tell me?
>
> *Euclid.* No, indeed, not offhand; but I took notes of it as soon as I got home; these I filled up from memory, writing them out at leisure; and whenever I went to Athens, I asked Socrates about any point which I had forgotten, and on my return I made corrections; thus I have nearly the whole conversation written down.

---

66. E.g., *1 Clement* 13.2, 24.5, 46.8.
67. E.g., Ignatius, *To the Ephesians* 14.2.
68. Holmes, *Apostolic Fathers*, 23, 131.

Terpsion. I remember—you told me; and I have always been intending to ask you to show me the writing, but have put off doing so and now, why should we not read it through?[69]

It is evident that Euclid's reconstructed conversation is portrayed as including the main points of what was said, rather than as a complete transcript. Even his corrections are based on further conversations that he remembers, and then returns to write down. The limits of memory have shaped the record of the conversation. It is only a summary of what was said. At the same time, it is indeed based on, amplified by, and corrected by memory. Thucydides similarly remarks that the speeches in his *History of the Peloponnesian War* are historical reconstructions. He says, "I have found it difficult to remember the precise words used in the speeches which I listened to myself and my various informants have experienced the same difficulty; so my method has been, while keeping as closely as possible to the general sense of the words that were actually used, to make the speakers say what, in my opinion, was called for by each situation."[70] His ideal of reporting "the general sense" of real speeches would be an ancient ideal for historians to follow. This rephrasing of words is not a conscious invention, but an artifact of memory and comprehension. There is a trade off between the inauthentic impression that would be left by omitting a conversation, and the inauthentic impression that is left by the fact of the conversations being approximations. Which representation leaves the reader with the most authentic portrait? This depends upon the skill, judgment, and care of the historian or biographer.

Ancient readers would not expect a perfect rendition of what was said, or a perfect memory of events, but many would object to the invention of miraculous events (or invented evidence supporting its miraculous character) in the attempt to tell the story. In the telling of a miracle story, a reputable historian would limit his reconstructions to what seemed historically likely, or to what he clearly indicated was beyond his strict historical intention. This in turn means that a reputable historian would not invent essential details of the miracles if the historian really didn't believe that the miracles occurred. If John believed in the resurrection of Jesus, this is no justification under ancient canons to invent stories of Jesus' appearance to the disciples, or of the sight of the empty tomb that greeted the beloved disciple. Some essential details about the miracles in the Fourth Gospel would not seem "historically likely" to the Evangelist on the sole basis of knowing that a miracle occurred. These details are better regarded as part of the miracle tradition accepted by the Evangelist. We will not understand how the Evangelist can reconstruct what he regards as a probable scenario, if we do not first understand what he considers to be the known facts on which this probability is based.

As another expression of the expected historical inaccuracy in John's Gospel, we may consider the movement of time in the various narratives. It is evident from a reading of Jesus' dialogues and discourses that early readers would understand these as mere summaries. The dialogue of Jesus with the woman of Samaria, for example, can be read

---

69. Plato, *Theaetetus* 142d,143a (Jowett).
70. Thucydides, *History*, 48.

in two minutes, give or take half a minute. Jesus is ostensibly speaking to this woman because his disciples are off in town, yet they return at the end of his conversation with the woman. The brevity of dialogue would suggest that they are within two minutes walk, very likely within sight, when he begins his conversation with the woman. The assumption that the conversation is a complete transcript thus violates the implied setting of the story. Similar problems arise if one assumes that Jesus' discourses in the temple represent all that he says there. The reader is not intended to take the conversation as a full transcript of what was said, but merely as a select summary of what was said, perhaps as highlights of major confrontations between Jesus and the temple authorities. A similar indication of the schematic presentation of conversations is found in any comparison of parallel passages in the Synoptic Gospels. Neither the Four Evangelists nor early readers saw any significant contradiction among the parallel passages in the Synoptic Gospels simply due to the addition of dialogue in one Gospel, or in the change of vocabulary between Gospels. Neither did they find the addition of material in Luke and Matthew to be invalidated by Mark's shorter Gospel. Selection and interpretation have shaped the dialogues in all these Gospels, but the Evangelists do not consider their accounts to be fictions in consequence, nor do they expect to have their readers treat their accounts as fiction or as unworthy of belief. That would be a misunderstanding of the author's expressed intention.

Departures from strict historical accuracy will never be carried so far as to become misrepresentation, unless the author is dishonest or incompetent. The author shares the common command of language that enables him to communicate his meaning; the author knows how his words will be understood and the honest author does not violate that understanding. It is conceivable that some new readership might understand a literary work without a knowledge of the original conventions of that genre, and that the author would not have anticipated such a reading of his work. However John's Gospel is the work of an Evangelist experienced in Christian polemic. By the continued influence of his work, it is evident that he knew quite well how many readers would understand it.

The Evangelist expresses amazement (John 12:37–40) that the miracles of Jesus did not lead the Jewish leadership to believe in him. This is quite natural if the Evangelist believes the miracles are authentic. On the other hand, it is hard to be amazed that people don't believe your miracle stories, when you know they are illustrative, rather than factual. It is also hard to be amazed that people don't believe your miracle stories when the only factual miracles you know of are not even convincing to yourself. The person who invents stories is normally hesitant to put them in writing for public review, or to include detailed descriptions, or to back up false stories with false but detailed proofs that the stories are true. This would be particularly true in the context of legal controversies and government inquiries, which are of evident concern to the Evangelist and his audience.

P. Gardner-Smith expresses the view that allegories were the basis for some Christian traditions adopted by the Fourth Gospel, but there is no inherent plausibility that the Evangelist himself would have actually invented miraculous events to supplement allegories.[71] Miracle stories are meaningful and dramatic primarily because they are believed to be historical acts of God, which consequently reveal God's purposes. Their non-miraculous significance is only secondary, and could always be better set forth as a parable or homily than as an allegory of a miracle. To discount the miraculous element is anachronistic, for miracles are included as signs of the divine precisely because of their miraculous character. Evidence that a miracle was false would be precisely the evidence used to discredit a messianic claimant. Allegories have no purpose that would be inherently likely to spur the invention of fictional miracles. Even if they did, there is no reason that an allegory should be set forth so that it was confused for history. Even if that happened, there is no reason to add details that proved the miracle to have occurred.

Our conclusion at this point is that each of the miracles in the Fourth Gospel are presented as nonfiction, and are set forth by the Evangelist as essentially historical events, rather than as merely representative of similar miracles which Jesus had performed. This conclusion holds other implications about the extent of nonfiction in John's Gospel, both regarding the nonfictional character of Jesus' claims, and the nonfictional character of the proofs that he advances in support of the miracles' authenticity.

NONFICTIONAL MIRACLES AND NONFICTION IN JESUS' CLAIMS

The evangelistic purpose of John is evident in the varieties of persuasion used in the Gospel, and provides significant limits to the extent of intentionally fictional embellishments that the Evangelist could plausibly have woven into his sources. In particular, the Evangelist's purpose is to use the miracles of the signs tradition as one proof that Jesus is the Christ. This proof entails several claims. First, it claims that the miracles of the signs tradition are essentially historical. Second, it claims that Jesus performed the miracles, so that it is Jesus' identity that is validated by the miracles. Third, it claims implicitly that Jesus was a man who followed God and kept the laws of God, rather than one who followed some other god; apart from this the signs would have no persuasive power with Jewish readers. Fourth, it claims that Jesus, as portrayed in the Fourth Gospel, is essentially the same Jesus as known to the readers by other traditions; this identification is implicit in the Evangelist's purpose that his readers believe in Jesus.

These four claims by themselves, however, could only show that Jesus is "come from God as a teacher," as Nicodemus says (John 3:2), but not that he is the Messiah and Son of God. The specific evidence that he is the Messiah and Son of God lies either in his own claims about his identity, or in the uniquely great power of his miracles. The latter idea is suggested by his resurrection, which causes Thomas to say, "My Lord and my God" (John 20:28). It is also suggested by the words of the blind man, "Since the beginning of time it has never been heard that anyone opened the eyes of a person born blind"(John 9:32). However various characters in the Gospel believe in Jesus before seeing such great miracles, and all of the characters in the Gospel have some knowledge of Jesus besides his miracles. Thomas, being a disciple, knows Jesus well. The blind man knew Jesus' reputation, which was why the blind man washed his eyes as Jesus had di-

---

71. Gardner-Smith, *Saint John*, 11, 98.

rected him. So when Jesus asks people to believe in the works even if they don't believe Jesus' own claims (John 10:37–38), this does not mean that they are to believe without knowing what his claims or reputation were. The evidence that Jesus is the Messiah does not rest, then, in the miracles alone, but in Jesus' claims as well. These claims must be claims Jesus makes about himself, in order to show that Jesus claims to be more than a prophet. The claim to be God's Son is made explicit in two other passages (John 5:18; 10:36). The former passage infers the claim simply from Jesus' reference to God as "my Father" (John 5:17). The term "Son of God" has distinctive messianic overtones (cf. 2 Sam 7:14), though this is carried further by the reference to the Son's previous existence outside the world. God sent "the Son into the world" (John 3:17) as the light which "has come into the world" (John 3:19). It is also carried further by the Son's status as God's representative, invested with the authority of God (John 5:18, 22, 23, 26).

In summary, the claims entailed in the use of the signs tradition include, along with the four claims listed above, Jesus' own claim about his identity. In the Evangelist's thought, Jesus claims to be "the Christ, the Son of God" (John 20:31). A fifth claim is implicitly included in all of the other four claims: the particular details of the miracle narratives are considered sufficient to establish each of the other four claims as grounds for the reader to believe. This means, for example, that Jesus' claims to be Christ and Son of God are considered by John to be essentially historical claims.

NONFICTION IN JOHN'S OFFERED PROOFS OF MIRACLES

Given that John's persuasive and polemic purpose would forbid him from inventing miracles, we may similarly argue that it would prevent him from inventing proof of the miracles' occurrence. As mentioned earlier, Meier thinks that John's Gospel includes a tendency to "heighten the miraculous element." For Meier, one example of this tendency must be the changing of water into wine at Cana, a miracle narrative that he regards as "for the most part" the creation of the Evangelist. However any attempt to "heighten the miraculous element" implies that the Evangelist does not consider the signs tradition to offer, as it stood, sufficiently compelling reason to believe. If this were his perspective, the Evangelist need not have included from the signs tradition any signs that he regarded as unconvincing. Instead of this perspective, the Evangelist presents Jesus' signs as grounds for belief in Jesus, and he evidently does this because he personally finds the tradition of these miracles already persuasive. This is shown particularly in his expression of wonder that people did not believe in Jesus "though he had performed so many signs before them" (John 12:37), a response which the Evangelist can only explain as blindness (John 12:40). That John should have accepted the signs tradition as essentially historical is not surprising, considering the success of miracle traditions within the earliest Christian writings. Given that the Evangelist finds the signs tradition persuasive, it is not credible that he perceives fundamental weakness in the tradition and then knowingly replaces those traditions with more compelling fictions.

The citation of miracles in religious contexts is inherently polemic and persuasive, so that the detailed evidence for miracles in John's Gospel would be a natural part of an early miracle narrative. John's heightened attention to miracles he considered proven need not mean that he invented the supporting details. In most or all cases he could have offered significantly more convincing evidence if he were free to invent without the constraints of tradition. Instead, his selection of miracles which have stronger claims to being proven may arise from his own experience in public evangelistic discourse, perhaps in part because of his experience in addressing audiences with a more Hellenistic outlook.

Another reason to doubt that the Evangelist would heighten the miraculous character of the signs is that he might consider it impious to do so. If one grants the Evangelist's sincerity and his acceptance of the signs tradition, would not the Evangelist have thought it impious to evaluate such traditional miracles as markedly unconvincing? If he accepts the miracles in the tradition as the work of God, would he really consider the miracles in need of improvement? Since the Evangelist himself portrays Jesus as doing only the works "he sees the Father doing" (John 5:19), why would the Evangelist himself knowingly ascribe to Jesus compelling works that he thought Jesus (and the Father) had not done? The "tendency of John's Gospel to heighten the miraculous element," noted by Meier, does not show that John has invented elements to make an unconvincing tradition more persuasive.[72] Instead it indicates that John has selected the most persuasive reports from within the tradition.

Though some might assume that the Evangelist wanted to make the miracle narratives more persuasive than they were in the Signs tradition, there is reason to think that the Evangelist had no such interest. While belief in the reality of some miracles was common in the ancient world, belief in particular miracle claims could face stiff opposition in the ancient world, as the Evangelist acknowledges in the case of the blind man's healing (John 9). If the Evangelist was free to invent any detail at all, and simply wrote to make the miracles as persuasive as possible, he could certainly have made improvements that he did not make. Why not set the religious leaders in the presence of the blind man while he is healed? Why not make them long time acquaintances of the blind man? Why not include the direct presence of the opposing Jewish leadership at Lazarus' or Jesus' resurrection? Why not portray Jesus as granting the miracle of giving manna from heaven (John 6)? Jesus is there uninterested in simply performing miracles upon request, as many commentators have noted. Why, then, should we think that the Evangelist is interested in providing as many proofs for miracles as his readership seemingly desired, rather than portraying a Jesus whose miracles have proofs that are constrained by other concerns? But given these constraints, it is more plausible to acknowledge that the signs tradition from which John drew acted as both an authority for and constraint upon his portrayal of Jesus' miracles.

In support of such a constraint, it is notable that the miracles in John's Gospel are not markedly greater than the miracles found in the Synoptic Gospels, but rather are given more supporting evidence for being genuine miracles. John's nature miracles include turning water into wine (John 2) and the multiplying of the loaves (John 6). These

---

72. Meier, *Marginal Jew*, 698.

are equaled in the Synoptic account of the multiplication of the loaves and fishes. The healing of the official's son from a distance (John 4) is matched by the healing of the centurion's slave (Luke 7). The healing of a lame man (John 5) is matched by the healing of a paralytic (Mark 2). The healing of a blind man (John 9) is found also in the Synoptic Gospels (Mark 10). The resurrection of Jairus' daughter (Luke 8) and the son of the widow of Nain (Luke 7) equal the raising of Lazarus (John 11). The resurrection of Jesus is of course present in all four Gospels. John does not include the stilling of the sea (Mark 4), though including the resulting question, "Who then is this, that even the wind and the sea obey him?" might well have proved amenable to John's purpose. Similarly, John does not include the transfiguration, or any casting out of unclean spirits. John himself notes that he has selected only some of the miracles known to him, but that these are sufficient for his purpose of evoking belief in Jesus as the Christ.

John's inclusion of more supporting evidence is made possible by his longer vignettes, which is related to the fewer number of miracles. While Mark has about twenty specifically described miracles, John has about one third that number in a gospel that is somewhat longer. This ratio holds even when the passion narratives (which essentially have no miracles) are excluded from consideration.

John gives additional supporting evidence to show that each miracle was really necessary, and that each miracle really occurred. He notes the large quantity of water that was turned into wine, and that it was the servants who placed the water in the jars (John 2). There is too much wine for this to have been a mistake, and the servants were witnesses that the jars were filled with water. John emphasizes that the royal official's child was healed at the exact time Jesus spoke, to exclude a coincidental recovery (John 4). He also notes the resulting belief of the official and his household in Jesus. The lame man at the pool of Bethesda was lame for 38 years, so there could be no mistake that he was lame (John 5). The disciples mention that 200 denarii of bread would be needed to feed the multitude, so there were in fact a lot of people (John 6:7). There are twelve baskets of fragments left over after the loaves are multiplied, and the people try to make Jesus a king in consequence. The blind man was blind from birth, as testified to by his own parents (John 9). Lazarus has been dead and in a tomb for four days, and his sister's grief and the presence of the mourners shows that he was considered dead (John 11). The need for assistance to remove the stone and the bindings about his hands and feet, all prove (along with their dramatic effect) that there is no mistake about Lazarus having been dead. Similarly, the Evangelist takes pains to show that Jesus was really dead from the thrust of the spear, water and blood flowing out, all being testified to by a witness (John 19:34, 35). The evidence for the risen Jesus includes the sight of his hands and side, where the nails and spear were thrust, showing that it is really the one who died (John 20). This occurs along with other evidence, as will be discussed below. In summary, John does not have greater miracles than the Synoptic Gospels, but rather provides more evidence that there can be no mistake about the miraculous character of Jesus' signs. That John should have better supporting evidence, but not either greater or lesser miracles, is important evidence that he adopts accepted miracle traditions rather than inventing his own. There is no obvious reason to think that John did not pass on the supporting evidences in this tradition essentially as he heard them.

We conclude, then, that John intended not only his miracles, but also the evidence for them, to be understood as essentially nonfiction, and actually regarded them as essentially historical and reliable. This view is like that of scholars who hold that John intended the miracles, both source and editing, to be understood as nonfiction. One example of this group would be Brendan Byrne.[73]

Byrne's article addresses only the miracle of Jesus' resurrection. Speaking of the beloved disciple, Byrne says the Evangelist "goes to considerable lengths in his description of what was to be seen in the tomb" and wants "to associate this vision very closely with the disciple's coming to faith."[74] While the other disciples believe in the resurrection because they see the risen Jesus, the beloved disciple "comes to faith on the basis of what he sees in the tomb."[75] What was seen in the tomb was only "the face cloth which had been on his head, not lying with the linen wrappings but rolled up in a place by itself" (John 20:7). Byrne, noting that Lazarus needed assistance to have the face cloth removed after his resurrection, says that the location of the cloth in Jesus' tomb showed in contrast that ". . . Jesus has actively raised himself. The neatly folded, separately placed facial cloth would appear to be the culminating indication of this totally self-possessed, majestic act of Jesus."[76]

Byrne refers to this folded cloth as a "sign," but it is better to think of it as evidence that a sign occurred. It is perhaps always true that a sign in John's Gospel includes the evidence for its occurrence. There was extra wine at the wedding at Cana; there was bread for the 5,000; those who were healed afterward had healthy bodies. However the Evangelist does not use the term *sēmeion* to refer to the observable effects of a miracle, apart from the miracle itself. The grave clothes, then, should not be considered a sign distinct from the miracle of the resurrection itself, at least not in the sense in which the Evangelist uses the term *sēmeion*. Rather, all the evidence of the resurrection, including evidence of its particular character, would be considered part of the sign of the resurrection.

The beloved disciple already believed in Jesus, but here he came to believe in Jesus' resurrection. Belief in the resurrection is indeed closely identified with belief in Jesus, so that refusal to believe in the resurrection might ultimately preclude belief in Jesus. However the two beliefs are not identical, unless we suppose that no disciple believed in Jesus throughout the course of Jesus' ministry, a view specifically denied by Jesus (John 17:8, 20).[77]

Byrne's emphasis on the Evangelist's evidence for the resurrection indicates that the Evangelist was concerned to evoke a belief in the historical character of this evidence. Byrne thinks the Gospel was composed "largely to give subsequent generations of believ-

73. Byrne, "Faith of the Beloved Disciple," 83–97.
74. Ibid., 83.
75. Ibid., 89.
76. Ibid., 88.
77. See the earlier discussion about "Signs" for a full argument against this denial of the apostles' faith.

ers access to the central events of Jesus' life, death, resurrection and return to the Father"; it is only in this way that Byrne considers it possible for later generations to "have an encounter with Jesus every bit as valid" as those who saw him. This means that, for Byrne, the encounter is essentially through the historical tradition. Whatever may be thought of the reliability of the Evangelist's account, this is the way he intended to be read.

CHAPTER CONCLUSIONS: THE NONFICTIONAL INTENTION OF JOHN

Given the sincerity of the Evangelist, his evangelistic polemic shows that he held certain elements of his Gospel to be "essentially" nonfiction. His persuasive purpose, to elicit and confirm belief in Jesus, depends upon those elements being understood as nonfictional. As argued above, this included both the signs, claims about the one who performed them, and the proofs of those signs. Such "essential" nonfictional elements in each miracle would have to support the following beliefs of the Evangelist:

1. *The narrated miracles really claim to show a change in the normal and regular and expected course of life, and they are promoted as being essentially historical.*

2. *The highly irregular changes attributed to miracles could not be plausibly explained as the result of a natural cause.* (This is necessarily the case for any who did not believe in natural causes, but instead that God directly orders every event in the world. For those who did believe in natural causes, a plausible natural explanation would be one for which a natural cause might be attributed, and for which such a cause would be antecedently or inherently probable to result in the change attributed to the miracle. An early Jewish belief in natural causation is indicated by God's use of instrumental means, as when (Exod 14:21) "The LORD caused the sea to go back by a strong east wind.")

3. *The exercise of the divine power of God provides a plausible explanation for the change.* (Again, a plausible divine explanation is one that is inherently or antecedently probable given the nature of God, as revealed in the Hebrew Scriptures. It must accordingly be consistent with God's moral character, his purposes for doing such miracles, his reasons for doing miracles rarely, and all other considerations that he might be expected to take into account. This does not mean that the actual decision to perform a particular miracle is fully predictable; it only means that some kinds of miracles would be precluded or unexpected. This is analogous to our limited ability to predict what kind of story an author will write, what kind of picture an artist will paint, what kind of speech an orator will give, or what kind of friend a person will choose.)

4. *No being or power other than God provides a plausible cause for the event.* (Again, by plausible cause, this means one that is inherently or antecedently probable given the nature of such causes. Here this means that Jesus was not performing his miracles by demonic powers.)

5. *Jesus was a righteous man who observed the laws of Moses faithfully.* (This means that he would not be a follower of other gods, or in league with evil powers.)

6. *The miracles were performed by Jesus' own word or act or both, or in his name.* (This makes Jesus the intermediary of miraculous power, so that we have grounds to trust in Jesus as the representative of God. Jesus himself prays to God for Lazarus's resurrection, just as Elijah (1 Kgs 17:21) earlier prayed for the life of the widow's child.)
7. *The miracles are gifts granted by divine favor, which also give hope of a better age to come.* (In that age, divinely provided life, healing, and provision would free us from the evils of this world.)
8. *The special proofs that the miracles occurred are generally reliable nonfiction, and every supporting detail that is essential to the miracle having occurred is represented as fully reliable.*

Other nonfictional claims that are implied by the Evangelist's persuasive use of the signs are as follows:

9. *Jesus claimed to be the Messiah and Son of God.* (Without Jesus' claims, the miracles provide insufficient grounds to believe. With his claims, the miracles provide sufficient grounds.)
10. *The nonfictional claims of John that are essential to justify belief in Jesus are historically credible, even if there may be errors or elaboration in nonessential details.*
11. *The Evangelist himself is basically credible.*
12. *The Jesus of history is, in essence, represented correctly in the Gospel.* (The Evangelist could not inspire belief in Jesus by presenting another Jesus who had nothing in common with the historical Jesus but the name. In practice, believing in Jesus could not be separated from joining with others who believed in Jesus, including others who knew Jesus from other historical traditions.)
13. *Those characters in John's Gospel who believe in Jesus do so for reasons that the Evangelist hopes will also persuade the reader to believe in Jesus.*
14. *Jesus' defense before his opponents was "essentially" valid.*

The conclusions reached here may be controversial, but they are more extensive than necessary for our purpose. That immediate purpose is simply to show the extent to which the miracles in John's Gospel should be understood as having a nonfictional core. This is not an argument to show that the Evangelist was right to believe this core was nonfiction, but merely to show that this was his own belief, and a belief that he sought to inculcate in his readers. The Evangelist's understanding of epistemology cannot be clearly discussed without reference to a body of knowledge that has a clearly nonfictional intention. The importance of the signs as nonfiction will serve as a basis for the next discussion.

9

John's Use of Miracles as Grounds for Belief in Jesus

GIVEN THE ESSENTIALLY NONFICTIONAL character of miracles in John's Gospel, we are now in a position to review the relation between knowledge of these miracles and belief in Jesus as the Christ. We will proceed by describing a variety of opinions expressed in the literature, and evaluating their supporting arguments. To give a sense of historical context, the authors will be discussed here in chronological sequence of publication.

MCCASLAND ON MIRACLES AS GROUNDS FOR BELIEF IN JESUS

S. Vernon McCasland's view of the relationship of faith to miracles was that Jesus did not "base his appeal on signs and wonders."[1] He showed this by Jesus' refusal to gain adherents merely by performing signs, even though Jesus was tempted to do this by the devil in the wilderness (Matt 4:1–6 et al). Similarly, in John's Gospel, Jesus refuses to provide manna from heaven as Moses had done (John 6:30–45). However for McCasland, this refusal to gain adherents solely by the use of signs was a denial that signs have any legitimate role at all in supporting or encouraging belief. In contrast to McCasland's view, John's Gospel should be understood as following the more positive assessment of miracles that is found in the Old Testament.

The Old Testament already acknowledged both the value of signs for evoking belief, and the inability of signs to secure the continuation of that belief. There is no reason to assume that the Evangelist does not accept this perspective, since he regards the Old Testament as a divine authority. The Psalmist complains after the miracles of the Exodus, "Our fathers in Egypt did not understand your wonders . . . but rebelled by the sea, at the Red Sea" (Ps 106:7). After their enemies were covered by the Red Sea, "Then they believed his words; They sang His praise. They quickly forgot his works; they did not wait for his counsel, but craved intensely in the wilderness, and tempted God in the desert" (Ps 106:12–14). Similarly, another Psalm says, "He brought forth streams also from the rock, and caused waters to run down like rivers. Yet they still continued to sin against Him, to rebel against the Most High in the desert" (Ps 78:16, 17). These Psalms draw in turn

---

1. McCasland, "Signs and Wonders," 152.

from the Pentateuch, which tells of numerous lapses of the people of Israel even after the signs of the Exodus and the provision of manna in the wilderness. These lapses are summarized in Moses' words at the end of the forty years, "from the day that you left the land of Egypt until you arrived at this place, you have been rebellious against the LORD" (Deut 9:7). It is not the signs that are inadequate, but the human response.

Knowledge of these miracles and of their failure to evoke faithful adherence to God would be well known to many Jews in the first century. Scripture was so familiar as to be often cited by characters in the Gospels, and the Exodus narrative was memorialized among Jews in the annual Passover celebration.[2] It is generally acknowledged either that John was Jewish, or at least that he had a comparable knowledge of Jewish thought. Consequently it is hardly necessary to follow McCasland so far as to deny that Jesus or John saw any positive role for the miraculous, just because miracles did not always secure a continuing faith.

HINDLEY ON MIRACLES AS GROUNDS FOR BELIEF IN JESUS

J. C. Hindley offers a discussion that is important because of his detailed attention to the grounds for belief in Jesus. While he asks many of the right questions, different answers will be given here. Hindley argues that "the appeal to miracle as a ground of faith" is an idea that would conflict with Jesus' refusal to gain adherents by performing miracles.[3] In support, Hindley cites Jesus' refusal to perform miracles during the temptation in the wilderness, as described in the Synoptic Gospels. In John's Gospel also, Jesus declines to miraculously provide manna from heaven, a miracle that is proposed by his hearers as a condition for them to believe Jesus (John 6:30–31). Commenting that the Fourth Gospel miracles at times seem to produce faith, Hindley sees this effect of miracles as a contradiction to Jesus' refusal to perform miracles to secure faith. He warns that Jesus "will not rely upon naked miracle to coerce belief."[4]

However for the Evangelist miracles only coerce belief in the miracle's occurrence, they cannot coerce a lasting belief in Jesus. Many who acknowledge Jesus' miracles do not believe in Jesus. Those who see his miracles at the temple do not prove faithful. Those who see the feeding of the five thousand are not satisfied with that sign. The authorities who see the blind man healed respond by accusing Jesus. Some who see Lazarus raised merely report it to Jesus' enemies. After the resurrection of Lazarus, even Jesus' enemies eventually say, "this man is performing many signs" (John 11:47). They do not, however, become his adherents. Hindley's idea that miracles necessarily cause belief in Jesus also ignores the limited ability of miracles in the book of Exodus to secure belief in God, from either Egyptian or Israelite. That Old Testament perspective is adopted by the

---

2. cf. Exod 12:24–27; John 2:13; 11:55. Also, Mishnah *Pesahim* 10:4,5 ascribes to the first century R. Gamaliel the pronouncement that the events of the Passover must be recited.

3. Hindley, "Witness," 329.

4. Ibid.

Evangelist, and specifically alluded to by his reference to the "grumbling" of the people (John 6:41).[5]

While the Evangelist would agree that miracles by themselves do not provide a sufficient ground of faith, he differs from Hindley in seeing miracles as a proper ground of faith provided that other conditions are also satisfied. Jesus himself implicitly acknowledges the existence of these other conditions by refuting charges against his own character. In particular, the Mosaic command to turn from false prophets who perform miracles (Deut 13:1–3) required some showing that Jesus held faithfully to the teachings of Moses. Some essential idea of Jesus' teaching and claims is also a condition, since a miracle worker with no message would be a mere curiosity rather than a prophet. For many characters in the Gospel, those other conditions of belief are already satisfied, so their belief in Jesus results immediately upon learning of a miracle. This is the case with the disciples of Jesus after they observe the wedding miracle at Cana. It is the case with the servants of the royal official. It is also the case with many who were present at the raising of Lazarus. The Evangelist often seems to allow people time to come to believe in Jesus, even after learning of his miracles. The other conditions for belief recognized by the Evangelist are often satisfied in the allowed time. Often it rests upon having a better understanding of Jesus' claims or message. This is the case with those Samaritans who did not believe until they heard Jesus for themselves (John 4:41), and with the man born blind (John 9:35–38). The Evangelist even seems to concede the right of the Jewish authorities to confirm that the blind man's healing occurred, for the Evangelist does not blame them until after they have established that the miracle occurred (John 9:13–41). Given that the Evangelist narrates more than one or two miracles, it seems that some readers are similarly allowed time for coming to believe in Jesus. The time is not unlimited, however, as Jesus' opponents are condemned for persecuting Jesus.

Hindley, however, attempts to resolve the apparent contradiction of faith arising from miracles in another way. He argues that miracles produce true faith only when seen as *signs* (Greek *sēmeion*) apart from their miraculous element. Accordingly to Hindley, when miracles are used "for their evidence-value, they are not the basis of true faith"; their glory is revealed only as "signs" and this only "to those who are *already* believers."[6] He emphasizes the main sense of the word *sēmeion*, which like the English word *sign*, refers primarily to *meaning* or *significance*. In particular he declares, ". . . it is possible to witness a miracle without seeing a sign."[7] Hindley fails to observe, however, that the *significance* of Jesus' miracles cannot be separated from their miraculous character. This is especially clear if we are to understand such *significance* as being the basis for faith, as Hindley suggests.

But what does Hindley mean in specific cases by his reference to the *significance* of signs as a basis for belief? What is the *significance* of turning water into wine, such that the disciples consequently come to believe in Jesus at that time, unless it includes

---

5. As noted, for example, by Beasley-Murray, *John*, 88, 93.
6. Hindley, "Witness," 331.
7. Ibid., 329.

John's Use of Miracles as Grounds for Belief in Jesus

his genuine miraculous power and his willingness to use that power in history? The Evangelist indicates that their faith was evoked by the miraculous, saying, "and his glory was revealed and his disciples believed in him" (John 2:11). There is nothing in Jesus' actions at Cana which could plausibly be described as "revealing his glory," apart from the miraculous.[8] The glory was revealed in the miraculous character of the sign. If this glory was revealed through the divine gift or promise[9] given in the sign, there would be nothing genuinely revealed unless the miracle had genuinely occurred. A mere fiction about a divine gift suggests that the promise and hope signified by that gift may also lie outside of history, and outside the real future life of the reader. Again, apart from the actual gift of the healing, what is the *significance* Hindley sees in Jesus' healing the man born blind, such that the man should come to believe in Jesus? If we are to say it was the revelation of Jesus' divine identity,[10] this is surely revealed primarily by the actual gift of healing, which was miraculous. It is a mistake to imply, as Hindley does, that the actual healing was not a cause of the man's coming to faith, even though it was not the sole cause. Again, what is the significance Hindley sees in Jesus' resurrecting Lazarus, apart from the actual miracle of Lazarus's resurrection? What is this significance that resulted in people coming to believe in Jesus (John 11:45)? To read this as a nonphysical resurrection is to impose a different idea upon John's narrative. The significance of miracles cannot be divorced from their miraculous character in the Fourth Gospel, just as the significance of the signs of the book of Exodus were not divorced from their miraculous character. It is the miraculous character of the sign that makes it a sign from God. John himself refers to miracles consistently by the term *sēmeia*, even when they are regarded especially in terms of their miraculous character. As mentioned above, Hindley says that only believers perceive the sign of a miracle. Against Hindley's reading, at the feeding of the five thousand, the Evangelist says that even those who would not believe in Jesus "saw the sign" (John 6:14).[11] What, apart from the miraculous in each sign, does Hindley think is the *significance* of signs, which is such that perception of it could result in genuine belief? Hindley gives no answer. If the miraculous element is so peripheral to the significance of the signs, why would either God or the Evangelist risk distracting people from the true significance of signs by including the miraculous element with them? John himself does not suggest that only believers see miracles as signs. John's emphasis when using the term *sēmeion* is not on the significance of a sign that only a believer can observe, but on the significance which is apparent to all.

By his claim that only believers see the signs, Hindley underestimates the real understanding that John attributes to all who see Jesus, whether believer or not. Here he expresses a Barthian (and Kierkegaardian) concern to show that revelation is beyond human reason.[12] It is true that the Evangelist credits Jesus' followers with a knowledge

---

8. Hindley, "Witness," 331.

9. As noted, for example, by Beasley-Murray, *John*, 36.

10. As suggested by Dodd, *Interpretation*, 329: "The works which Christ performs are manifestly divine activities." Cited in Hindley, "Witness in the Fourth Gospel," 325.

11. Hindley, "Witness," 329.

12. Ibid., 319.

that others do not have. Jesus says, "I am the good shepherd; and I know my own, and my own know (γινώσκουσί) me" (John 10:14). However there is also a kind of insight that John attributes to both believers and Jesus' enemies alike, and this insight comes in part through Jesus' miracles. Jesus says, "If I had not done among them the works which no one else did, they would not have sin, but now they have both seen and hated both me and my Father also" (John 15:24). They have seen Jesus. According to this text, Jesus himself was revealed to them in the miracles. Just as they have seen Jesus, in some real sense, they are said to *know* who Jesus is, "You both know (οἴδατε) me and know where I am from" (John 7:28). So they have both seen and known Jesus.

Hindley characterizes the common knowledge that comes from miracles as "inference." Citing Nicodemus' acknowledgment of Jesus' miracles, Hindley says, "it is to this attempt to proceed by argument and inference that Jesus says, 'You must be born again.'"[13] But if, as the Evangelist has said, they *see* and *know* Jesus by these miracles (by direct modes of perception), then how is such knowledge to be construed as a futile process of "argument and inference"? The miracles of Jesus revealed Jesus himself to his enemies, and it is Jesus himself whom they consequently "have both seen and hated." Hindley acknowledges that "arguing from evidence" has the positive value that it "may lead to perceiving the sign." He says this is why people are culpable (cf. John 15:24) for "not using this amount of rational insight" so as to become inquirers.[14] However the term "rational" should not be allowed here. The "insight" of the people, whether rational or revealed, makes them culpable. This insight, while not as full as that given to a genuine follower of Jesus, includes their ability to *see* and *know* Jesus by his miracles and words.

Consequently, it may be argued further that the knowledge of Jesus which is given to people generally through the miracles and other spoken testimony is, in John's Gospel, considered a sufficient basis for belief in Jesus. If Jesus' opponents "have seen and hated both me and my Father as well," then God himself has been revealed to his opponents in Jesus, and has himself been rejected by them. The Evangelist indicates in several ways that Jesus has revealed God to the entire world. Jesus is presented as "the light of people" that "enlightens all people" (John 1:4, 9). The condemnation of mankind is that "the light has come into the world and people loved the darkness rather than the light because their deeds were evil" (John 3:19). Similarly, people are condemned because Jesus "came and spoke to them" (John 15:22) and did miracles "among them which no one else did" (John 15:24). Jesus is the one who has "shown God" to all the people (John 1:18), so that to see Jesus is to see the Father (John 12:45; 14:9). Jesus' miracles are really the work of the Father (John 5:17,20). Jesus' public teaching is really the Father's (John 7:16). The people have seen Jesus in a way that might have been expected to result in belief in him (John 6:36, contrasting John 6:40). Jesus' miracles and works constitute a sufficient basis for belief, as is indicated by those who do believe in Jesus because of his word and works. In John's Gospel, no character comes to belief in Jesus apart from such general

---

13. Ibid., 330.
14. Ibid., 331.

knowledge of his word and deeds. Even the reader is encouraged to believe on the basis of the Evangelist's recounting of Jesus' words and deeds.

It is important to note further that, for the characters in John's Gospel, no private and internal revelation ever constitutes the sole ground for belief in Jesus. This is even true of John the Baptist, whose testimony that Jesus is the Son of God (John 1:34) evidently alludes to the tradition that the voice from heaven publicly declared Jesus to be "my Son" (Matt 3:17; Mark 1:11; Luke 3:22). For Hindley, "spiritual insight" apparently is the result of revelation, by which God speaks "in the heart" of a person.[15] The revelation from which faith arises must then be either a revelation of God through his public words, or of God directly. However we see from the discussion above that Jesus directly reveals God and God's words publicly, so that such a private revelation could actually not reveal anything essential that has not already been revealed publicly in Jesus. Consequently, any inner revelation should be understood primarily as recognition of the public revelation's validity and significance, made possible by the removal of sin and its resulting blindness. Hindley agrees with this so far as to say that "the internal assent of the heart" is the revelation that "enables a man to accept Christ."[16] However a private inner revelation itself is never portrayed by the Evangelist as the sole cause of faith in Jesus or in God.

The idea that there is a publicly available knowledge of Jesus better supports Hindley's claim that knowledge of miracles "is a step on the way, and may lead to perceiving the sign" or significance of the miracle.[17] If perception of the significance of a miracle was only possible by a private revelation, it is hard to see how "inferential knowledge" could ever be a "step along the way" to this "spiritual insight" of revelation. This is especially so since, for Hindley, "it is to this attempt to proceed by argument and inference that Jesus says, 'You must be born again.'"[18] Another problem this idea alleviates is that the purpose of Jesus' public words and deeds need not be seen as empty, as if they were incapable of evoking genuine belief. Instead they bring some people to a life-giving faith. Hindley criticized a person like Nicodemus for attempting to believe "by argument and inference," without the "spiritual insight" given by revelation. But how does Jesus' informing Nicodemus of this "fault" enable him to gain "spiritual insight"—unless the public words of Jesus to Nicodemus are themselves revelation rather than mere grounds for "inference"? The idea that revelation is public also explains why having "spiritual insight" would always be accompanied by a fundamental change in any person's character or way of life. There is no human reason, at least, to think that spiritual insight would necessitate a change in character. Hindley must simply assume a divine link between spiritual insight and character change. While possible, this explanation does not follow as naturally. Even the divine "gift" and "drawing" of followers to Jesus (John 6:37, 44, 65) can be understood with less difficulty as a change of heart, than as a private and internal revelation.

In identifying the main concepts in John's thought about signs, Hindley has not considered adequately the influence of Old Testament ideas upon John and the read-

15. Ibid., 326.
16. Ibid.
17. Ibid., 331.
18. Ibid., 330.

ers he addresses. Because of John's citations of and allusions to the Old Testament, and particularly his comparisons of Jesus to Moses,[19] it should be presumed that John would adopt a Jewish view about the value of signs, or at least address such a viewpoint. As will be argued below, the Old Testament does not support Hindley's idea that miracles justify only the inference that "divine power is at work."[20] Neither does it support the idea that the miracles have a "sign-value" or significance that can stand separately from their historical "evidence-value." Hindley gives no compelling reasons to think that John has departed from this traditional Jewish conception of the value of miracles.

The Exodus narratives alone show that the "knowledge by inference" which comes from miracles provides much more knowledge than merely the understanding of Hindley that "divine power is at work." Pharaoh, who is never represented as having the spiritual insight of one who believes in the LORD, says at one point to Moses "I have sinned this time; the LORD is the righteous one, and I and my people are the wicked ones. Make supplication to the LORD" (Exod 9:27–28). In response to this Moses says, "as for you and your servants, I know that you do not yet fear the LORD God" (Exod 9:30). Pharaoh's request is later repeated (Exod 10:16–17). The effect of these plagues is that "the Egyptians shall know that I am the LORD, when I stretch out my hand on Egypt, and bring out the sons of Israel from their midst" (Exod 7:5). Even though his knowledge of miracles never results in adherence to the LORD, Pharaoh does at times acknowledge that Moses is a prophet sent by the LORD. This means that all Moses tells him about God is implicitly accepted: that the LORD is a god, that this God has spoken to Moses, that this God wants his people to leave Egypt and offer sacrifices to him, that God has performed these miracles to force Pharaoh to let the people go, and that Pharaoh himself is under the power, and therefore owes obedience to this God. This is knowledge of far more than that "divine power is at work." In John's Gospel, such knowledge of God would have been comparable to momentary acknowledgments by all the Jewish leaders that Jesus was a prophet and teacher from God, as Nicodemus initially says (John 3:2). Similar to Pharaoh's intransigence in the face of miracles, Elijah's calling down fire from heaven at Mt Carmel in public view does not preclude Jezebel from seeking his execution (1 Kgs 18:38; 19:2).

That signs could justify inference about the knowledge of God is shown also in the case of the Israelites after the Exodus. They initially acknowledge Moses on the basis of the miraculous signs he performed and the promise of deliverance from Egyptian servitude. However at the end of forty years Moses says to Israel, "from the day that you left the land of Egypt until you arrived at this place, you have been rebellious against the LORD. Even at Horeb you provoked the LORD to wrath, and the LORD was so angry that he would have destroyed you" (Deut 9:7–8). And Moses particularly points out that he says this to those who had personally seen God's "signs and wonders which he did in the midst of Egypt to Pharaoh the king of Egypt and to all his land" (Deut 11:3). The Israelites are portrayed as knowing and believing that these signs occurred, and yet this

---

19. John 1:17; 5:45–47; 6:32; 9:28–30. See, for example, Meeks, *The Prophet-King*.
20. Hindley, "Witness," 330.

has not prevented them from repeatedly rebelling against God, showing that they did not fully trust Moses as God's prophet, or in God as sovereign over the world. Because they had seen the signs, they were especially blamed by Moses for acting as they did. John has incorporated this same theme.

Apart from Hindley's focus on the relation of belief to knowledge in John's Gospel, his most instructive insight is his recognition that the reader must respond along with the characters in the Gospel to Jesus' revelation. Hindley says, "One may ask in each situation, (a) what has this person found, or to what does he bear witness? (b) what is the *ground* of that response to Jesus?"[21] Here Hindley anticipates in part the literary approach of Culpepper.[22] While reliance upon the narrator distinguishes the reader's own situation from that of each character, the Evangelist clearly uses the reader's evaluation of each character's response to elicit the response of faith from the reader. Hindley says, "It is better to take these as types of possible response, than as exterior authorities upon whose testimony to historical facts we may rely."[23] This may be the right viewpoint for certain academic purposes, however the Fourth Gospel's direct claim to be reliable testimony shows a different expectation for the reader. The signs in the Gospel are all given first of all for the characters within the Gospel, but the Evangelist specifically includes them for the sake of the reader as well. Similarly, the Evangelist indicates the significance of the signs for these characters, but indicates that same significance for the sake of the reader. The signs are offered to the reader as inducements to believe, and the grounds for the characters' faith are offered as sufficient grounds for the readers also to believe in Jesus. The Evangelist, of course, knows by long experience as an evangelist that not everyone will believe his testimony. However he offers his testimony as deserving belief. The claims and apologetic given by Jesus to the public of his own day are offered to the reader as well.

FORTNA ON MIRACLES AS GROUNDS FOR BELIEF IN JESUS

Robert Fortna offers a different view of signs and belief. According to Fortna, John accepted signs as a legitimate basis for faith, but only when the sign was understood as a sign rather than as a mere wonder, a distinction he considers essential. Fortna says, for example, that "John reaffirms and clarifies the pre-Johannine understanding when he rules out wonder as a basis of faith"; and further, "I take 4:48 as a denunciation not of signs faith in general, but only of faith *requiring* the miraculous."[24] This separation of signs and miracle, advocated earlier by Hindley, was criticized in the above discussion of Hindley's work. In particular, the people of John 4:48 are criticized by Fortna for "faith which *demands* the miraculous, faith based on 'signs understood as wonders'—for so

---

21. Hindley, "Witness," 332.
22. Culpepper, *Anatomy*.
23. Hindley, "Witness," 332.
24. Fortna, "Source and Redaction," 153.

understood they cease to be truly signs."[25] Fortna carefully points out that John "takes for granted" that faith can arise from miracles.[26]

Fortna distinguishes signs from wonders by the "symbolic meaning" given "to every one of the signs."[27] In Fortna's view, John was concerned that miracles would not be seen in a way that evoked faith, instead being understood apart from their "symbolic meaning," and seen as "arbitrary."[28] What is this symbolic meaning apart from which a sign would be a mere wonder that could not evoke faith? The symbolic meanings that Fortna says are crucial include:

> Judaism contrasted with Christianity (2:6b); salvation as "life" (4:53a); Jesus' "working" (5:9b ff.); the Christian Passover (6:4); God's universal concern (6:12); Jesus' presence as dispelling the darkness (6:17b); "the bread of life" (6:27 ff.); "day" and "night" and the light of the world (9:4; cf. 11:9 f.); Jesus' mission (9:7); sight and blindness (9:8ff.); and "I am the resurrection" (11:21 ff.).

The meanings Fortna finds seem hardly to justify the superiority of sign over wonder, or to explain why all these elements are crucial to evoke genuine faith. For example, in John 2:6b, the disciples' faith in Jesus does not arise because "Judaism is contrasted with Christianity." The blind man's faith in Jesus does not arise on the grounds that the Pharisees are the ones who are truly blind. Even if we differently construe the "symbolic meanings" of these chapters, there is no obvious symbolic meaning that explains the rise of faith separately from the miraculous character of the signs. Fortna is more convincing when he says that the significance of the signs is that they reveal Jesus' "divine sonship" and "Jesus as the ultimate sign."[29]

While Fortna acknowledges that John accepts miracles, he fails to say that, for John, disbelief in reports of miracles as wonders precludes belief. It is not clear when he says that John denounces faith that *requires* miracles, if Fortna is saying that, for John, belief in reports of miracles is not essential to faith. This would violate the implications of the stories of Thomas, of Lazarus, and of the royal official. It also brings into question Fortna's explanation, which distinguishes signs from wonders. Is Fortna saying that the Evangelist did not think belief in reports of miracles was necessary to genuine faith? Some might understand the "symbolic meanings," which Fortna finds in the signs, to be devoid of a claim to the miraculous. This would be an imposition upon the Evangelist's thought. Fortna says, ". . . for John any request for a miracle, whatever the circumstances, is improper. . . . Jesus rebukes the nobleman seeking to save his son's life.[30] This seems hardly a credible reading of the Evangelist's viewpoint, or of the Jewish practice of prayer as expressed in the Psalms. Such writings have always encouraged prayers for healing and the preservation of life.

25. Ibid., 158.
26. Ibid., 156.
27. Ibid., 158.
28. Ibid., 158.
29. Ibid., 154, 165.
30. Ibid., 157.

On this basis Fortna goes on to discuss the relation between seeing the signs and believing. Fortna rightly points out that "demand to *see* a sign" is criticized. He also claims rightly that signs are a valid basis of faith for John, saying "the only place where belief on seeing signs is treated as invalid is in John 2:23–25, and there is no indication that it is the Jerusalemites' having *seen* the signs that nullifies their faith. Rather it is something 'in man' that calls this faith in question."[31] Fortna observes further that ". . . the situation of the second, or later, generation Christian (as John perceives it) is that he *cannot* see, but is dependent on the witness of others . . . Belief on the basis of concrete evidence is satisfactory, but belief without seeing is commendable." Here Fortna distinguishes the testimony of others from concrete evidence (e.g., seeing). He fails to say that not believing the cogent testimony of others is not satisfactory.

Fortna also claims that faith comes in degrees. He argues that "belief without seeing signs is a superior form of faith" and he argues that, unlike the earlier source, John sees degrees of faith.[32] Fortna does not make clear how these degrees of faith relate to the faith that gives eternal life. As argued in the chapter on belief, life-giving faith is, for the Evangelist, an either-or state.

FREED ON MIRACLES AS GROUNDS FOR BELIEF IN JESUS

Edwin Freed's opinion about the accepted basis for belief in John is overshadowed by his judgment that the text has no coherent theology. He declared that "in the Johannine material the theology is confusing to the degree that it is often unfathomable" and that it has contradictions "even in passages dealing with crucial questions of theology."[33] The contradictions he perceives include variations in the themes of "Jesus bearing witness," "seeing God," and "being Jesus' disciples." Freed thinks that the Signs-source "viewed Jesus' performance of signs and his subsequent crucifixion and resurrection as proofs of his messiahship," so that "in the source Jesus' signs are for the express purpose of making men believers."[34] He considers this view to be in contrast to the Synoptic Gospels, where "miracles are effective only for those who already have faith." Here Freed does not distinguish between believing in Jesus and believing that he will heal. Also, this neglects the evident use of the Synoptic miracle accounts for their influence upon the readers, as well as their influence generally in oral tradition. He thinks this interest of John in sign faith is unique, and is related to the Signs-source's use of the term *sēmeion*, perhaps implying that the term is used precisely in its miraculous sense. That would directly contradict Hindley's argument that *sēmeion* refers to the non-miraculous element of wonders.[35] John's inclusion of the Signs-source implies an acceptance by John of the Signs source's purpose for including miracles—especially because of the prominent place in which he locates or retains John 20:30–31, describing why the book was written. Freed can only

---

31. Ibid., 161.
32. Ibid., 162, 163.
33. Freed and Hunt, "Fortna's Signs-Source in John," 566.
34. Ibid., 574.
35. Hindley, "Witness," 329–30; Freed and Hunt, "Fortna's Signs-Source," 574.

deny this on the assumption that John was inconsistent in his ideas, but his case for that claim is cursory.

SMITH ON MIRACLES AS GROUNDS FOR BELIEF IN JESUS

D. M. Smith's assessment of the signs was that, "the purpose of the sign source was to demonstrate that Jesus was the expected Messiah by displaying his miraculous power."[36] Smith does not state whether the Evangelist shared this purpose by incorporating the sign source into his own material, but that seems to be suggested. Smith does not regard the evidence of signs as sufficient alone to convince people to believe. He thinks there would remain an apologetic need to answer questions about why Jesus was condemned to death as a criminal, a realization that also would have been forced upon both the author of the sign source and subsequently upon the Evangelist. The Gospel's account of Jesus' innocence of the capital charges against him would form the other reasons needed to believe in Jesus.

BYRNE ON MIRACLES AS GROUNDS FOR BELIEF IN JESUS

Brendan Byrne's assessment of the signs was that "the testimony about Jesus provided for subsequent generations by this gospel is precisely a testimony about his signs and it is testimony designed to promote faith through the recounting of these signs—a true and genuine 'sign' faith."[37] For Byrne, "sign faith" is not a proof like seeing, and does not have the stigma that others (e.g. McCasland) have attributed to it. Byrne contrasts faith that arises from signs with faith that arises from seeing.[38]

Byrne, similarly to Hindley, argues that John's Gospel was written so that later generations "can nonetheless join the pilgrimage of the first disciples." Just as the beloved disciple believed in Jesus' resurrection without seeing a sign, "so the subsequent generations through the gospel's witness to the signs of Jesus can come to faith in similar fashion without direct vision of him."[39] Byrne contrasts the apostles who have seen the risen Jesus with the later generations "who believe without having personally seen the Lord."[40]

PAINTER ON MIRACLES AS GROUNDS FOR BELIEF IN JESUS

John Painter's assessment of the signs was that both the Evangelist and the Signs Source accept faith based on signs. Against Bultmann and Haenchen's view that only the Signs Source advocated this idea, Painter says, "the evangelist *chose* to use the source."[41] Painter sees the historical claims about the signs as part of the earliest missionary preaching of the church. Painter points out that it is not so clear that the Evangelist regarded "faith *based*

---

36. Smith, "Setting and Shape," 235.
37. Byrne, "Faith of the Beloved Disciple," 90.
38. Ibid., 92.
39. Ibid., 90.
40. Ibid., 92.
41. Painter, "John 9 and Interpretation," 35.

on signs alone" as either durable or as perceiving the true nature of Jesus, and suggests that the failure to endure may even have proceeded from an inadequate Christology.[42] Painter also says, "the evangelist was critical of faith based on signs *alone* and the approach that made signs *necessary* for faith (20.29)." As Painter sees it, "faith based on signs was a real beginning, even if only a beginning."[43] He also says that John "was not opposed to faith based on signs as is sometimes supposed. Rather he saw such faith as a starting point and a real advance on unbelief or even 'neutrality' (John 10:37–38)."[44] What seems lacking in this is the Evangelist's more positive view of miracles and their major persuasive role throughout the Gospel.

From this point Painter's epistemology of belief is unclear. On the one hand he says of revelatory symbols, "While they enable faith to see, they condemn unbelief to blindness."[45] This suggests that only believers see the revelatory symbols. He refers similarly to blindness saying, "all men are blind, in the darkness, including those who *imagine* that they can see, that they have the light (9.39ff.)."[46] This suggests that men are blind in such a way as to have no real fault consequent to Jesus' revelation. However Painter also says, "the revelation provokes response, but the nature of the response is not determined. It can be for or against the revelation."[47] This indicates that men have, at the same time as blindness, a certain genuine vision. This seems to be implied in Jesus' implied criticism of those he calls blind—as though their blindness was willful. Painter gives an impressive discussion of symbols, and how the Evangelist uses those that touch the heart of human need. Since these symbols (bread, water, light, etc.) are not themselves the sources that satisfy life, they point to God who is beyond them.[48]

JOHNS AND MILLER ON MIRACLES AS GROUNDS FOR BELIEF IN JESUS

Johns and Miller present another article directly addressing the relation of signs to belief in Jesus.[49] As Johns and Miller see it, scholars have resolved, in a variety of ways, contradictory ideas about the value of "signs" as a basis for belief. Some scholars ascribe differing ideas to different sources, so maintaining "the independent integrity of distinct voices within the text."[50] Others ascribe the differences to unresolved complexities in the thought of the author. Other scholars deny that there is any tension regarding signs in the Fourth Gospel, but have not engaged with the specific critical problems in the text. Johns and Miller argue, out of rhetorical considerations, "the signs consistently play a positive

---

42. Ibid.
43. Ibid., 36.
44. Ibid., 43.
45. Ibid., 52.
46. Ibid.
47. Ibid., 54.
48. Ibid., 49.
49. Johns and Miller, "Signs as Witnesses," 519–35.
50. Ibid., 520.

role for faith in the Fourth Gospel."[51] This seems to mean that the Evangelist claimed to tell of historical signs of some kind.

Johns and Miller argue that each episode is narrated to show which protagonist is right, and that each episode stands as evidence "designed to persuade the reader."[52] Both works and signs constitute part of this evidence. The *works*, it is argued, are in several cases clearly miraculous acts; they give testimony about Jesus' identity as sent by God; they condemn those who do not believe in Jesus.[53] The term *sign*, it is claimed, "is used in the Fourth Gospel only of Jesus' miracles. They further point out that, in the Mosaic narratives alluded to by the Fourth Gospel, God provided "signs" in response to Moses' question, "Suppose they do not believe me or listen to me, but say, 'The LORD did not appear to you.'"[54] Johns and Miller conclude, "Like Moses, Jesus was commissioned by God, and like Moses, Jesus performed signs which were his credentials."[55] They note that "the Egyptians will 'know that [he is] the Lord' when signs and wonders are produced among them (Exod. 7:3–5; cf. 11:9–10)."[56] They conclude, "it is *necessary* that people be introduced to the signs or other witnesses in order to believe, yet it is possible for them to see the signs *without* believing."[57] For Johns and Miller, some evidence is required for faith.

STIBBE ON MIRACLES AS GROUNDS FOR BELIEF IN JESUS

Mark Stibbe's discussion of the raising of Lazarus incorporates a different view of the relation of miracles to belief in Jesus. Stibbe acknowledges the rhetorical intention of the miracle narratives to persuade the reader, although it is not clear that for him this intention refers to history, rather than to metaphysical realities. He says,

> the miracles of Jesus are, to the reader, a sign of glory. They are observable phenomena that reveal a greater reality. The miracle in John 11 is semiotic insofar as it discloses something of the authority and power of the Father and the Son over the great human enemy, death.[58]

Stibbe contrasts the "carnal, or superficial meaning" of the miracle of Lazarus' resurrection with the "secret or latent meaning" which is the disclosure "of the *doxa* [glory] of God and of his Son, Jesus Christ."[59] For Stibbe, the disclosure of God's glory is given in the promise of spiritual life. He says that it is the promise of "spiritual life," above the promise of "physical life," which is the fuller meaning given only to the perceptive reader

---

51. Ibid., 521.
52. Ibid., 524.
53. Ibid., 525.
54. Ibid., 526.
55. Ibid., 527.
56. Ibid., 531.
57. Ibid., 534.
58. Stibbe, "Tomb with a View," 49.
59. Ibid., 50.

(cf. John 11:25–26).[60] It is remarkable that Stibbe finds this kind of spiritual meaning to be the text's prime concern, when there is no incident of conversion upon which the author focuses attention. Or if, by spiritual life, Stibbe refers to the afterlife of the soul, there is no indication that John is separately promising that kind of life in this resurrection, or that the characters in the narrative who do believe would understand the promise in this way. Instead, there is enormous attention focused upon the reality of Lazarus' physical death and physical resurrection, as well as the political consequences to Jesus arising from this miracle. The glory of Jesus is shown only in the resurrection of Lazarus, and a concern primarily for Lazarus' "spiritual life" seems anachronistic.

MEIER ON MIRACLES AS GROUNDS FOR BELIEF IN JESUS

John Meier has a more supportive view of the value of miracles. He thinks miracles are definitely used as nonfiction. Meier says, "For all his rejection of crass faith based on 'miracles-on-demand,' Jesus obviously appreciated the value of miracles as pedagogy, as propaganda."[61] He says furthermore, "The belief in Jesus as a prophet who was at the same time a miracle-worker—a belief that goes back to his ministry—furnishes an important key to understanding who people thought Jesus was and perhaps even who *he* thought he was."[62]

Meier considers the possibility of miracles to be a philosophical or theological question, which lies outside the province of historiography and the historian. In particular, since he defines a miracle as an act of God, he does not think it is within the bounds of historical judgment to say that God caused any event, even if there was no human or natural power to which it might be plausibly ascribed or otherwise explained.[63] Comparing similar evidence of alleged healings at Lourdes in our own day, Meier argues for the historical probability that people at all times may have claimed to have been cured by divine power. As he puts it, "one cannot assert *a priori* that Jesus never performed inexplicable cures, claimed by some to be miracles."[64] This rule applies by historical analogy to Jesus' miracles, in spite of the far greater limitations in the evidence. Meier's restriction of the expert role of the historian is illuminating.

For the Evangelist, however, the conclusion that Jesus was not sent by God is one that the Jewish leaders could not have made reasonably, even though they held a different theological orientation. In Jewish scripture, miracles were seen as a sign of supernatural power, but not necessarily a sign that the prophet was from God. False prophets, who would lead people away from God, could also perform miracles (e.g., Deut 13:1–5; Mark 13:22). The occurrence of a miracle is regarded as simply observable, and does not require any particular faith orientation or entail any faith commitment to acknowledge that the miracle occurred. It probably does require belief in supernatural powers, or at

---

60. Ibid., 51.
61. Meier, *Marginal Jew*, 2:1043.
62. Ibid., 2:1044.
63. Ibid., 2:514.
64. Ibid., 2:516.

least acting as if one had such a belief. For example, the Egyptians were expected to act as if Moses' warnings of the plagues, however inexplicable according to one's religious views, deserved to be heeded. Pharaoh suffered the judgments of God because Pharaoh would not acknowledge the power invested in Moses. The person who does not find Moses' claims compelling is not considered a neutral party, but rather one whose view of reality prejudicially prevents acknowledgment of what is plainly evident. Even if the miracles are not absolute proof that God's power is invested in Moses, they constitute overwhelming evidence that it is so. The unreasonableness of Pharaoh's actions is described as being stubborn (or hardened). Similarly, the Evangelist ascribes the denial of Jesus' power to blindness (John 12:37–40).

LABAHN ON MIRACLES AS GROUNDS FOR BELIEF IN JESUS

Labahn thinks that miracles may lead to a perception of Jesus' glory, but warns that they "can also lead to a misunderstanding and a defective or unreal belief."[65] He says that belief from signs comes only when the *doxa* of Jesus is perceived in the sign. For Labahn, this means that the high Christology of the Gospel's prologue must be seen in the miracle. He says, "The one who understands the miracle only as a miraculous deed does not grasp the theological and christological depth of the *semeion*."[66] If we look at the characters' perception of this *doxa*, it is not evident that Jesus' deity is consciously perceived. The disciples do see Jesus' glory (John 2:11, cf. John 1:14) at Cana in the miracle, but do they recognize it as God's glory or are they like Phillip, who in Jesus has seen the Father, but doesn't realize it? The woman of Samaria does see Jesus as a great Messiah, but perhaps not as more.

Labahn, like Byrne, sees a strong call to faith for the reader "in the light of the Johannine characters taking part in these conflict stories."[67] He says, "With the help of the compositional order of the miracle stories and the various signals to guide the reader, the Fourth Evangelist tries to lead the implied reader into making a decision for the Son of God (cf., e.g., 4:48; 6:6)."[68]

LINCOLN ON THE VALIDITY OF TESTIMONY

Given the Evangelist's historical claims about specific miracles, it is appropriate to consider again the validity of testimony as grounds for belief. Andrew T. Lincoln has an important review of recent scholarship on the critical use of testimony. The problem Lincoln outlines is that the Gospel requires its testimony to be accepted, while critical scholarship has often insisted that, "valid knowledge is only knowledge discovered by people for themselves."[69] Lincoln argues for the possibility of actual knowledge arising

---

65. Labahn, "Tradition and Literary Art," 189.
66. Ibid.
67. Ibid., 181.
68. Ibid., 202.
69. Lincoln, *Truth on Trial*, 355.

from testimony. He notes in particular an insightful study by Coady[70] in which it is demonstrated that "reliance upon testimony is as fundamental to the justification of belief as perception, memory, and inference are"[71] so that even "the individual historian has to rely on the observational and empirical experience of many other people."[72] Lincoln summarizes Coady's view of history as saying that "in practice there will often be reasons to think particular witnesses are untrustworthy in particular respects but their cross-examination and sometimes rejection will take place within a framework that recognizes the vital nature of testimony for historical knowledge, and is initially positive, rather than skeptical, toward its value."[73] It is evident that without an "initially" positive view, we would never know anything by testimony, so this is the proper attitude with which to begin. Lincoln also notes Brueggermann's work on the idea of testimony in the Old Testament. Lincoln characterizes this work as calling for "a break with positivistic epistemology and a different attitude to certitude."[74] This is relevant to John's epistemology because he draws his conception of knowledge largely from the Old Testament.

The value of both testimony and the critical judgment of testimony are similarly advocated by the Evangelist. This is to be expected because he writes in a polemic environment in which he cannot simply expect his audience to believe him because he makes a claim. An audience who believes everyone will believe the Evangelist's opponents as well. Instead, the Evangelist accepts a certain reserve in the judgment of those who are considering his claims. He does not protest against the Samaritans who withhold belief until they hear Jesus' own words (John 4:39–42). He does not criticize the Pharisees for demanding testimony from the blind man's parents that their son was really born blind (John 9). Yet he does not criticize people for believing on the basis of miracles as evidence. Rather he repeats the miracle claims in his gospel to evoke such belief, and even claims that this is his purpose for including the miracles. Jesus even acknowledges some validity in the need for critical judgment of his own claims, saying, "if I bear witness about (περί) myself, my testimony is not true" (John 5:31). Similarly, Jesus says "If I do not do the works of my Father, do not believe me, but if I do them, though you do not believe me, believe the works, that you may know and understand that the Father is in me, and I in the Father" (John 10:37–38). Indeed, it is the credulousness of his opponents that Jesus criticizes, saying "I have come in my Father's name, and you do not receive me; if another shall come in his own name, you will receive him" (John 5:43). As Lincoln indicates, the claim for the autonomy of human reasoning over authentic testimony is illusory, and the unreasonable denial of authentic testimony will lead to dependence upon sources of knowledge that are even less reliable than testimony.[75]

---

70. Coady, *Testimony*.
71. Lincoln, *Truth on Trial*, 359.
72. Ibid., 361.
73. Ibid.
74. Ibid., 363.
75. Ibid., 367.

CHAPTER CONCLUSIONS: SIGNS AS A GROUND FOR BELIEF IN JESUS

Drawing from and critiquing this diversity of scholarly views, a more coherent picture has emerged, showing the way that John uses miracles as grounds for belief. John has a favorable idea of the relation of signs to belief in Jesus. Based on the arguments made earlier, the following conclusions can be made about the Evangelist's views. Against McCasland, the Evangelist thinks that belief in Jesus is limited by human failings, not by the nature of signs. The inadequacy of miraculous signs to evoke from everyone alike a continuing belief in Jesus is regarded by the Evangelist as due to the faulty character of individual people, not due to any inherent deficiency in the evidential value of signs. This is a theme that the Evangelist adopts from the Old Testament Exodus traditions. It was not because of any inherent deficiency in the value of signs that Jesus did not always use signs to attract followers. Similarly, Jesus did not always speak, but this does not make his words an inadequate basis for belief. Against Hindley, it was argued that the Evangelist did not regard miracles as capable of compelling people to believe in Jesus, but only to believe that a miracle occurred. Further, it was argued that miracles could be a proper ground of faith, provided other conditions are already satisfied. These conditions would include knowledge that Jesus adhered to the laws of Moses, and that he had a credible message and credible claims. It was further argued that the signs of Jesus cannot be separated from their miraculous character, since this is essential to making the sign a sign. It was the miraculous character of the signs which particularly revealed Jesus' divine authority, mediated a divine gift, and which served as the pledge of a divine promise. It was also argued that these signs have a public character, and that the signs, as signs, are visible to all alike. Again, John adopts this view of the public character of signs from the Old Testament Exodus traditions. Though in a more familiar sense Jesus' followers alone know him, even Jesus' opponents are thought by John to have seen and known Jesus well enough to hate him. The knowledge of Jesus and God, which is given through the signs and other testimony, is sufficient to justify genuine belief in Jesus. Jesus has revealed God, not merely to those who believe in him, but to the world, thus eliminating any essential need for private internal revelation. This eliminates the problem of determining what the content of such internal revelation might be. The miracles tell all people alike more than just the bare fact that God has acted. They show that Jesus is a prophet and teacher from God. As Hindley indicates, the reader is asked by John to decide, along with each character in the Gospel, in favor of belief in Jesus. The signs and words of Jesus, his claims and apologetic, are offered to the reader just as they are offered to the other characters, as sufficient grounds to believe. As Fortna indicates, Jesus denounced setting, as a condition for believing in Jesus, the requirement of seeing miracles. Faith arising from acceptance of the Evangelist's testimony about miracles is not criticized; in practice the wonders are never seen by themselves, but in the context of Jesus' performance of them. The significance or meaning of the signs rests in Jesus' revelation in them as the Son of God. Perhaps going beyond Fortna, this revelation of Jesus is not separate from the miraculous element in the signs, or from their character as a historical gift and promise. In John's thought, disbelief in the miraculous element of the signs precludes belief in the

John's Use of Miracles as Grounds for Belief in Jesus

sign. A request for a miracle is not improper, provided it is not a mere test of power, but requested to meet a genuine need. In the discussion with Freed, it was pointed out that believing in Jesus is not identical to every kind of belief, such as believing that Jesus can perform miracles. The object of belief must be made clear to avoid confusion. The Signs traditions are included in John because he accepts signs as a reason to believe, and as a valid way to persuade his readers to believe. Against Freed, the spiritual meaning of the miracles is not separate from the physical miracle, but is communicated through them. Beyond Meier's views, the mere observance of miracles is not dependent upon holding to any particular religious orientation or belief. The decision not to acknowledge Jesus' miracles was considered by John to be an unreasonable act, just as the miracles of the Exodus traditions are considered by those traditions to demand acknowledgment by the nation of Egypt.

We have been careful to found this basic understanding of John's epistemology upon the Evangelist's essential historical claim about Jesus miracles, and not upon any separate historical claim about any particular words of Jesus in John's Gospel. Epistemological claims by John cannot be understood apart from a clear identification of the statements that are to be taken as nonfiction and historical. Since the Johannine vocabulary and Christology are distinctive, and many have expressed doubt about the historical and nonfictional character of the words of Jesus in this Gospel, it is unnecessary at this point of our argument to rely upon the historicity of Jesus' words in John's Gospel as a basis for understanding John's epistemology. For our purposes here, we only need to know that the Evangelist believed that Jesus did have a message, and that the signs bore witness to Jesus' identity as a teacher from God and to his message. This is the same understanding of miracles found in Jewish monotheism.

Admittedly, this gives a restricted view of the miracles in John's Gospel. The miracles typically function as a staging ground for narrative that will persuade the reader to believe in Jesus. The first miracle results in the disciples coming to faith (John 2:11), which is given as an example to the reader. The narrative about the healing of the official's son teaches the reader not to demand "seeing for oneself" as a condition for trust in Jesus (John 4:46–53). Such a demand is considered unreasonable, when there is already reasonable evidence for trust. The healing at Bethesda becomes the setting for a defense of Jesus' Sabbath miracles as works by God, and for a declaration and defense of Jesus' high status as God's agent (John 5). The loaves that were multiplied are reminiscent to the multitude of the manna given under Moses, leading to their request for manna, and to Jesus' claim to be the bread that gives eternal life (John 6). In the healing of the blind man, the opposition of the religious leaders to the evidence of the miracles is also set forth. The lesson to the reader is that the blind are those who refuse to reasonably acknowledge God's miracles attesting to Jesus, and so remain in their sin (John 9). At the raising of Lazarus, Jesus declares himself to be the resurrection and life, the one in whom all should hope (John 11). Jesus' own resurrection appearance becomes a proclamation that he is "my lord and my God" (John 20:28). About half the miracles are themselves used symbolically. But it is only by associated teachings that this extended symbolism of the miracles is set forth, the miracle alone does not communicate the fuller meaning.

While the multiplied loaves (and heavenly manna) can support the natural life, Jesus is the bread from heaven that gives eternal life. Lazarus' resurrection is only back into mortal life, but Jesus is the continuing source of and promise of eternal life.

In response, one further argument might be raised. The Evangelist himself comments that in the first miracle Jesus "made his glory appear" (John 2:11). The reference to Jesus' glory (rather than "God's glory") appearing in this miracle alludes to the Evangelist's earlier comment that "the word became flesh and dwelt-in-a-tent (ἐσκήνωσεν) among us, and we beheld his glory" (John 1:14). Just as "the glory of the LORD filled the tent (σκηνή)" (Exod 40:34 LXX), so the glory of God appeared in flesh. This might be thought to show that some kind of direct perception of God's glory in the miracles gives, to the Evangelist's mind, a knowledge of God.

This argument for direct knowledge does not seem to hold up under examination. The glory of God does appear in miracles, but this means that the miracles of Moses and Elijah also genuinely revealed the glory of God. Even though Jesus' glory is manifested in the wedding miracle, the disciples themselves do not seem to consciously recognize the glory of God as Jesus' glory. Jesus later says to Philip, "Have I been so long with you and yet you have not come to know me Philip? He who has seen me has seen the Father" (John 14:9). For these reasons it is difficult to be sure that the miracles alone, apart from Jesus' words, should be used as a basis for claiming more about John's epistemology of miracles.

This approach of using the evidence of miracles alone, apart from any trust in Jesus' claims, follows the Gospel's saying, "If I do not do the works of my Father, do not believe me, but if I do them, though you do not believe me, believe the works, that you may know and understand that the Father is in me, and I in the Father" (John 10:37–38). This is the perspective of Jesus toward his opponents, a perspective that John therefore implicitly advocates. By the miracles alone, without otherwise knowing that Jesus' claims are true, people can know something objective about Jesus and God. By the miracles alone, some of the Evangelist's epistemology of belief can consequently be identified. Although the Evangelist considers this evidence incomplete, he considers it to be at least a proper beginning. Belief that the miracles occurred is not identical to belief in Jesus, but tends to evoke such faith.

Once the divine origin of the miracles is conceded, Jesus' words can no longer be so easily disregarded. Yet following the Evangelist's own priorities, it is evident that belief in some of Jesus' words in this Gospel is of more importance than belief in other words. It is not necessary to assume that these words of Jesus that elaborate on the meaning of the miracles are of the first importance. To understand the Evangelist's idea of the grounds for believing Jesus' words requires a different argument, to which we next turn.

10

The Essential Words of Jesus as Nonfiction in the Gospel of John

OUR PREVIOUS DISCUSSION FOCUSED on the way that John set forth miracles as a basis for belief in Jesus, and on the epistemological implications of evoking belief on this basis. This discussion was based in turn on an extended argument that the miracles of Jesus are set forth in John's Gospel as essentially miraculous and essentially nonfictional. In other words, the Evangelist regards them as genuine historical miracles, not as symbols only. The claim here was not that the miracle accounts are historically reliable, but rather that the Evangelist so regards them, or so portrays them to his readers. In contrast, several scholars have regarded John's miracles as possibly being a literary fiction. If the miracles are regarded as fiction, the accompanying dialogues are also likely to be regarded as fiction. Fiction provides an uncertain basis for determining the Evangelist's idea of how one can have knowledge. It was necessary to establish the nonfictional character of the miracles, before discussing how the accompanying dialogues or sayings of Jesus can be regarded as nonfiction, and as grounds for belief.

The Evangelist, however, does not regard the miracles of Jesus as the only ground, or even the primary ground, for belief in Jesus. Jesus says, "Believe me that I am in the Father and the Father in me; otherwise believe on account of the works themselves" (John 14:11). In this saying, Jesus refers to miracles as a merely secondary basis for belief, a basis that is not strictly necessary. In the Evangelist's mind, Jesus' credibility stands independently of the miracles. This credibility rests on several factors. However, it will be simplest to look first at the way that the Evangelist thinks that Jesus' essential message provides an independent basis for belief in Jesus. Jesus says, "If I had not come and spoken to them, they would not have sin, but now they have no excuse for their sin" (John 15:22). The Evangelist sets forth the message of Jesus, even apart from the miracles, as sufficient reason for people to believe in Jesus and turn to God. This message, along with certain implicit claims, such as Jesus' status as a righteous Jew, is set forth as a basis for belief that is separate from miracles.

THE EPISTEMOLOGICAL BASIS FOR BELIEF ACCORDING TO JOHN'S GOSPEL

VARIOUS VIEWS ABOUT HISTORICITY AND FICTION IN JOHN'S GOSPEL

There has been a considerable history of argument about the message of Jesus in John's Gospel. As we shall discuss below, many have argued that the Gospel is substantially unhistorical, without any credible historical tradition that is independent of the Synoptic Gospels. Various views have consequently arisen about the extent to which the Gospel is fictional. A few have declared explicitly that the Gospel is substantially fictional, but more have simply left an implicit doubt that any part of the Gospel, including Jesus' message, could be confidently regarded as nonfictional. In 1820, Karl Gottlieb Bretschneider argued, "It is accordingly quite impossible that both the Jesus of the [first] three Gospels and that of the Fourth can at the same time be historically true, . . . but it is quite believable that the author of the Fourth Gospel could have created his Jesus."[1] James Drummond wrote of Bretschneider's work, "all the main lines of attack are already laid down, and the conclusion is reached that the Gospel was fraudulently written by a Gentile in the name of John in the beginning or middle of the second century."[2] Drummond notes further that, there were "a number of replies, and Bretschneider himself retracted his objections."[3] Although Bretschneider retracted his views, David F. Strauss and Ferdinand C. Baur took up the arguments again. Kümmel says that in Baur's view the Gospel of John, "is also dismissed as a source of no consequence for the history of Jesus, without thereby ceasing to be the 'witness of a genuine evangelical spirit.'"[4] Here Baur may vaguely be alluding to the authentic essence of Jesus' message, yet there is no clear limit to the extent of fiction. Arguments for and against the historicity of John's Gospel were set forth throughout the nineteenth century. In C. H. Dodd's assessment, "The debate over 'the historicity of the Fourth Gospel' had pretty well reached a position of deadlock by the opening decade of the twentieth century. All the important arguments had been canvassed; only minor points could be added."[5]

Dodd's *Historical Tradition in the Fourth Gospel* offered new arguments that this Gospel contains independent historical tradition. For example, Dodd argued that the Old Testament scriptures cited by John are of the same character as scriptures cited in the other Gospels. He wrote, ". . . the Johannine body of testimonies provides the *same* key as the other forms of Passion narrative. They do not reflect the interpretation that is peculiar to the Fourth Gospel. For this interpretation he has provided no testimonies out of scripture."[6] Rather than being John's invention, these scriptural testimonia are evidence of an accepted tradition that shaped and controlled John's narrative. The testimonia used by John are not always those best suited for John's purpose. As Dodd observed, "By no means *all* prophecy that was, or could be, regarded as 'messianic' is exploited by writers of the New Testament. . . . large sections of 'messianic' prediction . . . are absent from the

---

1. Bretschneider, *Probabilia*, cited in Kümmel, *New Testament: Problems*, 85–86.
2. Drummond, *Character and Authorship*, 68.
3. Lücke, *Commentar*, cited in Drummond, *Character and Authorship*, 89, 100.
4. Kümmel, *New Testament: Problems*, 137.
5. Dodd, *Historical Tradition*, 3.
6. Ibid., 46–47.

The Essential Words of Jesus as Nonfiction in the Gospel of John

picture of Jesus in the gospels. These traits are either ignored or relegated to prophecies of the future. Not only so, even within those passages which are used as sources for testimonies not every detail is alleged to have been fulfilled."[7] On this basis, it appears that a core of John's narrative is determined by tradition. This at least supports the possibility that the message of Jesus in John's Gospel is also partially controlled by tradition. Dodd concluded that John's Gospel contains an independent tradition that "was shaped (it appears) in a Jewish-Christian environment still in touch with the synagogue, in Palestine, at a relatively early date, at any rate before the rebellion of A.D. 66."[8]

Dodd's argument also invoked other lines of evidence. He cited a number of texts in John's Gospel, which are also paralleled in the Synoptic Gospels, but which have a form that seems more likely to have originated from oral tradition than from the Synoptic parallels. An example of this type is John's saying, "The one loving his life shall lose it, and the one hating his life in this world shall keep it for eternal life" (John 12:25).[9] Dodd also cited parables, which are similar in form to some of the Synoptic parables, but which have no parallel outside of John's Gospel. These include, for example, the parable of the Grain of Wheat (John 12:24) and the parable of the Shepherd and the Thief (John 10:1–6).[10] Dodd further concluded that John "had at his disposal a body of traditional sayings, parables, and dialogues."[11] In Oscar Cullmann's assessment, "there is now a reaction on the part of many very critical New Testament scholars against a systematic exclusion of the Gospel [of John] as a source about the life of Jesus. A reversal has taken place in this respect."[12]

In spite of Dodd's work, the older critical position, which denied the presence of any significant historical tradition in the Gospel, continues to be voiced. Kümmel says, "And, while the Gospel of John cannot be used as a source for the history of Jesus, there can be no question of the historical reliability of the synoptic tradition of Jesus."[13] However, Kümmel does not explain the evidence that Dodd brought against such a blanket assessment. Kümmel's work on the history of New Testament investigation is restricted entirely to scholars who are German, and who worked before 1940, even though Kümmel himself writes a full generation later. In the opinion of Raymond Collins, Dodd, "has been rightly called the leading British New Testament scholar of this century."[14] Kümmel's failure to respond to Dodd's work undermines confidence in Kümmel's assessment.

More recently, Maurice Casey has argued that "the essential historicity of John's Gospel" is "demonstrably false" and this "beyond all reasonable doubt."[15] According to Casey, "The outstanding problem with the critical view has been its failure to explain

7. Ibid., 47–48.
8. Ibid., 426.
9. Ibid., 338.
10. Ibid., 366, 382.
11. Ibid., 430.
12. Cullmann, *The Johannine Circle*, 23.
13. Kümmel, *New Testament: Problems*, 175.
14. Collins, *Introduction to New Testament*, 58.
15. Casey, *Is John's Gospel True?*, 1.

how and why so much secondary material has been attributed to Jesus, particularly when this Gospel has been regarded as the work of one or more eyewitnesses of his ministry."[16] Casey calls this objection "the outstanding problem," and offers a new argument to remove the objection. In this way, he treats the objection as an understandable cause for doubt. But if the objection is understandable, is it not a cause for "reasonable doubt"? This suggests that, in Casey's view, understandable doubt about the falseness of John's essential historicity has only recently become impossible, perhaps impossible only because of Casey's new arguments. Since critics of John's historicity have already made similar claims to certainty over the last century and a half, the claim to have solved an "outstanding problem," only at this late date, requires examination.

As it happens, Casey's arguments are not sufficient to prove his case, for he fails to address all principal opposing arguments. As a prime example, Casey does not offer any detailed explanation of Dodd's evidence for independent historical tradition in John's Gospel. Casey's argument is weakened by his primary dependence upon chronological discrepancies to show that John is essentially unhistorical. Following the view of Dodd, many scholars would recognize an independent underlying tradition that is essentially historical, irrespective of chronological displacements in the Gospel; the historical scope is only reduced by such displacements, not eliminated. It is doubtful that Casey has disproven the "essential historicity" of John's Gospel, until he has substantively answered Dodd's argument for a controlling tradition, especially since the tradition includes both sayings and a pattern of ancient *testimonia*.

Similarly, in Casey's argument for three major chronological displacements in John's Gospel, his arguments are not decisive, because they do not address all major objections. For example, one of Casey's arguments is that, while Mark sets the Last Supper at a Passover Meal, John wrongly sets the Last Supper one day earlier than the Passover. The Passover meal was eaten each year in the night following the fourteenth day of the moon, in the month of Nisan. Casey argues that the change of date originates "from the authors' theological symbolism."[17] This is a proposal that J. Norval Geldenhuys has attributed originally to the Tübingen school under F. C. Baur.[18] Geldenhuys, however, listed 25 modern expositors who had more confidence in the earlier date, and he characterized their position as the majority view among critical scholars.[19] These other expositors typically questioned the plausibility of various events during the Passover Feast, on the grounds that Jewish law strictly forbids work (such as necessary to carry out Jesus' trial and crucifixion) during the Feast (cf. Exod 12:16; Lev 23:7; *m. Pesahim* 4:1, 6). While Casey's date is plausible, he fails to discuss these objections, so it is difficult to take seriously his claim to have decided the issue "beyond reasonable doubt." Casey also includes no discussion of the possibility that different Jews may have observed the

---

16. Ibid., 1–2.

17. Ibid., 25.

18. Geldenhuys, *Gospel of Luke*, 649.

19. Ibid., 650, 657. Expositors cited include Dibelius, Burkitt, Howard, Streeter, Sanday, Taylor, Moffatt, Hoskyns, and Manson. Geldenhuys himself does not accept the earlier date, but summarizes the views of Zahn and J. B. Lightfoot in favor of a different reading of John's chronology.

Passover on different days, at least for that year. Matthew Black has stated, "we can be certain that the Qumran sectarians or Essenes . . . did celebrate the Passover in the year of the Crucifixion at a different time from the official time promulgated by the Jerusalem Temple authorities."[20] Casey's failure to address all the plausible alternative explanations undermines confidence in the conclusiveness of his argument.

Even though Casey argues that John's Gospel is not historical, he sometimes supports the nonfictional character of the Gospel. In support of the Johannine date of the crucifixion, many expositors have noted the strong second century tradition attesting a celebration on the Passover (14 Nisan) by churches in Asia Minor, to celebrate Jesus' crucifixion as the new paschal sacrifice.[21] Casey himself says, "It is possible that this tradition is significantly older than the final composition of the fourth Gospel."[22] However, if the Evangelist is using an older tradition, then the Evangelist does not regard this tradition as a fiction, nor his dating of the Crucifixion as fictional. Rather, John regards his chronology as historical—even if he should be mistaken in thinking so.

In view of all this, Schnackenburg's assessment of the state of the debate about fiction in the Fourth Gospel remains pertinent. He says, "There is a big difference therefore between the two approaches. One holds definitely that the discourses of Jesus in John have been freely (and consciously) invented as 'discourses of Christ.' The other holds that according to the intention of the evangelist they are discourses of Jesus, which have indeed passed through the medium of faith." [23] This latter position holds that the Evangelist believes the discourses are, in an essential respect, authentic discourses by Jesus, even if the substance of Jesus' own message is expressed in the vocabulary and understanding of the Evangelist.

Our argument here will not be that Jesus' essential message, as given in John's Gospel, is actually historically reliable, but rather that the Evangelist considers it to be so. The Evangelist, consequently, sets forth this message as nonfiction, and as a message that the reader will identify as nonfiction. Fiction provides an uncertain basis for determining the Evangelist's idea of how one can have knowledge, for it may not fully reflect the Evangelist's real ideas about how one has knowledge in the real world. We will therefore attempt to identify the essential nonfictional message of the Evangelist. On this basis we will discuss his epistemology.

THE ESSENTIAL NONFICTIONAL MESSAGE OF JOHN

Where the Evangelist promotes a message that causes characters in his Gospel to turn away from Jesus, the message is meant as nonfiction. A driving evangelistic and polemic purpose of the Evangelist is to promote belief in Jesus. Essential nonfictional claims about Jesus are necessary to evoke belief in Jesus; fiction alone cannot evoke such belief. John would not confuse his message by representing people as turning away from Jesus

---

20. Black, *Scrolls and Christian Origins*, 200–201; cited in Morris, *Gospel According to John*, 694.
21. Eusebius, *Ecclesiastical History*, 5.24.6 (NPNF2 1:242).
22. Casey, *Is John's Gospel True?*, 25.
23. Schnackenburg, *Gospel According to St John*, 1:23–24.

because of a fictional message, or because of the Evangelist's fictional embellishment or invention. Rather, such an offensive message is meant as a nonfictional claim about Jesus, a claim that the characters and readers together are encouraged to accept.

John must regard such divisive messages, not only as nonfiction, but also as ultimately essential to his proclamation, essential to authentic belief in Jesus. Where John represents people as turning away from Jesus because of Jesus' message, this cannot mean that the people turn away because they do not understand Jesus correctly. Were that so, they might be won back by a simple explanation, for they would have turned away only because of a misunderstanding; at heart, they would not really have rejected Jesus. However, for the Evangelist, this turning away from Jesus shows how "people loved darkness rather than light." The perverse character of this decision hinges on the people having a genuine understanding of Jesus' message and of Jesus. The Evangelist's natural concern would be that people genuinely turn away from Jesus, and this is what he portrays. Consequently, John's true *kerygma*, or proclamation, is to be found particularly in the messages that John promotes, even though they cause such offense that characters or readers turn away from belief in Jesus.

A survey of the Gospel of John shows that it promotes the following messages that cause people to turn from Jesus. While the messages may embody John's interpretation of the essential kerygmatic tradition, the Evangelist is convinced that his interpretation is essential to that tradition, rather than a secondary imposition or innovation. The messages are, in his thought, essential for authentic belief in Jesus:

1. **Essential Message**: Jesus claims that God is distinctively his own Father. By this, Jesus claims to be the Son of God, God's full representative on earth. (As Raymond Brown remarks, citing 2 Samuel 7:14, *Son of God* is one of those titles "that do not in themselves imply divinity," however a "more exalted use of the title," indicating divinity, is also possible.)[24]

    1.1. *Texts with this Message*: Jesus "was calling God his own Father, making himself equal with God" (John 5:18). In response to Jewish objections, Jesus says that his authority is entirely derivative (John 5:19–30) since "the Son can do nothing of himself" (John 5:19) and since "the Father" is the one "who sent him" (John 5:23). Jesus also notes that the Father supports Jesus' claim to be the Son in two ways: by miracles (John 5:36) and by scripture (John 5:37–47). Jesus also confesses that true glory comes from "the only God" (John 5:44). Jesus also says, "Do you say of him, whom the Father sanctified and sent into the world, 'You are blaspheming,' because I said, 'I am the Son of God'?" (John 10:36).

    1.2. *People offended*: Those Jews who "were seeking all the more to kill him" (John 5:18). Jews who "were seeking again to seize him" (John 10:39).

---

24. Brown, *Community of the Beloved Disciple*, 25. The adjuration at Jesus' trial, requiring him to declare whether he is the "Son of God" (Matt 26:63; Mark 14:61), may have been intended to evoke the kind of response Jesus gave, which the council declared to be blasphemy, and which formed the basis for their sentence. This suggests that a "more exalted use" of the title was in mind. The particular sense of the title must be determined by context.

1.3. *Meaning of the texts*: The claim to be God's Son draws from Messianic language used about the Son of David. "I will be a Father to him, and he will be a son to Me" (2 Sam 7:14; cf. Ps 2:7,12). The associated claims over all mankind (to judge and give life) may draw from ideas about the Son of Man found in Dan 7:13–14. Jesus claims a status equal to God in this sense: that God has made Jesus His representative, to wield the supernatural power of God over the natural world, death, and life, and to wield full authority to judge how life and death are to be dispensed. This is so even though this authority and power is entirely derivative from God, and even though in his judgment of humanity Jesus obeys only the Father's will.

2. **Essential Message**: Jesus says that his own life (e.g. Jesus' incarnate life) is the only means by which eternal life is given to us.

2.1. *Texts with this Message*: ". . . as I live because of the Father, so he who eats me, he also shall live because of me" (John 6:57); ". . . he who believes has eternal life . . . the bread also which I shall give for the life of the world is my flesh" (John 6:47,51); ". . . an hour is coming and now is, when the dead shall hear the voice of the Son of God; and those who hear shall live. For just as the Father has life in himself, even so he gave to the Son to have life in himself" (John 5:25–26); "Truly, truly, I say to you, if anyone keeps my word, he shall never see death" (John 8:51).

2.2. *People offended*: Disciples who don't walk with Jesus anymore. "As a result of this, many disciples withdrew, and were not walking with him anymore" (John 6:66). Jesus' opponents similarly say, "Now we know that you have a demon. Abraham died, and the prophets; and you say, 'If anyone keeps my word, he shall never taste of death.' Surely you are not greater than our father Abraham, who died? The prophets died too; whom do you make yourself out to be?" (John 8:52–53).

2.3. *Meaning of the texts*: Life comes to all people from Jesus, just as his own life comes in turn from the Father. One mode of this dispensing of life is through Jesus' sacrificial death. However, John's interest is in the broader underlying principle of why Christ's death becomes a means of life; John finds this source in the divine life already within Jesus. This is evident, for example, in the prologue's saying, "All things came into being by him, and apart from him nothing came into being that has come into being. In him was life, and the life was the light of men" (John 1:3,4). Whether this life is held as a future promise (cf. John 3:36; 7:38–39), or is instead a possession offered at the moment when Jesus speaks, it is a sharing of Jesus' life. Calvin says that John 6 speaks of "the perpetual eating of faith" which is also "figured and actually presented to believers in the Lord's Supper. . . . This is also the reason why John makes no mention of the Lord's Supper."[25]

3. **Essential Message**: Jesus says that he is in the Father and the Father is in him, as proven by this: Jesus' miracles are his Father's miracles.

---

25. Calvin, *Gospel of John*, 1: 170, cited in Ridderbos, *The Gospel of John, A Theological Commentary*, 237.

3.1. *Texts with this message*: "believe the works, that you may know and understand that the Father is in me, and I in the Father" (John 10:38).

3.2. *People offended*: "The Jews took up stones again to stone him.... They were seeking again to seize him" (John 10:31,39).

3.3. *Meaning of the texts*: Again, the derivative character of Jesus' power means that this text is not making Jesus into another god, but is declaring that God in his full power is acting through Jesus, so that they act as one, which means that God is fully present in Jesus. By doing the Father's works, Jesus justifies his claim that "I and the Father are one" (John 10:30).

4. **Essential Message**: God authorized Jesus' baptism of others (by the hand of Jesus' disciples).

4.1. *Supporting Texts*: "... behold, he is baptizing, and all are coming to him. John answered '... He must increase, but I must decrease'" (John 3:26,30); "although Jesus himself was not baptizing, but his disciples were" (John 4:2); "Jesus answered, 'Truly, truly, I say to you, unless one is born of water and the Spirit, he cannot enter into the kingdom of God'" (John 3:5).

4.2. *People Offended*: This is implicit in the earlier rejection of John's baptism, "Why then are you baptizing, if you are not the Christ, nor Elijah, nor the Prophet?" (John 1:25). Also, "Unless one is born of water and the spirit, he cannot enter into the kingdom of God" (John 3:5). The reference of this second saying may not be limited to baptism, but it includes baptism. John refers to Baptism as purification (John 3:25; cf. Exod 19:10).

4.3. *Meaning of the Message*: Jesus' opponents rejected the practice of baptism, as though it were a new rite that was unauthorized by God. Nevertheless, this rite was normatively required by Jesus to be observed. Strictly speaking, it was the practice of baptism that caused offense, not the declaration that it should be practiced. However it is included here as an indication of Jesus' thought which was maintained even though considered offensive.

5. **Essential Message**: Jesus said that he existed in heaven before his birth in this world, and said he was destined to return there.

5.1. *Supporting Texts*: Jesus existed before his birth: Jesus says, "before Abraham was, I am" (John 8:58); "Does this cause you to stumble? What then if you should behold the Son of Man ascending where he was before?" (John 6:61–62). Peter does not only confess that Jesus' message is a message from God, but confesses further that Jesus himself is God's appointed messenger, saying to Jesus "you have the words of eternal life," and saying that Jesus is "the holy one of God" (John 6:68–69; cf. Mark 1:24, where this title is acknowledged by a demon). John says that the light has come into the world (John 1:9; 3:19; 8:12; 9:5; 12:46). The idea of Jesus' preexistence is even repeated by John the Baptist (John 1:15,30).

5.2. *People Offended*: "'Does this cause you to stumble?' . . . many of his disciples withdrew and were not walking with him anymore" (John 6:61, 66); "Jesus therefore said to the twelve, 'You do not want to go away also, do you?' Simon Peter answered him, 'Lord to whom shall we go?'" (John 6:67–68).

5.3. *Meaning of the text*: Jesus came to earth from a prior existence in heaven.

6. **Essential Message**: Jesus shares in the divine nature of God.

6.1. *Supporting Texts*: Jesus existed before his birth: Jesus says, "before Abraham was, I am" (John 8:58). Jesus is the divine word made flesh (John 1:1, 14).

6.2. *People Offended*: "Therefore they picked up stones to throw at him, but Jesus hid himself and went out of the temple" (John 8:59).

6.3. *Meaning of the texts*: As a punishment for blaspheming the name of God, the Law of Moses required that "the congregation shall certainly stone" the guilty party (Lev 24:16). Blasphemy did not always include a reference to the divine name itself, but could be any claim to an honor belonging only to God. For example, we read that to "make yourself God" is blasphemy (John 10:33). Jesus' opponents evidently regard his claim (John 8:58) as blaspheming, since they are preparing to stone him. Consequently, most scholars have understood Jesus' words "before Abraham was, I am" as a reference either to the divine name (Exod 3:14), or to the divine claim "I am he" in Isaiah (e.g., Isa 41:4; 43:10).[26] Since the Evangelist says, "before Abraham was, I am" rather than "before Abraham was, I was," it is evident that this is not a simple claim to preexistence. The Evangelist would not have used language that others found offensive, unless it were essential to his message, since to do so turned people away from Jesus. Consequently, the offensive features, especially the allusion to the name or identity of God, are essential to John's message. This offensiveness is here portrayed as the first impression upon Jesus' hearers, which is why they wish to condemn him for blasphemy. Although the charge of blasphemy is soon abandoned, this may be because Jesus' language is intentionally phrased with insufficient clarity to be proven blasphemous in a court of law. Similarly, we read the later complaint, "If you are the Christ, tell us plainly" (John 10:24). The essential message is therefore Jesus' claim to be, not only greater than Abraham and the one who can annul death, but one who somehow shares in the divine nature of the one God.

7. **Essential Message**: Jesus' call for obedience to himself, must be followed. The requirements for obedience to Jesus are known to the Evangelist, and to his readers. This would include the commandment that his disciples "love one another."

7.1. *Supporting texts*: "He who does not obey the Son shall not see life." (John 3:36) Jesus says, "If you love me, you will keep my commandments . . . . He who has my commandments and keeps them, he it is who loves me; and he who loves me

---

26. Ridderbos, *The Gospel of John*, 322. For the literature and discussion, see Ball, *"I Am" in John's Gospel*. See also Williams, *I am He*, and Bauckham, *God Crucified*.

shall be loved by my Father, and I will love him, and will disclose myself to him" (John 14:15, 21). "If anyone loves me, he will keep my word . . . He who does not love me does not keep my words . . . (John 14:23–24). "If you keep my commandments, you will abide in my love, just as I have kept my Father's commandments and abide in his love" (John 15:10–11). "This I command you, that you love one another" (John 15:17).

7.2. *People offended*: "You seek to kill me, because my word has no place in you" (John 8:37). "He who does not love me does not keep my words" (John 14:24).

7.3. *Meaning of the texts*: Since John considered it essential to his message that everyone follow the way of life commanded by Jesus, he must either have communicated this way to his audience, or believe that they know the way. John himself observes this way of life, so he knows this way. In his view the authentic tradition has always been regarded as essential, and so this way of life has been handed down from the beginning.

The following can also be included as an essential message of the Evangelist, although it is strictly only a particular facet of all John's essential messages:

8. Essential Message: In John's mind, the essential messages listed in the above headings do not arise from the innovation or misunderstanding of either the Evangelist or the Church. Instead, they were (at least implicitly) parts of the authentic essential message proclaimed by Jesus, a message that gives eternal life.

8.1. *Supporting Texts*: Jesus says, "The words that I have spoken to you are spirit and are life" (John 6:63); Peter says to Jesus, "you have the words of eternal life" (John 6:68–69); Jesus says, "If anyone keeps my word, he shall never see death" (John 8:51). The Evangelist says that Jesus is the "light that has come into the world" (John 1:9; 3:19; 8:12; 9:5; 12:46). Jesus says, "He who rejects me, and does not receive my sayings, has one who judges him; the word I spoke is what will judge him at the last day" (John 12:48). Jesus says, "For the words which you gave me, I have given to them; and they received them . . ." (John 17:8).

8.2. *People Offended*: In the essential messages cited above, people turn away from Jesus specifically because he himself proclaims teachings that the people do not accept.

8.3. *Meaning of the texts*: Any message that Jesus did not teach, at least implicitly, cannot be an essential expression of his authentic proclamation. John cannot plausibly have thought that his *kerygma* was not essential in the time of Jesus, or that Jesus preached a message that did not include (at least implicitly) John's *kerygma*. John believes that his *kerygma* is an authentic expression of the kerygmatic tradition handed down to him. John's *kerygma* cannot be a new revelation by the Holy Spirit at the time of the Gospel's writing, for a new *kerygma* would mean that the historical *kerygma* of Jesus was incapable of giving eternal life.

In summary, the essential message of Jesus includes the following: Jesus is the Son of God, God's full representative on earth, and God, in turn, is distinctively Jesus' own

Father. Jesus' own life (e.g., Jesus' incarnate life) is the only means by which eternal life is given to people. Jesus is in the Father and the Father is in him, as proven by this: Jesus' miracles are his Father's miracles. God authorized Jesus to baptize others (by the hand of Jesus' disciples). Jesus existed in heaven before his birth in this world, and was destined to return there. Jesus somehow shares in the divine nature of God. Jesus called people to obey him, and he must be followed. The requirements for obedience to Jesus are known to the Evangelist, and to his readers. This includes the commandment that his disciples "love one another."

OBSERVATIONS ABOUT JOHN'S ESSENTIAL MESSAGE

As outlined above, the Evangelist regards each part of this message as essential to hold, even if it means that some people will consequently turn away from Jesus. The Evangelist also declares that his own message is essentially the same as the message that Jesus proclaimed. The offense of John's message cannot be attributed solely to John's use of an innovative form of expression, as though the authentic core of the message was, in contrast, not offensive. Where John's form of the message is the primary cause of offense, the Evangelist regards this form as essential to any authentic expression of the message.

It is not plausible to suppose that John held to his controversial kerygmatic teaching lightly, rather than as an essential aspect of Christian faith and Christian communion. John's distinctive Christological emphasis must have been particularly offensive to many Jews of his time, just as he portrays Jews of Jesus' time being offended. Casey acknowledges that "Jewish allegations of blasphemy" within the Gospel reflect the "real historical events" arising from the proclamation of John's Christology during the later time when the Gospel was written.[27] The teaching that offends Jesus' opponents in the Gospel was one that many Jewish readers would find offensive, yet the Evangelist does not soften his claims. Since the claims that turn characters away from Jesus would also turn away some readers, the Evangelist's inclusion of these divisive messages also shows that he considers the messages essential to authentic belief in Jesus.

The seriousness of the Evangelist toward his distinctive *kerygma* is evident also in the way he judges even Jesus' disciples by their response. At one point the Evangelist portrays, not just Jesus' opponents, but also many of Jesus' own disciples, as those who do not walk with Jesus any longer. They leave because they do not accept the teaching that Jesus is the bread of life, come from heaven (John 6:61, 66). John says their departure from the Christian community was inevitable, "for Jesus knew from the beginning who they were who did not believe" (John 6:64). In contrast, John claims Peter and the rest of the twelve (apart from Judas) as adherents of this teaching (John 6:67–71). In effect, John claims that all the true disciples of Jesus, all who would continue to believe, accept this teaching, whether implicitly or explicitly.

Following these and earlier arguments, the above summary of John's essential message, a message we may think of as his essential proclamation or *kerygma*, should be understood as nonfiction. The term *nonfiction* does not mean here that the message was

---

27. Casey, *Is John's Gospel True?*, 2.

historically accurate, but merely that the Evangelist believed it was. The Evangelist considers it essential to authentic belief in Jesus that one regard these essential words of Jesus (in the outline summary above) as true, not as false, fictional, unreliable, or objectionable. The Evangelist portrays people dividing about Jesus, not because only some believe a *fictional* message about Jesus, but because only some believe a *nonfictional* message. It is a nonfictional message for the readers of the Gospel, just as for the characters in the Gospel.

This conclusion about the traditional character of John's *kerygma* is consistent with C. H. Dodd's view of the way that material in the Gospels was formed. Dodd counts it incredible that all authentic tradition about Jesus should have been forgotten, only to be replaced by invented traditions. He proposes instead that there was a "process of selection" from a "wider mass of material," in which "much was dropped which was of no immediate utility for the practical purposes of κήρυγμα [proclamation], διδαχή [teaching], or liturgical worship."[28] Here it is proposed, going beyond Dodd, that the distinctive proclamation (κήρυγμα) which John counted traditional was preserved by John in his Gospel, where it was set forth as nonfiction.

Our argument that John's essential message is entirely nonfiction stands in opposition to the view mentioned above that "the discourses of Jesus in John have been freely (and consciously) invented as 'discourses of Christ.'"[29] The messages in John's discourses are constrained by his *kerygma*, his proclamation, and to this extent his discourses can be neither free nor invented. John cannot consciously regard this *kerygma* as his own invention, for this would be to acknowledge that his *kerygma* is not the *kerygma* of Jesus. Furthermore, if characters were turning from Jesus only because of the way that John's expression of the gospel differs from the form found in the Synoptic Gospels, John could hardly be unaware that it was his own expression of the gospel that was the cause of offense. John regards his *kerygma*, especially in the way it causes offense, as equivalent to Jesus' own proclamation, and as an authentic expression of the *kerygma* that John has received by tradition. Freedom and fiction are not equally possible for the Evangelist at every level of meaning, certainly not at the fundamental level of his *kerygma*.

John's *kerygma* includes important Christological ideas, such as Christ's preexistence, and the idea that Jesus has come from heaven to be the means by which God gives life. These ideas are distinctive features of John's *kerygma*, not explicitly part of Jesus' *kerygma* as we know it in the Synoptic Gospels. Jesus' *kerygma* can be epitomized there in the words, "The time is now fulfilled, and the kingdom of God is at hand. Repent, and believe in the good news" (Mark 1:15). This is an indication of the difference from John's perspective.

---

28. Dodd, *Historical Tradition*, 216.

29. Schnackenburg, *Gospel According to John*, 1: 23–24. This is not the view of Schnackenburg, but is his characterization of the view.

VIEWS ON THE NONFICTIONAL QUALITY OF JOHN'S ESSENTIAL MESSAGE

Not all would agree with this view that nonfiction in John's Gospel extends to such a broad reading of his essential *kerygma*. The Christological claims in particular have been questioned. Some have claimed that John's *kerygma*, as outlined and summarized above, must have been an innovation, made either by the Evangelist, or by a circle of Christians from whom he drew his ideas. We have already noted Kümmel's claim (following F. C. Baur) about John's Gospel, that "in relation to the Synoptics it possesses no special historical tradition, but that probably its historical matter is contrived out of the idea of the divine dignity and glory of Jesus. This shows that John has no desire at all to give a historical report, but wants to express an idea."[30] If John's Gospel has "no special historical tradition" as Kümmel says, then the distinctive elements of John's essential *kerygma* must also be read as fiction. The weaknesses of Kümmel's views have already been discussed. However, it will be instructive to consider a few other views of John's Christology, particularly where these include objections to or affirmation of our claim that key elements of John's Christology are part of his nonfictional *kerygma*.

CASEY'S VIEW OF JOHN'S ESSENTIAL MESSAGE

As a recent example of objections to our outline of John's *kerygma*, we may consider the views of Maurice Casey. Casey has disputed John's account (John 5:18–26) that Jesus publicly claimed to be the Son of God. He has consequently disputed John's account that, in Jesus' own time, this claim was a cause for offense at Jesus' message. In particular, Casey denies that Jesus' use of the expression "my Father" in John's Gospel could have been historically authentic, on the grounds that "it never occurs in authentic sayings of Jesus" since, it occurs "never in Mark; in Q, only in . . . the entirely secondary Mt 11.27// Lk 10.22" and is rare "except in the editorial work of Matthew."[31] Casey acknowledges that the expression sometimes occurs in Luke's Gospel as well as in Matthew's and in John's and in the Q material, but judges all these instances to be secondary. Casey then argues more broadly, "Had this been part of Jesus' public preaching, both it and the disputes consequent upon it would have featured in the synoptic Gospels."[32]

However, Casey's claim that Mark never includes the expression "my Father" is misleading. The idea of Jesus' unique sonship is present in Mark's Gospel, even if the exact expression "my Father" is not. Mark writes that Jesus said to the multitude, "For whoever is ashamed of me and my words in this adulterous and sinful generation, the son of man will also be ashamed of him when he comes in the glory of his Father with the holy angels" (Mark 8:38). Here the reference to God as "his Father," while not identical to the phrase "my Father," embodies the same special claim to fatherhood. The claim is made publicly. Jesus claims that he will come "in the glory of" God, which hardly claims less than does the use of the expression "my Father." In another text (Mark 11:25), when addressing his disciples, Jesus refers to "your Father," rather than to "our Father." Jesus

---

30. Kümmel, *New Testament: Problems*, 137.
31. Casey, *Is John's Gospel True?*, 9, 230.
32. Ibid., 9.

also refers to himself as "the Son" when he warns his disciples privately, "But of that day and hour no one knows, not even the angels in heaven, nor the Son, but the Father alone" (Mark 13:32). Mark writes too of a voice from heaven saying, at Jesus' baptism, "You are my beloved son" (Mark 1:11). Jesus also addresses God intimately as "Abba, Father" (Mark 14:36), in a way that is consistent with a unique relationship of sonship. In summary, Mark's Gospel does portray Jesus as Son of God. Mark's Gospel is not, as Casey's claim would suggest, clearly different from the other three canonical Gospels in this respect.

Casey treats the sonship passages in all the canonical Gospels as secondary interpolations by the church, but he never explains how such a pervasive influence on all the canonical Gospels can have originated, or how we can be confident that an authentic tradition about Jesus' message does not underlie this influence. After all, while Paul later persecuted Jesus' followers for religious reasons, with support from Jewish authorities, Jesus himself was condemned to death by the Sanhedrin on the charge of "blasphemy" (Mark 14:64). Jesus' authentic teaching was evidently offensive to the Jewish religious authorities, and this was not only when he was brought to trial.

Casey's case is also weakened by his assumption that reference to God as "my Father" would always be understood as causing disputes.[33] This imposes on the phrase "my Father" an excessive precision and consistency of usage.[34] None of the Evangelists consistently portrays the phrase as openly offensive. Indeed, only John indicates in any context that the phrase "my Father" was offensive (e.g., John 5:18; 10:36; 19:7), and then only offensive to the Jewish religious authorities in Jerusalem, and John's account is the one Casey considers to be the least reliable. Yet even John does not always portray the phrase "my Father" as offensive.

For example, in John's account of the temple cleansing, Jesus publicly refers to "my Father's house." If calling God "my Father" was in itself extraordinarily offensive, we would expect the authorities to object to Jesus' words as blasphemous, or to question him about them. Instead, the authorities are portrayed as asking for proof of his authority to stop the sale of animals in the temple. If Jesus had clearly blasphemed by calling God his Father, the authorities would not even have voiced the possibility that Jesus had such authority. Initial ambiguity is indicated also by D. R. Catchpole's assessment, "the sanhedrin suspected that Jesus made claims to be the Son of God in an unusual sense."[35] The meaning of the expression "my Father" is, in the context of the temple cleansing, too vague to clearly mean anything more than a messianic claim—and not even clearly that in the Evangelist's mind, since Jesus is later asked in this Gospel to *clearly* say whether he claims to be the Messiah (John 10:24). The phrase "my Father" by itself was ambiguous, and could simply mean Messiah, since Hebrew scripture referred to the Messiah as God's son; the phrase was not necessarily considered offensive.[36] Casey imposes a uniform

33. Ibid., 9.
34. See the earlier footnote, with Raymond E. Brown's comment on "Son of God."
35. Catchpole, *The Trial of Jesus*, 141–48, cited in Marshall, *Gospel of Luke*, 851.
36. "He will cry to me, 'You are my Father, my God, and the rock of my salvation'" (Psalm 89:26). "I will surely tell of the decree of the LORD; He said to me, 'You are my son, Today I have begotten you.'" (Psalm

meaning on the expression "my Father" which this passage and John's Gospel as a whole cannot bear, mistaking the Evangelist's language for his meaning. Since Casey's linguistic argument against the authenticity of the phrase "my Father" depends on the assumption that the phrase would always be offensive, his linguistic argument collapses. He is left only with the argument that John sometimes used the phrase in a different sense than the authentic sense found in all the Synoptic Evangelists. However, that argument cannot show that John's sense of the expression is not authentic, but only that the original wording has not been preserved. An authentic expression has been invested with a meaning that it did not originally carry, but this is not surprising if the meaning is authentic and fit the other expression well. Consequently, Casey's linguistic argument against the authenticity of Jesus' claim to be God's Son is not decisive; there remains good reason at least to think that John regarded the claim as authentic, and in turn presented the claim as nonfiction.

SCHNACKENBURG'S VIEW OF JOHN'S ESSENTIAL MESSAGE

Schnackenburg expresses a more restrained objection, made in connection with one of the texts (John 5:18) we have identified above as communicating the Evangelist's essential *kerygma*. Schnackenburg says, "It is likewise hardly possible, in view of the Synoptics, that Jesus should have spoken openly, in front of unbelieving Jews, of the power given him (the Son) to give life and to judge (cf. 5:20–30), though some connection with the 'Son of Man' sayings in the Synoptics cannot be ruled out."[37] Schnackenburg does not detail his reasoning here. Perhaps his concern is that, in John's portrayal, Jesus quite early in his ministry makes statements which are like those that, according to the Synoptic Gospels, evoked his condemnation only later by the Sanhedrin (Mark 14:61–62).

However, the Synoptic Gospels also show a strong affinity toward the conception of Jesus as judge and mediator of life. Schnackenburg does not regard it as historically probable that Jesus "spoke publicly of himself" as mediator, although this is how John's Gospel portrays Jesus.[38] Nevertheless, Schnackenburg acknowledges that, "This role of Jesus as mediator of salvation is indeed presupposed in the Synoptics and (at least according to the faith of the primitive Church) also contained implicitly in the preaching of the Jesus of the Synoptics."[39] The Synoptic role of Jesus as mediator is particularly evident in the Last Supper, where the body and blood of Jesus are offered to his disciples. This symbol of Jesus as the paschal feast goes far beyond the idea that Jesus is a human prophet and a human king. Similarly, Jesus' call to follow himself, rather than merely to accept a message he brings from God, has an affinity to the idea that he stands as a mediator of salvation. These traditions are not innovations of the Synoptic Gospels, but arise from early tradition. If Jesus is understood as the final judge, as we will argue below, this also supports his role as mediator of salvation.

2:2, 7, 12). Hebrews 1:5 cites Psalm 2:7 and 2 Sam 7:14 in regard to Jesus.
   37. Schnackenburg, *Gospel According to John*, 22–23.
   38. Ibid., 22.
   39. Ibid.

Schnackenburg acknowledged a possible connection of a "Son of Man" saying to John's portrait of Jesus, where Jesus claims the power to judge men. A strong candidate for such a saying is Jesus' claim to be the future "son of man sitting at the right hand of power, and coming in the clouds of the heaven" (Dan 7:13,14; Ps 110:1; Mark 14:62 and parallels; cf. Acts 7:56). The Synoptic Evangelists set forth this claim as the basis on which the Sanhedrin justified their condemnation of Jesus under Jewish law. There must have been some reason given for delivering Jesus up to a Roman trial and execution. No other reason is as historically likely to have been used by the Sanhedrin. Although the Sanhedrin had concerns that Jesus would start an unsuccessful rebellion against Rome (e.g. John 11:48), he could not be condemned under Jewish law for deeds he had not yet committed. Condemnation on a religious basis is historically plausible, as evident from the consequent persecution of the politically impotent church by Paul, carried out with the support of Jewish religious authorities (e.g., Acts 9:1, 2; Gal 1:13, 14). Given that the condemnation was based on religious law, the plausibility of Jesus being condemned for blasphemy is supported by the fact that Jesus is condemned by agreement of both Pharisees and Sadducees. These parties had substantial disagreements of their own, but the Pharisees do not see in their support of Jesus' execution (or Stephen's, per Acts 7:56) a threat to their own rights, so Jesus must have been accused of a very grave violation of law, a violation that would also justify his execution. The idea that Jesus claimed to be the final judge thus has a reasonable basis in the tradition underlying the Synoptic Gospels. We will return later to a larger discussion of Christology in the Synoptic Gospels.

In a similar manner, Schnackenburg supposes that Jesus' message about himself, as given in the fourth Gospel, actually originated in John's own interpretation. Schnackenburg says, "historically speaking . . . Jesus never spoke publicly of himself in the way in which he constantly does in John. The self-revelation of Jesus in John . . . stems from a theological interpretation of the evangelist, which must be recognized as such. Whether it is legitimate or not is another question."[40] It is not clear what Schnackenburg means by "the way" that Jesus constantly spoke. In any case, it is precipitous to characterize Jesus' *kerygma* in John's Gospel on the same basis as all his teachings generally. The "way" in which Jesus spoke publicly of himself cannot, when it is the cause of offense, be distinguished from John's essential *kerygma*. John cannot plausibly regard this *kerygma* merely as his own "theological interpretation," nor is it plausible that he could fail to recognize that the larger Christian community did not share his interpretation, to the extent that he considers this interpretation part of his essential *kerygma*. The *kerygma* of John cannot be adequately explained on the same basis as all other sayings in John, as merely "the way" that Jesus speaks in John's Gospel. John's *kerygma* deserves a less superficial explanation.

---

40. Ibid.

BROWN'S VIEW OF JOHN'S ESSENTIAL MESSAGE

Raymond Brown has also made comments pertinent to the determination of the fictional character of John's *kerygma*, especially in regard to the *kerygma*'s Christological elements. Brown supposed that the prologue of the Gospel came from an already existing community hymn, which included the text, "The Word was God."[41] This suggests, at least, that the Evangelist believes himself to be passing on received tradition, rather than his own original interpretation. However, Brown apparently does not consider such a tradition authentic, even if the Evangelist thought it so. Brown thinks that the Evangelist's circle of tradition, rather than the Evangelist, may have read this theology into the tradition. For example, Brown believes that, "Since the exalted Christology of pre-existence never appears even on Jesus' lips in the other Gospels, its appearance in JBap's [John the Baptist's] proclamation is surely the product of Johannine theology."[42] Brown suggests that this arose from a misunderstanding of authentic sayings by John the Baptist.[43] In Brown's view, the circle of this "Johannine community" initially had "a relatively low Christology," while later "there appeared a higher Christology," though these two Christologies had "no exact demarcation."[44] In general, Brown supposes that the new ideas in John's Gospel are not consciously invented. Rather, "The material that came from the origins of the community was taken over because it was agreed with, and the new Johannine ideas were understood (correctly or incorrectly) as the true interpretation of the original material."[45] Brown seems to think, however, that John recognizes that his Christology is a new "interpretation" of the original "lower Christology," referring to John's recognition of "the audacity of the Johannine proclamation" as being justified only by "the concept of the Paraclete."[46] Since the Evangelist's message evidently took its form as a result of many years of teaching, Brown attributes John's distinctive Christology to this development. Brown argues as well that even Paul did not proclaim "the same kind of pre-existence christology as John," and he concludes that Johannine Christology "is quite foreign to the Synoptic Gospels."[47]

Although he terms the Johannine Christology "foreign" to the Synoptic tradition, Brown's view of the Johannine Christians seems to preclude a truly fundamental divide. In Brown's judgment, "the Johannine community, as reflected in the Fourth Gospel, had not really become a sect. They had not followed their exclusivistic tendencies to the point of breaking communion (*koinonia*) with these Christians whose characteristics are found in many NT works of the late first century."[48] This situation stands in contrast to the clear

---

41. Brown, *Community of the Beloved Disciple*, 47.
42. Ibid., 26.
43. Brown, *Gospel According to John*, 1:63–65.
44. Brown, *Community of the Beloved Disciple*, 25.
45. Ibid., 28.
46. Ibid., 28, 29.
47. Ibid., 48.
48. Ibid., 90.

break with the synagogue over Christology.[49] Similarly, Brown denies that John's Gospel originated in a gnostic community, affirming D. M. Smith's observation that "Irenaeus was able to accept the Gospel as orthodox, so that second-century usage is not a clear criterion of the sectarian status of Johannine thought in the first century:. . . ."[50] Brown also notes that a non-sectarian understanding of John's Gospel avoids any implication that the church "canonized the writings of groups who would not have acknowledged each other as true Christians."[51]

In a similar fashion, Beasley-Murray says, "the fundamental tradition of the Fourth Gospel is the kerygma of *the Church*, not simply that of the Johannine community (or communities)."[52] In respect to its historical origin, the "fundamental tradition" must necessarily be the authentic *kerygma* of the twelve, rather than a later development by John or his circle. However, John would naturally claim that the distinctive aspects of his *kerygma* were at least implicit in the "fundamental tradition" of the original *kerygma* of Jesus and the twelve. John's perspective is indicated by an absence of any argument against an opposing Christian message, or against the twelve, whether the new message originated on John's side, or on the side of other apostolic Christians. Brown's view is generally supportive of the possibility that John believed his essential proclamation was authentic tradition, and passed it on in his Gospel as nonfiction.

CULLMANN'S VIEW OF JOHN'S ESSENTIAL MESSAGE

Oscar Cullmann has also advocated a view that is supportive of a nonfictional Johannine *kerygma*. Cullmann begins with John's interest in showing that his Gospel's "type of Christianity goes back to the incarnate Jesus in the same way as the other types, and does so in a special way."[53] As Cullmann sees it, for John, "the narrative of what happened once is not an outer garment which could be stripped from the Gospel . . . . *history, facts,* are the *object* of theological consideration."[54] Cullmann even says that, "The evangelist is evidently convinced that he is reporting facts because he is relying on traditions or reminiscences which appear to him to be certain."[55] Cullmann understands the motivating principle of John as "a theological interest in demonstrating the identity between the historical Jesus and the eternal Christ" which, while it has a definite interest in historical facts, nevertheless puts that "history at the service of a theological interest" in the same way that occurs with the Synoptic Gospels.[56] This means that John does not consciously replace history with his theology, even if he should be wrong about the historical facts. Cullmann says, "The importance to the evangelist of the theological statement that 'the

---

49. Ibid., 43.
50. Smith, "Johannine Christianity," 224, cited in Brown, *Community of the Beloved Disciple*, 16.
51. Brown, *Community of the Beloved Disciple*, 14.
52. Beasley-Murray, *John*, xliv.
53. Cullmann, *Johannine Circle*, 15.
54. Ibid., 21.
55. Ibid.
56. Ibid., 22.

historical Jesus and the Christ present in the community are one' must have been a stimulus to him to portray the words and deeds of . . . the incarnate Jesus, as faithfully as possible."[57]

On this basis Cullmann finds a strong core of tradition underlying John's Gospel. In Cullmann's judgment, even such events as the wedding miracle at Cana are already part of an earlier tradition that John has accepted as authentic. Cullmann says, "The evangelist never *invents* an event or a person for allegorical ends. *For him* the historical character of events is a quite indispensable and fundamental element of his thesis."[58] Cullmann does not conclude from all this that John's Gospel is always historically reliable. He says, "This does not, of course, mean that we may expect him to have exercised critical control over traditions which he used about events of which he was not an eye-witness."[59] Nevertheless, Cullmann's assessment is strongly supportive of the claim that, to John's own mind, his *kerygma* was authentic. The Christian community may not have practiced modern "critical control," but this hardly means that the distinctive and identifying thought of the Christian community could be easily altered, or altered in every way. It certainly did not compromise with its Jewish opponents. Even if there were nonessential historical errors in the way that the Christian message was sometimes expressed, the community could not plausibly deny that Jesus was the Messiah, or that Jesus himself, not just a message that Jesus brought, was essential.

Cullmann's view is also supportive of the idea that the kerygmatic traditions in John's Gospel were already old. If the Evangelist had been a Christian for many decades, his knowledge of the Christian *kerygma* would reach back many decades before his gospel was written. If he had only been a Christian for a decade or two, he would still know older Christians and their *kerygma*. For John to regard his tradition as authentic, indicates that the higher Christology that he proclaims as essential to the authentic kerygma was already being taught, at least implicitly, around the time of the composition of the Synoptic Gospels.

The early character of Johannine Christology may receive some support from the work of F. M. Braun. Braun argued against the earlier view of J. N. Sanders, who had doubted the Gospel's use by the church in the first half of the second century.[60] T. E. Pollard has summarized the work of Braun, as showing, "by an examination of a far wider range of evidence than his predecessors could take into account," that "St John's Gospel was not only used but also held in high esteem in the church in Egypt, Asia Minor, Syria and Rome early in the second century."[61] Pollard notes in particular the use of Johannine symbolism in second-century art in Rome. Pollard also notes the presence of a Johannine Christology in the work of Ignatius. He cites, for example, Ignatius' saying: "There is only one Physician—of flesh, yet spiritual, born, yet unbegotten, God in a man" (Ign *Eph.* 7.2).

57. Ibid., 25.
58. Ibid., 74.
59. Ibid., 25.
60. Sanders, *Fourth Gospel*.
61. Pollard, *Johannine Christology*, 24, 33 citing François-Marie Braun, *Jean le théologien*, 69–300.

THE EPISTEMOLOGICAL BASIS FOR BELIEF ACCORDING TO JOHN'S GOSPEL

In Cullmann's view, John's distinctive Christological emphasis can be attributed to its origin among nonconformist Hellenistic Jewish Christians, even though the influence of official Palestinian Judaism remains considerable.[62] Cullmann notes the affinities that John's Gospel has with the Qumran texts, the Pseudo-Clementines, and Philo, along with the Gospel's affinities toward the interests of rabbinic Judaism and Old Testament themes.[63] More particularly, Cullmann notes the similarities between John's Gospel and the ideas that Stephen proclaims during his own trial (Acts 7), as well as the common points they both share with nonconformist Judaism (Qumran texts, John the Baptist, Samaritanism, Odes of Solomon). Cullmann remarks that openness to alien influences was not restricted to the Diaspora, but was "particularly marked in Palestine and Syria."[64] This all supports the plausibility of the idea that John's *kerygma*, though it has a different flavor than in the Synoptic Gospels, was still nevertheless authentic, or at least an old tradition. Cullman explains the differentiation of style from the Synoptic Gospels as following the "ethno-religious" boundaries between Judaism and Jewish Hellenism.

Cullmann also argues against a fundamental divide between John and other Christians, saying, "I would, however, differ from Käsemann when he supposes that the author was engaged in direct *polemic* against the mainstream church. . . . [John] never loses sight of the church in its *unity*; indeed, this is one of his most important concerns. As we shall see . . . Peter is never *attacked*."[65] Cullmann further concludes that, "In Johannine scholarship today there is a tendency to exaggerate the opposition between the Johannine group and the rest of earliest Christianity, making this a matter of open polemic."[66] Cullmann denies the existence of such polemic. Cullmann's view is supportive of our claim that the Christology of John, though differing from the Synoptic Christology, was not fundamentally opposed to it. The differences have been exaggerated. The Synoptic Tradition presents Jesus as making claims so grand as to be called blasphemous, and John's Gospel presents Jesus with a Christology in which "the Father is greater than I" (John 5:19–30), a theology which, in the words of Brown, "shows that the Johannine community had not made a rival God out of Jesus."[67] This acknowledgement of a common Christianity in turn avoids the otherwise intractable problem of explaining the acceptance of John's Gospel into the canon.

Cullmann's solution also avoids the problem of explaining how John could have introduced a fundamentally more divisive Christology, without causing a break within the Christian community. Although adding divisive messages may attract a few more people than would a simple proclamation about Jesus, the dominant effect of such messages will be to turn away both current and prospective adherents. Furthermore, few divisive messages would have any power to attract additional adherents, especially since the Evangelist expresses several such messages, and there must be sufficient coherence

---

62. Cullmann, *Johannine Circle*, 43.
63. Ibid., 32.
64. Ibid., 31.
65. Ibid., 15.
66. Ibid., 58.
67. Brown, *Community of the Beloved Disciple*, 53.

between them that the Evangelist's adherents can accept them all. The historical situation known to us is more easily explained without the supposition that the Christology of John brought about open division in the Christian community.

JOHN'S KERYGMA IN THE CHRISTIAN COMMUNITY

While John is often supposed to indulge in fiction, the implausibility of John bringing forth a new Christian *kerygma*, given the likely response of the larger Christian community, is not always considered. If John's essential views were genuine innovations, his claim that his views were essential would seem contentious at best. The existing church must already have thought that its belief in Jesus was authentic, and would give eternal life. Consequently, we could naturally expect that other Christian leaders would dispute demands to follow a new *kerygma*, pointing out either that the views were not authentic, or that such views were never regarded as of such great importance as to be a point of issue between Christians. If the kerygmatic teaching was by all accounts new to the community, and yet set forth as essential to Christian belief, it is predictable that some or most in the community would not accept it. Since John sets it forth as a teaching accepted by the apostles, his claim to authenticity, if an innovation, would be easily spurned by Christian leaders who had never heard such teachings, and who knew there was no tradition that the church had ever advocated such teachings. They would not accept John's representation of the true Christian community as limited to those who would hold his distinctive teaching, but would instead more naturally rebuff him for putting forth a new *kerygma* in God's name.

Similarly, adequate consideration is not always given to the lack of a sufficient motive for the Evangelist to set forth his own innovation as the *kerygma*. Given the Evangelist's view that this teaching is essential to authentic Christian belief, it is unlikely that he consciously regarded the teaching as his own innovation. If he called for adherence to a *kerygma* that had important innovations, the existing Christian community is bound to have pointed the innovations out to him. It seems impossible that John should have set forth, as a teaching essential to authentic belief, teaching which he himself regarded as one not yet held by the Christian community. To do so would mean he did not accept the belief of the existing Christian community as authentic. If no one had until John's time believed as John demanded, then the Christian community did not believe, the gospel of that community was defective, and the tradition of Christian baptism was an empty one. Martin Kähler noted the same problem arising when modern portraits of a historically authentic Jesus are set out as a replacement for the canonical portraits of Jesus. Kähler asked, "What would that imply with respect to our fellow Christians in the early period? If their contemplation and worship of the Jesus of the Gospels were distorted and deflected by those obscurities which the critic professes to find in their writings and feels bound to remove, then indeed they would not have known their Savior. And the same would be true of all subsequent Christians, including ourselves."[68]

---

68. Kähler, *So-called Historical Jesus*, 62.

John's claim to authenticity also tells against his kerygmatic message being a recent innovation. He portrays his controversial teaching as authentically Jesus' own message, and as a teaching that Peter and the apostles accepted (John 6). He might instead have simply portrayed his *kerygma* as a prophetic interpretation, but he makes the otherwise unnecessary claim that his *kerygma* is the authentic historic *kerygma*. As Cullmann notes, John does not criticize Peter or the apostles (as we might expect him to do if he were advocating a view in conflict with acknowledged tradition).[69] Instead, the Evangelist adopts the apostles as advocates of his own teaching.

Consequently, John must have thought that the existing Christian community already held to his controversial teachings, at least implicitly. If John anticipated any sharp objections to his distinctive *kerygma*, he saw this as arising from compromise with Judaism, and he was confident that a large part of the community would not sustain the objections. The entire picture indicates that John's *kerygma* is not indeed his own innovation, but is a traditional formulation that at least a portion of the Christian community explicitly acknowledged, and which the larger Christianity community already accepted as a valid expression of the apostolic *kerygma*. This situation would explain both the absence of polemic against alien groups who continued to follow Jesus, and John's apparent confidence that his teaching would not divide the Christian community. It also accords well with John's sole characterization of Christian division (John 6) as a full rejection of Jesus and (presumably) return to official Judaism, rather than as a rejection only of Johannine Christology.[70]

CHRISTOLOGY IN THE SYNOPTIC GOSPELS

For our purposes, it is only necessary to show that John himself believed his *kerygma* was authentic, and believed this even in respect to the distinctive Christological elements of his *kerygma*. We do not need to show that the *kerygma* really was historically authentic to show that John thought it authentic, and presented it as nonfiction.

It is worthy of note, however, that the Synoptic Gospels as we have them exhibit a Christology that has significant affinities toward John's Christology. As discussed below, the Synoptic Gospels themselves do not present Jesus merely as a human prophet-king. Consequently, it is not at all clear that the Synoptic Evangelists would have rejected John's *kerygma*. T. E. Pollard has said that, in the New Testament, distinct types of Christology often "stand side by side in the writings of the same author and, indeed intertwined with each other."[71]

This should make us hesitate to emphasize the distinctions too strongly, or to quickly characterize John's Christology as actually opposed to the Christology of the Synoptic Gospels.

69. Cullmann, *Johannine Circle*, 72.

70. Marinus de Jonge notes the recent dissertation of B. W. J. de Ruyter, which argues in part that John's polemic is aimed solely "against Christians," who are referred to as Jews, Pharisees, et cetera. As de Jonge observes, this idea cannot explain why figures of such varied religious inclination appear in the Gospel. See de Jonge, "Christology, Controversy and Community," 214–15.

71. Pollard, *Johannine Christology*, 4–5.

The Essential Words of Jesus as Nonfiction in the Gospel of John

It was stated in the outline above that the preexistence of Jesus is part of John's essential message. While the preexistence of Jesus is not generally evident in the Synoptic Gospels, they nevertheless have certain points of affinity with this idea. One of these is that Jesus portrays himself as the permanent king of the coming age. Jesus cites, for example, Daniel's vision of "the Son of Man . . . coming with the clouds of heaven" (Mark 14:62). This is a figure that, according to Daniel, has "an everlasting dominion" (Dan 7:14). As Ezra Gould observed, Jesus applies this language of Daniel to himself.[72] This figure's everlasting life shows an affinity with the idea of a preexistent life. This is especially so because it is hard to account for any mere man "coming with the clouds," which, as Ridderbos notes, is imagery "used elsewhere only of God."[73]

Another point of affinity is that it is hard to account for a mere man being given the role of everlasting dominion, and supreme everlasting status. God characterizes the Israelites' original request for a king as having "rejected me from being king over them" (1 Sam 8:7). The establishment of a human king seems to violate the ideal that God himself should rule. However, this problem of permanent kingship is sharpened in Jesus' discussion of the scripture, "The LORD said to my Lord, sit at my right hand, until I put your enemies beneath your feet" (Ps 110:1). Jesus asks how the Christ, the one at God's right hand, can be David's son if he is David's lord (Matt 22:42–44; Mark 12:35–37; Luke 20:41–44). The point of the question is that the Messiah is more than David's son, and that this must be explained. The unspoken alternative is that the Christ is not merely David's son, but also the Son of God. Use of the title 'Son' for the Messiah was already known from two texts of scripture: "I will be a father to him and he shall be a son to me" (2 Sam 7:14) and, "the rulers take counsel together against the LORD and against his anointed. . . . you are my son" (Ps 2:2, 7). Jesus' exalted view of the Messiah is made clear by his subsequent identification of this figure with Daniel's Son of Man (Dan 7:13). Jesus says, "you shall see the Son of Man, *sitting on the right hand of Power*" (Matt 26:64; Mark 14:62; Luke 22:69). Such a figure is exalted above the place of mortal men. Robert Gundry[74] and A. W. Argyle,[75] among others, see a claim of divine sonship in Matthew's account of this Psalm (Matt 22:42–44). Psalm 110:1 is the Old Testament text most frequently cited or alluded to in the New Testament (Matt 22:44; Matt 26:64; Mark 14:62; 16:19; Acts 2:34; 1 Cor 15:25; Heb 1:13; 10:13 and other references to the "right hand of God" like Acts 7:56). This indicates the early Christological use and wide influence of this text. The use of the Psalm in connection with Daniel's vision is not an innovation of any of the Synoptic Evangelists, but as James Dunn has said, existed at least at "a very early stage of Christian tradition."[76]

We may also note a few other indications that the Christology in the Synoptic Gospels has an affinity to John's Gospel. We have already discussed, in connection with Rudolf Schnackenburg, evidence in the Synoptic Tradition for Christ being the mediator

---

72. Gould, *Gospel According to Mark*, 279.
73. Ridderbos, *Gospel According to John*, 93.
74. Gundry, *Matthew, A Commentary*, 451.
75. Argyle, *Gospel According to Matthew*, 170.
76. Dunn, "Are You the Messiah?" 18.

of life from God. We may note also that Luke's Gospel says, concerning Jesus' supernatural conception by a virgin, that it was "for that reason the holy one begotten shall be called the Son of God" (Luke 1:35). As the phrase "for that reason" indicates, and as I. H. Marshall observes, the term "Son of God" is used here "in its full sense of one begotten by God" rather than by a human father.[77] To connect Jesus' birth without a human father to the title "Son of God," shows an affinity to John's kerygmatic idea of Jesus' preexistence. Similarly, in Luke's portrait, Jesus refers to the temple as his Father's (Luke 2:49). Marshall observes that, in the whole Lukan context, this goes beyond the usage of "a pious Israelite."[78] Even in Mark's Gospel, Jesus is presented as "son of God" (Mark 1:1; 3:11; 15:39), with no mention of Joseph. In Matthew's Gospel, Jesus says, "I am with you always, even to the end of the age" (Matt 28:20), so that Robert Gordon has remarked, "To talk about Jesus is, for Matthew if not for some of his modern interpreters, to talk of God—a perspective only more explicit in John's gospel."[79] Even Mark, at Jesus' stilling of the waves, portrays the disciples as "much afraid" and as asking, "Who then is this, that even the wind and sea obey him?" (Mark 4:41). For uncertainty about Jesus' *identity* to evoke fear indicates that Jesus is more than a merely human figure. Jewish thought typically viewed the natural world as evidently a province of God's control alone (e.g. Gen 1; Job 26:5–12; Ps 135:5–7; Isa 40:12–18, 21–26). For example, God asks Job, "Who enclosed the sea with doors . . . ? I placed boundaries on it and I set a bolt and doors, and I said, 'Thus far you shall come but no farther; and here shall your proud waves stop'" (Job 38:8, 10, 11). The agreement of all four Gospels that Jesus was accused of having blasphemed (Mark 2:7; 14:64 and parallels, John 5:18; 10:33) also indicates a shared perspective about his claims.

Admittedly, these affinities to the Johannine *kerygma* lie in the canonical forms of the Synoptic Tradition, but their pervasiveness through all the Synoptic Gospels indicates an earlier history as well. There is no depiction of Jesus as a mere prophet and king in the canonical Gospels, nor does their Christological perspective line up on a simple continuum from, say, Mark's viewpoint to John's. The variety in the four individual Christological perspectives, none of which saw Jesus as merely human, must instead be explained in terms of antecedent tradition. Whether or not the Christological affinities cited above can support the ultimate authenticity of John's *kerygma*, they support the argument that John did not see his own *kerygma* as departing from the authentic *kerygma* of the apostolic Christian community.

It might be objected that this result has assumed the literary unity of the Gospel as the work of one person. De Jonge criticized the work of P. N. Anderson[80] for assuming "an individual person responsible" for the Gospel, an evangelist rather than a group or school.[81] However, it is appropriate to begin with the presumption of a single *implied author*, and then to modify this slightly to account for any indications of an *implied editing*

---

77. Marshall, *Gospel of Luke*, 71.
78. Ibid., 129.
79. Gordon, "Sermon on the Mount," 169.
80. Anderson, *Christology of the Fourth Gospel*.
81. De Jonge, "Christology, Controversy and Community," 212.

(e.g., John 21:24). The real author must have expected the book to be read (by some) in this light, rather than on the basis of authorial information that was not generally available. It is only when, on this basis, we have understood the Gospel's ideas, that we could have sufficient data to support any more complex theory of the Gospel's authorship, since the ideas conveyed may shape that judgment. A determination of the author's fictional intent, especially at the level of his *kerygma*, is fundamental for an understanding of his meaning.

Furthermore, if we are to think of someone as editing the Gospel, are we also to think of an editing of the *kerygma* within it? This suggestion contains all the problems that we have raised already in regard to the introduction of a genuinely new *kerygma*. It is problematic to envisage a process by which the Gospel of John (or any literary work) could plausibly have been prepared without a single primary author. However, even if the Gospel were somehow the work of a school, its *kerygma* must be the *kerygma* shared by the school. A theory of multiple authors does not itself then undermine our conclusion that the Gospel has one *kerygma* which is set forth as nonfiction.

NONFICTION IN JOHN—BEYOND THE KERYGMA

The nonfictional character of John's Gospel extends further than John's essential *kerygma*. This is really to be expected, for it would be difficult to frame all non-kerygmatic material as fiction. Dodd's work on historical tradition gives many examples of nonfiction.[82] However here we will restrict ourselves to nonfictional material that, while not itself *kerygma*, gives further indications of the nonfictional status of the *kerygma*.

Since John represents the following eight messages as being true, and since their truth inherently depends upon John's retention of an authentic tradition, he must believe there is an authentic tradition, and must want his readers in turn to also believe that tradition. Italics have been added in the citations below to emphasize words that are most relevant to the argument.

1. *Nonfictional Message*: Jesus himself came and spoke to the world.

    a. *Texts with this Message*: Jesus says, "He who rejects me, and does not receive *my sayings*, has one who judges him; *the word I spoke* is what will judge him at the last day" (John 12:48). Jesus says, "If I had not come *and spoken to them*, they would not have sin, but now they have no excuse for their sin" (John 15:22). "Jesus answered him, '*I have spoken openly to the world; I always taught in the synagogue, and in the temple,* where all the Jews come together; and I spoke nothing in secret. Why do you question me? *Question those who have heard what I spoke to them; behold, these know what I said.*' And when he had said this, one of the officers standing by gave Jesus a blow, saying, 'Is that the way you answer the high priest?'" (John 18:20–22).

    b. *Significance of the Texts*: John represents Jesus himself as claiming to have spoken publicly. Jesus' essential proclamation forms the basis on which people

---

82. See also, Higgins, *Historicity of the Fourth Gospel*.

will be held accountable to God. This proclamation cannot be given for the first time, prophetically, through the Evangelist, since that would deny Jesus' historical proclamation.[83] Neither can the word be other than the word of Jesus. John recognizes the historical reality that Jesus did proclaim a message, and consequently John regards Jesus' own message as the sufficient basis on which God will judge all people.

2. **Nonfictional Message**: John cannot be setting forth his own word in place of the word of Jesus, since he regards Jesus' own word as the essential word.

   a. *Texts with this Message*: Jesus says, "He who *hears my word and believes him* who sent me, has eternal life" (John 5:24). Jesus says, "I have come *in my Father's name*, and you do not receive me; *if another shall come in his own name, you will receive him*"(John 5:43). Jesus says, "The words that *I* have spoken to you are spirit and are life" (John 6:63). The officers answered, "never did a man speak the way *this man* speaks" (John 7:46); this saying can hardly be John's description of his own narrative. Jesus says, "If anyone *keeps my word, he shall never see death*," to which his opponents respond, "whom do you make yourself out to be?" (John 8:51, 53). Jesus says, "For I did not speak *on my own initiative*, but the Father himself who sent me has given me commandment, *what to say, and what to speak*. And I know that his commandment is eternal life, therefore the things I speak, *I speak just as the Father has told me*" (John 12:49–50). Jesus says, "and *the word which you hear is not mine, but the Father's who sent me*" (John 14:24). Jesus says, "If you abide in me, and *my words abide in you*, ask whatever you wish, and it shall be done for you" (John 15:7). Jesus says, "*If you keep my commandments*, you will abide *in my love*; just as I have kept my Father's commandments, and abide in his love" (John 15:10). Jesus says, "You are my friends if you do what *I command* you" (John 15:14). Jesus says, "For the words which you gave *me, I have given to them;* and *they received them*, and truly understood that I came forth from you, and *they believed* that you sent me" (John 17:8). Jesus says, "I have given them *thy word*" (John 17:14a). There are similar sayings under section 1 of nonfictional messages above, and sections 6 and 7 below.

   b. *Significance of Texts*: John does not regard the sayings of Jesus in his Gospel as John's own words, but as authentically the sayings of Jesus. This is not to say that they are unaffected by John's vocabulary or concepts, but rather that they are not affected in such a way that John considers them inauthentic.

3. **Nonfictional Message**: Since John portrays Jesus as the revelation of the Father, John's portrait cannot be an inauthentic portrait of Jesus and still be an authentic revelation of the Father.

---

83. Cullmann has suggested that Jesus' words in John's Gospel are, in some cases, the Evangelist's "own words." By this Cullmann seems to mean that John gives, beyond an interpretation of Jesus' original words and teaching, new revelations from Jesus. However, Cullmann does not claim that such additional teaching replaces Jesus' original message. See Cullmann, *Johannine Circle*, 18.

a. *Texts with this Message*: "The Word was made flesh, and dwelt among us" (John 1:14). "*He has made him known*" (John 1:18). Jesus says, "I speak *the things which I have seen with my Father*" (John 8:38). Jesus says, "He who believes *in me* does not believe in me, but *in him who sent me*" (John 12:44). Jesus says, "He who beholds *me* beholds the One who sent me" (John 12:45). Jesus says, "If you had known *me*, you would have known my Father also; from now on you *know him*, and have seen him" (John 14:7). Jesus says, "He who has *seen me* has seen the Father" (John 14:9).

b. *Significance of the Texts*: In John's thought, the *Word* of God "was made flesh" in Jesus Christ, to make God Himself known to the world, and to do so in a way which prophecy alone could never have done. Only witnesses saw or heard this incarnate Word, but witnesses in turn made him known, as they handed on an authentic tradition about Jesus. Just as John regards Jesus as the authentic representation of God, so John regards the tradition he hands on as an authentic representation of Jesus. Jesus even speaks "the things I have seen with my Father" which, since they are known by Jesus only because he is God's Son, cannot merely be things that the Evangelist has seen prophetically, but are representations of Jesus as known in the tradition.

4. **Nonfictional Message**: God and Jesus are revealed primarily through history and historical tradition, rather than directly by the Holy Spirit (as in prophetic visions).

   a. *Texts with this Message*: "The Word *was made flesh*" (1:14). "*He has* made Him known" (1:18). Jesus says, "I have many *more* things to say to you, but you cannot bear them now. . . . the Spirit . . . will guide you into all the truth, for he will not speak on his own initiative, but whatever He hears, He will speak; and He will disclose to you what is to come. He shall glorify *me*; for he shall take of mine and shall disclose it to you" (John 16:12–14). Jesus says that the Holy Spirit would "*teach you all things, and bring to your remembrance all that I said to you*" (John 14:26). "*But this he spoke of the Spirit, whom those who believed in him were to receive, for the Spirit was not yet given, because Jesus was not yet glorified*" (John 7:39).

   b. *Significance of the Texts*: John does not regard the prophetic word of the Spirit of God as able to replace or equal the authentic tradition about Jesus. Instead, John regards Jesus, and Jesus as he is known in the authentic tradition, as the unprecedented expression of God. The prophetic Spirit can only interpret, not replace, this Word. The Evangelist does not ignore this revelation of the incarnate Word, as though his own prophetic insights could equal or supersede that unprecedented revelation. Just as the Spirit's teaching to each disciple does not make the Evangelist's words needless, so the Spirit does not teach the Evangelist in such a way as to make the authentic tradition needless to the Evangelist. The Spirit brings Jesus' words to remembrance, rather than bringing direct revelation that makes such remembrance needless. The Spirit is only to teach what was too hard for the disciples to bear at that time. This cannot include the authentic *kerygma* of Jesus, although the need to suffer for this *kerygma* might itself be a disclosure that has been postponed.

5. *Nonfictional Message*: Jesus was a witness.

   a. *Texts with this Message*: Jesus says that he and his disciples "*bear witness of that which we have seen; and you do not receive our witness*" (John 3:11). John the Baptist says, "He who comes from above is above all, he who is of the earth is from the earth, and speaks of the earth. He who comes from heaven is above all. *What he has seen and heard, of that he bears witness*; and no man receives his witness (John 3:31–32). Jesus says, "The world cannot hate you; but *it hates me* because *I testify of it*, that its deeds are evil" (John 7:7). "... others were saying, 'No, on the contrary, *he leads the multitude astray*' " (John 7:12). [Jesus could not be thought to mislead without any teaching.] "*You seek to kill me because my word* has no place in you" (John 8:37). [Here Jesus is addressing those who will try to execute him by stoning that same hour.] "But as it is, you are seeking to kill me, a man *who has told you the truth*, which *I heard from God*" (John 8:40). "But *because I speak the truth*, you do not believe me" (John 8:45). "If *I* speak truth, why do you *not believe me*? He who is of God hears *the words of God*; for this reason you do not hear, because you are not of God" (John 8:46–47). "There arose a division again among the Jews because of these words. And many of them were saying, "He has a demon and is insane. Why do you listen to him? Others were saying, 'These are not the sayings of one demon-possessed. A demon cannot open the eyes of the blind, can he?" (John 10:19–21). "Lord, *who has believed our report*?" (John 12:38). Jesus says, "*For this I have been born, and for this I have come into the world, to bear witness to the truth.* Everyone who is of the truth hears *my voice*" (John 18:37).

   b. *Significance of Texts*: Jesus is portrayed as a witness from heaven. John thinks that Jesus really did proclaim a message and that John's portrait of Jesus' message is authentic. Similarly, John portrays the animosity against Jesus as arising from Jesus' message, which is a historically sound portrayal. The elements of Jesus' message that caused offense would naturally be preserved in the tradition of his message, they cannot be regarded as peripheral to its essence. Jesus' says his entire purpose for being born is to be a witness of the truth, so John's Gospel must preserve the essentials of this witness.

6. *Nonfictional Message*: Jesus was sent to speak God's words.

   a. *Texts with this Message*: The Evangelist writes, "He who has received his witness has set his seal to this, that God is true. For *he whom God has sent speaks the words of God*; for he gives the Spirit without measure.... He who does not *obey* the son shall not see life, but the wrath of God abides on him" (John 3:33–36). "Jesus therefore answered them, and said, 'My teaching is not mine, but his who sent me. *If any man is willing to do his will, he shall know of the teaching, whether it is of God, or whether I speak from myself. He who speaks from himself seeks his own glory*" (John 7:16–18). Jesus says, "'... the things which *I heard from him, these I speak to the world.* ... I do nothing on my own initiative, but *I speak these things* as the Father taught me.' ... As he spoke these things, many came to believe in him" (John 8:26, 28, 30). To those who will try to execute him by stoning in that same hour Jesus says, "But as it is, you are seeking to kill me, a man *who has told you the truth*, which *I heard from God* (John 8:40). Jesus says, "*The words that I say to you* I do not speak on my own initiative, but the Father abiding in me does his works" (John 14:10). Jesus says, "but I have called you friends, for *all things that I have heard from my Father I have made known to you*" (John 15:15). Jesus says, "*if they kept my word, they will keep yours also*" (John 15:20). Jesus says, "If I had not come *and spoken to them*, they would not have sin, but now they have no excuse for their sin" (John 15:22). Jesus says, "For the words which *you gave me* I have given to them, and *they received them* and truly understood that I came forth from You" (John 17:8). Jesus says, "*I have given them your word*; and the world has hated them" (John 17:14).

   b. *Significance of Texts*: In the mind of the Evangelist, Jesus was sent by God to speak God's message to the world, so Jesus' message cannot have been without importance to the tradition or to the Evangelist. It is the message of one who receives the Spirit "without measure," not just the message of the Evangelist who is taught by the Spirit. The message must be obeyed, which means that the message must have been known. Just as Jesus says the teaching "is not mine," so the Evangelist in turn must regard the teaching as God's, and not his own. The disciples are represented as having received Jesus' word, which are God's words given to Jesus.

7. **Nonfictional Message**: Jesus is the teacher and lord of his disciples, so he must have taught and commanded them.

   a. *Texts with this Message*: "And they said to him, 'Rabbi' (which translated means *teacher*)" (John 1:38). Jesus, says, "If you abide in *my word*, you are truly disciples of mine" (John 8:31). Jesus says, "You call me Teacher and Lord, and you are right, for so I am. If I then, the Lord and the Teacher, washed your feet, you also ought to wash one another's feet" (John 13:13–14). Jesus says, "If you love me, you will keep *my commandments*. ... He who has my commandments and keeps them, he it is who loves me; and he who loves me shall be loved by my Father, and I will love him, and will disclose myself to him" (John 14:15, 21). Jesus says, "If anyone loves me, he will keep *my word* ... He who does not love me does not keep *my words* ..." (John 14:23–24).

   b. *Significance of the Texts*: Jesus must have taught his disciples a message and way of life. His status as teacher and lord of his disciples would be empty if the authentic tradition of Jesus' words were eclipsed or superseded by John's interpretation or some new *kerygma*.

8. **Nonfictional Message**: Jesus commands his disciples to remember his words.
   a. *Supporting Texts*: "*Remember the word that I said to you, 'A slave is not greater than his master'*" (John 15:20). In this regard, there is also Jesus' saying that the Holy Spirit will "*bring to your remembrance* all that I said to you" (John 14:26).
   b. *Significance of the Texts*: John must have in mind an existing tradition of Jesus' essential teaching, since John represents Jesus' disciples as normatively remembering this teaching.

The following messages also indicate that the nonfictional tradition of Jesus' teaching is more extensive than the *kerygma*.

9. **Nonfictional Message**: Where Jesus' words in miracle accounts are essential to the miracle being recognized as a sign, the words must also be regarded as essentially nonfictional.
   a. *Supporting Texts*: Jesus "said to him, '*Go, wash in the pool of Siloam*' (which is translated, Sent). And so he went away and washed and came back seeing" (John 9:7).
   b. *Significance of Texts*: If Jesus had not told the man to wash, the miracle (as it is portrayed) could not have been ascribed to Jesus' power, and so would not be a sign that Jesus was sent by God. Given our earlier argument that the miracles are set forth as nonfiction, such words must also be set forth as nonfiction.

10. **Nonfictional Message**: Jesus is portrayed as foretelling future troubles, to give his disciples confidence that those difficulties are part of the plan of God.
    a. *Supporting Texts*: Jesus says, "From now on *I am telling you before it comes to pass*, so that when it does occur, *you may believe* that I am he" (John 13:19). Jesus says, "These things I have spoken to you, while abiding with you. But the Helper, the Holy Spirit, whom the Father will send in my name, he will teach you all things, and *bring to your remembrance* all that I said to you" (John 14:25–26). Jesus says, "And now I have told you *before it comes to pass*, that when it comes to pass, you may believe" (John 14:29). Jesus says, "But these things I have spoken to you, *that when their hour comes, you may remember that I told you of them*. And these things I did not say to you at the beginning because I was with you. But now I am going to Him who sent me" (John 16:4–5).
    b. *Significance of the Texts*: While it is conceivable that the Evangelist is creating fiction when he represents Jesus foretelling events, and thus preparing his disciples for the events, fiction would misleadingly indicate that the disciples were comforted by Jesus in a way which, in fact, never occurred. There is no

11. ***Nonfictional Message***: Jesus' words were often given in obscure or parabolic speech, but he promises in his farewell discourse that he will soon begin to speak more plainly.

    a. *Supporting Texts*: Addressing his disciples, Jesus says, "These things I have spoken to you in figures of speech; an hour is coming when *I will speak no more to you in figures of speech, but will tell you plainly* of the Father" (John 16:25). Of the multitude John says, "*They did not realize* that he had been speaking to them about the Father" (John 8:27). The Jews say, "How long will you keep us in suspense? If you are the Christ, *tell us plainly*" (John 10:24). At the last supper, addressing Judas, "Jesus therefore said to him, 'What you do, do quickly.' Now *no one of those reclining at the table knew* for what purpose He had said this to him. For some were supposing, because Judas had the money box, that Jesus was saying to him, 'Buy the things we have need of for the feast'; or else, that he should give something to the poor" (John 13:27–29).

    b. *Significance of the Texts*: The Evangelist often portrays Jesus' speech as obscure, rather than giving a clarified interpretation of its meaning. The obscurity is sometimes marked by an explanatory comment from the narrator. The Evangelist's representation of Jesus' language as "figures of speech," as language that was not "plain," is portrayed as something that would change in the future. What can be the significance of such a change in the Evangelist's mind? It does not mean that the Evangelist sees his own later account of Jesus' words as differing from Jesus' real words in either their obscurity or transparency. There is no indication that the Evangelist regards his work as expressing the "plain" words of either the risen Christ or the Holy Spirit. This retention of obscurity is naturally understood as showing the Evangelist's faithfulness to a tradition he regards as authentic.

We may summarize these additional claims of the Evangelist as follows. These are not claims of such importance that people turn from Jesus because of them, but they are claims that tell us what the Evangelist thought about his own *kerygma*, and about other nonfictional words of Jesus. They are given without further comment:

> The Evangelist represents that Jesus came and spoke to the world. The Evangelist cannot plausibly be thought to be setting forth his own word as the word of Jesus, since he represents Jesus' word as God's Word. Since the Evangelist portrays Jesus as the revelation of the Father, the Evangelist's portrait cannot be an inauthentic portrait of Jesus and still be an authentic revelation of the Father. God and Jesus are not revealed directly by the Holy Spirit, and apart from history and human historical tradition. For example, Jesus is not revealed to

the Evangelist or to the reader in a prophetic vision, the same way that he appears in the first chapter of the Book of Revelation. A direct revelation would make Jesus' own earlier words superfluous. The Evangelist says that Jesus was a witness. Similarly, the Evangelist says that Jesus was sent to speak God's words. Jesus' words in some miracle accounts must also be regarded as essentially nonfictional, for the miraculousness of the account depends in some cases on Jesus having spoken in the way indicated. Jesus is the teacher and lord of his disciples, and the authentic tradition of Jesus' words is not substantially eclipsed by John's new interpretation or some new revelation. Some of Jesus' words are represented as spoken in advance, to give confidence that all that will happen is in the plan of God. This is a misrepresentation if they were not spoken in advance. Jesus commands his disciples to remember particular things he has said. If Jesus himself did not give these commands, their inclusion as fiction would misrepresent Jesus. The Evangelist often represents Jesus' words as obscure, rather than as plain enough to be understood, but the Evangelist still gives an explanation as narrator.

CONCLUSION: JOHN'S ESSENTIAL MESSAGE IS NONFICTIONAL

This nonfictional characterization of John's *kerygma* stands in opposition to the view that John's theological innovations or fictions can adequately and fully explain the origin of all his distinctive material. John cannot be unaware that he is setting forth distinctive material as essential to his *kerygma*. Consequently, the distinctive material in John's essential *kerygma* cannot be explained as John's own innovation, for it cannot be essential *kerygma* in John's mind if it is his innovation. In important respects, such as its higher Christology, the above outline and summary of the Evangelist's essential proclamation comprises a more extensive claim for nonfiction than is always acknowledged in the literature on John's Gospel. According to Kümmel, it is probable that the Fourth Gospel's "historical matter is contrived out of the idea of the divine dignity and glory of Jesus."[84] Yet important Johannine ideas about the "divine dignity and glory of Jesus" are part of the Evangelist's expression of the *kerygma*. The Evangelist could hardly dare to express those ideas as being essential to the authentic *kerygma*, if he knew they were his own invention, or if the Christian community would perceive the ideas as a change to the authentic *kerygma*. This does not prove that John's distinctive ideas are in fact historically authentic tradition, but it does show that the Evangelist thought they were (at least implicitly) accepted tradition, and that in his time they were not generally considered to be a change to the essential authentic *kerygma*.

Even Schnackenburg's description of John's contribution was too free. Schnackenburg said that, in the less skeptical view of the composition of John's discourses, "Tradition was permeated and interpreted by the light of faith, and the only difference in John is that this process has here reached its climax, so that the fourth Gospel is a presentation com-

---

84. Kümmel, *New Testament: Problems*, 137.

pletely dominated by the vision of faith."[85] To speak of "complete domination" ignores the objective control of the *kerygma*. Where John's *kerygma* is expressed in his Gospel, it cannot be essentially changed by his own interpretation, insight, or form of expression. A change in what is essential to the message constitutes a different message.

The *kerygma* of John acts as a canon or rule within his Gospel. Brevard Childs warns of the common error of ignoring the control exerted by a canon, "The basic error involved arises from the assumption that the literature was shaped by historical, literary, sociological, and history-of-religion forces, but that the theological struggle of its tradents with the literature's normative function was insignificant. . . . The tradents of the developing New Testament were themselves being shaped by the content of the material which they in turn were transmitting, selecting, and forming into a scriptural norm."[86] This same error has been made with John's *kerygma*.

In an earlier chapter we argued that, according to John, one can know something about God by his signs in history. This chapter extends the basis for knowing God to John's essential message about Jesus. This proclamation, a message from which many turn, is set forth as nonfiction, and so as a basis for knowing God.

---

85. Schnackenburg, *Gospel According to John*, 23–24.
86. Childs, *New Testament as Canon*, 22.

11

John's Essential Message as Grounds for Belief in Jesus

THE LAST CHAPTER HAS argued that John the Evangelist sets forth his essential message, a message that includes important and controversial Christological claims, as nonfiction. We may now discuss the grounds on which John expected his audience to believe his message. The Evangelist indicates some of these grounds explicitly, and some implicitly. These grounds themselves are not direct causes of division from other Jews, but their nonfictional intention is, nevertheless, generally evident from their use as the recognized grounds for belief in John's nonfictional message. Identification of John's recognized grounds for belief, together with an explanation showing how his reasoning seemed plausible, will also give further support to our argument that John intended his essential message to be understood as nonfiction, since the presence of a systematic apologia is more indicative of nonfiction than of fiction.

The Evangelist not only sets forth his essential Christological claims as nonfiction, but he also sets forth grounds in the Gospel on which characters (and by implication the readers) should find these claims warranted (e.g., John 5:31–47). Jesus himself makes the essential claims, but Jesus concedes that others cannot know on the basis of his testimony alone that what he says is true (John 5:31). However, the claims are not of the sort that can be verified by everyone alike (John 5:37). They can only be known to be true (apart from the miracles) by some form of revelation (John 5:34). Consequently, Jesus can only appeal to the testimony of others who would be in a position to know. He cites the testimony of John the Baptist, and of Moses (John 5:33, 46). However, each of these witnesses relies ultimately upon revelation from God for the knowledge about which they are called to testify. Jesus also cites the testimony of the Father (John 5:37), and the testimony of the Scriptures (John 5:39, 46), the latter again depending upon the inspiration of the prophetic knowledge given to its authors. This dependency upon revelation creates strong doubts in the modern mind. These doubts make it difficult to seriously suppose that Jews of the first century would not find new revelation inherently doubtful. Consequently, to understand the force of John's argument, we must first understand how the thought and plausibility of John's arguments draw largely from Jewish beliefs about the grounds for knowledge of God, beliefs that were widely accepted among first century Jews. These include the belief that God had communicated with real language, the belief that revelation was not discredited by its anthropomorphic appearance, the belief that God's communication with people was limited because of his majesty, and the belief that God's use of prophetic intermediaries did not prevent people from having a true knowledge of God.

JEWISH RELIGIOUS EPISTEMOLOGY: A GOD WHO SPEAKS

The belief that people know God by his words and acts was a fundamental first century Jewish belief that John adopted. In Jewish thought, God's ability to speak to people was a mark that he is a living God, whereas the inability of idols to speak was one mark that they are not gods at all, but are merely wood or stone (Ps 115:3–8; Jer 10:5; Acts 17:29–30). Any god who neither speaks nor acts had no valid claim to be a god. Indeed, in this view, people can only know God through his speech and acts; there is no way to know more directly about any god's reality and nature. This does not mean that human knowledge of God, being indirect, is not real knowledge of God himself. In Jewish thought, God is genuinely present in and known through his words. When God creates the world by speaking (Gen 1), it is Almighty God himself who creates the world, not God's words acting separately. When God speaks to people, it is God they hear, not just God's words.

John describes the presence of God in God's word by the statement, "the word was with God, and the word was God" (John 1:1). Even in the original Greek, the two opening words of John's Gospel, "in (the) beginning" (Ἐν ἀρχῇ) are identical to the two opening words of Genesis, as found in the Septuagint. Furthermore, in John's milieu, where Jewish scriptural texts are often cited, these two words could hardly fail to be recognized as paralleling the beginning of the Jewish scriptures, given the subsequent topic and allusions: the creation of all things by God, creation by means of God's word, and the contrast of light and darkness. The naming of Jewish prayers and texts of Scripture by their beginning words is documented in the Mishnah, compiled at the end of the second century AD. For example, Danby's translation of Tractate *m. Ta'anit* 4.3 is, "On the first day they read from *In the beginning* . . . to *Let there be a firmament*."[1] As Karl Barth observed, "in unmistakable allusion to Gen. 1:1,"[2] John draws this idea of God's self-revelation from the first lines of the Book of Genesis (cf. Gen 1; John 1:3). In some respects, God is to be identified with his word, just as other individuals are identified with their own words. It is only in God's words and acts that he is known.

In Jewish thought, the word and acts of God are revealed as his own when there is no other plausible explanation for their origin. This means first that a divine being provides the most plausible explanation for the existence, variety, qualities, and order of the world, and of one's life in it. Job says, "But now ask the beasts, and let them teach you; and the birds of the heavens, and let them tell you . . . Who among all these does not know that the hand of the LORD has done this" (Job 12:7, 9). Philo of Alexandria

---

1. For examples of other texts cited by their beginning words, see Tractates *m. Berakhot* 2.2; *m. Pesahim* 10.4–6; *m. Megillah* 2.3). For an important discussion of John's prologue as a commentary on Genesis, see Borgen, "Observations on the Targumic Character," 288–95. Ridderbos offers balancing considerations in *Gospel of John*, 24.

2. Barth, *Witness to the Word*, 19.

writes, "He therefore who comes into that which is truly the greatest of cities, namely, this world, and who beholds all . . . would he not naturally, or I should rather say, of necessity, conceive a notion of the Father, and creator, and governor of all this system?"[3] This same Jewish reasoning is taken up by Paul when he says, "since the creation of the world his invisible attributes, his eternal power and divine nature, have been clearly seen, being understood through what has been made, so that they are without excuse" (Rom 1:20). Under this view, the creation of the one world cannot be explained as the work of the many pagan gods, for as Luke explains, "we ought not to think that the divine nature is like gold or silver or stone, an image formed by the art and thought of man" (Acts 17:29; cf. Isa 40:18–26). Furthermore, God's action is sometimes the most plausible explanation of the cause of certain events (including miracles). For example, God says that the departure of Israel from Egypt by means of great plagues against the Egyptians will make the people of Israel "know that I am the LORD your God" (Exod 6:7).

Similarly, God's word through a prophet is revealed as God's own word when there is not a more plausible explanation of the prophecy than that the word is authentically from God. John's belief in prophets, individuals who heard God's words and spoke in turn to the people, is also a thoroughly Jewish conception. Throughout the Hebrew Scriptures, God speaks through prophets. Most significantly, as we shall discuss below, Moses acted in a prophetic role when he gave the law of God to the people of Israel.

The scriptural narrative about the giving of the Ten Commandments (Exod 20; Deut 5) illustrates the Jewish conception of God's words as objectively real. After God himself "came down on Mount Sinai to the top of the mountain" (Exod 19:20) and "spoke these words," the people of Israel,

> perceived the sounds and lightning flashes and the sound of the trumpet and the mountain smoking; and when the people saw, they trembled and stood at a distance. Then they said to Moses, "Speak with us yourself and we will listen; but let not God speak with us, lest we die." . . . So the people stood at a distance, while Moses approached the thick cloud where God was. (Exod 20:18, 19, 21)

Here God speaks to the people directly, not through a prophet. The words spoken by God have the same objective reality as audible speech, for each person hears directly what God says, and falls under a sense of dread at God's presence. In the case of the Ten Commandments, God's speech is probably to be understood as audible speech (as also for Num 7:89 per Niehaus).[4] This may not be the case elsewhere (e.g., Gen 1). However, the essential point is not that God speaks audibly, but that God's speech is as objectively spoken as audible language.

In the first century, it was an accepted Jewish view that when God spoke the Ten Commandments, his words had the same objective reality as human speech. Philo writes, "And a voice sounded forth from out of the midst of the fire which had flowed from heaven, a most marvelous and awful voice, the flame being endowed with articu-

---

3. Philo of Alexandria, *The Special Laws 1* 34, (Yonge) 537. See also, *The Special Laws 1,* 32–35, Philo's *On the Creation* 7–12, and Josephus *Antiquities*, Preface.

4. Niehaus, *God at Sinai*, 206.

late speech in a language familiar to the hearers, which expressed its words with such clearness and distinctness that the people seemed rather to be seeing than hearing it."[5] Josephus says, "And they all heard a voice that came to all of them from above, insomuch that no one of these words escaped them, which Moses wrote on two tables."[6] In his last words, the martyr Stephen is portrayed as saying before a court that Moses "was in the congregation in the desert with the angel who spoke to him on Mount Sinai, and with our fathers; and he received living words to pass on to us" (Acts 7:38). The Letter to the Hebrews similarly says in reference to Mt. Sinai, "they did not escape when they refused him who warned them on earth" and "his voice shook the earth" (Heb 12:25, 26). All of these texts understand the words of God as an objective reality.

We also observe in this passage on the Ten Commandments (and in the rest of the Mosaic Law) that God's speech conveys sufficiently numerous and complex ideas that it must be understood as language, not as mere impressions, realizations, insights, or judgments of conscience. Instead, the words are portrayed as God's direct speech and as God's own words. The words of the Law are not even explicable as reflections or commentary upon God's word. John Baillie observed that a broad theme in twentieth century writing about revelation was that "all revelation is given, not in the form of directly communicated knowledge, but through events occurring in the historical experience of mankind . . . which therefore engender in the mind of man such reflective knowledge as it is given him to possess."[7] Unless we understand God's speech as an event, first century Jews did not regard the Law of God as knowledge "engendered in the mind of man" from the events of the Exodus. The Law in all its detail is not explicable as a reflection on the visible events of the Exodus. Rather, God's speech is itself an object upon which people reflect. The first century Jewish idea that God spoke with a real language when giving the Law does not require that the exact original wording has been preserved, but it does require that the words of law given in scripture accurately represent or summarize those original words. Otherwise, the words could not function in any particularity as binding law, as they evidently did for first century Jews. We read in the Rule of the Community used in first century Qumran that those who enter the community must "walk with perfection on all the paths of God, conforming to all he has decreed concerning the regular times of his commands and not turn aside, either left or right, nor infringe even one of his words."[8] Obedience to all of God's commands was a matter of grave concern among first century Jews, for it was thought that the curses of the Law had fallen upon Israel, and would continue to fall if the Law was not kept. We read in the Halakhic Letter from Qumran, "And we are aware that part of the blessings and curses have occurred that are written in the b[ook of Mo]ses."[9] Evidence of first century Jewish concern about the threat of impending judgment can also be found in the canonical Gospels, most notably in the warnings of John the Baptist (Matt 3:7–9). This all indicates a first century Jewish

---

5. Philo of Alexandria, *Decalogue* 46 (Yonge).
6. Josephus, *Antiquities* 3.90 (Whiston).
7. Baillie, *Revelation in Recent Thought*, 62.
8. 1QRule of the Community (1QS), Col. III, 10 (Watson) 6.
9. 4QHalakhic Lettere, frg. 1=4Q398 = 4QpapMMTe (Watson) 84.

acceptance that God gave the Law using real language. John Baillie has criticized the idea that revelation is to be understood as conceptual knowledge about God.[10] However, language is a category that includes far more than dogmatic knowledge, for language can express and make known the person who speaks. As Karl Barth said, "The word is the unassuming but incomparably true form in which people simply impart themselves, no more and no less, to others."[11]

JEWISH EPISTEMOLOGY: GOD'S SPEECH AND ANTHROPOMORPHISM

Some might suppose that even in Jewish thought it would be considered naively anthropomorphic to think God's speech at Sinai was actually in the form of language. Julius Wellhausen asked, "Who can seriously believe that Yahweh wrote the ten commandments on stone . . . and even thundered them down at the assembled people with his own voice from the mountaintop?" Wellhausen suggests that this is poetic license.[12] However, first century Jewish use of the Law of Moses seems inexplicable if Jews did not believe that God spoke using language. The Law is cited as binding, and the application of the Law can depend upon a single word. The problem of anthropomorphism is, however, deeper than even Wellhausen's remark indicates.

In the first century, Jews would not have denied that God speaks using language, since they accepted even more anthropomorphic representations of God in connection with theophanies. The theophanies are momentous and often terrifying appearances of God. These appearances differ from the universal presence of God that is relied upon by those who pray or offer sacrifice. God's appearances are marked by their limitation to a particular place and time, by otherwise inexplicable phenomena, and by the fear that weighed upon those to whom God appeared. We have already noted these characteristics in God's coming to Mount Sinai. Similarly, when the LORD appears to Moses from within the burning bush, "Moses hid his face, for he was afraid to look upon God" (Exod 3:6). The mortal danger of seeing God explains part of its dread. When Moses later asks to see God's glory, the LORD responds, "You cannot see my face, for no man can see me and live"(Exod 33:20; cf. Exod 19:21–22). Isaiah expresses this same sense of dread, when he sees a vision of the LORD, and says, "Woe is me for I am ruined, because I am a man of unclean lips, and I live among a people of unclean lips, for my eyes have seen the King, the LORD of hosts" (Isa 6:5). Indeed, each one of the seraphim "covered his face" at this sight, calling out, "Holy, holy, holy, is the LORD of hosts" (Isa 6:2–3). God also appeared to others, including Abram (Gen 12:6–7), and Elijah (1 Kings 19:13). In the Hebrew Scriptures, there are many examples of such appearances.[13] In most of these appearances, God speaks, and his words are recounted. Jeffrey Niehaus has even noted

---

10. Baillie, *Revelation in Recent Thought*, 83–108.

11. Barth, *Commentary on John 1*, 26.

12. See Wellhausen, *Israelitische und jüdische Geschichte*, 12–13, cited as translated in Niehaus, *God at Sinai*, 50.

13. For the recent literature, see Niehaus, *God at Sinai*. See also Kuntz, *The Self-Revelation of God*, and Kline, *Images of the Spirit*.

that, without any pronouncement by God, the "theophany would go unexplained."[14] These appearances have features that are anthropomorphic. Nevertheless, the evidence indicates that first century Jews accepted these appearances as nonfiction. Philo says of the burning bush, "And in the middle of the flame there was seen a certain very beautiful form, not resembling any visible thing, a most Godlike image, emitting a light more brilliant than fire, which any one might have imagined to be the image of the living God. But let it be called an angel, because it merely related the events which were about to happen."[15] Josephus says the people were brought near to Sinai "that they might hear God himself speaking to them."[16] The Gospels likewise refer to what "God said" in the burning bush (Matt 22:31; Mark 12:26).

While accepting the reality of theophanies, Judaism of the first century regularly denied that, in an ultimate sense, anyone could really *see* the unseen God. According to Philo, Herod Agrippa's appeal to the Emperor Caius said, "Now pictures and images are only imitations of those gods who are perceptible to the outward senses; but it was not considered by our ancestors to be consistent with the reverence due to God to make any image or representation of the invisible God."[17] That the true God was unseen was an active point of friction between Jews and their pagan neighbors, and Christians adopted the Jewish idea. There are strong indications that many Jews thought that, in one sense, God himself cannot be seen, even in his appearances.[18] John himself writes, "No man has seen God at any time" (John 1:18). God's appearance was itself regarded as only a partial representation of his full reality. Similarly, just as Hebrew scripture used the expression, "the Angel of the LORD" in connection with God's appearance at the burning bush, so theophanies are sometimes referred to in the first century as an angel.[19] Nevertheless, the other passages cited above show that first century Jews thought God had really appeared and spoken in the theophanies, even if he appears in angelic form. As God himself was heard in his word, God himself is seen in the phenomena of his appearances.

For first century Judaism, the theophanies seemed plausible. It was only by accepting some anthropomorphism that God could be known as a god who speaks. The phenomena of the theophanies are often integral to God's message, for they identify who is speaking. As mentioned above, God's ability to speak to people was a mark that he is a living God, whereas the inability of idols to speak was one of the marks that they are not gods at all (Ps 115:3–8; Jer 10:5). If God's use of language seems to make him too much like a human person, the lack of speech seemed to many Jews to make a god too much like inanimate wood or stone. Furthermore, to deny that God speaks using language is arguably a denial of God's ability to speak or communicate, since most communication can be represented only as language. Denial that God speaks using language is not a

14. Niehaus, *God at Sinai*, 29.
15. Philo of Alexandria, *Life of Moses 1*, 66 (Yonge) 465. Cf. Philo's *On the Decalogue* 46–47.
16. Josephus, *Antiquities* 3.89 (Whiston) 85.
17. Philo of Alexandria, *Embassy to Gaius* 290 (Yonge), 783.
18. See John 1:18; 6:46; Rom 1:20; Col 1:15; 1 Tim 6:16; 1 John 4:12. For the opposite sense, see Matt 5:8.
19. See Acts 7:30–38 and the references by Philo of Alexandria quoted above.

merely literary judgment; it is a theological judgment about the character of God and of the way that people can relate to God. Given that theophanies were accepted in Jewish thought, it is doubtful that Jews of the first century would have disbelieved in God's use of language simply because language has human qualities.

JEWISH EPISTEMOLOGY: GOD'S SPEECH AND INTERMEDIARIES

The Hebrew Scriptures regard the fearful presence of God's appearances as a major reason that God speaks to people indirectly through prophets. After hearing the Ten Commandments directly, the people of Israel are terrified of God's presence. In order to alleviate this fear, the people of Israel asked Moses to stand as an intermediary, hearing God's words and passing them on to the people. Niehaus describes this as "an appropriate human fear of Yahweh's holy presence."[20] Indeed, the people to whom God appears typically express a fear of impending death, for they stand on the brink of an unendurable revelation of God. Even Moses, however, could only endure a certain proximity to God. We read,

> "The cloud covered the tent of meeting, and the glory of the LORD filled the tabernacle, and Moses was not able to enter the tent of meeting because the cloud had settled on it, and the glory of the LORD filled the tabernacle." (Exod 40:34–35)

Similarly, we read that when Moses asked to see God's glory, God told Moses, "No man can see my face and live" (Exod 33:20). For this reason God's appearance and speech are always partial revelation.

In the Hebrew Scriptures, God normally speaks to the people of Israel only through prophets, and only on momentous occasions. Direct speech to all the people was a rare exception used for the giving of the Ten Commandments. Reflection on the meaning and implications of God's words might be an implicit part of a prophetic message, but it was always derivative from the prophetic message. The few people with whom God speaks verbally are usually people who follow God. However, God's most important messages are not spoken to all pious people directly, but rather are spoken indirectly through prophets. That this was the accepted first century Jewish view is indicated by Jewish reverence for the Law, and for Moses as the prophet who gave them the Law, and for the later prophets. This reverence pervades the Qumran documents, Philo,[21] the New Testament, Josephus, and the Mishnah. For example, we read from Qumran, "And whoever enters the council of the Community shall make a binding promise to re[vert] to the Law of Moses with all that it decrees, with whole heart and whole soul."[22] When God does speak to prophets, it seems usually to be only for matters of considerable (often national or historic) importance, not only for the person directly addressed. Given that the appearance of God is an occasion for fear and trembling, it is consistent with the unbearable weight of God's glory that he does

---

20. Niehaus, *God at Sinai*, 221.
21. E.g., Philo, *Embassy to Gaius* (210–212) and Philo, *On the Life of Moses*.
22. E.g., 4Q258 (4Q Rule of the Communityd) 5, 6. (Watson) 22.

not speak to everyone alike, or at all times. It is foreign to Jewish thought to expect the Creator of heaven and earth, whose word of power created the world, to speak to every person directly. Fitting to the majesty of his almighty power, God speaks to people primarily through his chosen prophets. At the giving of the Ten Commandments, the people of Israel are amazed, saying, "we have seen today that God speaks with man, yet he lives" (Deut 5:24). The people had never before personally *experienced* that direct speech was possible, having always known God's speech indirectly through Moses. The people fear to have this experience repeated ever again.

That God rarely speaks except through a prophet is also indicated by Moses' unique role as the regular intermediary for the delivery of God's words. At God's first appearance to Moses, God says to Moses that Aaron "shall speak for you to the people; and it shall come about that he shall be as a mouth for you, and you shall be as God to him" (Exod 4:16). Similarly, God says to Moses, "See, I make you as God to Pharaoh, and your brother Aaron shall be your prophet. You shall speak all that I command you, and your brother Aaron shall speak to Pharaoh that he let the sons of Israel go out of his land" (Exod 7:1, 2). God tells Moses that he will speak to the people at Mount Sinai "in a thick cloud, in order that the people may hear when I speak with you, and may also believe in you forever" (Exod 19:9). After the Ten Commandments are given, Moses' leading prophetic role is again emphasized. We read, "Whenever Moses went in before the LORD to speak with Him, he would take off the veil until he came out; and whenever he came out and spoke to the sons of Israel what he had been commanded, the sons of Israel would see the face of Moses, that the skin of Moses' face shone" (Exod 34:34–35a). Even while removed from a direct encounter with the divine presence, the people are still afraid of Moses because his face would shine after he had spoken with God. Moses wears a veil on his face when he speaks to the people so they will not be afraid of him (Exod 34:35b). Josephus, from within first century Judaism, supports this tradition of Moses as intermediary, as does the New Testament (2 Cor 3:7, 13). Josephus writes that, after the construction of the tabernacle, "Moses went no longer up to Mount Sinai, but went into the tabernacle, and learned of God what they were to do and what laws should be made, which laws were preferable to what have been devised by human understanding."[23] In the account of Aaron and Miriam's complaint against Moses, Moses' unique knowledge of God is emphasized,

> Hear now my words: If there is a prophet among you; I, the LORD shall make myself known to him in a vision. I shall speak with him in a dream. Not so, with my servant Moses, he is faithful in all my household; With him I speak mouth to mouth, even openly, and not in dark sayings, and he beholds the form of the LORD, Why then were you not afraid to speak against my servant, against Moses? (Num 12:6–8)

Moses' unique relationship with God shows that the Prophet who would be like Moses is also conceived of as a dominant figure. As Jeffrey Niehaus remarks, "Moses as covenant

---

23. Josephus, *Antiquities*, 3.222–23 (Whiston) 94.

mediator sees Yahweh in a way that no one else does. He has an unparalleled exposure to the divine glory.[24]

JEWISH EPISTEMOLOGY: INTERMEDIARIES AND AUTHENTICATION

The indirect revelation of God's word is a source of epistemological difficulty, since a prophet's claims could not always be trusted. It is to be emphasized that Jewish scripture had for centuries recognized that (even Jewish) people would at times follow prophets of other gods (Deut 13:2; 1 Kgs 18:16–24), or trust false prophets of the true God (Jer 28:15; 29:8, 9, 31). First century Jewish recognition of the existence of false prophets is evident from a document found at Qumran that says, "They prophesied deceit in order to divert Israel from following God."[25] The Hebrew Scriptures did not interpret the real existence of false prophets as justifying complete skepticism about the possibility of knowing the words of God. Rather, like the Jewish judicial system, the Hebrew Scriptures offered precedents for judging and confirming controversial claims. Indeed, the Law of Moses required that one examine prophets, so this was a properly judicial task. Prophets were not to be trusted without regard to evidence, but rather because the facts were somehow considered sufficient to warrant trust. In Jewish thought it was accepted that trust in a prophet must be warranted. Indeed, this is why it was possible for the Jewish leadership to reject Jesus, and why John takes pains in his gospel to vindicate Jesus of the charges made by the Jewish leadership. The charges would otherwise justify the Jewish leadership in their rejection of Jesus. In the ancient Jewish view, the reality of false prophetic claims does not eliminate the possibility of knowing that some prophetic testimony is authentic.

Instead of responding to such prophetic claims with religious skepticism, the Hebrew Scriptures provided guidelines that identified false prophets by their false claims. A primary guideline of this type, as might well be expected, was to expect that new claims about God or God's demands should be coherent with what could be separately known of God. For example, the prophet who called people to follow a foreign god was not to be given heed, for this call violated the demands of God which were already made known by the prophet Moses (Deut 13:2). Similarly, any prophet who wrongly foretold what would happen was not to be heeded after his words were shown to be inconsistent with the facts (Deut 18:22). These kinds of guidelines only act negatively, identifying particular instances when prophets were not to be believed. Similarly, the real existence of false prophets is conceived of as giving rise to the negative concern, "How shall we know the word which the LORD has not spoken?" (Deut 18:21). Considering the complexities of applying Jewish law, which are evident from the Mishnah, a wide variety of reasons might have been found to discredit a prophet.

The complexities of identifying a false prophet are illustrated by Jeremiah's response to the false prophet Hananiah (Jer 27). Jeremiah initially concedes that a prediction by

---

24. Niehaus, *God at Sinai*, 212.

25. 4QDamascus Documentd (formerly 4Q269 but now renumbered as 4Q267) (Watson) 36. The reading is confirmed by the later Cairo Genizah manuscript CD–A Col. VI, 1.

Hananiah may be authentically from God, for he allows Hananiah to publicly remove the yoke that Jeremiah had placed on his own neck as a prophetic symbol of impending judgment. However, Jeremiah recognizes that Hananiah's prediction has a contrary appearance to the prediction of earlier prophets, so he instructs the people to remember that fulfillment of predictions is the final test of authenticity. Jeremiah tells the people to neither believe nor disbelieve Hananiah, but to wait and see. The reason for this reluctance, however, is that Hananiah's prediction has this contrary appearance. Yet Jeremiah was not sure that it really was contrary, for he could not be sure that God had not changed his mind for some reason. Otherwise, Jeremiah would not have called for the confirmation of Hananiah's words. For our purposes it is not necessary to fully describe or show the validity of any method used to examine prophets, but only to show that first century Judaism thought in principle that it could be done.

JEWISH EPISTEMOLOGY: WARRANT VERSUS PROOF

The Hebrew Scriptures regarded it as possible for knowledge of God to come by means of other people's knowledge of and testimony about God, even though testimony is not always reliable. The mere existence of false prophets was not itself considered a reasonable cause for doubting all prophetic testimony; rather, there must be specific evidence that warrants doubt of a prophet's word. This could include, for example, practical experience of many people making false claims. Apparently there were never large numbers of such claims. Even though the acceptance of testimony (after sufficient public examination) does not itself absolutely eliminate deception or error as a logical or an actual possibility, those possibilities are often excluded as lacking any probability, due to the absence of specific and substantive evidence warranting belief that error or deception has actually occurred. The ultimate reason for accepting testimony as factual was that testimony often seemed reliable, and so was a nearly undeniable source of knowledge. Failure to discredit false prophets was attributed to unfaithfulness to God's revelation through Moses. Despite the existence of false prophets, the legal guidelines were apparently stringent enough that spurious claims could generally be recognized. This acceptance of examined testimony is more closely related to judicial criteria for determining the truth "beyond reasonable doubt," than to criteria that are skeptical of testimony as a means of knowledge.

GROUNDS FOR BELIEF IN JESUS: A DISCUSSION WITH HINDLEY

Given this Jewish background about the grounds on which belief in a revealed message was considered credible, we will now describe and evaluate the views of J. C. Hindley about the grounds for belief expected in the Fourth Gospel. Hindley gives the most detailed published discussion available about the Fourth Gospel's expected grounds for belief.[26] He centers his argument on the use of testimony (*martyria*) in the Gospel. Hindley sees three primary sources of testimony, "the self-witness of Jesus, the witness

---

26. Hindley, "Witness in the Fourth Gospel."

of the Father [about Jesus], and the witness of the works."[27] Since we have discussed in a previous chapter Hindley's comments about Jesus' miracles as testimony, we will focus here on the testimony of Jesus and the Father.

Hindley characterizes Jesus' witness about himself as testimony that "cannot be in any way checked or controlled" so that Jesus' "heavenly origin is not proved."[28] For this view, Hindley cites Bultmann's support. However, our prior discussion about Jesus' miracles shows that the Evangelist does represent Jesus' miracles as a way to check Jesus' testimony. In this Gospel, Jesus says, "If I do not do the works of my Father, do not believe me" (John 10:37; cf. John 5:36). Similarly, the Evangelist clearly understands John the Baptist as one who was "sent by God to bear witness" independently of Jesus (John 1:6–8,34). The Evangelist also considers the testimony of the Scriptures to be a check upon Jesus' claims (John 5:46). Hindley discounts these two latter controls, apparently because he believes their evidence is historically or rationally problematic. However, this is to assume that John shared modern doubts about the validity of such evidence. Given John's belief in miracles, his acceptance of John the Baptist as a prophet, and his acceptance of Moses' authority as preserved in the scripture of the community, there is little reason to suppose this was so.

Hindley next argues that the testimony of the Father to Jesus is "the internal assent of the heart which leads to belief, as E. F. Scott maintained."[29] Hindley argues largely from Jesus' words in the following text:

> . . . these works which I do bear witness about me that the Father has sent me. And the Father who sent me, he has borne witness of me. You have neither heard his voice at any time, nor seen his form. And you do not have his word abiding in you, for you do not believe him whom he sent. (John 5:36b–38)

Herman Ridderbos, similarly, understands the witness of the Father in this text as something beyond the perception of Jesus' opponents. Ridderbos writes, "It seems rather that here again the reference is to 'seeing' and 'hearing' that are attributable only to the Son of God, and from the vantage point of which *he* speaks (cf. 1:18; 3:11; 5:19, 20; 6:46; 7:29)."[30]

Against Hindley's view, there is good reason to regard the Father's testimony as publicly accessible. Beasley-Murray says, "The Father's witness in this paragraph [John 5:37–40] is *his word in the Scriptures* (so Schlatter, 157; Bultmann, 266, Hoskyns, 273)."[31] This view makes better sense of John's text, especially if we think more narrowly of those scriptures that simply record God's words spoken directly to Moses. The reference to not seeing the Father's form or hearing his voice is, in the context of Judaism, a reference to a theophany, not to reason or conscience. Jesus' point is not that God never spoke in a way which could be known, but is rather that the Jews of Jesus' day could only know God by

27. Ibid., 320.
28. Ibid., 321.
29. Ibid., 326.
30. Ridderbos, *The Gospel of John*, 204.
31. Beasley-Murray, *John*, 78.

means of testimony from one to whom God had spoken directly. Most significantly for Jews, their scriptures said that God had not even given his Law directly to the people of Israel. Instead, he gave his Law to Moses, who then gave the Law to Israel (Deut 5:23–31). Moses was also thought to have heard God's voice (at Mount Sinai), and to have "seen his form" (e.g., Exod 33:23), and to have been the appointed mouthpiece for the delivery of the Law. Jesus' then charges that his opponents have turned from this Law, saying, "you do not have his word abiding in you." This language is drawn from Ps 119, where it refers to obedience to the commandments of God (e.g., Ps 119:11, 57, 67, 74, 101). Jesus' point, then, is that since his contemporaries could not expect to hear God directly, it was only their obstinacy that prevented them from believing the ones (Jesus and Moses) to whom God had spoken. This is why, in the dialogue following this text, Jesus emphasizes that his opponents cannot believe in him. They already have shown, in his estimation, unwillingness to consider with any seriousness the testimony of God spoken to Moses,

> This is according to all that you asked of the LORD your God in Horeb [at Mount Sinai] on the day of the assembly, saying, "Let me not hear again the voice of the LORD my God, let me not see this great fire anymore, lest I die. And the LORD said to me, they have spoken well. I will raise up a prophet from among their countrymen like you, and I will put my words in his mouth, and he shall speak to them all that I command him. (Deut 18:16–18)

These words, at least, are the Father's testimony in support of Jesus' claim. That this text, at least, is in mind is indicated by Jesus' claim that Moses "wrote of me" (John 5:46). There is no other obvious reference in the Torah to such a prominent figure as Jesus claims to be. The Prophet like Moses is a well known figure to John, for John does not bother to explain his identity when the figure is mentioned in the Gospel, and he portrays this figure as well known to the people (John 1:21; 6:14; 7:40).

Hindley next remarks that Jesus' "heavenly origin is not proved," but this statement is misleading.[32] The unqualified use of the term "proved" invokes modern ideas about the standard of proof that can warrant belief. This is an imposition on John's own idea of proof, for under many modern standards of proof (which question testimony as a means for knowledge), it would be impossible to prove that any divine revelation ever occurred. John does not recognize such standards of evidence as reasonable. Like the Jews of his time, he accepted the laws given through Moses as authentically from God. Under Jewish standards of evidence, this did not require an absolute proof, but rather it required only that the supporting testimony be sufficient to warrant belief. Although no independent witness confirmed the individual laws given through Moses, Jews still accepted the laws as authentically from God. They did so on at least two grounds. First, Moses' status as God's representative was confirmed when God himself spoke the Ten Commandments at Mount Sinai, and the whole community "heard his voice." Moses' testimony is also confirmed for later generations by the people directly hearing God's voice at Mount Sinai, given so that, as God says to Moses, "the people may hear when I speak with you, and may also believe in you forever" (Exod 19:9). Second, Moses' status

---

32. Hindley, "Witness in the Fourth Gospel," 321.

was confirmed by the miracles God performed in the sight of the entire community, and similarly by the public evidences of God's presence—such as the cloud which stood over the tabernacle—where Moses received the Law from God. The scriptures telling of this are regarded as the community's preserved tradition. As with Moses, Jesus' status was confirmed by miracles. Since the community accepts the words given to Moses as authentic, they should accept the promise of God that he would raise up a Prophet who had a similar revelatory function to Moses (Deut 18:16–19).

Hindley acknowledges that Jesus' claim to a heavenly origin is backed up in John's Gospel by limited arguments, but he says these arguments "would *not* prove the tremendous assertions in the eyes of any impartial jury."[33] Hindley cites several such arguments (John 10:34, 8:50; 8:28). His conclusion, however, is far different from the assessment of the Evangelist. It is doubtful that the early Christian community would agree that those dissenting from belief were justly or impartially doing so. The Evangelist is instead amazed that people reject Jesus, even in the face of Jesus' miracles, and can only attribute such rejection to blindness (John 12:37–40). The Evangelist recognizes no grounds that justify a settled doubt of Jesus' claims, even if the Evangelist does not provide absolute proof (such as seeing, rather than testimony). The Evangelist thinks his evidence that God sent Jesus is sufficient to have placed the burden of proof on those who would disbelieve Jesus. Hindley notes further that these evidences "are plainly not logically compelling, and in fact they are rejected by many in the Gospel."[34] This assumes, however, that Jesus' rejection shows there was a deficiency of evidence, rather than an opposing purpose. The phrase "logically compelling" also suggests a modern standard of evidence that was alien to John and to his audience. Hindley's assessment shows no detailed understanding of the force that John's argument held for an ancient Jewish audience.

Hindley offers a second basis for denying that others could know Jesus' heavenly origin. Hindley cites Jesus' words, "you do not know from where I come or where I am going" (John 8:14). Hindley thinks this statement means that knowledge of Jesus' heavenly origin is not available to those who do not have faith in him. However, in a sister passage Jesus says, "You know both me and where I am from, and I have not come of myself" (John 7:28). In another we read that Jesus says to his disciples, "And you know the way where I am going. Thomas says to him, 'Lord, we do not know where you are going, how do we know the way?'" (John 14:5). These passages are better reconciled as indicating merely that Jesus' opponents know in a general way that Jesus has come from God (and so should follow him), but have no clear or detailed conception of how this is true.

Hindley's work offers two important observations. First, Hindley notes perceptively that the Evangelist "is concerned with the logical structure of the revelation in Jesus and its acceptance."[35] This is evident from the Evangelist's interest both in the nature of revelation and in the use of testimony as a theme. It is a theme that ties together the prologue

33. Ibid., 321, 323.
34. Ibid., 324.
35. Ibid.

John's Essential Message as Grounds for Belief in Jesus

in a way that other approaches do not. Second, Hindley notes that those who believe in Jesus gain access to other evidences for Jesus' authority. Hindley says, "they imply certain experiences of 'life', and so forth in the lives of those who respond."[36] This view is supported by the Evangelist's claim that Jesus' opponents do not "know" God (John 8:55) and that the knowledge of God is eternal life (John 17:3). Similarly, the Holy Spirit is sent to teach and to bring remembrance of all that Jesus said (John 14:26) and to bear witness of Jesus (John 15:26). As Ridderbos has argued, this is not intended to eclipse what Jesus said in his earthly ministry, but to make its implications clear.[37] Hindley is right to recognize the importance of subjective testimony, however it is important as well to recognize the use of objective testimony in this Gospel.

CONCLUSION: GROUNDS FOR BELIEF IN JOHN'S KERYGMA

From this chapter's review of the first century Jewish idea of revelation, and from consideration of Hindley's work, we can better understand the grounds on which the Evangelist expected people to believe his essential message. This message included a strong Christological claim which, in evangelistic or apologetic argument with the main Jewish community, made it necessary to appeal to the most fundamental Jewish ideas about revelation. One of these fundamental ideas was that God reveals himself in the manner he chooses. The facts made known by God's self-revelation are the only way that people can have any knowledge of God, so people must allow the facts to guide their human understanding. Jesus had come and made claims that required examination as prophetic testimony. The Evangelist believed he could rightly interpret the miracles and words of Jesus only as being authentic revelation. In accord with the Jewish view of revelation, the Evangelist had to interpret Jesus' words and miracles together with other accepted facts of revelation. These other facts of revelation included both the created world and the revelation from God given through Moses. The revelation through Moses was attested by miracles and by the Jewish community's preservation of the tradition about Moses found in their scripture. In general, Jews thought such facts of revelation, such as the sayings and miracles of Moses, could be credibly communicated by testimony. This is why the Evangelist also tells of the essential words and miracles of Jesus. Though such facts could be made known by sufficient testimony, sufficient testimony does not usually have the character of being incontestable. The Evangelist did not think that the facts of revelation would force in everyone a consequent trust and acceptance of Jesus; rather, they only provided a sufficient basis to warrant trust. John believed he could only explain the facts of Jesus' works and message, especially Jesus' claims, as an appearance of God himself in human form (John 1:14). Yet, since God is unseen, John conceived of this more strictly as the word of God appearing in the flesh. In Jewish thought, God's appearances and speech always seemed anthropomorphic to some degree, yet this was the only way that people could be thought to have knowledge of a God who speaks. Consequently, there were no compelling reasons on Jewish grounds to deny that God could appear in human

---

36. Ibid., 323.
37. Ridderbos, *Gospel according to John*, 15.

form if he wished, provided that by this no one claimed to have seen God (John 1:18). The purpose of the Incarnation also made its innovative character more plausible. By appearing in human form, God expressed himself in a way that could speak to our full human nature. The glory of God was seen, bringing life and salvation to the world.

12

Conclusions

JOHN THE EVANGELIST WRITES for a catechetical and evangelistic purpose. He portrays Jesus' divine attestation by miracle and scripture as sufficient evidence that all should accept Jesus as one sent by God. John portrays the denial of Jesus' claims as evidence of ill will, comparable to a rejection of Moses and the Law that God gave to Moses, and so amounting to a rejection of God. In Jewish thought, a rejection of God's full representative could only result in God's judgment.

John's epistemology cannot be understood without some prior determinations of the intended historical and fictional character of the Gospel. In particular, many scholars doubt the historicity of the miracle accounts, and some scholars have supposed that the Evangelist intended the miracles to be understood as fiction or as merely symbolic. However, many professional philosophers today still vigorously advocate the possibility of miracles, so that it is unreasonable to assume that the Evangelist, in the first century, would necessarily find miracle accounts incredible. Ancient readings of John's Gospel show that the miracles were not understood as fictional or merely symbolic. Miracle reports were widely credited by early Christian authors, and there is no sufficient reason to think that John would be an exception. John's interest in miracle accounts is what would naturally be expected from one who saw significance in miracles. While some have claimed that John depreciates belief that arose from miracles, this is not confirmed by exegesis of the texts usually cited in support. Depreciation of belief arising from miracles is also antipathetic to first century Jewish thought, which accepted the miracle accounts of the book of Exodus as grounds on which Pharaoh should have believed Moses.

The credibility of miracle reports is often denied on the grounds that belief in such reports demands absolute certainty, and that certainty is attainable only by logical reasoning rather than sensory knowledge. Perceptions and reports of others' perceptions are denied as sources of warranted belief and knowledge. Such views first came into prominence near the beginning of the nineteenth century. Kierkegaard rejected philosophical skepticism about knowledge that arises apart from human reasoning, maintaining that knowledge could arise separately by divine revelation. The Evangelist, as well, accepts divine revelation, but in addition he has a higher regard for observation and testimony as a source of knowledge and warranted belief. His view has more affinity with the acceptance of testimony by courts and society, than with the demand by skeptical philosophers for absolute certainty.

While modern scholars have varying understandings of the Fourth Gospel's miracles, the Evangelist regards the miraculous element in each of his miracle accounts as essentially historical and nonfictional. Because the Evangelist offers the miracles as a reason to believe, his credibility depended on each miracle account being accepted as genuinely miraculous, the miraculous character being adequately supported by details he regarded as authentic, including Jesus' own performance of the miracle. This does not require that he regarded his account as entirely accurate, but it does require that he regarded it as essentially historical. Any supposed elaboration of his account for literary purposes cannot have interfered with or undermined his essential nonfictional claim.

Consequently, the Evangelist portrays belief in Jesus as being warranted by the evidence of the miracles, together with other public evidence. This other evidence would include God's revelation through Moses and the Prophets, public knowledge that Jesus was observant of God's law, and public knowledge of the character of Jesus and his teachings. For the Evangelist, the miracles themselves also stand as public evidence, just as Moses' miracles stood as evidence for Pharaoh. In John's thought, there is no credible alternative explanation for the miracles other than that God performed the miracles, showing that God sent Jesus. The revelation from God given through miraculous signs is public, not an internal revelation given only to some. Failure to believe in Jesus is regarded as arising from human stubbornness, rather than from any supposed inadequacy of the miracles as evidence. John regards miracles as observable events, so that belief in the occurrence of a miracle is compelled by evidence. However, belief in Jesus cannot be compelled, since this requires not just a belief that Jesus performed a miracle, but also an inference that Jesus was sent by God. The Evangelist thought that this inference was compelling, but could be resisted by those whose hearts were stubborn. The attitude of Pharaoh in the face of Moses' miracles is a parallel to John's conception of the rejection of Jesus.

Many scholars also broadly doubt the historicity and nonfictional character of Jesus' words as they are portrayed in John's Gospel. Nevertheless, there is at least one part of the Evangelist's messages that cannot be intended as nonfiction. The Evangelist advocates certain messages, even though he portrays these messages as the grounds on which many Jews rejected Jesus. Such advocacy by the Evangelist shows that he regards such messages as essential to belief in Jesus; if he did not think them both essential and true, he would not promote messages that turned many people from Jesus and from God. Consequently, these divisive messages constitute at least a portion of John's kerygma. They include elements of John's distinctive Christological expression, including Christological claims that the Evangelist regards as so essential that they must be included even though they were treated by Jesus' opponents as blasphemous (John 8:58).

For several reasons, it is not plausible that John's essential kerygma could have been his own innovation. The Christian community around him could hardly have accepted a new expression of Christianity as "essential" to a saving belief in Jesus, since this would be an implicit rejection of the kerygma and tradition they already held and of the church already in existence. At most, John emphasized certain elements in the accepted kerygma of the church. Even this emphasis cannot have been so striking that there were significant factions of the church that rejected John's message. John fails to defend himself from any criticism other than that which was raised by Jewish opponents and by former disciples of Jesus. John specifically claims that the eleven apostles held to elements of his distinctively Johannine kerygma; that claim would have undermined John's credibility if it were known to be false. This in turn shows that John's kerygma was not his own innovation, but reflected accepted tradition. While it has been widely suggested that the Synoptic Gospels have a Christology that opposes the Christology of John's Gospel, examination shows the deep affinities between the Christology of all the canonical Gospels. The tendency to read distinctive features in John's vocabulary, concepts, and literary structure as evidence for a fictional origin of every part of John's message is simplistic, for it cannot hold up with respect to John's kerygma. Given the nonfictional character of John's kerygma, it is further evident that John's nonfiction is not limited to controversial messages in his distinctive kerygma, but includes other messages as well.

Since John considers his divisive message to be essential and nonfictional, on what grounds does he expect his audience to believe this message? The Evangelist admits that Jesus' words must be somehow confirmed, and thinks that they can only be confirmed by appeal to others who have had revelation from God. These others include John the Baptist and Moses. The scriptures are also cited as authorities, but for John these in turn depend on prophets who spoke by prophetic revelation.

Dependence upon divine revelation for proof is alien to the modern mind, as Kierkegaard observed. However to the first century Jewish mind, the revelation of God's Law through Moses was confirmed by the miracles of Moses and by God himself speaking the Ten Commandments to the whole nation from Mount Sinai. All of these events were thought to lie within the capacity of credible historical report, and so the scriptures were accepted. Since hearing God directly was terrifying, the full Law of God was declared to Moses rather than directly to the nation. Moses in turn announced to the nation the laws that God had given. Jews regarded Moses' declaration of the laws as credible grounds for belief, because of the attestation of miracles and the divine voice at Mount Sinai. Testimony about divine revelation had certain controls, for it had to be checked against testimony of any previous revelation. For this reason, all prophets after Moses had to be consistent with Moses to be recognized. Jews did not recognize the mere possibility of error as a legitimate ground for doubting testimony, whether it was prophetic testimony, accounts of prophetic testimony that were handed down as scripture, or human testimony generally. Evidence of error was required to justify doubt.

The Evangelist credits prophets because he accepts the Jewish idea that God sometimes communicates to people using human language. Speaking in a language seems anthropomorphic, but in Jewish thought the denial of a god's ability to speak was a denial that the god was real (Ps 115:5). These anthropomorphic features were accepted rather than deny that God could communicate. However, since God's appearances were terrifying, and perhaps because it seemed inappropriate that the One who created the heavens by his word should speak to every person directly, it was understood that God normally spoke to people through prophets as intermediaries.

The Evangelist supports his Christology from what he considers to be facts of revelation. These include the miracles and words of Jesus, the tradition of the miracles and words of Moses, the words of the Prophets, and the order of the created world. John regards testimony given by prophetic revelation as provisionally credible (like other testimony), even though it must be checked against other revelation. He thought the knowledge arising from this revelation warranted belief in Jesus. However since such belief in Jesus required trust, those who were unwilling could instead fasten upon some implausible explanation of the revealed evidence. To John's mind revelation always had limited anthropomorphic features, but it was not for man to decide how God should reveal himself, and the evidence for Jesus' claims was sufficient to justify belief in Jesus as the Word of God appearing in the flesh.

From the argument of this thesis, a number of consequences deserve note. First, the basic structure of John's epistemology has been described with significant new detail. This structure gives serious attention to the Evangelist's own arguments and ideas about the proper warrants for belief. In particular, Jesus' miracles, and the prophetic character of the claims of Jesus stand as evidence of importance to the Evangelist. In accord with Jewish thought, John regards both prophetic testimony, and reports about miracles and prophetic sayings, as provisionally credible, just like testimony about other events is provisionally credible. He regards reports of miracles and prophetic sayings as provisionally credible, even if the reports are received from earlier generations. This structure recognizes the importance that John's epistemology had for his catechetical or evangelistic purposes, especially when dealing with Jewish believers.

Detailed arguments have clarified the discussion about John's use of miracles. First, it has been argued that John expected his miracles to be understood as nonfiction. Second, a detailed argument, with exegesis, has been given against the idea that John does not accept or promote Jesus' miracles as warranting a saving belief in Jesus. John thought the miracles did warrant belief, if accompanied by knowledge of Jesus' character and message, and by knowledge of Jewish ideas about God and prophetic revelation.

The argument also shows that John intends his divisively controversial claims to be understood as nonfiction. These claims include elements of John's distinctive formulations of Christology. Use of controversial claims in John's Gospel, together with his assertions that these elements are authentic, shows that the author's controversial claims could not be claims newly proposed by the author. Instead, they are claims that the Christian community must already have widely accepted, at least implicitly, and without substantive Christian dissent. Consequently, the claims are drawn from the community's advocacy of those controversial claims, including important elements of John's Christology. These arguments extend Dodd's argument about historical tradition in John's Gospel, by showing the state of tradition when the Gospel was published. This result also removes considerable confusion, which has resulted from the assumption that the miracles recounted by John, and the controversial elements of John's message (including controversial elements of his distinctive Christology), might be intended as essentially fictional, or as his own embellishments.

A detailed explanation has been offered to show that, in accord with Jewish thought, John finds divine revelation (using human language) inherently plausible. For John, revelation offers a certain kind of objectivity. Distinctively Christian claims do not rest upon evidence that is perceived only by Christians, but rather on divine revelation, which stands as public evidence, to be considered with other public divine revelation as found in the Jewish Scriptures, and reasonable examination. The epistemic stance and concerns of the author assume as authorities one Creator, whose speech through prophets has been recorded in Jewish scripture. This is evidence strongly favoring a Jewish, rather than a Greek mindset, in the author. It further suggests an intended audience largely limited to Christians, Jews and Jewish proselytes. The arguments in the Gospel show the seriousness with which revelation was regarded as a source of evidence, in the polemic between Jewish Christians and other Jews. This epistemological stance pervades John's Gospel, and stands as evidence supportive of the literary unity of the work. It is for these reasons that the Gospel begins with the theme of the revealing Word of God.

Bibliography

Abbott, Edwin Abbott. *Johannine Grammar.* London: Black, 1906.
———. *Johannine Vocabulary.* Diatessarica 5. London: Black, 1905.
Aland, Kurt, editor. *Synopsis quattuor evangeliorum: locis parallelis evangeliorum apocryphorum et patrum adhibitis.* Stuttgart: Deutsche Bibelgesellschaft, 1985.
Alston, William. *Perceiving God: The Epistemology of Religious Experience.* Cornell: Cornell University Press, 1991.
Anderson, Paul N. *The Christology of the Fourth Gospel: Its Unity and Disunity in the Light of John 6.* Valley Forge, PA: Trinity, 1997. Reprint, Eugene, OR: Wipf & Stock, 2010.
The Ante-Nicene Fathers. Edited by Alexander Roberts and James Donaldson. 1885–1887. 10 vols. Repr. Peabody, MA: Hendrickson, 1975.
Argyle, Aubrey William. *The Gospel According to Matthew.* New York: Cambridge University Press, 1973.
Augustine. *The City of God Against the Pagans.* Translated by David S. Wiesen. Loeb Classical Library 411. Cambridge: Harvard University Press, 1957.
Aune, David Edward. "Magic in Early Christianity." In *Aufstieg und Niedergang der römischen Welt.* Edited by H. Temporini and W. Haase. Part II, 23/2. 1507–57. New York: Walter de Gruyter, 1980.
Baillie, John. *The Idea of Revelation in Recent Thought.* Bampton Lectures in America 7. New York: Columbia University Press, 1956.
Ball, David Mark. *"I Am" in John's Gospel: Literary Function, Background, and Theological Implications.* Journal for the Study of the New Testament Supplement Series 124. Sheffield: Sheffield Academic, 1996.
Bareille, G. "Gaius." In *Oxford Dictionary of the Christian Church*, edited by F. L. Cross and E. A. Livingstone, 544. Oxford: Oxford University, 1988.
Barrett, Charles Kingsley. *Essays on John.* Philadelphia: Westminster, 1982.
———. *The Gospel According to St John: An Introduction with Commentary and Notes on the Greek Text.* 2nd ed. London: SPCK, 1978.
Barth, Karl. *Church Dogmatics.* Translated by G. T. Thompson et al. Edinburgh: T. & T. Clark, 1936–77.
———. *Witness to the Word, A Commentary on John 1.* Translated by Geoffrey Bromiley. Grand Rapids: Eerdmans, 1986.
Bartholémy, Dominique, and Jozef Tadeusz Milik. *Discoveries in the Judean Desert.* Vol. 1. Oxford: Clarendon, 1955.
Basinger, David. "Miracles." *The Routledge Encyclopedia of Philosophy,* edited by Edward Craig, 6:411–16. New York: Routledge, 1999.
Bauckham, Richard. *God Crucified: Monotheism and Christology in the New Testament.* Didsbury Lectures. Grand Rapids: Eerdmans, 1999.
Bauer, Walter. *A Greek English Lexicon of the New Testament and Other Early Christian Literature.* 2nd ed. Translated by William F. Arndt and W. Wilbur Gingrich. Chicago: University of Chicago Press, 1979.
Beasley-Murray, George Raymond. *John.* Word Biblical Commentary 36. Waco: Word, 1987.
Black, Matthew. *The Scrolls and Christian Origins: Studies in the Jewish Background of the New Testament.* Chico, CA: Scholars, 1983.
Blass, Friedrich, Albert Debrunner, and Robert Walter Funk. *A Greek Grammar of the New Testament and other early Christian Literature.* Chicago: University of Chicago Press, 1961.
Borg, Marcus. *Jesus, a New Vision: Spirit, Culture, and the Life of Discipleship.* San Francisco: Harper & Row, 1987.

Bibliography

Borgen, Peder. "Observations on the Targumic Character of the Prologue of John." *New Testament Studies* 16 (1970) 288–95.

Braun, François-Marie. *Jean le Théologien et son Évangile dans l'Église Ancienne.* In Études bibliques. Paris: J. Gabalda, 1959.

Bretschneider, Karl Gottlieb. *Probabilia de Evangelii et Epistolarum Joannis Apostoli Indole et Origine.* Lipsiae: J. A. Barth, 1820.

Brooks, James A., and Carlton L. Winbery. *Syntax of New Testament Greek.* Washington, DC: University Press of America, 1979.

Brown, Colin. *Miracles and the Critical Mind.* Grand Rapids: Eerdmans, 1984.

Brown, Raymond E. *The Community of the Beloved Disciple.* New York: Paulist, 1979.

———. *The Gospel According to John.* 2 vols. The Anchor Bible 29. New York: Doubleday, 1966–1970.

———. *New Testament Essays.* New York: Doubleday, 1968.

Bultmann, Rudolf. "γινώσκω." In *Theological Dictionary of the New Testament.* Vol. 1. Edited by Gerhard Kittel and Gerhard Friedrich, 689–719. Translated by Geoffrey W. Bromiley. Grand Rapids: Eerdmans, 1964–76.

———. *The Gospel of John: A Commentary.* Translated by G. R. Beasley-Murray. Philadelphia: Westminster, 1971.

———. "New Testament and Mythology." In *Kerygma and Myth: A Theological Debate,* edited by Hans Werner Bartsch. Translated by Reginald H. Fuller, 1–44. London: SPCK, 1953.

———. "πιστεύω." In *Theological Dictionary of the New Testament.* Vol. 6. Edited by Gerhard Kittel and Gerhard Friedrich. Translated by Geoffrey W. Bromiley, 174–228. Grand Rapids: Eerdmans, 1964–76.

Burrows, Miller, translator. *The Dead Sea Scrolls.* New York: Viking, 1955.

Byrne, Brendan. "The Faith of the Beloved Disciple and the Community in John 20." *Journal for the Study of the New Testament* 23 (1985) 83–97.

Byrskog, Samuel. *Story as History, History as Story.* Wissenschaftliche Untersuchungen Zum Neuen Testament 123. Tübingen: Mohr Siebeck, 2000.

Calvin, John. *Commentary on the Gospel of John.* 2 vols. Edited by David W. Torrance and Thomas F. Torrance. Translated by T. H. L. Parker. Grand Rapids: Eerdmans, 1993.

Cameron, Ron, editor. *The Other Gospels: Non-Canonical Gospel Texts.* Philadelphia: Westminster, 1982.

Casey, Maurice. *Is John's Gospel True?* New York: Routledge, 1996.

Catchpole, D. R. *The Trial of Jesus.* Leiden: Brill, 1971.

Childs, Brevard S. *The New Testament as Canon: An Introduction.* Philadelphia: Fortress, 1984.

Clement of Alexandria. *Christ the Educator.* Translated by Simon Wood. Fathers of the Church 23. Washington: Catholic University Press, 1954.

Coady, C. A. J. *Testimony, a Philosophical Study.* Oxford: Clarendon, 1992.

Collins, Raymond F. *Introduction to the New Testament.* New York: Doubleday, 1983.

Cover, Jan A. "Miracles and Christian Theism." In *Reason for the Hope Within,* edited by Michael J. Murray, 345–74. Grand Rapids: Eerdmans, 1999.

Cullmann, Oscar. *The Johannine Circle.* Translated by John Bowden. Philadelphia: Westminster, 1976.

Culpepper, R. Alan. *Anatomy of the Fourth Gospel: A Study in Literary Design.* Philadelphia: Fortress, 1983.

De Jonge, Marinus. "Christology, Controversy and Community in the Gospel of John." In *Christology, Controversy, and Community.* Edited by David R. Catchpole, David G. Horrell, and Christopher M. Tuckett, 209–30. Supplements to Novum Testamentum 99. Boston: Brill, 2000.

Dodd, Charles Harold. *Historical Tradition in the Fourth Gospel.* Cambridge: Cambridge University Press, 1963.

———. *The Interpretation of the Fourth Gospel.* Cambridge: Cambridge University Press, 1953.

Drummond, James. *An Inquiry into the Character and Authorship of the Fourth Gospel.* New York: Charles Scribner, 1904.

Dunn, James D. G. "'Are You the Messiah?': Is the Crux of Mark 14.61–62 Resolvable?" In *Christology, Controversy, and Community.* Edited by David R. Catchpole, David G. Horrell, and Christopher M. Tuckett, 1–22. Boston: Brill, 2000.

Ellis, E. Earle. "Gospels Criticism: A Perspective on the State of the Art." In *The Gospel and the Gospels,* edited by Peter Stuhlmacher, 26–52. Grand Rapids: Eerdmans, 1991.

Evans, C. Stephen. "Empiricism, Rationalism, and the Possibility of Historical Religious Knowledge." In *Christian Perspectives on Religious Knowledge*, edited by C. Steven Evans and Merold Westphal, 134–60. Grand Rapids: Eerdmans, 1993.

Fanning, Buist M. *Verbal Aspect in New Testament Greek*. Oxford: Clarendon, 1990.

Fortna, Robert. "Source and Redaction in the Fourth Gospel's Portrayal of Jesus' Signs." *Journal of Biblical Literature* 89 (1970) 151–66.

———. Review of Gilbert Van Belle, *The Signs Source in the Fourth Gospel*. *Review of Biblical Literature* (6/26/2000). Online: http: //www.bookreviews.org /bookdetail.asp?TitleId=2809&CodePage=2809.

Freed, Edwin and Russell Hunt. "Fortna's Signs-Source in John." *Journal of Biblical Literature* 94 (1975) 563–79.

Gaffney, James. "Believing and Knowing in the Fourth Gospel." *Theological Studies* 26 (1965) 215–41.

García Martínez, Florentino, editor. *The Dead Sea Scrolls Translated*. 2nd ed. Translated by Wilfred Watson. Grand Rapids: Eerdmans, 1996.

Gardner-Smith, Percival. *Saint John and the Synoptic Gospels*. New York: Cambridge University Press: 1938.

Geldenhuys, J. Norval. *Commentary on the Gospel of Luke*. Edinburgh: Marshall, Morgan & Scott, 1950.

Gerhardsson, Birger. "The Gospel Tradition." In *The Interrelations of the Gospels. A Symposium led by M. E. Boismard, W. R. Farmer, F. Neirynck, Jerusalem 1984*, edited by David L. Dungan, 497–545. Bibliotheca ephemeridum theologicarum lovaniensium 95. Leuven: Peeters, 1990.

———. *Memory and Manuscript, Oral Tradition and Written Tradition in Rabbinic Judaism and Early Christianity*. Grand Rapids: Eerdmans, 1998.

Goodacre, Mark. Review of Lawrence Wills, *The Quest of the Historical Gospel*. *Journal of Biblical Literature* 119 (2000) 134.

Gordon, Robert. "Towards a Critical Appropriation of the Sermon on the Mount: Christology and Discipleship." In *Christology, Controversy, and Community*. Edited by David R. Catchpole, David G. Horrell, and Christopher M. Tuckett, 157–92. Supplements to *Novum Testamentum* 99. Boston: Brill, 2000.

Gould, Ezra P. *A Critical and Exegetical Commentary on the Gospel According to Mark*. International Critical Commentary 27. New York: Scribners, 1913.

Green, Ronald. "Kierkegaard's Philosophical Fragments: A Kantian Commentary." In *International Kierkegaard Commentary; Philosophical Fragments and Johannes Climacus*, edited by Robert Perkins, 169–202. Macon, GA: Mercer University, 1994.

Gundry, Robert. *Matthew, A Commentary on His Literary and Theological Art*. Grand Rapids: Eerdmans, 1982.

Habermas, Gary. "Did Jesus Perform Miracles?" In *Jesus under Fire*, edited by Michael Wilkins and J. P. Moreland, 117–40. Grand Rapids: Zondervan, 1995.

Haenchen, Ernst. *John: A Commentary on the Gospel of John*. Edited by Robert W. Funk. Translated by Robert W. Funk. 2 vols. Philadelphia: Fortress, 1984.

Helms, Randel. *Gospel Fictions*. Buffalo: Prometheus, 1988.

Hesse, Mary. "Miracles and the Laws of Nature." In *Miracles*, edited by Charles F. D. Moule, 33–42. New York: Morehouse, 1966.

Hick, John. *Philosophy of Religion*. 4th ed. Prentice Hall Foundations of Philosophy. Englewood Cliffs: Prentice Hall, 1990.

Higgins, Angus J. B. *The Historicity of the Fourth Gospel*, London: Lutterworth, 1963.

Hindley, J. Clifford. "Witness in the Fourth Gospel." *Scottish Journal of Theology* 18 (1965) 319–37.

Holland, Roy Fraser. "The Miraculous." *American Philosophical Quarterly* 2 (1965) 43–51.

Holmes, Michael, editor. *The Apostolic Fathers*. Grand Rapids: Baker, 1999.

Hoskyns, Sir Edwin Clement. *The Fourth Gospel*. 2nd rev. ed. Edited by Francis Noel Davy. London: Faber & Faber, 1956.

Houston, Joseph. *Reported Miracles: A Critique of Hume*. Cambridge: Cambridge University Press, 1994.

Hume, David. *Enquiries Concerning Human Understanding and Concerning the Principles of Morals*. 3rd ed. Edited by L. A. Selby-Bigge. Oxford: Clarendon, 1975.

Jeanrond, Werner. "After Hermeneutics: The Relationship between Theology and Biblical Studies." In *The Open Text: New Directions for Biblical Studies?*, edited by Francis Watson, 85–102. London: SCM, 1993.

Bibliography

Johns, Loren and Douglas Miller. "The Signs as Witnesses in the Fourth Gospel: Reexamining the Evidence." *Catholic Biblical Quarterly* 56 (1994) 519–535.

Jónsson, Jakob. "Humour and Irony in the New Testament" in *Beihefte der Zeitschrift für Religions und Geistesgeschichte* 28. Leiden: Brill (1985).

Josephus. Translated by H. St. J. Thackeray et al. 10 vols. Loeb Classical Library. Cambridge: Harvard University, 1978.

———. *Antiquities of the Jews*. Pages 27–542 in *The Works of Josephus*. Translated by W. Whiston. Peabody: Hendrickson, 1991.

Kähler, Martin. *The So-called Historical Jesus and the Historic Biblical Christ*. Translated by Carl E. Braaten. Philadelphia: Fortress Press, 1964.

Kant, Immanuel. *The Conflict of the Faculties*. Translated by Mary J. Gregor. New York: Abaris, 1979.

Kee, Howard Clark, edited. *Miracle in the Early Christian World*. New Haven, CT: Yale University Press, 1983.

Keller, Ernst, and Marie-Luise Keller. *Miracles in Dispute*. Translated by Margaret Kohl. Philadelphia: Fortress, 1969.

Kierkegaard, Søren. *Philosophical Fragments*. Translated by David Swenson. Princeton: Princeton University Press, 1962.

Kirchschlaeger, Peter. "A Literary and Historical Approach to John." In *What We Have Heard From the Beginning: The Past, Present and Future of Johannine Studies,* edited by Tom Thatcher, 145–48. Waco, TX: Baylor University Press, 2007.

Kirn, Otto. "Faith." In *The New Schaff-Herzog Encyclopedia of Religious Knowledge*. Vol. 4. Edited by Samuel McCauley Jackson, 267–70. Grand Rapids: Baker, 1977.

Kittel, G., and G. Friedrich, editors. *Theological Dictionary of the New Testament*. Translated by Geoffrey W. Bromiley. 10 vols. Grand Rapids, Eerdmans, 1964–1976.

Kline, Meredith. *Images of the Spirit*. Grand Rapids: Baker, 1980.

Koester, Helmut. *Ancient Christian Gospels*. Philadelphia: Trinity, 1990.

Konstan, David. "The Invention of Fiction." In *Ancient Fiction and Early Christian Narrative*, edited by Ronald F. Hock, J. Bradley Chance, Judith Perkins, 3–17. SBL Symposium Series 6. Atlanta: Scholars, 1998.

Kümmel, Werner Georg. *The New Testament: The History of the Investigation of its Problems*. Translated by S. McClean Gilmour and Howard Clark Kee. Nashville: Abingdon, 1972.

Kuntz, J. Kenneth. *The Self-Revelation of God*. Philadelphia: Westminster, 1967.

Kysar, Robert. *The Fourth Evangelist and his Gospel: An Examination of Contemporary Scholarship*. Minneapolis: Augsburg, 1975.

———. "The Fourth Gospel: A Report on Recent Research." *Aufstieg und Niedergang der römischen Welt*, 2.25/3:2389–2480. Edited by H. Temporini. New York: de Gruyter, 1985.

Labahn, Michael. "Between Tradition and Literary Art; The Miracle Tradition in the Fourth Gospel." *Biblica* 80 (1999) 178–203.

Larmer, Robert A. H. *Water into Wine: An Investigation of the Concept of Miracle*. Kingston, Ontario: McGill-Queen's University Press, 1988.

Larmer, Robert A. H. *Questions of Miracle*. Montreal: McGill-Queen's University Press, 1996.

Larson, Edward J. "Leading Scientists Still Reject God." *Nature* 394 (1998) 313.

Larson, Edward J., and Larry Witham. "Scientists and Religion in America." *Scientific American* 281.3 (1999) 88.

Lauterbach, Jacob Z. *Mekilta de-Rabbi Ishmael*. Philadelphia: Jewish Publication Society of America, 1935.

Leloir, Louis. "Le Diatessaron de Tatien." *L'Orient Syrien* 1 (1956) 208–31.

Lincoln, Andrew T. *Truth on Trial: The Lawsuit Motif in the Fourth Gospel*. Peabody, MA: Hendrickson, 2000.

Locke, John. *Essay Concerning Human Understanding*. Edited by P. H. Nidditch. Oxford: Clarendon, 1975.

Lücke, Friedrich. *Commentar über das Evangelium des Johannes*. Vol. 1. 3rd ed. Bonn: Weber, 1840.

Mackie, John Leslie. *The Miracle of Theism*. Oxford: Clarendon, 1982.

MacRae, G. "Miracle in the Antiquities of Josephus." In *Miracles*, edited by Charles F. D. Moule, 129–47. New York: Morehouse, 1966.

Marshall, I. Howard. *The Gospel of Luke: A Commentary on the Greek Text*. Grand Rapids: Eerdmans, 1989.

McCasland, Selby Vernon. "Signs and Wonders." *Journal of Biblical Literature* 76 (1957) 149–52.

Bibliography

Meeks, Wayne. *The Prophet-King: Moses Traditions and the Johannine Christology.* Supplements to *Novum Testamentum* 14. Leiden: Brill, 1967.

Meier, John P. *A Marginal Jew: Rethinking the Historical Jesus.* 2 vols. Anchor Bible Reference Library. New York: Doubleday, 1991.

The Mishnah. Translated by Herbert Danby. Oxford: Oxford University Press, 1933.

Moore, George Edward. *Philosophical Papers.* New York: Macmillan, 1959.

Moreland, James Porter. *Christianity and the Nature of Science: A Philosophical Investigation.* Grand Rapids: Baker, 1989.

Morris, Leon. *The Gospel According to John.* The New International Commentary on the New Testament. London: Marshall, Morgan & Scott, 1972.

———. *The Gospel According to John.* Rev. ed. The New International Commentary on the New Testament. Grand Rapids: Eerdmans, 1995.

Moule, Charles F. D. *Miracles.* New York: Morehouse, 1966.

Moulton, James Hope, and George Milligan. *The Vocabulary of the Greek Testament: Illustrated from the Papyri and Other Non-Literary Sources.* Grand Rapids: Eerdmans, 1976.

Neill, Stephen, and Tom Wright. *The Interpretation of the New Testament, 1861–1986.* 2nd ed. New York: Oxford University Press, 1988.

Nestle, Eberhard, and Kurt Aland. *Novum testamentum Graece.* Stuttgart: Deutsche Bibelgesellschaft, 1988.

The Nicene and Post-Nicene Fathers. Edited by Philip Schaff and Henry Wace. Grand Rapids: Eerdmans, 1982.

Niehaus, Jeffrey J. *God at Sinai: Covenant and Theophany in the Bible and Ancient Near East.* Studies in Old Testament Biblical Theology. Grand Rapids: Zondervan, 1995.

Painter, John. "The Idea of Knowledge in the Johannine Gospel and Epistles." PhD diss., University of Durham, 1968.

———. "John 9 and the Interpretation of the Fourth Gospel." *Journal for the Study of the New Testament* 28 (1986) 31–61.

Pannenberg, Wolfhart. *Theology and the Philosophy of Science.* Translated by Francis McDonagh. London: Darton, Longman & Todd, 1976.

Peterson, William L. "Tatian's Diatessaron." In *Ancient Christian Gospels*, edited by Helmut Koester, 403–30. Philadelphia: Trinity, 1990.

———. *Tatian's Diatessaron: It's Creation, Dissemination, Significance, and History in Scholarship.* Supplements to *Vigiliae Christianae* 25. New York: Brill, 1994.

Philo of Alexandria. *The Works of Philo.* Translated by C. D. Yonge. Peabody: Hendrickson, 1993.

Plantinga, Alvin. *Warranted Christian Belief.* New York: Oxford University Press, 2000.

Plato. Translated by W. R. M. Lamb. 10 vols. Loeb Classical Library. Cambridge: Harvard University Press, 1990.

———. *The Collected Dialogues.* E. Hamilton and H. Cairns, ed. Princeton: Princeton University Press, 1999.

———. *The Dialogues of Plato.* Translated by Benjamin Jowett. Great Books of the Western World, vol. 7. Chicago: Encyclopedia Brittanica, 1952.

———. *Theaetetus.* Edited by Bernard Williams. Translated by M. J. Levett. Indianapolis, Ind.: Hackett, 1992.

Pollard, T. E. *Johannine Christology and the Early Church.* Society for New Testament Studies Monograph Series 13. New York: Cambridge University Press, 1970.

Prickett, Stephen. *Words and The Word: Language, Poetics and Biblical Interpretation.* New York: Cambridge University Press, 1986.

Purtill, Richard L. "Defining Miracles." In *In Defense of Miracles: A Comprehensive Case for God's Action in History*, edited by R. Douglas Geivett and Gary R. Habermas, 61–72. Downers Grove, IL: InterVarsity, 1997.

Quinton, Anthony "Knowledge and Belief." In *Encyclopedia of Philosophy*, edited by Paul Edwards, vol. 4, 345–52. New York: Macmillan, 1967.

Reimarus, Hermann Samuel. "The Intention of Jesus and his Teaching." In *Reimarus: Fragments*, edited by Charles Talbert, translated by Ralph Fraser, 59–269. Chico, CA: Scholars, 1985.

Bibliography

Ridderbos, Herman N. *The Gospel According to John: A Theological Commentary*. Translated by J. Vriend. Grand Rapids: Eerdmans, 1997.

Sanders, E. P. *Jesus and Judaism*. Philadelphia, Fortress, 1985.

Sanders, J. N. *The Fourth Gospel in the Early Church*. Cambridge: Cambridge University, 1941.

Schepens, Guido. *L' 'autopsie' dans la méthode des historiens grecs du Ve siècle avant J.-C.* Verhandelingen van de Koninklije Academie voor Wetenschappen, Letteren en Schone Kunsten van België, Klasse der Letteren, Jaargang 42, no. 93. Brussel: Paleis der Academiën, 1980.

Schmeling, Gareth. "The Spectrum of Narrative." In *Ancient Fiction and Early Christian Narrative*, edited by Ronald F. Hock, 19–29. SBL Symposium Series. Atlanta: Scholars, 1998.

Schnackenburg, Rudolf. *The Gospel According to St John*. 3 vols. Translated by Kevin Smyth and Cecily Hastings. New York: Crossroad, 1982.

Schneiders, Sandra. "Remaining in His Word." In *What We Have Heard From the Beginning: The Past, Present, and Future of Johannine Studies,* edited by Tom Thatcher, 261–76. Waco, TX: Baylor University Press. 2007.

Schweitzer, Albert. *The Quest of the Historical Jesus*. London: Black, 1936.

Sloyan, Gerard S. *What Are They Saying About John?* New York: Paulist, 1991.

Smith, D. Moody, Jr. "Johannine Christianity: Some Reflections on its Character and Delineation." *New Testament Studies* 21 (1974–75) 222–48.

———. "The Problem of History in John." In *What We Have Heard From the Beginning: The Past, Present, and Future of Johannine Studies,* edited by Tom Thatcher, 311–20. Waco: Baylor University Press, 2007.

———. "The Setting and Shape of a Johannine Narrative Source." *Journal of Biblical Literature* 95/2 (1976) 231–41.

Smith, Morton. *Jesus the Magician*. San Francisco: Harper & Row, 1978.

Stibbe, Mark. "A Tomb with a View: John 11:1–44 in Narrative-Critical Perspective." *New Testament Studies* 40 (1994) 38–54.

Strauss, David Friedrich. *The Life of Jesus Critically Examined*. Edited by Peter C. Hodgson. Philadelphia: Fortress, 1973. [Originally *The Life of Jesus Critically Examined*. Translated by Georg Eliot. London: Chapman, 1846. Translation of *Das Leben Jesu*. 4th ed. Tübingen: Osiander. 1840.]

Stroll, Avrum. *Moore and Wittgenstein on Certainty*. New York: Oxford University Press, 1994.

Swinburne, Richard, editor. *Miracles*. Philosophical Topics. New York: Macmillan, 1989.

Theissen, Gerd. *The Miracle Stories of the Early Christian Tradition*. Translated by Francis McDonagh. Edinburgh: T. & T. Clark, 1983.

Thompson, Paul. *The Voice of the Past*. 3rd ed. New York: Oxford University Press, 2000.

Thucydides. *History of the Peloponnesian War*. Translated by Rex Warner. New York: Penguin, 1985.

Twelftree, Graham. *Jesus the Miracle Worker*. Downers Grove, IL: InterVarsity, 1999.

Van Belle, Gilbert. *The Signs Source in the Fourth Gospel: Historical Survey and Critical Evaluation of the Semeia Hypothesis*. Biblioteca ephemeridum thelogicarum lovaniensium 116. Louvain: Leuven University Press, 1994.

van der Loos, Hendrik. *The Miracles of Jesus*. Supplements to *Novum Testamentum* 9. Leiden: Brill, 1968.

Watson, Francis, editor. *The Open Text: New Directions for Biblical Studies?* London: SCM, 1993.

Wellhausen, Julius. *Israelitische und jüdische Geschichte*. 2nd ed. Berlin: Georg Reimer, 1895.

Westcott, Brooke Foss. *Gospel According to St. John*. 2 vols. Grand Rapids: Erdmans, 1954.

Westphal, Merold. "Johannes and Johannes: Kierkegaard and Difference." Vol. 7. In *International Kierkegaard Commentary; Philosophical fragments and Johannes Climacus*, edited by Robert L. Perkins, 13–32. Macon, GA: Mercer University Press, 1994.

Wilkins, Michael, and J. P. Moreland, editors. *Jesus under Fire*. Grand Rapids: Zondervan, 1995.

Williams, Catrin H. *I Am He: The Interpretation of Anî Hû in Jewish and Early Christian Literature*. Wissenschaftliche Untersuchungen zum Neuen Testament 2 Reihe 113. Tübingen: Mohr Siebeck, 2000.

Wills, Lawrence. *The Quest of the Historical Gospel*. London: Routledge, 1997.

Wood, Simon. *Clement of Alexandria: Christ the Educator*. Fathers of the Church, vol. 23. Washington, DC: Catholic University Press, 1954.

Ancient Documents Index

OLD TESTAMENT/ HEBREW BIBLE

Genesis
1	172, 183, 184
1:1	183
5	60
12:6–7	186

Exodus
3–14	44
3:6	186
3:14	157
4:1–9	9
4:1	vi
4:16	9, 189
6:7	184
7:1–2	189
7:1	9
7:3–5	142
7:3	86
7:5	136
7:9	86
9:27–28	136
9:30	136
10:1–2	43
10:2	vi
10:7	vi
10:16–17	136
11:9–10	142
11:9	86
12:16	152
12:24–27	131
14:21	128
16:10	90
19:9	6, 9, 189, 193
19:10	156
19:20	184
19:21–22	186
20	184
20:18–19	184
20:21	184
33:20	186, 188
33:23	193
34:34–35	189
40:34–35	188
40:34	148

Leviticus
1:2	68
23:7	152
24:16	157

Numbers
7:89	184
12:6–8	189
14:11	43

Deuteronomy
4:34	86
5	184
5:23–31	193
5:24	189
5:27–33	8
6:22	86
7:19	86
9:7–8	136
9:7	131
11:3	86, 136
13:1–5	75, 143
13:1–3	132
13:1	86, 89
13:2	86, 190
18:16–19	194
18:16–18	193
18:18–19	8

Ancient Documents Index

Deuteronomy (*cont.*)

18:21	190
18:22	190
26:8	86
28	10
28:1	9
28:15	9
28:46	86
29:3	86
30:15	6, 9
31:19	68
34:10–12	9
34:11	43, 86

1 Samuel

8:7	171

2 Samuel

7:14	124, 154, 155, 162, 171

1 Kings

17:21	129
18:16–24	190
18:21	129
18:38	136
19:2	136
19:13	186

1 Chronicles

28:9	31

Nehemiah

9:10	86

Job

12:7	183
12:9	183
26:5–12	172
38:8	172
38:10	172
38:11	172

Psalms

2:2	162, 171
2:7	155, 162, 171
2:12	155, 162
78:16–17	130
78:43	86
89:26	162
105:27	86
106:7	130
106:12–14	130
110:1	164, 171
115:3–8	183, 187
115:5	199
119:11	193
119:57	193
119:67	193
119:74	193
119:101	193
135:5–7	172
135:9	86

Isaiah

6:2–3	186
6:5	186
8:18	86
20:3	86
40:12–18	172
40:18–26	184
40:21–26	172
41:4	157
43:10	157

Jeremiah

10:5	183, 187
27	190
28:15	190
29:8	190
29:9	190
29:31	190
32:20–21	86

Daniel

7:13–14	155, 164
7:13	171
7:14	171

∼

APOCRYPHA

Wisdom

8:8	86
10:16	86
13	31

Baruch
2:11	86

1 Maccabees
1	75

2 Maccabees
5:21—7:42	75

NEW TESTAMENT

Matthew
3:7–9	185
3:17	135
4:1–6	130
5:8	187
8	107
9:8	73
10:7	59
10:17	35
11:27	161
22:31	187
22:42–44	171
22:44	171
23:34	35
24:24	86
26:63	154
26:64	171
28:12–15	35
28:20	172

Mark
1:1	172
1:4	16
1:11	135, 162
1:15	160
1:24	156
1:28	59
1:45	59
2	126
2:7	172
3:11	172
3:15	59
4	126
4:41	172
5:20	59
6:12	59
6:15	59
7:36	59
8:38	161
10	126
11:25	161
12:26	187
12:35–37	171
13:22	86, 104, 143
13:32	162
14:36	162
14:61–62	163
14:61	154
14:62	164, 171
14:64	162, 172
15:39	172
16:16	16, 19
16:19	171

Luke
1:35	172
2:49	172
3:22	135
5:1–11	112, 116
5:4	112
6:6–11	48
7	126
7:17	59
8	126
8:13	12
10:8	59
10:22	161
20:41–44	171
22:69	171
23:20	18
24:36–43	75
24:37	71

John
1:1	157, 183
1:3	155, 183
1:4	134, 155
1:6–9	10
1:6–8	192
1:9	134, 156, 158
1:11	35
1:12–13	16
1:12	18, 29
1:14	90, 144, 148, 157, 175, 195

John (*cont.*)

1:15	156
1:17–18	8
1:17	136
1:18	134, 175, 187, 192, 196
1:21	193
1:25	156
1:30	156
1:33	18
1:34	135, 192
1:38	15, 82, 177
1:48	81
1:49–50	74
1:50	83
2	44, 125, 126
2:6	138
2:9	24
2:11	14, 43, 72–74, 88, 90, 133, 144, 147, 148
2:13–25	43
2:13	131
2:18–21	63
2:18	87
2:22	19
2:23–25	12–13, 17, 79, 81–83, 139
2:23–24	106
2:23	12, 14, 16, 43, 74, 79, 81
2:24	79
2:25	14–15, 83
3:1–2	13
3:1	14
3:2	14, 43, 78, 82, 87, 89, 123, 136
3:3	64
3:5–10	64
3:5	14, 156
3:6	13–14
3:9–11	13
3:11–12	24
3:11	14, 74, 89, 176, 192
3:12	14, 21
3:15–16	10, 18
3:15	20
3:16–21	98
3:16	18, 20, 78–79, 81, 116
3:17	20, 124
3:18–19	10
3:18	16, 18–21, 98
3:19–20	98
3:19	10, 124, 134, 156, 158
3:25	156
3:26	156
3:30	156
3:31–32	176
3:33–36	176
3:36	10, 18, 20, 155, 157
4	26, 44, 110, 126
4:1–42	56
4:1–2	79
4:2	156
4:9–24	74
4:10	64
4:14	64
4:18	56
4:29	74, 84
4:32	64
4:39–42	71, 83–84, 145
4:41	11, 132
4:42	79
4:45	79
4:46–54	84–86
4:46–53	147
4:46–50	65
4:48	21, 79, 84, 86, 88, 137, 144
4:50	84, 86
4:53	74, 84, 86, 138
4:54	73
5	113, 126, 147
5:9	138
5:16	64, 75
5:17	124, 134
5:18–26	161
5:18	75, 106, 114, 124, 154, 162, 163, 172
5:19–30	154, 168
5:19	125, 154, 192
5:20–30	163
5:20	74, 134, 192
5:22–23	124
5:23	154
5:24	18, 20, 174
5:25–26	155
5:26–29	74
5:26	124
5:28–29	64
5:31–47	182
5:31	145, 182
5:33–36	74
5:33	182

John (*cont.*)

5:34–36	84
5:34	182
5:36–38	192
5:36	74, 154, 192
5:37–47	154
5:37–40	192
5:37	182
5:38	21
5:39	74, 182
5:40	74
5:42	81
5:43	145, 174
5:44	21, 154
5:45–47	136
5:46–47	21, 74
5:46	vi, 9, 182, 192, 193
5:47	11
6	125, 147, 155, 170
6:2	79
6:4	138
6:6	144
6:7	126
6:12	138
6:14–59	86–87
6:14–15	87
6:14	74, 79, 133, 193
6:17	138
6:26	87
6:27	138
6:30–45	130
6:30–31	60, 79, 131
6:30	87
6:32	136
6:33–41	64
6:35	18
6:36	21, 134
6:37	135
6:40	18, 134
6:41	132
6:44	135
6:46	187, 192
6:47	18, 19, 155
6:51	155
6:53–54	20
6:57	155
6:58–66	87
6:61–62	156, 157
6:61	159
6:63	158, 174
6:64	10, 19, 21, 159
6:65	135
6:66	155, 157, 159
6:67–71	159
6:67–68	157
6:68–69	156, 158
7:5	21
7:7	13, 176
7:12	64, 75, 89, 176
7:16–18	177
7:16	134
7:17	vi, 24
7:20	64
7:23–24	75
7:23	64
7:28	98, 134, 194
7:29	192
7:31	60, 74, 79, 89
7:34	64
7:37–39	64
7:38–39	155
7:38	18
7:39	18, 19, 175
7:40–41	74
7:40	193
7:46	174
7:47	64, 75
7:48	21
7:51–52	75
7:51	74
8:12	156, 158
8:14	194
8:19	98
8:24	21
8:26–27	64
8:26	177
8:27	179
8:28	177, 194
8:30–31	16
8:30	74, 177
8:31	12, 19, 177
8:37	24, 158, 176
8:38	175
8:40–47	13
8:40	176, 177
8:41–42	31
8:43	29

John (cont.)

8:45–49	74
8:45–46	21
8:45	176
8:46–47	176
8:46	9
8:50	194
8:51	155, 158, 174
8:52–53	155
8:53	174
8:55	195
8:58	156, 157, 198
8:59	114, 157
9	25, 26, 44, 55, 57, 70–71, 84, 108, 112, 113, 115, 125, 126, 145, 147
9:4	74, 138
9:5	156, 158
9:7	138, 178
9:8	113, 138
9:13–41	132
9:16	75, 79, 87, 89
9:18–23	65
9:18	11, 21, 35, 113
9:20	23
9:24–25	75
9:24	24
9:25	23
9:28–30	136
9:29	24
9:30–33	74
9:30–31	74
9:30	24
9:31–33	89
9:32–33	87
9:32	123
9:34	75
9:35–38	132
9:35	81
9:39–41	74
9:39	24, 27, 88, 141
9:41	98, 110
9:42	59
10:1–6	151
10:14	134
10:19–21	74, 176
10:20	65
10:21	74, 87, 89
10:24	157, 162, 179
10:25–26	21
10:25	74
10:30	156
10:31	114, 156
10:32	74
10:33	157, 172
10:34	194
10:36	75, 124, 154, 162
10:37–38	2, 21, 73, 124, 141, 145, 148
10:37	vi, 74, 192
10:38	72, 74, 78, 87, 108, 156
10:39	154, 156
10:41–42	43
10:42	74
11	25, 26, 84, 108, 126, 147
11:8	106, 114
11:9	138
11:11–13	64
11:17	44
11:21	138
11:25–26	18, 143
11:25	10, 20, 106
11:26–27	65
11:26	20
11:45–48	75
11:45	74, 79, 133
11:46–53	106
11:47	79, 87, 113, 131
11:48	87, 164
11.53	114
11:55	131
12:9–11	43
12:9	24
12:10–11	74
12:12–19	82
12:17–18	114
12:24	151
12:25	20, 151
12:36	20
12:37–43	59, 79, 110
12:37–40	83, 122, 144, 194
12:37–39	21
12:37	14, 21, 88, 124
12:38–40	24
12:38	176
12:39	21
12:40	27, 74, 89, 98, 124
12:42	12, 14, 16
12:44	18, 20, 21, 175
12:45	134, 175

John (*cont.*)

12:46	18, 156, 158
12:48	158, 173
12:49–50	174
12:49	9
13:10	13
13:13–14	177
13:19	178
13:27–29	179
14:5	194
14:7	175
14:9–11	74
14:9	134, 148, 175
14:10	74, 177
14:11	72, 74, 78, 88, 149
14:12	18
14:15	158, 177
14:18	77
14:21	158, 177
14:23–24	158, 177
14:24	174
14:25–26	178
14:26	175, 195
14:29	178
15:7	174
15:10–11	158
15:10	174
15:14	174
15:15	177
15:17–25	13
15:17	158
15:20	177, 178
15:22	134, 149, 173, 177
15:24	98, 134
15:26	195
16:4–5	178
16:9	21
16:12–14	175
16:25	179
17:2	10
17:3	22, 195
17:4	73
17:8–9	10
17:8	19, 20, 29, 79, 127, 158, 174, 177
17:14	79, 174, 177
17:18	79
17:20	18, 127
17:25	22
18:2	114
18:20–22	173
18:21	24
18:30	75
18:33	74
18:37	176
19	82
19:7	162
19:33–35	72
19:34–35	44, 126
19:35	70
19:38–42	82
19:39	14
20	71, 123
20:7	127
20:8	72, 110
20:20	71
20:24–31	87–88
20:25	35, 75
20:26–29	74, 80
20:27	65, 110
20:28	126, 147
20:29	19, 72, 85, 88, 141
20:30–31	59, 139
20:30	9
20:31	10, 12, 15, 19–21, 23, 65, 70, 74, 78–79, 81–82, 108, 110, 116, 124
21	112, 114, 116
21:24–25	117
21:24	70, 172

Acts

2:34	171
2:38	16
2:41	59
2:44	18
7	168
7:30–38	187
7:38	185
7:56	164, 171
9:1–2	164
9:42	59
16:31–33	16
17:29–30	183
17:29	184
17:32	36
19:17	59
23:6–10	74
23:8–9	36

Ancient Documents Index

24	74

Romans
1:16	17
1:20	184, 187
3:22	17
4:5	17
4:11	17
4:24	17
9:33	17
10:4	17
10:10–17	59
10:11	17

1 Corinthians
15:3–8	80
15:25	171

2 Corinthians
3:7	189
3:13	189
11:24	35
12:12	59

Galatians
1:13–14	164
1:13	35
1:22	35
5:11	35
6:12	35

Philippians
3:6	35

Colossians
1:15	187

2 Thessalonians
2:9	104
3:17	43

1 Timothy
6:16	187

James
2:14	12

1 Peter
3:21	16

1 John
1:1	63
3:6–7	17
4:7–8	17
4:12	187
4:16	11
5:13	16

Hebrews
1:5	162
1:13	171
2:4	59
10:13	171
12:25–26	185

~

DEAD SEA SCROLLS

(In bibliography: see García-Martínez)

1QS
[Rule of the Community]
Col III, 10	185

4Q258
[4Q Rule of the Community]
5, 6	188

4Q267
[4Q Damascus Document]
Fragment
2	190

4Q397 [4Q MMT 92]
Fragments
14–21	74

4Q398 [4QHalakhic Letter
=4QpapMMTe]
Fragment
1	185

Cairo Genizah
Damascus Document
CD-A
Col VI, 1	190

RABBINIC WRITINGS

Mekilta de Rabbi Ishmael
Exod 21.1   68

Mishnah
m. Berakhot
2:2   183

m. Megillah
2:3   183

m. Pesahim
4:1   152
4:6   152
10:4–6   183
10:4, 5   131

m. Ta'anit
4.3   183

Talmud
b. Bava Metzi'a
85b   68

b. Ketubbot
103b   68

GRECO-ROMAN WRITINGS

Josephus
Antiquities
Preface   184
1.82   60
3.89   187
3.90   185
3.222–23   189
12.246–56   75

Wars
2.184–98   75
6.288–309   104

Philo
Decalogue
46–47   187
46   185

Embassy to Gaius
210–212   188
290   187

Life of Moses I
All   188
66   187

On the Creation
7–12   184

Special Laws I
34   184
32–35   184

Plato
Theaetetus
142d   120
143a   120

Meno
80   94
85   94
86   94

Thucydides
History: Peloponnesian War
1.22–24   70
1.22   100
47   118
48   121

EARLY CHRISTIAN WRITINGS

(In bibliography: see *Ante-Nicene Fathers* or *Nicene and Post Nicene Fathers* for many of these.)

Augustine
City of God
10.12   39

Ancient Documents Index

Faustus the Manichaean
26.3 — 39

Genesis
6.13.24 — 39
6.18.29 — 40
9.18.33 — 40

Clement of Alexandria

Fragments — 63
Hypotyposes — 62
Instructor
1.2 — 63

Clement of Rome

1 Clement
13.2 — 119
24.5 — 119
46.8 — 119

Epiphanius

Panarion
51.3 — 61

Eusebius

Ecclesiastical History
4.29.6 — 61
6.14 — 62

Ignatius

Ephesians
7.2 — 167
14.2 — 120

Irenaeus

Against Heresies
1.26.1 — 62
2.22 — 62
3.3.4 — 62
3.9.1 — 62

P. Egerton 2 — 61

Origen

Gospel of John
10.2–6 — 109

Tatian

Diatessaron — 61
Fragments — 61

Names Index

Abbott, Edwin Abbott, 15, 16, 18, 19
Aland, Kurt, 61
Alston, William, 48
Anderson, Paul N., 172
Aquinas, Thomas, 11, 39, 40
Argyle, A. W., 171
Austin, J. L., 26
Ayer, A. J., 25

Bahrdt, Carl, 45
Baillie, John, 185, 186
Ball, David Mark, 157, 188
Barrett, Charles Kingsley, 12–14, 16, 43, 72, 73, 81, 83, 100
Bareille, G., 62
Barth, Karl, 11, 183, 186
Basinger, David, 48
Bauckham, Richard, ix–xi, 2, 157
Bauer, Walter, 10, 42, 43, 56
Baur, Ferdinand C., 100, 150, 152, 161
Beasley-Murray, George R., 13, 62, 132, 166, 192
Bennema, Cornelius, 2
Black, Matthew, 153
Blass, Friedrich, 18
Borg, Marcus, 37, 56, 183
Borgen, Peder, 183
Bradley, Frances H., 51
Braun, François-Marie, 167
Bretschneider, Karl Gottlieb, 150
Brooks, James A., 18, 19
Brown, Colin, 39, 45, 50, 51
Brown, Raymond E., 14, 43, 154, 162, 165, 166, 168
Bultmann, Rudolf, ix, 13–17, 28–30, 34, 47, 54, 57, 70–73, 77, 78, 80–84, 87, 104, 111, 112, 140, 192
Burrows, Miller, 31
Byrskog, Samuel, 36, 66–70, 117–19

Byrne, Brendan, 127, 128, 140, 144
Calvin, John, 13, 16, 39, 78, 79, 90, 155
Casey, Maurice, 151–153, 159, 161–63
Catchpole, D. R., 162
Childs, Brevard S., 181
Chillingworth, William, 45
Clifford, W. K., 27
Coady, C. A. J., 99, 101, 145
Cover, J. A., 52
Cullmann, Oscar, 151, 166–68, 170, 174
Culpepper, R. Alan, 137

Darwin, Charles, 46
Daub, Carl, 46
De Jonge, Marinus, 170, 172
Debrunner, Albert, 18
Descartes, Rene, 27
Dibelius, Martin, 47, 66, 152
Dodd, Charles Harold, 29–31, 58, 106, 133, 150–52, 160, 173, 200
Drummond, James, 150
Duhem, Pierre, 92
Dunn, James, 171

Evans, C. Stephen, 2, 96

Fanning, Buist M., 17
Feuerbach, Ludwig, 46
Fichte, Johann, 46
Freed, Edwin, 110–12, 116, 139, 147, 160
Fortna, Robert, 110–16, 137–39, 146

Gadamer, Hans-Georg, 32
Gaffney, James, 27–30
García-Martínez, Florentino, 74
Gardner-Smith, P., 122, 123
Geldenhuys, J. Norval, 152
Gerhardsson, Birger, 68, 69
Goodacre, Mark, 57

Names Index

Gordon, Robert, 172
Gould, Ezra, 171
Gundry, Robert, 171
Gunkel, Hermann, 47

Habermas, Gary, 37, 56
Haenchen, John, 112, 140
Healy, Mary, 2
Hegel, G. W. F., 46, 99
Helms, Randel, 47, 57
Herbert, Lord of Cherbury, 45
Hesse, Mary, 42
Hick, John, 47, 48, 93, 184, 189
Hindley, J. C., 104, 106, 107, 113, 131–37, 139, 140, 146, 191–95
Higgins, Angus, J. B., 173
Hodges, David, 2
Hogg, H., 60, 61
Holland, R. F., 48
Holmes, Michael, 120
Hoskyns, Sir Edmund Clement, 12, 14, 15, 16, 152, 192
Houston, Joseph, 39–42, 47–52, 99
Hume, David, 39, 41, 45, 47–52, 93
Hunt, Russell, 111, 112, 116, 139

Jeanrond, Werner, 32
Jeremias, Joachim, 66
Johns, Loren, 141, 142
Jónsson, Jakob, 63

Kähler, Martin, 169
Kant, Immanuel, 45, 46, 49, 95
Käsemann, Ernst, 47, 66, 168
Kee, Howard Clark, 45, 55
Keller, Ernst and Marie-Louise, 38, 45, 46
Kierkegaard, S., 6, 45, 93–101, 106, 133, 197, 199
Kirn, Otto, 11
Kirchschlaeger, Peter, 55
Klein, G., 88
Kline, Meredith, 186
Koester, Helmut, 57, 58, 61, 66, 78, 206, 207
Konstan, David, 56
Kümmel, Werner Georg, 150, 151, 161, 180
Kuntz, J. Kenneth, 186
Kysar, Robert, 103
La Placette, Jean, 45
Labahn, Michael, 110, 111, 113–15, 144

Larmer, R. A. H., 48
Larson, Edward, 48
Leibniz, Gottfried, 45
Leloir, Louis, 60
Lessing, Gotthold, 45, 93, 94, 96, 97
Lewis, C. I., 25
Lincoln, Andrew, 119, 144, 145
Locke, John, 39–41, 50
Lücke, Friedrich, 150

Mackie, J. L., 47, 49
MacRae, George, 42
McCasland, s. Vernon, 104, 105, 107, 130, 131, 140, 146
Malatesta, Edward, 2
Malcolm, Norman, 26
Marshall, I. H., 162, 172
Meeks, Wayne, 136
Meier, John P., 52, 58, 92, 105, 107–10, 114, 124, 125, 143, 147
Miller, Douglas, 141, 142
Moore, G. E., 25, 26
Moreland, J. P., 48
Morris, Leon, 13, 18, 153
Moule, C. F. D., 42, 66
Mosser, Carl, 2

Neill, Stephen, 60
Niehaus, Jeffrey J., 184, 186–90

Pannenberg, Wolfhart, 48
Painter, John, 79, 110–14, 140, 141
Parry, Robin, 2
Penelhum, T., 47
Peterson, William, 60, 61
Plantinga, Alvin, 48, 92
Pollard, T. E., 167, 170
Prickett, Stephen, 32
Purtill, Richard L., 42

Quinton, Anthony, 22–27

Reimarus, Hermann, 37, 38, 45, 55, 94
Reisner, Rainer, 69
Ridderbos, Herman M., 155, 157, 171, 183, 192, 195
Rowe, William, 48
Russell, Bertrand, 25
Sanders, E. P., 35, 37, 47

Names Index

Sanders, J. N., 167
Schepens, Guido, 67
Schleiermacher, Friedrich, 46
Schmeling, Gareth, 57
Schnackenburg, Rudolf, 43, 54–56, 58, 81, 83–86, 114, 153, 160, 163, 164, 180, 181
Schneiders, Sandra, 55
Schurmann, Heinz, 68
Schweitzer, Albert, 46, 47, 56, 57, 66, 100
Sloyan, Gerard, 103
Smith, Dwight Moody, 55, 111, 112, 140, 166
Smith, Morton, 37, 105
Spinoza, Baruch, 45
Stibbe, Mark, 104–7, 142, 143
Strauss, David F., 6, 37, 38, 44–46, 55–57, 93, 94, 96, 97, 99, 100, 150
Stuhlmacher, Peter, 48
Swinburne, Richard, 38, 48

Taylor, A. E., 50
Taylor, Vincent, 66, 152
Theissen, Gerd, 59, 88
Thompson, Paul R., 66, 67
Thulstrup, Neil, 45, 94, 97
Twelftree, Graham, 38, 92
Troeltsch, Ernst, 51

Van Belle, Gilbert, 2, 115
Van der Loos, Hendrik, 38, 42, 45

Watson, Wilfred, 185, 188, 190
Wellhausen, Julius, 186
Westcott, Brooke Foss, 12, 13, 16, 18, 19
Westphal, Merold, 97
Williams, Catrin H., 157
Wills, Lawrence, 57
Winbery, Carleton L., 18, 19
Witham, Larry, 48
Wittgenstein, Ludwig, 26
Wright, Tom, 60

Subject Index

belief. *See also* belief in Jesus.
  credulity different from, 145
  defined as assent, 10–11, 40
  defined as trust, 10–11, 21, 40
  warrant (evidence) needed for, 2, 27, 191
belief, basis for. *See* belief; knowledge; epistemology, Jewish religious; miracles; testimony and records
belief in Jesus. *See also* epistemology, Jewish religious.
  belief in Moses similar to, 5–10
  eternal life given by, 10, 17–21
  eternal life not given by, 11–19
  needed, reason, 5, 6, 8–10
  stable or unstable, 12–19
  varieties of, 10–21

certainty. *See* doubt
Christology in the Gospel of John
  essential, 153–70, 199–201
  secondary, 173–81
Christology in the Synoptic Gospels, 170–73, 199
conversation partners, 2, 80, 103

doubt. *See also* knowledge; historical knowledge; knowledge, John's view of.
  acceptable ways to, 71, 190–191
  certainty and, 25–26, 51, 92, 99
  historical skepticism and, 6, 93–97, 99–102
  inductive knowledge versus, 24–26, 50–51
  justification needed for, 25–26, 51, 99–100, 199
  perception versus, 24–26, 32–33, 50, 94
  reasonable versus unreasonable, 26, 32–33, 50–51, 191

epistemology in John's Gospel. *See also* epistemology, Jewish religious.
  conclusions about, 197–201
  Jewish basis for, 5–10, 182–91, 197–201
  nonfictional basis required for, 3–4, 34, 54, 102, 153
epistemology, Jewish religious. *See also* hearing God; knowledge of God.
  anthropomorphism, 183, 186–87, 195
  belief and doubt alike require warrant, 27, 191
  existence of God, 5, 7, 183–84
  God's appearances, 184–88, 195
  God speaks to prophets, 7, 188–89
  God speaks using language, 183–88
  God's actions, 42, 60, 183–84
  miraculous events, 5, 42, 60, 183–88
  Moses as the standard, 5–9, 132, 188–89, 199
  prophets need authentication, 84, 190–92
  theophanies, 186–88, 195
essential message of Jesus per John
  Christological claims in, 153–60
  disputed historicity of 150–53, 161
  elements of, 154–59
  grounds for belief in, 195–96
  innovations can't include, 169–70
  Johannine scholars' views of, 161–68
  nonfictional character of, 21, 149–61, 180–81
  offends people, 7, 153–59

faith. *See* belief.
fiction. *See also* fiction versus nonfiction.
  definition of, 3, 54
  in Greco-Roman historians, 118–22
  historical intent defines, 3
  in historical novels, 3, 37, 57–60, 115, 119

Subject Index

fiction (*cont.*)
  in literary elaboration, 34, 115–18, 180–81
  in metaphors, 3–4, 63–66, 74–78
  in misleading fabrications, 37
  in symbols, 34, 58, 141
  in symbolic miracles, 54, 63–66, 77–78, 138
  in theological elaboration, 55, 112–13, 152, 180
fiction versus nonfiction. *See also* fiction.
  definitions for, 3
  earliest readers recognized, 60–66
  essential message of Jesus as, 149–73,
  historical intention expressed by, 2–4, 34, 55–60, 103–29, 153–54
  limited in Jesus' words, 3–4, 149–81
  limited in John's miracles, 3–4, 116–29
  minor messages of Jesus as, 173–81
  miracles as, 38, 103–29
  oral history and, 66–70
  persuasive purpose and, 4, 8, 21, 123–29, 153–54

ginōskō, 23, 28–29
God. *See also* knowledge of God.
  existence, 5, 7, 39, 183–84
  capacity for speech and action, 186–89
  speech and action necessarily anthropomorphic, 186–88
Gospel of John
  catechetical or evangelistic purpose of, 5, 8–9
  implied author versus real author of, 2, 172–73
  literary unity of, presumed, 2, 172–73
  primary author of, 2
Greek terminology, 10–11, 28

hearing God. *See also* epistemology, Jewish religious.
  a priori possibility, 183–88
  anthropomorphism, appearance of, 186–87, 199–200
  coherency with other knowledge, 190–91
  confidence in human senses and mind, 24–26, 32–33, 50
  evidence needed to know, 5, 186–87
  identifying God as speaker, 187
  rarity of the experience, 188–89
  reasonable doubt, 24–26, 32–33, 50–52, 144–45, 191
Hebrew terminology, 29
historical knowledge. *See also* knowledge; epistemology, Jewish religious; testimony and records.
  agreement not required for, 74–75, 91–93
  John's confidence about, 97–100
  testimony and, 99, 144–45
  as proof, 92, 123–25, 191–94
historicity of John's Gospel, always controversial, 35–36
historiography of John, comparison of modern views with, 91–102

Jewish religious epistemology. *See* epistemology, Jewish religious.

kerygma (proclamation), 80, 154–73, 195–99
knowledge. *See also* historical knowledge; knowledge of God; knowledge, John's view of.
  belief not a kind of, 23
  certainty and, 25–26
  courtroom understandings of, 23–27, 74, 92, 94, 99
  definitions of, 23–24
  from inference, 24–26, 94–96
  Kierkegaard on, 93–100
  kinds of, 22
  from perception, 24–26, 32, 50, 94–96
  of persons and arts, 22, 32
  provisional justification of, 24–27, 50
  that a proposition is true, 22
  from testimony or records, 23–25, 99, 144–145
knowledge, John's view of.
  as a concept, 27–30
  Gaffney on, 27–30
  of God, 30–33
  Greek vocabulary for, 28
  as provisionally justified, 32
  from seeing, 24, 28–29, 32–33
  from testimony or records, 23–25, 32
  of persons, 22, 32
knowledge of God. *See also*, God; knowledge; epistemology, Jewish religious.
  from miracles, 136

knowledge of God (*cont.*)
   John's concept of, 22, 30–34
   Kierkegaard's view of, 95–97
   from needless order in the universe, 5, 7, 183–84
   from prophetic testimony, 182–84, 191, 195
message, essential. *See* essential message of Jesus per John.
messages, non-essential,
   nonfiction in, 173–80
miracle reports. *See also* miracles; testimony and records.
   a priori discrediting of, 44–53
   as historical claims per earliest readers 60–66
   fictional intention in John's, 54–76
   historicity of, 35–38
   historical intention in John's, 58–66
   historical reliability of, 70–75
   historicity versus agreement about, 35, 91–92
   Hume and Houston's critiques of, 49–52
   no consensus against, 48–52
   nonfictional character of, scholarly views on, 103–18
   as nonfictional in their essentials, 6, 54–66, 104–29
   philosophy alone can discredit all, 47, 52–53
   as test case for historical intention, 36–37
   tested like other reports, 7, 51
miracles. *See also* knowledge of God; miracles as grounds for belief; miracle reports.
   a priori possibility of, 48–53
   defined, 37, 39–44
   God's existence not proven by, 39
   historical challenges against, 44–48
   John's concept of, 42–44
   modern conceptions of, 39–42
   natural law and, 39–42, 50–52
   as signs, 42–44
miracles as grounds for belief. *See also* miracle reports; miracles.
   Bultmann on, 77–84, 87–88
   demands to see, 86–88
   denied as invalid, 77–78, 81, 130–31
   generally, 77–80, 88–90, 146–48
   Hindley on, 131–37
   human unreliability and, 81–83
   Johannine scholars on, 77–88, 130–44
   in John 2 (Jesus doesn't trust all belief), 81–83
   in John 4 (Samaritans delay believing), 83–84
   in John 4 (healing not visible), 84–86
   in John 6 (miracle not given), 86–87
   in John 20 (belief conditioned on seeing), 87–88
   Schnackenburg on, 81, 83, 85–86
Moses, 5–10, 136–37, 183–200

nonfiction. *See* fiction and nonfiction.

oida, 23, 28–29

pisteuō, 10–11
prophets. *See* epistemology, Jewish religious.

revelation. *See* knowledge of God.

signs. *See* miracles.

testimony and records
   as sources of knowledge, 5, 23–26, 99–101
   and coherency with other information, 52, 107, 190
   as grounds for belief, 149, 191–96
   perception as basis of, 9, 24–25, 32–33, 50
   permissible to test, 71, 145
theophanies. *See* epistemology, Jewish religious.

words of Jesus. *See* essential message of Jesus per John.

yada', 29

www.ingramcontent.com/pod-product-compliance
Lightning Source LLC
Chambersburg PA
CBHW080431230426
43662CB00015B/2239

www.ingramcontent.com/pod-product-compliance
Lightning Source LLC
Chambersburg PA
CBHW080431230426
43662CB00015B/2239